The Cultural Roots of Strategic Intelligence

Philosophy and Cultural Identity

Series Editors: Michael Krausz and Andreea Deciu Ritivoi

Editorial Board: Stephen Angle, Kwame Anthony Appiah, Costica Bradatan, Noel Carroll, Aurelian Craiutu, Christoph Cox, David Crocker, Cora Diamond, Edward Dimendberg, Fred Evans, John Gibson, Lydia Goehr, David Goldberg, Gary Hagberg, Rom Harré, Ian Jarvie, Christine Koggel, Thomas Leddy, Bo Mou, Amelie Rorty, Henry Rosemont, Paul Snowden, Kok Chor Tan, Mary Wiseman, David Wong

Philosophy and Cultural Identity encourages new scholarship in cross-cultural philosophy, exploring topics such as cultural memory, cultural membership, cultural obligations, cultural pluralism and universalism, ethnocentrism, cosmopolitanism, cross-cultural dialogue, cross-cultural experience, personal identity, single and multiple identities, single and multiple selves, and self-realization. The series is especially interested in works that address contemporary problems, situated in a broad theoretical and/or historical perspective. Interdisciplinary approaches are welcome. The series encourages submissions of monographs, collections, and dialogues.

Titles in the Series

The Cultural Roots of Strategic Intelligence, by Gino LaPaglia
What Is a Public Education and Why We Need It: A Philosophical Inquiry into Self-Development, Cultural Commitment, and Public Engagement, by Walter Feinberg
Against Individualism: A Confucian Rethinking of the Foundations of Morality, Politics, Family, and Religion, by Henry Rosemont Jr.
In Search of Just Families, by Chhanda Gupta

The Cultural Roots of Strategic Intelligence

Gino LaPaglia

LEXINGTON BOOKS
Lanham • Boulder • New York • London

Published by Lexington Books
An imprint of The Rowman & Littlefield Publishing Group, Inc.
4501 Forbes Boulevard, Suite 200, Lanham, Maryland 20706
www.rowman.com

6 Tinworth Street, London SE11 5AL, United Kingdom

Copyright © 2020 by Gino LaPaglia

All rights reserved. No part of this book may be reproduced in any form or by any electronic or mechanical means, including information storage and retrieval systems, without written permission from the publisher, except by a reviewer who may quote passages in a review.

British Library Cataloguing in Publication Information Available

The hardback edition of this book was previously catalogued by the Library of Congress as follows:

Library of Congress Cataloging-in-Publication Data Available

ISBN: 978-1-4985-8831-7 (cloth)
ISBN: 978-1-4985-8833-1 (pbk.)
ISBN: 978-1-4985-8832-4 (electronic)

To the loves of my life, James, Nino, and Poppy Ann

The views expressed in this book are those of the author and do not reflect the official policy or position of the Department of Defense, the U.S. military, or the U.S. Government.

*At many things, of wonders and terrors we are awestruck
But at nothing more than man, cleverest of all...
Who catches through cunning in deadly nets,
Flocks of birds, prides of beast, and schools of fish,
And masters beasts with ruse, harnesses horses, and the bull.*

Sophocles (497-406 BCE)
Antigone, Scene 1 lines 373-392.

Contents

Preface	xi
Acknowledgments	xv
Notes on Translation, Conventions, and Abbreviations	xvii
1 Cultural Genealogy: Theory and Method	1
2 Greco-Roman Strategic Intelligence: Strategic Heroes, Divine, and Human	21
3 Greco-Roman Strategic Intelligence: Beasts and Philosophers	47
4 The Legacy of Judeo-Christian Strategic Intelligence	71
5 The Patrimony of Medieval & Renaissance Strategic Intelligence	97
6 Toward a Cultural Genealogy of Chinese Strategic Intelligence	129
7 The Endowment of Chinese Strategic Intelligence: Strategic Officialdom	159
8 *Thick Black Theory* 厚黑學: Annotated Translation	191
Conclusion	217
Bibliography	223
Index	239
Author Biography	245

Preface

What exactly is Strategic Intelligence? What is Strategic Culture? Where do they come from? And what makes them ultimately legitimate and authoritative in human affairs?

This book is the result of my search for the answers to these questions.

Interest in the art and science of strategy appears to be growing, as evidenced by the increasing number of graduate programs and professional societies dedicated to it. But I have noticed during my time teaching at the National Intelligence University in Washington D.C., the center of academic life for the U.S. Intelligence Community, a curious lacuna in the articles produced by theorists of strategy in the public and private sectors about the long history and intellectual foundations of strategic thought, and what exactly makes it meaningful. The objective of this book is twofold: (1) to enable contemporary strategists in all domains of practice to identify themselves within a rich cultural legacy which philosophical underpinnings arise in the necessity of life itself and (2) to spark broader interest in strategic thought in culture.

In contrast to many strategic practitioners who, inspired by debates in the Philosophy of Science, ground their disciplines in scientistic epistemology, I reconnect the art of strategy with its roots in the living of life itself. I advocate for a theory of Strategic Intelligence and Strategic Culture that is informed by philosophical naturalism, hermeneutic philosophy, psychology, and existentialism, and the power, values, and meaning that inform political and cultural subjectivity. In response to the alienation generated from the human engagement with mystery (what the Existentialist Psychoanalyst Ernest Becker referred to as "death terror"), the threat of finitude to the expansion of human life force, and legitimated by human experience and the necessity of life itself, Strategic Intelligence emerges historically as a heroic form of hope that promises the possibility of strategic advantage, value, dignity, freedom, the achievement of objective, and the fulfillment of potential in hostile environments.[1] Paradoxically, it also has the potential to deny these outcomes when wielded by a skillful adversary.

The identity of the heroic strategist is a culturally validated role that promises strategic advantage in life. Becker famously understood heroic roles as "vital lies": they are vital for human life, but they never actually result in immortality. Arising in human experience, encoded as value, and born by culture as a strategic resource, I demonstrate that the strategic aspect of reason has been encoded as heroically strategic values that have been memorialized in culturally authoritative sources for over 2,500 years. These sources validated a strategic orientation in the world, legitimized the strategist as a heroic identity and a culturally validated meaningful role, and transmitted a coherent worldview that enables the heroic strategist to overcome asymmetric threat through the development of interpretation, foresight, and appropriate adaptation. By excavating the provenance of strategic thought expressed in the cultural identity of heroic strategists in the most culturally authoritative mythological, literary, philosophical, and religious sources, and excavating the underlying strategic values expressed in cultural products, I demonstrate that the strategic aspect of human rationality is one of the most fundamental dynamics in human meaning, and that the transmission of this strategic way of life offers hope for the underdog in the game of life.

By the means of a cultural genealogy, I trace the roots of Strategic Intelligence back to a metaphorological paradigm that articulates an understanding of life that is both enabled and constrained by finitude. The awareness of physical death to one's identity is so traumatic, Becker taught, that it is repressed psychologically. This nameless threat, that *life is death*, functions as a paradox and a metaphorical paradigm. Life is not merely constrained (and enabled) by the fact of physical death—the expansion of life is also threatened by anything that might symbolically oppose it. In this way, symbolic death might be anything that opposes one's ambition, value, chosen heroic role, or sense of meaning. While the exact phrase *life is death* is never explicitly articulated, in being paradigmatic, it nevertheless functions as a blackhole or forcefield that shapes our conceptual and linguistic worlds; informs human orientation in the universe as a worldview; and validates, explains, and predicts certain human behaviors.

The threat of symbolic finitude, sometimes expressed figuratively as ensnarement and entrapment (Greek: *dólos/δόλος*, chapter 2) by the threat environment, sets the condition for the possibility of attaining self-actualization, human dignity, liberty, freedom, and strategic advantage. In this book, I have assembled a series of narratives about heroic strategic thought drawn from across many Eurasian cultures which share an uncanny resemblance and common features, which point us to their underlying strategic values. In lieu of a linguistic definition of Strategic thought, I have identified a constellation of common features, which includes an orientation to an antagonistic environment, and which in turn necessitates the just, legitimate, and heroic utilization of opportunism and timing; resourcefulness; expediency; adaptability; covert behavior that includes dissimulation, dissembling, deception, and trickery; exposure; and foresight. All of the sources analyzed in this book depict these features. I explain this resemblance of features in these sources by means of positing a preexistent paradigm and common set of strategic values: the threat of figurative death (finitude) to the expansion of life is what necessitates strategic thought.

Like previous scholars who have looked at the data comparatively, I chose primary sources from a variety of modes and domains in two cultural legacies, Western and Chinese, that demonstrate that Strategic Intelligence and strategic cultural values are both prevalent, culturally validated (just, legitimate, and authoritative), and therefore a *root* of contemporary life as well. An epigenetic understanding of the cultural transmission of the metaphorological paradigm understands that, in response to the nuances of a given threat environment, the particular response is psychologically, historically, culturally, and linguistically conditioned, which accounts for variation across strategic cultures.

I wrote this book with three audiences in mind: current and future practitioners of strategy in the public (national security) and private (business and competitive intelligence) sectors, academic theorists of strategy, and for the general public whose narratives are increasingly populated by victims, a trend which is indubitably reflective of the ongoing twenty-first century American culture wars. It is my hope that the strategic worldview presented here will reintroduce heroic agency by orienting future generations of strategists to their own antagonistic environments, to strategic values, and to the potent tool that they might command in the pursuit of freedom, liberty, and advantage.

This book pays homage to the pioneering research of intellectual giants Marcel Detienne, Jean-Pierre Vernant, and Lisa Raphals, without whose scholarly contributions to the study of cunning intelligence this study would not have been possible.[2] In contrast to their approaches which utilized analytic frameworks informed by Structuralism, Philology, and Epistemology, and which emphasize the analytic variables of language and concept, I interpreted the cultural data through the lenses of Hermeneutic Philosophy, Axiology, and Psychoanalysis, emphasizing metaphor and paradox, values and meaning. My goal is to reinterpret Greek *metic* and Chinese *zhì* 智 intelligence as culturally, linguistically, and historically conditioned articulations arising from a common metaphorical wellspring. Through the course of my research it became clear that the cultural data covered by these researchers often appeared in a political-existential frame, which led me to think more broadly about the ways in which cultural sources re-present subjectivity and agency.

My choice to label the phenomenon under observation in this book as Strategic Intelligence derives from my dissatisfaction with how we talk about and value this worldview in contemporary discourse. *Metic intelligence* feels too clinical, and *phronesis, prudence*, and *practical wisdom* are terms of art that mean too little to the general public, and too much to professional philosophers. The term *strategic* as used in industry and government to express the value of future-oriented deliberation, and which integrates foresight, *ends, ways, and means*, and appropriate action, is largely not at odds with this purpose of this book. Moreover, the Greek philosophical legacy points to the strategic: the heroic exemplar of *phronesis* provided in book six of Aristotle's *Nichomachean Ethics* is the figure of the heroic statesman Pericles, who is remembered primarily for his identity as *strategos*, general, and who is contrasted with the professional philosopher Anaxagoras.[3] I think Aristotle would concur that Pericles' Strategic Intelligence is an example of the type of rationality and excellence (virtue) that he describes as the "eye of the soul."[4] But Aristotle's exploration of the morality and ethics of *phronesis* has diverted attention from its more ambiguous aspects: like the philosopher of the *will to power* and of life itself, Friedrich Nietzsche, I also take inspiration from what pre-Aristotelian and pre-philosophic sources refer to as heroic denial and deception, a mode of strategic wisdom that is celebrated for being *snare-aware* (*dolophronéōn δολοφρονέων*) and *crafty* (*dolómētis δολόμητις*). While there are certainly examples of Strategic Intelligence from other cultures, I have chosen to limit the scope of my research for this book to Eurasian sources because of my expertise in these languages and cultures. As I will demonstrate in the following pages, strategic values are, and have always been, core to culture.

NOTES

1. Ernest Becker, *The Denial of Death,* (New York: Free Press Paperbacks/Simon & Schuster, 1973).

2. Marcel Detienne and Jean-Pierre Vernant, *Cunning Intelligence in Greek Culture and Society*, trans. Janet Lloyd (New Jersey: Humanities Press, 1978); Lisa Raphals, *Knowing Words: Wisdom and Cunning in the Classical Traditions of China and Greece* (Ithaca: Cornell University Press, 1992). Marcel Detienne and Jean-Pierre Vernant, *The Cuisine of Sacrifice among the Greeks*, trans. Paula Wissing (Chicago & London: University of Chicago Press, 1989), 21–86.

3. Aristotle, *Nichomachean Ethics*, 5:1149, 5:1141.

4. Aristotle, *Nichomachean Ethics*, 6:12.

Acknowledgments

I owe a great deal to many teachers, too many to name, who have patiently taught me over the years. I am most grateful for the friendship and intellectual support provided by Jo Ann Moran Cruz, Frank Ambrosio, Carol Benedict, and James Millward, all who provided invaluable feedback on multiple drafts. I'd like to thank students and colleagues at the National Intelligence University, editors at Rowman and Littlefield for their diligence, and the anonymous reviewers who provided helpful advice. Books do not get written without an extensive network of support and the generous gift of "alone" time—a most precious resource. I am indebted both to superiors who enabled me to focus on this project, and to my immediate family and friends for their continued support and love.

Notes on Translation, Conventions, and Abbreviations

This book is primarily a book about life, not a book about other books. I recognize that most readers will not have had the leisure to read the many books cited, but they are included in chapters 2–8 as evidence that supports my argument about Strategic Intelligence as a life philosophy and worldview.

With regards to translating Chinese philosophical and cultural terms, I both emphasized the practical, emotive, and affective aspects of the strategic tradition that I interpreted through the lens of Lǐ Zōngwú thought. For example, I translated the Ruist value of rén 仁, conventionally translated as humaneness or benevolence, as empathetic response, and the value of yì 義 as rightness. Sometimes I downplayed some philosophical aspects of terms, such as the term shēn 身 "body," which over the long course of Chinese cultural history sometimes refers to embodiment as in the Theory of Body-Reverence (zūnshēnlùn 尊身論) advocated by some Late Imperial philosophers, and sometimes in terms that cover the semantic range of identity, personhood, and self (such as as Hán Fēi's' discussion of the power of personal intactness shēnquán 身全 in Chapter 6). At times, I translated tiān 天 as "heaven," or as "nature" depending on my interpretation of the context. Lastly, I refer to what is known in the West as Confucianism by its indigenous name, Ruism (rúxué 儒學), which I understand in terms of a broad East Asian cultural trajectory, with a real or imagined continuity, that includes a diverse yet normative set of heroic values, beliefs, aesthetic practices and protocols, traditions, discourses, and texts, the identities of those that have not historically been always defined in opposition to other traditions. For consistency, I have rendered all Chinese terms in traditional script (fántǐzì 繁體字), and have almost always used the standard pīnyīn 拼音 romanization system—the most notable exceptions occur for the representation of Chinese names of authors who have published with other romanization schemes, which I tried to respect. Foreign language citations and definitions are documented in the endnotes. All errors remain my own.

Chapter 1

Cultural Genealogy
Theory and Method

The adjective *strategic,* prepended to the terms *Strategic Intelligence* and *Strategic Culture* which gesture to relatively new paradigms for analysis in International Relations theory, seems to be a feature common also to political and military science, business management, and executive leadership. Figure 1.1 features a Google Ngram analysis of these terms and demonstrates the increasing prevalence and importance of these terms in English. A query in WorldCat for "Strategic Culture" and "Strategic Intelligence" returns about 3,000 titles for each. The spike of interest in the late 1970s in the concept of Strategic Intelligence as applied to international relations theory may be related to Jack Snyder's 1977 Rand report "The Soviet Strategic Culture: Implications for Limited Nuclear Options," which provided an early definition for Strategic Culture as the "sum total of ideals, conditional emotional responses, and patterns of habitual behaviour that members of the national strategic community have acquired through instruction or imitation and share with each other with regard to . . . strategy."[1]

Both terms have since become an analytic lens used by many researchers in International Relations (IR) theory, and the popularity of this analytic paradigm has been humorously compared to a "Philosopher's Stone for policy and strategy" and "the magical element that will transform ignorance into knowledge," and judged as "foolish" by one observer since the field lacks consensus on the exact meaning of these terms.[2] Informed by opposing trends, both by the linguistic and cultural turn in the Humanities and debates in the Philosophy of Science, IR theorists have sought to understand their object of inquiry with regards to the exact relationship of Strategic Culture to the strategic behavior of grand strategy and policy-making, and of the relationship of strategic theory to praxis in general. For example, borrowing from the epistemological concerns of the Philosophy of Science, the scholar

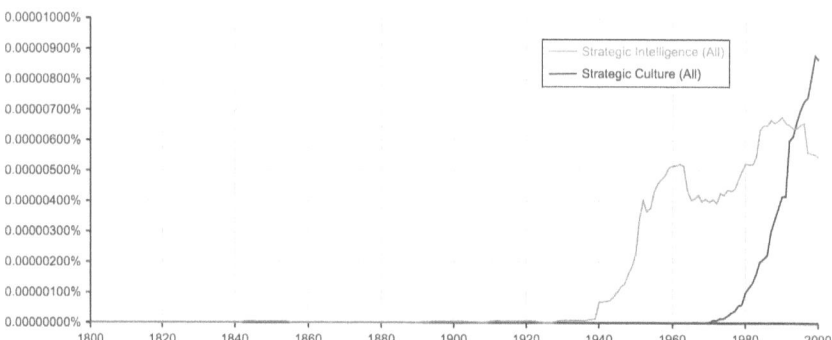

Figure 1.1 Google Ngram Analysis of Terms Strategic Culture and Strategic Intelligence. Reprinted with permission of Google http://books.google.com/ngrams.

of Chinese grand strategy Alastair Iain Johnston has grounded his approach to Strategic Culture in empirical method, scientific testability, ability[3]; and those who oppose have staked out theoretical positions informed by post-positivist hermeneutics and social constructivism.[4]

Journals dedicated to Strategic Intelligence have documented the state of the fields; for example, *The Journal of Strategic Intelligence*, an online periodical created in 2016 by the US National Intelligence University (NIU), one of a handful of universities that trains students in Strategic Intelligence for the purposes of national security, defines Strategic Intelligence as a field which offers "a comprehensive understanding of current or emerging regional and transnational issues broadly that will significantly impact national security or interests."[5] The *Strategic Culture Foundation*, an online journal created in 2005, provides "a platform for exclusive analysis, research and policy comment on Eurasian and global affairs"; that platform includes global analysis in the political, economic, social, and security domains.[6]

Strategic Intelligence is not limited to the national-international level of analysis. In the business world, Strategic Intelligence is synonymous with competitive and business intelligence, and is closely related to strategic management and strategic planning. The Bureau of Industry and Security (BIS) of the US Department of Commerce has a Strategic Intelligence Division, which mission is to provide "all-source information regarding foreign end-users of U.S.-controlled items to BIS and interagency partners to determine potential diversion risks when making licensing decisions."[7] In 1986, Strategic Intelligence practitioners formed the Strategic and Competitive Intelligence Professionals (SCIP) group, a 501(3)(c) nonprofit professional society comprised of business experts across industry, academia, and government, with fifty-three chapters for "professionals engaged in strategic, integrated and competitive intelligence and related organizational decision influencing disciplines." The expressed goal of SCIP is to "be the premier advocate for the skilled use of intelligence to enhance business decision-making and organizational performance to create competitive advantage."[8] The Association for Strategic Planning, founded in 1999, is a nonprofit professional society that helps business, nonprofit, and government organizations "succeed through improved strategic Thinking, Planning and Action."[9]

At some point in their professional training, many students of strategy in the United States, especially those in the national security domain, are exposed to the writings of the Prussian military strategist Carl von Clausewitz (1780–1831 CE), whose adage "war is the continuation of politics by other means," and whose emphasis on ends, ways, and means provides the principles for forming strategies that result in success. Concurrent with the historical rise of China, academic programs are increasingly requiring their students to read Sūnzi's famous text *Art of War* as a cultural manifestation of Chinese Strategic Intelligence that contrasts considerably with the European type exhibited by Clausewitz'.[10]

Since the turn of the twenty-first century, a robust debate has ensued in some circles about the appropriate philosophical foundation of strategic thought and competitive advantage. There is a growing anxiety on the part of some theorists about the intellectual foundations, philosophical legitimacy and authority, and appropriate justification of strategic thought. For example, the U.S. Office of the Director of National Intelligence convened a conference in 2005 that, amongst other items, explored the intellectual foundations of Strategic Intelligence.[11] Researchers for the US Army have recently asserted that "strategic thinking in today's military" is an "imperative," even though there is a general "confusion about the definition of strategic thinking," which is "exacerbated by the confounded concepts of strategic thinking, strategic planning, strategy, and the strategic thinker."[12] The stakes for a self-reflective understanding of strategy are high; one writer characterized the "deficit of strategy" as akin to a sickness from which the nation and its military needs to "recover,"[13] and a lost "art" that must be "rediscovered,"[14] for the consequence of miscalculation of the "strategic calculus" performed by the virtuosic strategist poses an existential threat to "our people and way of life."[15]

Theorists of strategic management in industry have also vigorously explored the intellectual roots of their discipline and have mostly attempted to legitimate their discipline within the epistemological philosophical framework of the Philosophy of Science, debating Bayesian induction, abductive inference, instrumentalist pragmatism, positivism, varieties of realism, and constructivism.[16] One theorist of strategic management noted that "strategy is an experiential arena where philosophy matters, and strategy research is beginning to recognize this connection."[17]

I concur; #PhilosophyofStrategyMatters.

What is salient to me as I review their articles is the absence of history and value. It is almost as if the identity of these strategic practitioners in different domains is disconnected from its historical, cultural roots, which have partially grown from the rich soil of the practical wisdom of deliberation (*phronesis*). And their putative objective of scientifically justifying their knowledge claims is reflective of their primary values. In other words, the question that jumps out is: to what degree has valorization of scientific knowing and of "knowing" in general predetermined their understanding of what strategy is?[18] Values therefore appear to precede knowing; what matters is not what you know—what matters is that what you value contributes to what you believe is worth knowing, how to succeed in knowing it, and how to be successful in your endeavors. Although the theorists of strategy in industry that I address above may disagree about nuances stemming from the philosophy of science and epistemology, it is clear that their shared culture enables them to express their shared values. Therefore, I recognize both the need for a type of analysis that incorporates values, new and different types of questions that we can ask of strategy, and a foundational approach to understanding Strategic Culture and Strategic Intelligence that is broad enough to orient the various communities that hope to employ them. Namely, what are the values of Strategic Intelligence? What is the connection of these values with the articulation of strategy as something that is valued as meaningful? What is the relationship between values, meaning, and culture? Where does strategy come from? What are its grounds? And, what makes it authoritative and legitimate?

CULTURAL GENEALOGY

To arrive at a more profound understanding of the dynamic of Strategic Intelligence at the level of values and meaning, and to query where it comes from, I adopted the interpretative framework of a Cultural Genealogy that enabled me to qualitatively evaluate meaning and appreciate the manner in which meaning is always historically and culturally conditioned.

Meaning is a term of art that denotes value and significance. To date, homo sapiens are the only species that we have discovered that have evolved to require a sense of meaning, and it has been argued that the human meaning-making apparatus is the system that has enabled humans to thrive because it integrates self-esteem, identity, human flourishing, and immortality.[19] What one values directly shapes those cultural roles that one feels are meaningful. For example, any female can be a biological mother if she gives birth to offspring, but motherhood is also a culturally validated meaningful role. As anybody who has interacted with tiger-, helicopter-, and Parent Teacher

Association-moms can attest, or as anybody who has observed the contemporary American "mom wars" can corroborate, the fierceness of the tiger mom stems from her critical need for meaning (gained often vicariously through her children). Humans are brilliant for the myriad creative ways that they contrive to live their lives heroically—the psychoanalyst existentialist philosopher Ernest Becker named this phenomena the *vital lie*—living out our heroic values is vital because humans cannot live without a sense of meaning, and it is a lie because ultimately the heroic role does not buy immortality. By analyzing specific projections of values articulated through the figures of heroes and villains, strategic heroes and villains in particular, one can begin to understand one way in which humans create meaning.

Genealogy itself is a genre practiced by authors hailing from many cultures, ancient and modern, who seek to make sense out of the present by tracing how the present descends from the past. It is therefore a literary means of documenting or inventing roots for the purposes of the present—Hesiod's (~750–650 BCE) *Theogony* and the biblical books of *Genesis* and the *Gospel of Matthew* are all types of genealogies. For philologists and philosophers like Friedrich Nietzsche (1844–1900 CE), and to some extent Michel Foucault (1926–1984 CE), genealogy is what Bernard Williams (1929–2003 CE) described as "a narrative that tries to explain a cultural phenomenon by describing a way in which it came about, or could have come about, or might be imagined to have come about."[20] A genealogical approach to *meaning* can be applied to study the ways in which humans at various times and places constructed a sense of significance and how it was expressed through values and worldviews. Likewise, a genealogy of Strategic Intelligence seeks to understand present strategic values by examining previous articulations via the figures of heroic and villainous strategists in cultural history.

What is salient about this genealogical way of legitimating knowledge is a recognition of the validity and authority of history. Evidence from the historical record is one way of verifying and authenticating perceptions of reality. For example, as early as the eighteenth century, the Scottish philosopher David Hume (1711–1776 CE) cast scorn on Social Contract theory as useful and prudent, but ultimately without any historical basis: "But would these reasoners look abroad into the world, they would meet with nothing that, in the least, corresponds to their ideas, or can warrant so refined and philosophical a system."[21] Nietzsche echoed Hume's criteria in the preface to his *Genealogy of Morality*, in which he undermined the authority of the English psychologists due to their lack of historical evidence. The result was that those responsible for the cultural tradition have failed at knowing themselves precisely because intellectuals have rarely sought themselves.[22] For Nietzsche, influenced by Charles Darwin's (1809–1882 CE) theory of evolution, history is a narrative that can help to explain why something useful in the present had a greater chance of surviving in culture.[23] Nietzsche's genealogical argument is a challenge—he posits that the project of "know thyself" and claims to interpreting reality are only valid if one can document the way in which the present descended from the past. Anything else is sheer speculation. For this reason, cultural evidence provided in the following chapters is authoritative because history itself is authoritative.

My interpretation has been highly influenced by Nietzsche's *Genealogy*. Like his study of the historical transvaluation of morality over time from its original and native social formation, the values of Strategic Intelligence also have their culturally genealogical provenance which have been entangled with cultural memory and amnesia, self-consciousness and ignorance. Both Western morality and Strategic Intelligence are embedded in a legacy of evolving social formations that reproduce or reject social hierarchies of domination. There is an interesting difference in findings though; whereas Nietzsche highlighted a historical process of transvaluation in morality, I point to a metaphorological paradigm that is consistently generative throughout the ages. With its emphasis on strategic rationality, it is quite possible that Strategic Intelligence is generated from the *ressentiment* of the "slave class" of priestly intellectuals, and is its greatest weapon. Nietzsche wrote:

> The priest is the first form of the more delicate animal that holds in contempt even more readily than it hates. He will not be spared waging war with the beasts of prey, a war of cunning (of the "spirit") more than of force, as goes without saying—to this end he will perhaps need almost to develop in himself, at least to signify, a new type of beast of prey—a new animal terribleness in which the polar bear, the lithe cold wait-and-see tiger cat, and not least of all the fox appear to be bound into a unity just as attractive as it is fear-inspiring.[24]

Indeed, as I will show, Strategic Intelligence has always been depicted in culture as a potent force for life.

Human values and human meaning cannot be measured quantitatively; one must use a qualitative, interpretative frame of analysis, what philosophers refer to as a hermeneutic approach, to get at them. A Cultural Genealogy then, is a hermeneutic approach to understanding value claims across a broad spectrum of historical cultural-intellectual domains, and it is an analytic framework that is particularly useful for identifying and interpreting the change and continuity of implicit features of meaning that underlie a worldview over time. Cultural Genealogy refers to the study of the evolutionary development of the meaning structures which constitute a worldview, and the value systems identifiable in the cultural history of human societies. What makes Cultural Genealogy a particularly insightful interpretative framework for analyzing these implicit features of meaning is the way that it attends to history, metaphor, ontology, and values. In this section, I begin by describing how these foci combine to make Cultural Genealogy a robust standard of objectivity, in order to explain why I understand the strategic as a form of hope molded primarily by a metaphorological paradigm.

METAPHOR, IMAGERY, AND FIGURES OF SPEECH

By leveraging metaphor, the Cultural Genealogical analytic framework provides a means for elucidating the human search for meaning. Metaphor in this instance does not just denote a literary turn of phrase; rather, metaphor articulates a paradigm by which humans perceive and construct reality.[25] Metaphors not only reveal new dimensions of human reality when one conceptual domain is juxtaposed with another, but they are central to thought itself—the more abstract the concept, the more complex the metaphor. Born in the human experience of embodiment, a metaphorological paradigm is a legacy that orients us in the world, informs how we relate to others, and how we ascribe significance to human life.[26] The imaginative aspects of reason, including metaphor and imagery, are the starting point of any philosophical anthropology, that is the study of what makes human life meaningful, and how humans construct a sense of meaning and value.[27]

In this study, I have been influenced by the German Philosophical Anthropologist Hans Blumenberg's (1920–1996 CE) notion of metaphorological paradigmatics. For him, the metaphorological is akin to, yet different from, both the emphasis on logocentric (linguistic) analysis often used by professional philosophers, and the focus on conceptual history utilized by intellectual historians.[28] The metaphorological, in being paradigmatic, preexists both, but is reducible to neither the terminological nor the conceptual. For Blumenberg, metapholorogy is an analysis of a type of nonconceptuality (*Unbegrifflichkeit*) that resists totalization and systematization—it is an excavation of the roots of human meaning in embodiment.[29] Metaphorological analysis is a philosophical query that seeks to excavate the substratum of language and concept through the manner in which it is projected.[30] This type of analysis is focused on observing, to the greatest degree possible, the ground of our existence (*daseinsgrund*), which nourishes the roots of concept formation in whatever media it is projected.[31]

Metaphors as paradigms can be organized into typologies of metaphor histories, the recovery of which may illuminate the historical provenance of human meaning.[32] Take the Copernican revolution for example; Blumenberg, quoting Johann Wolfgang von Goethe (1749–1832 CE), noted that "of all discoverers and opinions, none may have exerted a greater effect on the human spirit than the astronomical restructuring of the universe."[33] This threat to the cultural equilibrium of its time was not due to new scientific learning about astronomy—rather, it was a direct threat to astronomy's metaphorical status as an orienting model in which humanity could peg its cosmological significance or marginality, because humanity derives meaning first and foremost through embodied orientation in the world.[34] A change in a cosmological metaphor necessarily threatens human meaning because it introduces uncertainty and ambiguity into identity.

This is what I mean when I assert that the strategic is generated from a root metaphor functioning in culture. To trace the roots of Strategic Intelligence back to the ground of human existence (*daseinsgrund*), one must follow the cultural-archeological record backwards in time to the pre-Socratic and the pre-philosophic, past language and concept to more primeval forms of cognition such as metaphor and paradox; and beyond Aristotelian *phronesis* and Platonic care of the soul to the earlier *dolophronesis* (snare-awareness) and biological and bodily necessity. We must recall the first principles of our embodied humanity: that all life depends on the consumption of life, and that extending life is the first principle of human labor. This implies that death, which sometimes dissimulates as gift and sacrifice, enables life just as life necessitates death. *Life is death: death is life.* In this paradox lies the *mysterium tremendum* that is the root cause of human anxiety. This universal law is paradoxically just and unjust: we can recognize that it is the central dynamic of the universe, but it is unjust to human identity which yearns for infinity. The possibility of non-value and non-identity paradoxically sets the condition under which value and identity are made possible. And the roots of this biology-based principle extend themselves figuratively into the domains of the psychological; the sociocultural; the religious; the rhetorical; and the moral, ethical, and political aspects of the philosophical.

As I will show through my interpretation of 2,500 years of multicultural data, the strategic is generated from the paradoxical and metaphorological paradigm *life is death*. In the sense of insights arising from the study of epigenesis over the last twenty years, I understand that the root metaphor has been re-articulated in diverse forms as it has interacted with different historical, linguistic, and cultural environments. It is not that the environment or the past has determined that it should be so—rather this is merely explanatory of historical chance. In other words, a hostile environment provides the necessary stimulus to activate certain features transmitted via our cultural heritages. With this in mind, the metaphorological paradigm that underlies the strategic expresses antagonistic reality figuratively in a variety of ways, which include closure, entrapment, finitude, damnation, manipulation, fraud (trick, lie, ruse, artifice), deception, covert, concealment, darkness, unseen, unreal, ignorance, and illusion. In contrast, heroic hope is articulated as life, reality, infinitude, liberation, freedom, emancipation, salvation, escapement, self-actualization, enlightenment, self-esteem, dignity, movement, exposure, wisdom, and disclosure. The root metaphor is always wrapped up with cultural legacies of hierarchy, justice and injustice, order and disorder, the authoritative, and the illegitimate. I believe that we can track the root metaphor-paradigm in multiple cultural domains and genres, but that it is ultimately resistant to conceptual and terminological totalization. In other words, this metaphorological paradigm is itself *dolophronic* and *dolometic*: a reducible building block of the strategic escapes us![35] Like Blumenberg's monograph *Paradigms for a Metaphorology*, which has been characterized as focused on the "insights" and "strategies by which we cope with an otherwise alien and overpowering reality," the strategic is fundamental for the manner in which it structures our perception of reality and informs human meaning.[36]

An analysis of metaphor and imagery is one of the best ways to trace the human search for meaning. With regards to the power of metaphor, Francis Ambrosio in his text *Philosophy, Religion, and the Search for Meaning* wrote that metaphor

> can offer insights into the dynamics of human experience in its encounter with the mystery of existence as a whole, as well as suggesting new paths for inquiry. Used judiciously, these metaphors can serve as hermeneutic tools; that is, tools that are capable of opening up new possibilities of understanding at a level of meaning and truth that exceeds the scope and authority of the properly scientific. Metaphor is the most powerful tool that the human imagination can employ in relation to the mystery of reality as a whole. Metaphors make their own kind of truth claims, and I think we will discover in the course of our investigations that it is those truth claims precisely that are reached through metaphor; that are most powerful in their claim on human experience; and most rich in their contribution to the human search for meaning.[37]

Metaphors model and inform reality and perception, bundle values into prescriptive and normative cultural memory, and thus guide human behavior. For example, in his 1997 book *Moral Politics: What Conservatives Know that Liberals Don't*, the American Cognitive Linguist George Lakoff convincingly demonstrated the degree to which metaphor, values, and cultural politics are inextricably linked.[38] Synthesizing insights from Ernest Becker who saw that cultural politics was actually a battle of values that had been bundled into culturally validated "heroic roles," and the Prussian military strategist Karl Von Clausewitz who claimed that "war is the continuation of politics by other means," we can postulate that culture war is a life and death war fought for preferred metaphors and the human values that underlie them.[39]

Another aspect of metaphor that is particularly applicable to Cultural Genealogy lies in a metaphor's inherent ability to compare divergent domains. As all translators know from experience, in the cross-cultural context, metaphors such as "time is money" (or in our case, *life is death*) are full of both promise and peril because partaking of conceptual and linguistic features of a given language in a particular era makes it impossible to entirely capture all of the same nuances of a metaphor in the cultural, conceptual, and linguistic features of a different language of a different era. Because metaphors compare, the assertion of a preexistent paradigm enables us to examine their comparability across cultural, temporal, and linguistic barriers.

Metaphorical analysis is more conducive to the type of data that I examine in this book than Structuralist analysis. Whereas Structuralist approaches to cultural analysis can be quite powerful in their ability to explain complex cultural phenomena, they are also limited. Structuralist analyses in general rely on collecting, analyzing, and quantifying data represented explicitly on the surface form of the text, which it subjects to binary analysis. This methodology assumes an "either-or" essential contrast, and a true correspondence between linguistic utterance, concept, and value, which it articulates as "structure." Taking my inspiration from the Political Philosopher Leo Strauss who noted the esoteric aspect of much intellectual writing throughout history, I refer to the interpretative framework that I use as Cultural Cryptology. Cryptology is that field which studies the phenomenology of hiding and revealing (κρυπτός *conceal* + λόγος study of), and when applied to cultural data it is a mode of analysis sensitized to the covert aspects of meaning in a source, and sources as meaningful responses to what incited their creation.[40] In contrast to the assumptions in Structuralist approaches, I assume that meaning can also be hidden strategically beyond word-level evidence, that values in texts can be both explicit and implicit, that secret, silence, and invisibility in the surface of the source can be even more meaningful than what is explicitly expressed, and that meaning can be dispositioned paradoxically as "both-and," rather than "either-or."

All metaphors seem to both conceal even as they reveal aspects of reality. For example, when metaphors such as *time is money* become dominant, they tend to close off other aspects to awareness. Other than the apparent human unease with cognitive dissonance, there is no reason why the capitalist-influenced *time is money* metaphor cannot coexist with a medically inspired metaphor such as *time is bleeding away*. In this book, I assert that the paradoxical metaphor *life is death* is so cognitively dissonant that it is systematically erased from the surface form of the text, while still being functional as an underlying metaphorical paradigm. Cultural Cryptology enables us to see the strategic value that is functioning esoterically even if it is not articulated explicitly. This books aims to show students of Western strategic thought that the functional equivalent of *metic* intelligence continued to exist in a variety of cultures over time, even though its linguistic signifiers varied, or are not explicitly mentioned at all. Similarly, students of Chinese strategic thought may learn about the theoretical aspects of *discerning dynamics shì* 勢 from Sūnzi's *Art of War*. But literary texts, such as chapter 18 of Wú Jiǎnrén's *Uncanny Reality Witnessed over Twenty Years* which I discuss in chapter 7, demonstrate practically how a strategic master wields *shì* 勢 and strategic technique *shù* 術 virtuosically—without ever explicitly mentioning these terms in the text.[41] Cultural Cryptology enables us to recover implicit values functioning in the text in a way that Structuralism can not.

Cultural Genealogy is a hermeneutic framework that leverages insights from the fields of history (genealogy) and biology (phylogenesis, epigenetics). For example, I use the concept of phylogenesis from the field of biological science to explain metaphorically how certain value features descended in culture over time from common ancestors, which is imagined to be mapped as a tree of life. I do not claim that the ancestors themselves predetermined the future projections, but rather that the resurgence of certain features is better explained by the interaction of offspring with similarly antagonistic environments. By juxtaposing the metaphor of lines of cultural descent with these domain-specific fields, Cultural Genealogy itself leverages the features that makes the answers to these queries valid. Cultural Genealogy adopts a sophisticated apparatus that explains the appearance of similar projections in terms of descent and common experience, and bases its claims about reality (ontology) on experiential evidence excavated from the historical cultural record, marking it as both replicable and verifiable.

To reiterate, I do not claim that phylogenesis as a metaphor for cultural descent is deterministic. I think that the resurfacing of a specific projection has been made possible by, not determined by, the ancestor. I understand that the transmission of the values of the strategic are meaningful and strategically advantageous because of human interaction with a reality that is consistently exposed to be either hostile to or ambivalent about human life and ambition. An epigenetic-inspired understanding of phylogenesis tries to balance descent in history with environmental interaction over the mechanism of reproduction. Because I argue for the strategic in terms of both similarity and difference, I use the notion of a paradoxical metaphorological paradigm to explain the unity, and the metaphorical figure of rhizomatic sub-structures to represent the multiplicity of cultural expression.[42] But since I examine multiple metaphors and figures that have descended in multiple cultures, perhaps a more apt metaphor for the tree of life might be the *forest of life*. The forest of life of Strategic Intelligence is a map that exposes to view the general shape of the way in which Strategic Intelligence as a form of meaning has been continuously expressed. In the case of Strategic Intelligence, the repeated and aggregated evidence organized in a cultural genealogy illuminates a type of strategic identity found in multiple cultures, a consistent *Way* (*dào* 道) of human meaning, and the possibility of human advantage in an ambivalent and/or antagonistic environment.

LIMITATIONS

Utilizing the concept of phylogenesis metaphorically is but one heuristic technique to get at meaning. But as with any tool, it is limited by what it can do. In this sense, I include within the scope of this study the metaphorical use of phylogenesis as a philosophical means of excavating meaning. *Caveat emptor*, for those technical specialists whose reading strategies are shaped by current debates in their disciplines or by trends in academia at large, I make no strong claims of historical causality, and have scoped out an investigation of the historical process of cross-cultural diffusion and dissemination. This book actually began with numerous unsuccessful attempts on my part to explain to Western students the intricacies of the Chinese strategic worldview, a perspective that assigns great importance to their indigenous culture. I quickly realized that there was no Western cultural baseline of Strategic Intelligence with which to begin comparison as Americans, even the most educated, appear to be estranged from their own cultural heritage. And so I endeavored to excavate that genealogy first.

The separation of data into European and Chinese sections is not altogether arbitrary, but should not be taken as evidence of ethnocentrism or cultural stove piping. In the economy of meaning, there are always trade-offs—the cultural stovepipes are a consequence of my choice to demonstrate the recursive aspect of cultural evolution, a process in which producers of cultural products adapt elements from their cultural patrimony. Thus the reemergence of *Thickblackology* (chapters 7 & 8) at the end of the twentieth century and its birth at the end of the Chinese Imperial order at the beginning of that century is understood here within the Chinese strategic framework informed by cultural products that preceded it for thousands of years. This aspect comes at the cost of ignoring transcultural influences—although I perceive and explicitly gesture to a Nietzschean influence on *Thickblackology*, I barely pull that thread within the scope of this book.[43] Also, I tried to balance these cultural stovepipes by gesturing to a similar phenomenon in Islamic and South Asian cultural traditions. I mean these sections to be suggestive, but presently insufficient, and contingent on future research.

I divided the cultural evidence in light of the types of authorities that modern readers in various communities feel are important for two reasons. First, as opposed to assertions made by previous scholars, the cultural evidence demonstrates that Greco-Roman strategic values made their way into the Late

Antiquity, Medieval and Renaissance cultures of various Mediterranean and European polities.[44] Second, dividing the cultural data in terms of a religious or secular authority, although anachronistic and never entirely divisible, nonetheless aids in connecting with modern audiences who often perceive the world along said disjunctures. I readily and preemptively agree that the story could be told another way and that new insights could be and will be gleaned from that telling. My intent in dividing the cultural evidence in this way is to sidestep any facile East-West, least-best binary, and my interpretation of the cultural evidence produced by multiple Eurasian polities in multiple eras aims to balance continuity with disjuncture.

Biological evolution, which mode of transmission in practice is very different from cultural evolution, can nonetheless also be used metaphorically to set the basis and common theoretical background for understanding cultural descent. Whereas biological communication is relatively slow and limited by the laws of genetics in regards to which set of features that it can transmit forward, cultural transmission is fast; it is not limited by genetic and biological constraints, but instead is driven forward by the recursive capability of intellectual consciousness. Cultural transmission creates its own distinctively human environment and shapes the opportunities it provides. As Peter God-frey-Smith pointed out in his book *Philosophy of Biology*, concepts of change, adaptability, fitness, reproduction, survival, and strategic advantage for individuals and populations in various cultural ecosystems lend themselves well to Cultural Genealogy, especially to the cultural genealogy of strategic rationality, which informs the worldview of Strategic Intelligence that claims to enable the weak to reverse sociopolitical asymmetry.[45]

Although my emphasis on phylogenesis differs from the metaphor of cultural genetics utilized by Ambrosio, what he wrote below is still valid if we swap out the term "genetic" for the term "genealogical."

> The perspective of genetic explanation is fundamentally different from any and every type of metaphysical explanatory framework, including the framework of classical and modern science until the time of Darwin . . . the basic distinction between the genetic and metaphysical explanatory perspectives is the way of understanding the role of history in each perspective. In metaphysical terms, explanation proceeds on the basis of a "first cause" or a "prime mover" that must exist as an absolute principle in order to avoid the absurdity of an infinite regress. Logically, such an absolute principle must transcend every spatio-temporal condition; in other words, it must be beyond history and apart from history. A genetic explanatory framework, on the other hand, employs explanatory factors, all of which are correlative to all other factors—every one is connected to every other; nothing is beyond the system; nothing is absolute—because none operates above or beyond a spatio-temporal matrix; that is, none is outside of space and time. In other words, all genetic explanations function within the

horizons of history, and no appeal to or allowance for metaphysical transcendence beyond the historical is invoked in such explanation.[46]

Cultural Genealogy is an analytic framework that appropriately explains the continuity and change over time of human values at the level of meaning. Although it is true that meaning evolves over time and that the meaning of life has been adapted to various cultural ecosystems, this provides the dark backdrop against which we can more clearly see both the transmission of the values of strategic rationality in a consistently articulated identity and worldview through the ages and cultural lines of descent from common cultural ancestors themselves molded by the root metaphor.

ONTOLOGY

The third focus that makes Cultural Genealogy a particularly insightful analytic framework is its insistence on articulating a legitimate and verifiable ontology, that is to say, the way that one describes aspects of reality. An appropriate ontology is authoritative because it is existential—human articulation and interpretation of existence is predicated on direct experience, and experience creates artifacts in the historical-cultural record. Nietzsche alluded to the importance of the existential-historical in his own philosophical-historical hermeneutic method, such as when he emphasized that "which can be documented, which can really be ascertained, which has really existed, in short, the very long, difficult-to-decipher, hieroglyphic writing of the human moral past."[47] The American pragmatist philosopher William James (1842–1910) agreed, concisely noting that "truth has its paleontology."[48]

Replicable, verifiable evidence from the historical record is critical because it legitimizes any human interpretation of reality. In essence, history provides the touchstone upon which human knowledge of reality is culturally situated. Getting reality right is critical for the human for two reasons: (1) the right understanding of the world makes human existence meaningful, and (2) it provides strategic advantage in the domain of action through orientation. In other words, appropriately interpreting our ecosystem informs how we successfully navigate through it.

A values analysis enables us to interpret and theorize about aspects of our common humanity, the values aspect of human existence, that are not queryable through quantitative and empirical approaches. But how exactly, the reader may wonder, can values function as analytic variables if they are a "mystery," as the title of Axiologist Ludwig Grünberg's monograph *The Mystery of Values* suggests?[49] In the axiological ontology explored by

American philosopher-theologian Robert Neville, human knowing begins with embodied human experience. Human experience of the world leads to strategic advantage because of the power of imagination, which is an internal process of synthesis. Imaginative synthesis is a "primordial value" that integrates experience, feelings, thought, and memory.

> Imagination is the beginning of experience. Creatures without imagination might at any given time respond to particular stimuli; but without imagination, they cannot respond at a moment from the perspective of many moments. With imagination, for instance, it is possible to respond now from the perspective of a whole judgement that began a few moments ago and which vaguely aims off into the future.... It is imagination that makes it possible to respond to a subjective world with both spatial and temporal dimensions ... the most elementary function of imagination is gathering so as to constitute experience in the form of a world present to a subject.[50]

Imagination not only produces images that can be analyzed, but they are image-projections with value, significance, worth, and meaning for human existence.[51] Images are the expressed form of imagination, which is itself the output of the process that synthesizes experience.[52] Figures, as a type of image, articulate a legacy of human experience, and they may be understood as a framing device for values, as a pointer to a master narrative, and as a type of culture-based model or schema. As a specific mode of communication, figures preserve a level of ambiguity that defies and frustrates simple linguistic definition, semantic clarity, and deductive and inductive reasoning. In fact, understanding the meaning of figures and the values that they transmit may have more to do with how figures resonate with the type of cognition we now understand as emotional intelligence. In this book, I look for the meaning of strategy expressed through the figures of exemplary strategists, and the identity, heroic values, and ways of life that they express.

A forensic and interpretative analysis of underlying values is possible because values are born by the figures in cultural products, what the German philosopher Max Scheler (1874–1928 CE) described as a "value bearer" (*wertträger*). To the degree that the history of valued human experience expressed in image in both metaphors and figures of speech becomes the horizon for a given community, they become axiomatically meaningful at the level of culture. In this philosophy of culture, culture is defined primarily as a systematic realm of values, that "engenders common cultural assets for humanity and a common responsibility for their preservation or continuation."[53] Value is a "specifically human way of responding to the world through projections, attitudes, preferences, ideals."[54] Human value is the substrate of culture.

> Value is the ontological foundation of constitutive culture; it is the irreducible factor of human creativity. By way of its axiological propensity, culture is not only a continuation and amplification of nature by humankind; beyond a certain limit, culture is a source pursuing its own purposes, the biological cause of which cannot be found. Understood in the perspective of the axiocentric ontology of the human, culture is an autonomous realm of values with its opening toward the dilemmas of the human condition.[55]

In essence, the human species is itself the domain of values. Values are what makes us human in that we value and need to be valued in a certain way. We are simply "values-beings."[56] A proper interpretation and analysis of images expressed in the phenomenon of cultural products thus enables us to reconstruct the mystery of values operating at the core of humanity.

Together these foci come together in the analytic framework of Cultural Genealogy as a value-centric approach to questioning that can be characterized as qualitative and hermeneutical as opposed to approaches whose authority and legitimacy to answering questions are derived from metaphysics or empirically based scientific method. Empirical approaches do not have the capacity to analyze human value because they can only measure—we certainly may value measurement (although it cannot of itself have *meaning*), but measurement is incommensurable with human values and meaning.

My concern herein is with excavating human values, appropriately interpreting worldviews, and fleshing out the metaphorological paradigm that generates strategic thought in its many historical and culturally conditioned forms. As I aim to show, the worldview articulated though the metaphorical figures and cultural identities of various heroic strategists is one of the most ancient and most reproduced in the historical cultural record, and its line of descent can be tracked right back to the beginning of Eurasian civilization. It corresponds to what I consider as one of the most important of all the possible human journeys towards meaning, and quite simply the first wisdom—human enlightenment is nothing other than the awakening to the primacy of mystery, finitude, deception, the not-true, the not-real, the double, to fundamental uncertainty and the threat of contingency. This is the most profoundly disturbing of all human truth. Paradoxically, human security is ultimately an illusion, deception is the primary feature of life, life is framed by death, and existence by nonexistence. But there is hope—in such a dark reality, the cultural genealogy of Strategic Intelligence documents a heroic path in which the strategic virtuoso may appropriately interpret the strategic environment, which results in her foresight, adaptation, survival, and strategic advantage. Strategic Intelligence is heroic, existential, paradoxical, and hopeful.

CHAPTER SUMMARIES

After laying out the theoretical and methodological framework in chapter 1, I then trace the transmission of the values of strategic rationality that are born through figures of heroic strategists in cultural products excavated from more than 2,500 years of civilization. I explore in chapters 2–3 strategic values articulated in the heroic *dolophronic* and *dolometic* figures in Greco-Roman cultural products. In addition to the strategic values derived from the Greco-Roman heritage, I excavate in chapter 4 the strategic values transmitted via authoritative Judeo-Christian cultural sources. I demonstrate in chapter 5 the presence of strategic values through heroically strategic figures in important sources from various cultures throughout the Medieval and Renaissance periods. Lastly, I gesture to the potential universality of the paradoxical metaphorological paradigm that generates strategic thought in culture in chapters 7–8 by tracing a cultural genealogy of the heroically strategic in Chinese civilization, before concluding this monograph in chapter 9.

NOTES

1. Jack L. Snyder, *The Soviet Strategic Culture: Implications for Nuclear Options*, R-2154–AF (Santa Monica, CA: Rand Corporation, 1977). Alastair I. Johnston, "Thinking about Strategic Culture," *International Security*, 19:4 (Spring 1995), 32–64, accessed 27 April 2017, http://www.fb03.uni-frankfurt.de/45431264/Johnston-1995-Thinking-about-Strategic-Culture.pdf.

2. Colin S. Gray, "Out of the Wilderness: Prime Time for Strategic Culture," National Institute for Public Policy, United States Nuclear Strategy Forum, Publication No. 0004, National Institute Press, 2006, accessed 21 January 2019, http://www.nipp.org/wp-content/uploads/2014/12/CSG-Strategic-culture-paper-Marheine-pub.pdf.

3. For example, see Alastair Iain Johnston, "Strategic Cultures Revisited: Reply to Colin Gray," *Review of International Studies*, 25:3 (1999), 519–523. Colin Gray, "Strategic Culture as Context: The First Generation of Theory Strikes Back," *Review of International Studies*, 25:1 (1999), 49–69. Stuart Poore, "What is the Context? A Reply to the Gray-Johnston Debate on Strategic Culture," *Review of International Studies*, 29:2 (2003), 279–284. Based on their cultural analyses, well-known scholars on China such as Andrew Scobell have characterized China's Strategic Culture in terms of "a cult of defense," and in terms of cultural realism and realpolitik. Andrew Scobell, *China and Strategic Culture* (Carlisle, PA: Strategic Studies Institute, US Army War College, 2002), accessed 27 January 2019, https://www.globalsecurity.org/military/library/report/2002/ssi_scobell.pdf. Iain Johnston, *Cultural Realism: Strategic Culture and Grand Strategy in Chinese History* (Princeton, NJ: Princeton University Press, 1998).

4. Gray (*Wilderness*), for example, throws shade on scholars of the theoretical (such as Johnston) by noting that "Strategy is a practical business," but conceals awareness of the roots of the practical in the ancient Western tradition of prudence (*phronesis*). In *History* (note 13), he again alludes to the "the virtues of prudence," which cites Raymond Aron, *Peace and War: A Theory of International Relations* (New York: Doubleday, 1966), 285.

5. "Journal of Strategic Intelligence," National Intelligence University, accessed 26 April 2017, http://ni-u.edu/wp/csir/journal-of-stategic-intelligence/.

6. "Online Journal," Strategic Culture Foundation, accessed 26 April 2017, http://www.strategic-culture.org/articles/about.html.

7. "Strategic Intelligence Division," U.S. Department of Commerce, Bureau of Industry and Security, accessed 26 April 201, https://www.bis.doc.gov/index.php/enforcement/oea/sid.

8. "Mission Statement," Strategic and Competitive Intelligence Professionals, accessed 26 April 2017, http://www.scip.org/?page=missionstatement.

9. "About Us," Association for Strategic Planning, accessed 27 February 2018, https://www.strategyassociation.org/?page=aboutus_overview.

10. Sūnzi 孫子, *Art of War Bīngfǎ* 兵法. A view disputed by David A. Graff, "Brain over Brawn: Shared Beliefs and Presumptions in Chinese and Western 'Strategemata,'" *Extrême-Orient Extrême-Occident*, No. 38, *La Guerre en Perspective: Histoire et Culture Militaire en Chine/War in Perspective: History and Military Culture in China* (2014), 47–64.

11. Gregory F. Treverton, Seth G. Jones, Steven Boraz, Phillip Lipscy, "Toward a Theory of Intelligence: Workshop Report," Rand Corporation, 2006, accessed 27 February 2018, https://www.rand.org/content/dam/rand/pubs/conf_proceedings/2006/RAND_CF219.pdf.

12. *Exploring Strategic Thinking: Insights to Assess, Develop, and Retain Army Strategic Thinkers*, ed. Heather M. K. Wolters, Anna P. Grome, Ryan M. Hinds (Fort Belvoir, VA: US Army Research Institute, United States Army Research Institute for the Behavioral and Social Sciences), Research Product 2013-01, accessed 21 January 2019, https://ssl.armywarcollege.edu/dclm/pubs/Developing%20Army%20Strategic%20Thinkers.pdf.

13. Colin S. Gray, *What Should the U.S. Army Learn From History? Recovery From a Strategy Deficit* (Carlisle, PA: US Army War College Press, Strategic Studies Institute, 2017), accessed 21 January 2019, https://ssi.armywarcollege.edu/pubs/display.cfm?pubID=1360.

14. Daniel H. McCauley, "Rediscovering the Art of Strategic Thinking: Developing 21st century Strategic Leaders," *Joint Force Quarterly* 81 (2nd Quarter, April 2016), National Defense University Press, accessed 21 January 2019, https://ndupress.ndu.edu/JFQ/Joint-Force-Quarterly-81/Article/702006/rediscovering-the-art-of-strategic-thinking-developing-21st-century-strategic-l/.

15. Charles H. Jacoby, Jr., with Ryan L. Shaw, "Strategic Agility: Theory and Practice," *Joint Force Quarterly* 81 (2nd Quarter, April 2016), National Defense University Press, accessed 21 January 2019, https://ndupress.ndu.edu/JFQ/Joint-Force-Quarterly-81/Article/702009/strategic-agility-theory-and-practice/.

16. Kai-Man Kwan and Eric W. K. Tsang, "Realism and Constructivism in Strategy Research: A Critical Realist Response to Mir and Watson," *Strategic Management Journal*, 12:22 (2001): 1163–1168; Raza Mir and Andrew Watson, "Critical Realism and Constructivism in Strategy Research: Toward a Synthesis," *Strategic Management Journal*, 12:22 (2001): 1169–1173; Thomas C. Powell, "Competitive Advantage: Logical and Philosophical Considerations," *Strategic Management Journal*, 9:22 (2001): 875–888; Rodolphe Durand, "Competitive Advantages Exist: A Critique of Powell," *Strategic Management Journal*, 9:23 (2002): 867–872; Richard J. Arend, "Revisiting the Logical and Research Considerations of Competitive Advantage," *Strategic Management Journal*, 3: 24 (2003): 279–284; Thomas C. Powell, "Strategy Without Ontology," *Strategic Management Journal*, 3:24 (2003): 285–291.

17. Thomas C. Powell, "The Philosophy of Strategy," *Strategic Management Journal*, 23 (2002): 873–880.

18. By "knowing," I refer to philosophical queries that emphasize epistemology, the study of knowing.

19. Ernest Becker, *The Denial of Death* (New York: Free Press Paperbacks/Simon & Schuster, 1973).

20. Bernard Williams, *Truth and Truthfulness* (Princeton: Princeton University Press, 2002), 20.

21. David Hume, *Of the Original Contract, in Classics of Political & Moral Philosophy*, ed. Steven M. Cahn (Oxford: Oxford University Press, 2012), 640.

22. Friedrich Nietzsche, *On the Genealogy of Morality*, trans. Maudemarie Clark and Alan J. Swensen (Hackett: Indianapolis/Cambridge: 1998), 1.

23. Maudemarie Clark, "Introduction" Friedrich Nietzsche, *On the Genealogy of Morality*, trans. Maudemarie Clark and Alan J. Swensen (Hackett: Indianapolis/Cambridge: 1998), xxiii-xxvi.

24. Nietzsche, *Genealogy*, 90. Reprinted with permission, curtesy of Hackett Publishing Company.

25. George Lakoff and Mark Johnson, *Metaphors We Live By* (Chicago: University of Chicago Press, 1980).

26. Lakoff and Johnson, *Metaphors*, 3, 226–228.

27. George Lakoff, *Women, Fire, and Dangerous Things: What Categories Reveal about the Mind* (Chicago: University of Chicago Press, 1987), xi.

28. Hans Blumenberg, *Paradigms for a Metaphorology*, trans. Robert Savage (Ithaca: Cornell University Press, 2010), 77.

29. Blumenberg, *Paradigms*, 134–135.

30. Blumenberg, *Paradigms*, 5.

31. Blumenberg, *Paradigms*, 139.

32. Blumenberg, *Paradigms*, 77.

33. Blumenberg, *Paradigms*, 100–101.

34. Blumenberg, *Paradigms*, 11, 102.

35. These terms, *dolophronic* (δολόφρονε) and *dolometic* (δολόμητις), are discussed in (chapters 2–5). Ancient Greek Strategic rationality expressed the heroic strategic through the figure of the heroic strategist who was the master the art of ruse and stratagem.

36. Blumenberg, *Paradigms*, 146.

37. Francis Ambrosio, *Philosophy, Religion, and the Search for Meaning* (The Great Courses, 2013), 24.

38. George Lakoff, *Moral Politics: What Conservatives Know that Liberals Don't* (Chicago: University of Chicago Press, 1997).

39. Ernest Becker, *The Denial of Death* (New York: Free Press Paperbacks/Simon & Schuster, 1973).

40. The technique of leading by indirection, *ductus obliquus*, through noble lies and pious frauds, was mentioned by Leo Strauss in chapter 2 "Persecution and the Art of Writing," in Leo Strauss, *Persecution and the Art of Writing* (Chicago: University of Chicago Press, 1952/1988), 38.

41. Wú Jiānrén 吳趼人, *Uncanny Reality Witnessed over Twenty Years Èrshínián Mùdǔ zhī Guài Xiànzhuàng* 二十年目睹之怪現狀 (Běijīng: Rénmín Chūbǎnshè: Xīnhuá Shūdiàn Běijīng fāxíngsuǒ fāxíng, 1959), 1–6.

42. Peter Godfrey-Smith, *Philosophy of Biology* (Princeton & Oxford: Princeton University Press, 2014), 113.

43. Lǐ mentions the Nietzschean ubermensch in his *Psychology and Mechanics* (*Xīnlǐ yǔ Lìxué* 心理與力學).

44. See chapter 7, note 5.

45. Godfrey-Smith, *Philosophy, 35*, 46, 52.

46. Ambrosio, *Philosophy*, 23.

47. Nietzsche, *Genealogy of Morality*, 6.

48. William James, *Pragmatism, a New name for Some Old Ways of Thinking, Together with Four Related Essays Selected from the Meaning of Truth* (New York: Longmans, Green and Co, 1948), 37.

49. Ludwig Grünberg, *The Mystery of Values; Studies in Axiology* (Amsterdam, Rodopi: 2000).

50. Robert C. Neville, *Reconstruction of Thinking* (Albany: State University of New York Press, 1981), 135.

51. Neville, *Reconstruction of Thinking*, 17.

52. Neville, *Reconstruction of Thinking*, 219.

53. Neville, *Reconstruction of Thinking*, 56–57.

54. Neville, *Reconstruction of Thinking*, 57.

55. Neville, *Reconstruction of Thinking*, 58–59.

56. Robert Ginsberg, "Preface" to Ludwig Grünberg, *The Mystery of Values; Studies in Axiology* (Amsterdam, Rodopi: 2000), vii, xiii.

Chapter 2

Greco-Roman Strategic Intelligence
Strategic Heroes, Divine, and Human

Cultural products are rarely explicit—rather, they are often highly stylized in a manner that requires proper interpretation to uncover their latent lessons and hidden values. Before analyzing the strategic values expressed through ancient Greek sources, I begin this chapter by examining a relatively late North American artifact that I see as emblematic of Strategic Intelligence for the manner in which it bundles specific features that are common to these types of stories as a whole, and because they all respond to an unspoken understanding of life that is constrained by finitude, which in turn necessitates Strategic Intelligence. Disney's animated film *The Sword and the Stone* (1963) is just one of many examples of popular cultural products that demonstrate that strategic values are fundamental to culture. I then turn to ancient Greek narratives that express strategic values through the figures of heroically strategic gods, men, and animals.

Popular cultural products such as *The Sword and the Stone* (1963) serve as vehicles that articulate important cultural values to our most vulnerable and innocent demographic, our naïve young.[1] One of the most interesting ways that cultural products have articulated the values of Strategic Intelligence is through the motif of the antagonistic competition between predators and prey, and the presentation of the identity of the heroic strategist as a potent form of hope against physical and symbolic death. The wizard's duel in the film is a stylized representation of a zero-sum antagonistic reality, and the plot is peopled with an enlightened teacher who demonstrates heroic and strategically cunning intelligence, and an innocent protagonist who needs to learn fast. The entertaining lyrics of "Thats What Makes the World Go Round" clarifies that human reality is constituted of the antagonistic relationship between the strong and the weak, and that hope lies in the use of a mode of wisdom which I call Strategic Intelligence.

The wizard's duel between Merlin and the antagonistic and crafty hedge witch Madame Mim, is essentially a battle of wits. In a wizard's duel, masters engage in magical *kung fu* by transforming themselves into a series of creatures traditionally known to be related in a predator-prey relationship. During the duel, each mage dynamically responds to and anticipates his or her opponent's metamorphosis, and by so doing, each proves his or her know-how, and the virtuosic command of their strategic art.

The scene presents Strategic Intelligence as the means to victory against existential threat. It is a type of intelligence that is informed by sensitivity, experience, and clarity that leads to rapid adaptation and appropriate action. The great wizard's duel functions in the film as the final test of a practical curriculum in which young Prince Arthur becomes sensitized to the reality of the world. For example, Arthur first tastes love while transfigured into a squirrel, and he learns to be very wary of the unanticipated crisis of death, the elation of victory of brain over brawn, and the necessity of the mastery of the art of strategy when chased by a predatory pike while in the form of a minnow.[2] The capacity to adapt to contingency is the main theme of the scene, and success is evaluated by the practitioner's ability to rapidly attend to the unanticipated. After Mim takes the form of a crocodile for example, Merlin quickly responds by transforming into a snapping turtle that bites her. When Merlin metamorphoses into a hare, Mim responds with the shape of a fox. The two virtuosos subsequently transform into a walrus, an elephant, a mouse, a tomcat, a rattlesnake, a crab, a rhinoceros, a goat, a purple dragon, and a virus. Each metamorphosis manifests a type of intelligence that is informed by sensitivity to the opponent and the environment that directly leads to rapid reaction, and ultimately to strategic advantage.

The wizard's duel is a game of wit that is framed by ruse, stratagem, entrapment, and escape, and it is designed to prove both one's mettle and quality. It is, I think, what the ancient Greeks would have referred to as being *snare-aware* (*dolophrone* δολόφρονε), which I discuss at length in the next chapter. As the scene progresses, Merlin, and his voyeurs, becomes continuously sensitized to threat and insecurity through a series of fearful encounters. In addition to anticipating Mim's patterns, he also tactically interprets the features of the specific environment to gain strategic advantage. For instance, he transforms into a centipede when he spies a small hole in a hollow log from which he escapes crocodile-Mim, who subsequently transmogrifies into a chicken. Merlin proves his consummate proficiency in the end through ingenuity—he counters the asymmetric threat by leveraging knowledge that Mim does not have. Because Merlin has time-traveled, he has learned from the future about modern germ-theory—he unfairly weaponizes this knowledge by changing the very nature of the competition, and unexpectedly infects dragon-Mim with himself as a rare virus. This sneaky move vanquishes his foe to her sickbed, liberates his young protégée from Mim's clutch, cathartically releases tension, demonstrates the triumph of "good" over and "evil," exemplifies strategic values by manifesting the excellence of Strategic Intelligence, and teaches an important lesson both to his naïve prince Arthur and to the external voyeur.

I am interested here with understanding the nuances of this important lesson.

Many scenes from *The Sword and the Stone* depict the theme of the unanticipated encounter with contingency, finitude, mystery, and death. For Prince Arthur, this theme includes both the threat of physical death and the figurative threat to his ambition and self-esteem since it is not certain that young "Wart" will achieve his potential as the King Arthur of legend. The question that has driven the research for this book is simply why culture, in this case contemporary North American culture, has validated this as a legitimate topic to be embedded in a cultural product designed for the youngest demographic of North American society. My answer to this question, and the conclusion that I have reached after tracing this theme in cultural products produced by civilizations over the course of thousands of years, is that societies have legitimated and authorized this message time and time again because, when used in an exemplary fashion, Strategic Intelligence is a potent force against the unanticipated threats posed by antagonistic reality. Cultural products have always served as the preeminent vehicle in a curriculum of Strategic Intelligence that intends to habituate society's most vulnerable, the naïve, to strategic virtue in order to succeed in the game of life.

Cultural products are not just mere entertainment—they are *edutainment*. Cultural products that express strategic values communicate models and memories which have crystallized insights developed through embodied experience over millennia, as well as interpretive frameworks that enable practitioners of Strategic Intelligence to achieve strategic advantage by appropriately interpreting the threat features of an antagonistic reality. There is a common set of features in all of these stories which gestures to a cultural genealogy that can be traced for over two and a half millennia. These features highlight (1) personal experience as a means of sensitization to the threat features of any given antagonistic reality which is depicted as zero-sum, (2) this sensitization to the threat features leads to strategic vision, which is the capacity to interpret the nuances of any new threat environment, and (3) proper interpretation then enables appropriate adaptation and reaction, which leads to strategic advantage. Although they are rarely called out explicitly, other features of heroic Strategic Intelligence in the film include opportunism and timing, anticipation, resourcefulness, rapid adaptation, covert means, trickery, and deception.

In addition to being emotionally satisfying edutainment, there are three features that make the wizard's duel interesting. First, metamorphosis is a device, and the wizard's duel a framing mechanism that highlights the issues of the unanticipated and of contingency, and the threat that a violent and conflict-laden reality poses to an embodied being. Second, the scene promises hope in the form of power over the unknown—Merlin's Strategic Intelligence offers a type of symbolic immortality by portraying an exemplary and heroic mode of human action that is able to overcome existential threat. Third, the wizard's duel is emblematic of a mode of Strategic Intelligence with a long multi-cultural genealogy. The movie is itself a source that frames a profound question that one should ask when dealing with the unanticipated, and points to the answer: *WWMD? What Would Merlin Do?* The novice has learned vicariously that human ingenuity, which I call strategic rationality, when used in an exemplary fashion, enables life, ambition, and self-esteem in the face of finitude.

Stories of Strategic Intelligence are always framed by insecurity. Reality, otherwise known as the threat environment, is tyrannical. It is unfair, unjust, and illegitimate. Life in this worldview is sustained only by the death (literal and figurative) of others; nature is *red in tooth and claw*—conflict, violence, and murder are primary. History is full of stories that demonstrate that security is not even to be had within the confines of the family. The psychoanalyst Ernest Becker identified death terror in the dependence of infants on their mother, who had the power to deny life at any moment;[3] the theologian Søren Kierkegaard also made much of existential anxiety in the Biblical narrative of the sacrifice of Isaac by his father Abraham.[4] The leitmotif of familial murder in our culturally foundational religious, literary, and dramatic stories are striking, such as the cannibalism of Saturn; the exposure of Oedipus; the sacrifices of Isaac, Iphigenia, and Jesus; the fratricide of Cain and Abel; and the infanticide of Medea. The seer Isaiah captured this aspect of reality perfectly in the Old Testament: "Terror and pit and snare confront you, O inhabitant of the earth."[5]

Humans are always the underdog, since human life is transitory, ephemeral, and fragile—always vulnerable to the potential entrapment of *pit and snare* by the unknown, or the improperly interpreted environment. It is enough to both get your adrenalin flowing and to give you a complex. Psychologically, the threat of constant obliteration is so traumatic that it appears necessary to repress the profound tragedy of human finitude in the form of comedy. What can we do? With no safe harbor, what appropriate response is there for humanity but to laugh, cry, and rage? Most alarming about these stories is that when stripped of the entertaining escapades and the colorful details that delight the reader or listener, what is left is an extremely disturbing point: if you do not get smart, and fast, you will be murdered, by predators, gods, monsters, demons, nature, starvation, sickness, enemies, perhaps even friends and family, or the whimsy of unanticipated change herself (*fortuna*). This is the first lesson that culture imparts to our most innocent and vulnerable.

For the second feature, cultural history demonstrates that although reality is at best ambivalent about, or at worst terribly antagonistic to, human ambition, the species is not without hope. Hope here signifies increasing sensitivity that leads to the strategic vision which enables appropriate action and strategic advantage. Although insensitivity and ignorance to the dynamics of change in the mutable present can easily lead to one's unanticipated and premature end, *The Sword and the Stone* is authoritative cultural evidence that human hope lies in Strategic Intelligence. The sense that most evokes the heroically strategic is sight—strategic advantage here is first won through the acquisition of foresight when the hero can see through and anticipate, thereby properly interpreting the threat in order to rapidly adapt to it. It is sensitivity that is cultivated and honed through personal, practical experience. Strategic rationality is a deadly weapon that both enables and disables human dignity and freedom. Human agency is fundamentally enabled and constrained by the mastery of Strategic Intelligence as the human being itself may be both the producer and consumer, beneficiary and victim of death.

The wizards' duel described here is a device that reveals both the game of life which is violent and conflict laden, and the identity of the strategic hero herself, *homo ludens*, gaming man.[6] Gaming man overcomes the insecurity of the unanticipated by cultivating sensitivity to the unique features of any given threat. Sensitivity to the present is a type of strategic vision, or foresight, that enables one to see, to see through, to anticipate, to envision tactics and strategies that may even incorporate subterfuge. Sensitivity enables the knack of attending both to the face of change experienced as the unknown (and its corollary: the known that turns out to be false), to appearance (and its corollary: the thing seen which turns out to be mere illusion) and to exposure. Masters who wield Strategic Intelligence like a weapon dominate the contingent because they have the power to reveal and conceal, to entrap and liberate, to trick or enlighten, and even to trick in order to enlighten. In short, wisdom is power, and power is strategic advantage resulting from foresight, and the proper interpreting and leveraging of reality. Born in human embodiment, Strategic Intelligence is a type of wisdom with its own ethical framework and categorical imperative in which expediency is the most highly valued criterion. Expediency, or the *freeing of one's feet* (Latin *ex + ped*), is that which enables human dignity, freedom, and the achievement of ambition from the enclosure of snare and pit. In short, Strategic Intelligence is soteriological—the possibility of human salvation is born within, but must be cultivated.

Last, the wizard's duel as a device that frames the problem of contingency and adaptation is just one example of this worldview which has a long multicultural genealogy. The term *strategic culture* is redundant because culture, defined here as that which is worth remembering, is always strategic. Culture is the repository of strategic values deemed relevant to human advantage and thus transmitted through time. Constructed through generations of lived experience, cultural memory, and models remain relevant through time to the degree that they make us more adaptable in any given environment, because they enable strategic advantage. In addition to the wizard's duel discussed here, the problem of the contingent can be treated genealogically when we understand that it has been articulated under different but related and comparable metaphors in the culturally foundational stories of Eurasia, often in terms of journey, exile, aging, the vicissitudes of *fortuna*, regime transition, seasonal change, astrological wandering, and death.

It is striking that over the course of human cultural evolution this basic lesson has been developed and articulated as the elementary curriculum delivered to our most vulnerable in the form of animal fables and cartoons. In the North American cultural context of the twentieth and twenty-first centuries, the same setting of antagonistic reality and strategic use of intellect to thwart threat infuses the cartoons that we show our most naïve. I refer to the Loony Tunes characters upon which generations of Americans have been raised: Bugs Bunny and the hunter Elmer Fudd, Wile E. Coyote and Road Runner, Tweety and Sylvester, or Hanna and Barbera characters Tom and Jerry. Recall also the antagonistic characters Mowgli and Shere Khan or Rikki Tikki Tavi and Nag and Nagaina in Rudyard Kipling's *Jungle Book*. The message? Get smart or get eaten, smashed, or shot. These stories teach about the tyranny of reality which is terrifying, fraught with extreme uncertainty, unpredictable change, and insecurity. True wisdom is the awareness of the paradox that even though human life is not possible without a sense of meaning, that meaning is always at risk of being undermined by the absurdity of unexpected death, that mystery and meaninglessness shadow everything, and that mutability is the only constant.

Where is hope in such a dire reality?

Strategic Intelligence is a type of rationality born out of existential necessity—out of the human encounter with mystery, and its various articulations are generated from the paradoxical and psychologically traumatizing metaphorological paradigm that *life is death*. The values of Strategic Intelligence are important because Strategic Intelligence enables those who are vulnerable to finitude to achieve human meaning at its most elemental level, life itself, in the face of sudden, unanticipated existential threat. Strategic Intelligence is critical not because it exists as a category in the mind, but because it operates in the day-to-day world of prudent action, and it has been culturally validated since time immemorial. In short, Strategic Intelligence is meaningful because it functions as a form of hope that enables life.

The cultural models discussed here under the heading of Strategic Intelligence function as the theoretical component of a practical curriculum that taught humankind the means to success when faced with threat. As the psychoanalyst Alfred Adler (1870–1937) noted,

Only a science which is directly related to life, said the great philosopher William James, is really a science. It might also be said that in a science which is directly related to life, theory and practice become almost inseparable. The science of life, precisely because it models itself directly on the movement of life, becomes a science of living . . . . Such a science is of necessity oriented in a practical sense, for with the aid of knowledge we can correct and alter our attitudes . . . " [it] "is thus prophetic in a double sense: not only does it predict what will happen, but, like the prophet Jonah, it predicts what *will* happen in order that it should *not* happen.[7]

Strategic Intelligence is a type of strategic rationality informed by sensitivity, experience, and clarity that is performed—and the virtuosic performance of the art of Strategic Intelligence leads to human excellence. Whether articulated through the figures of purposeful trickster gods, heroically strategic humans, and plucky animals in historical narratives produced in cultures around the globe, or in the form of good manners and *savoir vivre*, Strategic Intelligence presents itself as a critical enabler to the historical cultures that advocated for it, and for contemporary times as well. With a didactic intent, these Mirrors for Princes (*specula principum*) served as a practical curriculum because they enabled *young princelings* to see. They enabled sight through experience, through experiencing vicariously the predicaments of shrewdly strategic heroes and villains. These stories also enabled *princelings* to learn the values of the kingly way—the exemplary utilization of strategic intellect in crisis situations enables strategic advantage under asymmetric threat—for both interpersonal and political governance. In other words, youth gained practical experience through suffering the experiences of the stories' heroes as case studies, for as the Greek wise men noted, *that which is suffered is learned*.[8] What is learned in this curriculum of case studies and models of heroic strategy is that power is a matter of sensitivity to power, and that power can both be gained or lost through the selection of appropriate means. The virtuosic utilization of Strategic Intelligence can both benefit and threaten the prince. It is paradoxically both brutishly comic and beautifully tragic.

THE CULTURAL GENEALOGY OF GREEK STRATEGIC INTELLIGENCE

"The wise naturally conspire with the great and mighty" wrote Plato (428–348 BCE) in his *Epistles*, "they are always mutually pursuing, seeking and consulting with each other."[9] Indeed, the linking of the masters of strategic wisdom with the chiefs of power is as old as humankind. Starting from the appearance of divine deceivers transmitted to the subsequent oral and textual tradition of myths and epics of the first millennium BCE, we can posit a much earlier valorization of Strategic Intelligence in human societies. What is most salient about this history is that we can detect a cultural genealogy of Strategic Intelligence articulated through the figures of strategic heroes of the various ancient cultures surrounding the Mediterranean basin. From the myths of pre-history, we can still appreciate the divinities, humans, and animals that exemplified the power of Strategic Intelligence in the figures of various masters and mistresses of ruse and stratagem, including tricksters, mages, and heralds. This cultural genealogy includes Enki/Ea, and Inanna and Inara of the Near Eastern cultures; the deities Isis and Seth in the Egyptian tradition; and many examples from Greek culture: Prometheus, Sisyphus, Cronos, Zeus, Metis, Autolycus, Mestra, Hermes, Odysseus (Ulysses), Athena, Circe, Hephaestus, Apollo, and Momus. We can add in Loki for the Nordic cultures, and a plethora of tricksters in the Judeo-Christian tradition, including the serpent in the Biblical story of the Garden of Eden, and many other eminent cultural heroes, including tricksters and prophets such as Moses, Jacob, Solomon, St. Peter—and even the son of God himself (chapter 4).

The label of trickster is, I fear, a misnomer that has obscured the central point of these cultural heroes—they are, in fact, heroic strategists who make use of the means of deception and trickery in order to attain their ends; the trick is never the end in itself. These strategic cultural heroes are crafty because of their mastery of strategic tools, which includes deception and strategic trickery. Carpenters use a hammer, but we do not call them hammerers because we perceive that there is something more central that points to the essence of carpentry. Likewise, the term trickster obscures the holistic tradecraft and toolkit of the strategist. In contrast to previous analyses which have emphasized the trickery of the trickster, I interpret these ancient figures in terms of Strategic Intelligence because the possibility of fraud sets the condition for human excellence in an antagonistic or ambivalent universe. The great deceivers of ancient philosophical and religious myth mark the birth of Strategic Intelligence because they compelled humanity to develop the strategic vision necessary to interpret the threat features of reality that they observed. My interpretation of the evidence shows that culture has always transmitted themes of deception because surprisingly, strategic trickery may be good for us—it somehow makes us better. Strategic trickery actually helps us *up our game*, so to say, because it makes us better at the game of life. In other words, vicarious exposure to stories about heroic strategists who use strategic trickery and narratives that expose ruses heuristically compel us to see. And through seeing, and through seeing through, the heroic strategist is able to preserve human meaning, identity, and dignity in a denied environment.

Before we analyze the images of Strategic Intelligence in ancient sources, it is worth mentioning that the strategic aspect of rationality was encoded in both the Greek and Latin languages. The Greek and Latin terms for reason, *ratio* and λόγος also communicated the concepts of measurement and value before being enshrined as terms of art by technical philosophers and theologians. Nowadays, we recall the rationalism of the Enlightenment and empirical scientific method when we hear *ratio* (reason/rationality), and reverence for the *Word* (λόγος) that is ritually proclaimed during mass, that "in the beginning was the λόγος, and the λόγος was with God, and the λόγος was God."[10] In a way, both are expressions of value and worth, of what is worthy, and of what is considered authoritative. Although these are the senses of the terms beloved by scholars throughout the ages—we can trace the pre-historic roots of both terms in the banal and the day-to-day.

What is concealed by the abstruse is revealed by etymological dictionaries—we may speculate that rationality was born in the functional requirement to measure, value, and interpret, which we now understand as the domains of metrology, axiology, and hermeneutics. Both terms signify the concepts of counting, reckoning, accounting, calculating, and computing. Appropriate accounting, of commodities, of the movements of the heavens in support of claims to political legitimacy, and of the right interpretation of omens, enabled the ancients to assign significance, meaning, value, and worth. These calculating masters were thus able to orient human experience in time and space, and provide strategic advantage through prediction as well as claims of legitimacy for a configuration of order that was grounded in the metaphysical. Thus, in this earliest stage, rational intelligence was defined by the practical activity of observing, calculating, and interpreting. By doing so, these intellectuals of accounting became the privileged arbiters of what counts, and their exclusive sacred lore only offered to the limited consumers of value, the religiously and philosophically initiated, and the aristocratically powerful.

In fact, we can postulate that the earliest art of interpretation, which subsequently developed into the discipline of hermeneutics, was a political art concerned with governance and power, especially war. Modern English still associates hermeneutic (the art of interpretation and exegesis) and the hermetic (the concealed) with the God Hermes, whom both Homer and Hesiod depicted as a strategic trickster. Many ancient Chinese texts, including the *Book of History,* the *Book of Rituals*, the *Master of Demon Valley*, and the *Exemplary Transmission of the Arts of Plastromancy and Yarrow Cleromancy* in the Hàn dynasty Grand Historian Sīmǎ Qiān's (206 BCE–220 CE) *Annals*, show that the appropriate interpretation of oracular data was believed to result in strategic advantage, and the ancestors of today's practitioners of Strategic Intelligence were those political diviners-courtiers who served a critical role in governance.[11] Similar to the etymological connection of the root *herm-* in English, Chinese also maintains the linkage of strategy with its roots in divinatory interpretation—the ancient Chinese term used for plastromancy and yarrow cleromancy (*guīcè* 龜策), which means divination by turtle plastron (*guī* 龜) or yarrow stalk (*cè* 策), lives on in the modern Chinese term *cèlüè* (策略), which denotes strategy, tactics, and ploys. In this stage of human cultural evolution, spirituality appears to be a servant of governance, and spiritual potency was leveraged for the mission of ordering.

In the West, the cultural obsession with universals over particulars never really left us—the hyper-valorization of the universal in Bronze Age astro-theology that we perceive in the gold-leafed material culture of goldhütes and skydisks, and the preference for astro-theological monumentality, such as Stonehenge and the pyramids, evolved into latter calculating equivalents such as the astrolabe and the antikythera mechanism. Sacred astro-theological lore evolved into an obsession with cosmological foundations, which we can call out in various forms, including Pythagorean mathematics, Platonic forms, cosmological and metaphysical religion, natural law, *sub species aeternitatis*, transcendent deontological ethics, theoretical totalization, philosophical holism, and theological perennialism. In the domain of human value and meaning, the values of a calculating rationality in human consciousness, what I call strategic rationality, also found expression discursively in the metaphors, images, and figures of culturally foundational stories produced by the heirs of that ancient sect of calculating intellectuals who also had to survive in this world. The values of this calculating Strategic Intelligence informed the myths, legends, and identities of heroic strategists who suffered the antagonistic sociopolitical reality of their present situations, and framed the types of responses that led to strategic advantage.

The strategic values underlying these heroically strategic divine figures come more sharply into focus in the great Greek epics of the first millennium BCE, conventionally understood as the foundation of Western civilization. In this section, I show that the paradoxical metaphorological paradigm of *life is death* was expressed long before Disney's *Sword and the Stone*, here in Hesiod's *Theogony* and *Works*. All are sources that seek to teach humanity the means of winning through the development of strategic vision that leads to strategic advantage.

STRATEGICALLY HEROIC GODS: THEOGONY

It is not difficult to perceive the culturally genealogical linkage between Disney's *Sword and the Stone* and Hesiod's *Theogony*, a culturally foundational text written nearly two and half millennia earlier in a very different social environment.[12] In lieu of the wizard's duel, Hesiod utilized the device of cosmogonic, intergenerational conflict as the game in which a god won over tyrannical reality by his use of Strategic Intelligence.[13] What the initiate to Strategic Intelligence observes in the epic poetry is a vision of antagonistic reality structured as successive political and familial conflict, and the development of the gaming god Zeus, whose power grows as his Strategic Intelligence matures. When we get down to brass tacks, we discover a rather stunning depiction of heroic Strategic Intelligence—the lesson of *Theogony* is that ambition is both enabled and stymied by Strategic Intelligence.[14]

The first depiction of Strategic Intelligence in *Theogony* occurs in the story about the self-liberating of Earth (Gaia) from excessively lusty, tyrannical, and intemperate Sky (Uranus), when their youngest child Cronos "of the infamous ruse" castrates dad with the help of mum. The second exemplar of Strategic Intelligence occurs shortly later in the text when Rhea connives with her youngest child Zeus, the master "of stratagems" and her mother-in-law Earth (Gaia) to overthrow *crooked* Cronos, who also recklessly raped his consort. The contest of wit between Zeus and the four excessively ambitious sons of Iapetus, Atlas, Menoetius, Prometheus, and Epimetheus, provides the third example of Strategic Intelligence. Zeus goes head to head with *crooked-wise* Prometheus who tries to trick him.[15] "Zeus, cloud-bearer, said to crafty Prometheus in rage, 'Son of Iapetus, most wily, you have not yet forgotten your deceptive arts!'"[16] Thus, Zeus shows himself to be *farsighted, forever seeing through machinations*, and the exemplar of Strategic Intelligence described in Greek as *dolophrone* (δολόφρονε), trap-wise.[17] A *dolophrone* is a strategic hero who can both see through a trick and set his or her own *snares*.[18] In essence, Zeus gained strategic foresight from experience. The Greek term προειδοποιήσει "foresight" aligns with its equivalent in Latin (*praemonitus*) and the many derivations in Western European languages (*prévenu, avvisato, avvertito, prevenido*). Strategic Intelligence is itself providential—and most importantly, it is the acquisition of strategic foresight that makes humanity god-like—we become strategic like the god Zeus through the cultivation of *providence*.

Hesiod's *Works*, another strategic primer, points out that reality is strife, which can be understood both as praiseworthy and blameworthy.[19] The philosopher Heraclitus (535–475 BCE), Aristotle noted, saw that strife in life was necessary. Criticizing Achilles' wish for peace in the *Iliad*, Heraclitus thought that the conflict of opposites was necessary in the world of flux. Strife as war is necessary, and war determines gods, kings, slaves, and the free. If war is the father of, and strife is the crucible in which the strategic is formed, then the god of war, Polemus, is the figuration of the principle that may lie under all discourse, concealing the polemical aspect of *Logos* (*Word*). In other words, meaning is always contested.

Like the *Sword and the Stone*, underneath Hesiod's *Theogony* lies the same points that I identified earlier, including a stylized representation of reality that is antagonistic, and a heroically strategic protagonist or assumed naïve pupil who develops strategic vision from personal experience which results in strategic advantage. In contrast to Zeus, his forebears Sky and Cronos, who are tyrannical, divine man-babies with poor impulse control and reckless ambition, portray antagonistic reality. Zeus, on the other hand, matures into the exemplar of the just, wise, and well-governed ruler who incorporates strategic deception and denial in order to accomplish his legitimate goals. For example, starting as a vulnerable infant, Zeus is saved first by Rhea and Earth's ruse to hide him in the dark depths. He learns more of Strategic Intelligence when the ruse of the swallowed *omphalos* stone functions as an emetic that forces Cronos to vomit up Zeus' siblings, which subsequently weakens the older deity. Just and strategic trickery thus underscores one of the earliest of soteriological doctrines in Western civilization. Zeus' heroic *anabasis*, or rising up from the depths, is an archetype of the victorious ascent of the underdog that echoes through the ages, such as in the depiction of escape from shadowy ignorance in Plato's cave to the true sight of eternal forms, when Jesus freed humanity from the bowels of the devil in the traditional story of the harrowing of hell (chapter 4), when Luke Skywalker emerges from the Dagobah cave, and Harry Potter resurrects and returns from the forbidden forest.[20]

Zeus still has a long way to go though—although his incontinence and temper flared up in the conflict with Prometheus, he is well on the journey to becoming more sensitive to ruse itself. Unlike his grandfather who imprisoned cosmogonic powers within the wombs of Earth, Zeus learns from his father Cronos' mistake by internalizing his own strategic power—it is only through the swallowing of the deity of Strategic Intelligence herself, Metis, an act itself accomplished through strategic trickery, that Zeus is able to become the paragon of Strategic Intelligence, what Homer called metieta, what I translate as "the Strategically Wise." By so doing, Zeus became the most cunning and strategic of the gods, a long-range thinker whose mode of power is equal to that of the divine general bright-eyed Athena, who is generated from his forehead. As the icon of Strategic Intelligence and as "a lover of war and wisdom," Athena's relationship with the strategic hero Odysseus provides the key to interpreting Homer's *Odyssey* as a primer of Strategic Intelligence.

Hesiod's *Theogony* has much to tell us about the religious, mythical, political, social, and cultural dimensions of the times in which it was written. But what is the ethical lesson of the text, if there is one? In *Theogony*, we discover little of the prevailing ethical paradigms one learns in Ethics 101, whether Consequentialist, Non-consequentialist, and Agent-centered theories. We see little of the deontological and utilitarian—there is neither a vision of grace, duty, virtue, nor Kantian maxims, or a categorical imperative. One may be tempted to see the ethics of *Theogony* as an early articulation of egoism, like that expressed by Thrasymachus, Thomas Hobbes, or Ayn Rand's virtue of selfishness. But it is not quite, for in these sources we cheer for the heroism of *homo ludens* and *homo aestimans* rather than *homo moralis*, for gaming and calculating man rather than moral man.

It is not that *Theogony* lacks an ethical lesson—rather, its ethical stance can only be recovered when we appreciate the normative values underlying the calculating worldview of Strategic Intelligence. Like *Sword and the Stone*, *Theogony* operates in the worldview of life lived as game. The earliest of categorical imperatives for *homo ludens* centered on the value of expediency and the obligation to win, where winning signifies survival and self-expansion. To be frank, the highest good and excellence of the art of human life for *homo ludens* experiencing a life *in extremis* is focused on the acquisition, maintenance, and expansion of life itself. The contest for meaning at this level is a zero-sum game that inherently constrains responsibility to other. Winning is achieved through knowledge and vision—the most important ethical obligation for gaming man is to cultivate strategic vision in order to achieve her purpose. What is salient about this paradigm is the natural integration of heroic strategy with the criteria of a risk management framework intent on mitigating harm and producing harm to other when necessity requires. What counts is the expedient and the efficacious rather than that which is understood in terms of a theoretical evaluative theory of the good or bad that is disassociated with the aims of life itself.

For the ancients, strategic vision and knowledge were interchangeable terms—strategic vision *was* knowing, and it was one of the most important ancient values. The Roman historian Polybius (200–118 BCE), following the insight of Heraclitus (535–475 BCE), wrote that "nature has bestowed on us two instruments of inquiry and research, hearing and sight. Of these sight is, according to Heraclitus, by far the truer; for eyes are surer witnesses than ears."[21] The sense of sight, as a metaphor of enlightenment, signifies the ability of the mind to see reality as it truly is. Sight is also the most strategic of the senses because it enables the organism to properly interpret its environment—farsightedness is strategic because it is anticipatory—it provides greater protection against threats further removed in space and time. *Theogony*'s divinely inspired bard is able to reveal the contours of reality, he tells us, through the indwelling power of the inspiration of the muses, and the mind of the listener of the epic is impregnated with Strategic Intelligence now that it beholds reality projected through the poem's images, which is presented as insight. What is most important about strategic vision is the capacity to change perspective—the power to receive divine insight is not the same as properly interpreting that insight—rather, truth and falsehood are two sides of the same coin.[22] The art of Strategic Intelligence lies in the most efficacious way of properly interpreting the portents.

This worldview formed the core of the Greco-Roman strategic tradition. In fact, Hesiod relayed to posterity that the emblem of Zeus' strategic trickery, the rock of ruse that induced Cronos' demise, became the bedrock of Greek religious life and divine revelation when it was placed as the foundation stone of the Pythian oracle at Delphi.[23] In other words, the cosmic trick is both the navel of the world and the core of cosmic ambiguity, which must be interpreted—as Heraclitus said, "the Lord of the Delphic oracle provides signs, neither revealing nor concealing."[24] In other words, not only is ambiguity cosmological, connecting Strategic Intelligence to metaphysical interpretation increases its value in an era in which metaphysical speculation was considered fundamental—although a sign may be given, strategic advantage results from proper interpretation of oracular ambiguity.

In conclusion, like the *Sword and the Stone*, Hesiod's *Theogony* and *Works* are primers and expressions of values associated with the kingly way. Intimately linked with personal and political change in the earliest Greek myths, the strategic is inseparable from the most fundamental and cosmological coordinates of meaning derived from human orientation to the particularities of time and space, and to the possibility of the *what might be otherwise if.* After listening to the epic poems, the initiate of the cult of Strategic Intelligence knew that the stakes were high, and that the consequences of losing were potentially devastating. Peter Paul Rubens' famous seventeenth-century masterpiece *Prometheus Bound* (Figure 2.1) is one example of an artifact that transmits the values of Strategic Intelligence via visual culture to the modern players of the game of life. In response to the question *WWZD? What Would Zeus Do?*, the novice now knows the potency of Strategic Intelligence through the model of heroically strategic Zeus, the role model of strategic planning and divine deception. Zeus in *Theogony* is a great example of the victory of heroic Strategic Intelligence over the reckless, the impulsive and the intemperate, through the cultivation of strategic vision.

STRATEGICALLY HEROIC MEN: THE ODYSSEY

In this earliest stage of Western civilization, Strategic Intelligence was as critical for enabling the young prince Zeus as it was for the heroic human kingship that we see exemplified in the story of the princeling Arthur. Strategic Intelligence therefore appears to gesture to ultimate political subjectivity, of divinely royal power and meaning, and to its use as a critical means of governance, justice, and order. Like *Theogony* and *Works,* a closer inspection of the strategic values that informs Homer's *Odyssey* reveals a cultural genealogical connection with Disney's *Sword and the Stone.*[25] Similar to the other two texts, Homer articulated the underlying metaphorological paradigm of *life is death* in the *Odyssey* via the trope of the alienation of voyage. *Odyssey* teaches the strategic lesson that hope for the ambitious person on the unstable

Figure 2.1 Prometheus Bound. Image provided for reprint with permission of Philadelphia Museum of Art, Purchased with the W. P. Wilstach Fund, W1950-3-1. Peter Paul Rubens, Prometheus Bound Begun c. 1611-1612, completed by 1618. Philadelphia Museum of Art, Purchased with the W. P. Wilstach Fund, W1950-3-1.

journey of life amongst insecurity and threat lies in Strategic Intelligence, and appropriate adaption born from the development of strategic vision, all of which are gained through lived experience.[26] More than 2,000 years later, the Spanish master strategist Juan Luis Vives (1492–1540 CE) echoed this sentiment when he described the fragility of life as a journey amidst unanticipated dangers, any one of which may end it without warning.[27]

The opening lines of this greatest of primers that teach about divine deception reveals both the import of the narrative and the secret of all secrets, of the potency of strategy—"Of the man, pray tell O Muse, of many places, driven far after sacking sacred Troy. Many the men he saw and insights learned, many the pains of ambition while on the vast sea." As opposed to the meaninglessness of a life lived by impulsive wrathful ambition in the *Iliad*, the opening lines of the *Odyssey* clarify that the adapted man, the man *made* adaptable through his experience of many places (*polytropos*), is superior to the brawny warrior driven by wrath and excessive ambition. Homer also reveals something more profound—the strategic endurance of present pain in the pursuit of aim and gain is a critical life-enabler. To put it in modern parlance, not only does personal experience enable strategic vision, but strategic advantage is won agonistically through the temporary acceptance of pain and degradation—and shame in the cases of Kings Wén and Gōujiàn (chapter 6). In addition to being a swashbuckling travelogue, biography, and penny dreadful, Homer's *Odyssey* is also the hagiography of a strategic virtuoso, an early pilgrim's progress if you will, a primer of the kingly way through which strategic values and strategic sight were incited in the minds of pupils everywhere.

In place of the wizard's duel and cosmogonic intergenerational rivalry discussed previously, Homer used the device of journey to represent both the painful experience of antagonistic reality and the experience of the new, the strange, and the dangerous as necessary to stimulate strategic insight in the mind to grow. Outward journey, as the device that stands for inner cultivation, is analogous to the way the ancients understood the journey of the sun through the great zodiacal houses over the course of the year—in actuality what counts is the journey.[28] The metaphor of journey is a mythical archetype that goes back to Gilgamesh and beyond, and is the most common ontology of modern gaming culture—Monopoly®, Chutes and Ladders®, Dungeons and Dragons® all use it. In fact, it is difficult to even imagine a contemporary first-person shooter video game that is not centered on some theme of alienating journey amidst enemies.

And what can be said of this strategically deceptive hero, King Odysseus, the great hope of humankind? What answer does *WWOD* provide? In short, Homer's *Odyssey* is the story of the master gamer who, through perseverance, temperance, strategic prudence, and adaptability, is able to endure every indignity that nasty reality can throw at him in order to win the long game.[29]

Odysseus exemplifies the lesson that the unexpected transformation of *homo ludens* into *homo impotens*, powerless man, is but a temporary setback for adepts of the kingly way, those who adapt themselves to the reality of the present and strategically await the possibility of future opportunity. Beggar-king Odysseus withstands all types of indignities throughout the epic—in addition to physical privation of long exile on the sea, resulting in the indignity of age, physical and material impoverishment, and enslavement to the tyranny of the stomach, he is emasculated, sexually objectified, unrecognized, jeered, derided, belittled, and treated as a delicious substitute for mutton. Although he comes under the stilettoed heel of two divine dominatrixes, that actually accentuates his internal virility and erotic power—it is significant that he was never sodomized nor cuckolded—both acts would have undermined the integrity of his Mediterranean masculinity.

Integrity in extreme poverty was an inspiring theme for the Stoics, and the Stoic philosopher Epictetus (50–135 CE) through the voice of Socrates asked, "Shall he not imitate Odysseus, who made no worse figure in rags than in a fine purple robe?"[30] More than 2,000 years later, the Italian master strategist Niccolò Machiavelli in his *Discorsi* described the figure of a great man in similar terms—great men remain the same whatever befalls. They remain steadfast in mind and conduct when fortune changes, and so all can see that they are invulnerable to the turn of the wheel of fortune itself.[31] By maintaining his integrity and virtue, Odysseus kept alive the ancestral glory and honor that would transfer to his progeny.[32]

Although Odysseus often bewails his lot, he slowly overcomes his reckless impulsiveness and learns to master strategy through temperance. He became a paragon of self-restraint for the ancients, which is significant in light of the passionate Mediterranean temperament that could be quick to anger and vengeance when honor was threatened, often resulting in multi-generational vendetta. Odysseus shares with his wife Penelope the singularity of purpose that enables him to survive by adapting in order to achieve the future.[33] This is the great hope of Strategic Intelligence.

King Odysseus, the heroic strategist, is the potential everyman, and Homer's *Odyssey* documents his development into a master strategist. Like Zeus and Prince Arthur discussed in the narratives before, the figure of Odysseus offers another example of the nurturing of heroic Strategic Intelligence through the development of strategic vision as the means to achieve appropriate action that leads to strategic advantage. Examples of his now-famous immature recklessness include the visit to the land of the lotus-eaters, the hypocrisy and disrespect shown to his host, the cyclops Polyphemus, the hubristic boasting with Polyphemus that resulted in further persecution, his miscalculation in not revealing to his crew that he had the west wind tied up in a bag, the risky encounter with the Sirens, and the idiocy of not forewarning his crew about the monsters at Scylla and Charybdis. Although he was much more cautious when he visited the island of the Laestrygonians, he still lost all of his men. It was not that Odysseus was a good or bad leader, or suffered from a character flaw—he was simply human, all too human. These episodes are cultural models that gesture to the problem of imprudence, defined as a miscalculation and poor interpretation of the threat environment due to the lack of experience. In the strategic worldview, imprudence results in a value judgment of inexpedient and the ineffective rather than the good or the evil.

We observe the maturation of imprudent Odysseus to the master strategist in the distance traveled from his encounter with the cyclops Polyphemus to his rendezvous with the Princess Nausicaa of the Phaeacians. The episodes in which Odysseus meets Polyphemus and Nausicaa of the Phaeacians are complementary, both because of the similarities and differences. Starting with the antagonistic cyclops Polyphemus, whose name means *many-sounds*, the episode is a model that highlights the integration of what is known through sight with what is appropriately done and said. Although Odysseus, with a clever double ruse, extricated himself out of the mess that he caused through his own over-reaching curiosity, he still had not mastered the art of dissimulation. The irony in the scene is that Odysseus is the one of too many words, not Polyphemus. The lesson learned is that Odysseus probably would have escaped scot free if he had just strategically remained quiet. But, he just could not leave well enough alone—his miscalculation and excessively imprudent taunting resulted in further damage, death and cursing. The strategic lesson here is comparable to many articulations in the wisdom literature of the Old Testament in which the tongue is suspect: "The tongue devises mischief; like a sharp razor, working deceitfully."[34]

"The end of all action," wrote Aristotle in a section of the *Nicomachean Ethics* dedicated *practical wisdom,* is to avoid extremes by aiming for the middle ground, which famously defines Aristotle's conception of the virtuosity of virtue; as Calypso advised in the *Odyssey* "steer the ship clear of yonder spray and surge."[35] The point is that proper interpretation of the features of the threat environment enables one to act and speak appropriately—thus appropriate interpretation of the external is enabled by internal virtuosity. This observation hits the mark, because we observe in the encounter with Nausicaa the exemplary model of a matured, strategically-minded King Odysseus, what the strategic goddess Athena indubitably proudly characterized as a man of "many machinations."[36]

In contrast to the encounter with Polyphemus, the Odysseus who met the Princess Nausicaa played by the rules of a very different game, the game of the strategic hunt. This is the masterly Odysseus whom the Roman intellectual Plutarch observed was the man "adept at speaking and a man of sense."[37] Interestingly, Homer integrated in the image of Nausicaa the intelligence of both the divine deceiver and strategist behind the infamous Trojan horse, General Athena, and the Virgin Huntress Artemis.[38] Homer layered the scene with many senses of the term game—Nausicaa was playing a game with her handmaidens when she roused the slumbering Odysseus from his sleep. Odysseus and Nausicaa were in a symbolic predator-prey game relationship since Homer portrayed Odysseus as a wild lion compelled to the hunt by insatiable hunger, stealthily staking his prey.[39] Reduced to his wits and his birthday suit, having learned from his experience with Polyphemus, the successful graduate from the school of hard knocks quickly decided to strategically use a discursive weapon, flattering the young princess and pleading his case. And his matron Athena helps him with a spell that glamored his onlookers—"then Athena, strategic daughter of Zeus, glamoured him, making him taller and stronger, with luxuriously curling locks cascading down."[40] His persuasive rhetoric is so effective that Nausicaa sees the revealed form of the thoughtful, cultured, and kingly man underneath the appearance made haggard by the vicissitudes of fortune commanded by the gods.[41] Potent indeed is the weapon of words delivered strategically!

Even though the man is slightly revealed, the episode of Odysseus with the Phaeacians highlights the potency of ruse and concealment, disinformation and misinformation, with Nausicaa and Athena going to great lengths to conceal his true identity. In essence, Odysseus, like Zeus before him, is saved and perfected by feminine Strategic Intelligence, expressed through the divine figures of Metis, Athena, and Nausicaa. His salvation is accomplished through his own excellence (virtue), as Heraclitus wrote that excellence is the outcome of appropriately interpreting reality so that one can speak and act accordingly.[42]

By the time that Odysseus finally reaches his kingdom of Ithaca, we observe the strategic master gamer who is able to heroically maintain the power of dissimulation and deception almost to the end of the story. In fact, the only two characters who see through his plot are his hunting dog Argos, and his wet-nurse Eurycleia. When Her High Holiness, the Mistress of Divine Deception herself, Athena, finally meets with Odysseus face to face as he is hiding his booty in a cave, she is simply charmed by the jolly good yarn that he spins. Revealing her true form, she "caressed him and smiled, and then said, 'One has to be pretty sharp to outdo you in trickery . . . Shame! You never tire of trickery, and you don't even give up your lies and deception on your own shores. Let us put this aside, for we both are masters amongst gods and men. . . . And now again here I am to help you in your schemes.'"[43] To highlight the degree to which Greek culture positively valued Strategic Intelligence as a divinely royal means of salvation, denial and deception as the core attribute of mother-son intimacy could not be more different than that relationship exemplified in Christianity by the Virgin Mary with her son, Jesus, even though Strategic Intelligence is also a defining feature of his kingship (chapter 4).

The Sword and the Stone, Theogony, Works, and the *Odyssey* all point to the values of an underlying and cohesive strategic worldview shaped by the metaphorological paradigm of *life is death,* in which adaptability and expediency are paramount criteria. But even in the classical age, the strategic dimensions of these sources that transmitted the values of Strategic Intelligence were not immediately understood by all, especially by those ancients who interpreted the model that the *Odyssey* provided in a moral framework rather than a strategic one that dramatized the conception of life lived as game. Greek cultural specialists were already contending about the worth of strategic values as early as the fifth century BCE.

For some, "godlike Odysseus" had much to teach humankind about how to win success in life in a hard world. The philosopher of moral virtuosity *par excellence* Aristotle cited the *Odyssey* in reference to a form of education "in which boys should be trained not because it is useful or necessary but as being liberal and noble; though whether there is one such subject of education or several, and what these are and how they are to be pursued."[44] And Polybius, (200–118 BCE) in the section "An Historian Needs Practical Experience" in his *Histories*, referred to King Odysseus as the endpoint of virtuosity—he is what the "man of light and leading should be"; the man of many experiences is "the exemplar to which professional historians need to attend."[45] To Polybius, practical experience was the pinnacle of learning, enabling the military historian, speechmaker, healer, and navigator. The soldier-philosopher and student to Socrates, Xenophon (430–354 BCE), in his *Symposium* agreed that the *Odyssey* was a type of practical primer— "You surely are aware that the sage Homer wrote about everything man needs to know." Anyone who wishes to master the art of strategy of the "householder, politician or general," or who wishes to become heroic like "Achilles, Ajax, Nestor, or Odysseus . . . should approach, for I understand such things."[46]

In addition to Xenophon, Plutarch (46–120 CE) too, saw much to imitate in the strategic paragon of King Odysseus. Xenophon compared the ascetic Socrates to Odysseus, who was able to strategically avoid undesirable metamorphosis into a swine through his self-restraint and avoidance of indulgence.[47] In *Advice for Bride and Groom*, Plutarch contrasted Odysseus' crew as dimwitted, degenerate swines and asses, in contrast to strategic Odysseus who was exceedingly loved by the sorceress Circe because he "had sense and showed discretion in her company."[48] In "On Garrulousness," Plutarch's praise of Odysseus as a paragon of temperance and prudence in service to his resolution to achieve his strategic objective is positively gushing:

> And the Poet has made the most eloquent Odysseus the most reticent, and also his son and his wife and his nurse; for you hear the nurse saying, I'll hold it safe like sturdy oak or iron. And Odysseus himself, as he sat beside Penelope, did pity in his heart his wife in tears, but kept his eyes firm-fixed within their lids like horn or iron. So full of self-control was his body in every limb, and Reason, with all parts in perfect obedience and submission, ordered his eyes not to weep, his tongue not to utter a sound, his heart not to tremble or bark: his heart remained enduring in obedience, since his reason extended even to his irrational or involuntary movements and made amenable and subservient to itself both his breath and his blood. Of such character were also most of his companions; for even when they were dragged about and dashed upon the ground by the Cyclops, they would not denounce Odysseus nor show that fire-sharpened instrument prepared against the monster's eye, but preferred to be eaten raw rather than to tell a single word of the secret-an example of self-control and loyalty which cannot be surpassed.[49]

Many later masters of strategy agreed with Plutarch, observing that strategic advantage was often enabled by opportunism, adaptability, and proper timing. The Spanish master strategist Vives taught that patient endurance transforms misfortune into fortune.[50] His compadre, the seventeenth-century Jesuit master strategist Baltasar Gracián recommended adapting to circumstance—"governing, reasoning, and everything else must be perfectly timed. Wait to do something when you can, for time and opportunity wait for no one."[51] The Italian master strategist Machiavelli thought that it was wise to adapt to the circumstances of the time, and that one's adaptability was what actually enabled good or bad fortune.[52] "How stupid would it be to play a game in which you might lose much more than you could possibly win?" asked Machiavelli's compatriot, the master strategist Francesco Guicciardini (1483–1540 CE).[53] "It would be a most dangerous proverb, should one not be aware of its subtlety, to take advantage of the moment, because one must act quickly when opportunity presents itself. But when you are in a tight spot, you can often free and illuminate yourself by procrastinating. Understood in this way, this saying is advantageous; otherwise it is dangerous."[54]

The values articulated by Odysseus' craftiness and deceit in Homer's epic were morally problematic for others. Although Plato was highly vexed by poets and wished to banish most of them from his republic, he still nonetheless recognized their divine insight even if they were not able to interpret the meaning of their portent. And in the *Lesser Hippias*, after an incredibly insightful analysis of a scene in the *Odyssey*, Plato's favorite character Socrates surprisingly advocated for the *integrity* of Odysseus over the *deceit* of Achilles.[55] Like in *Theogony*, Pindar (522–443 BCE) also alluded to the falsehood, doubting what Homer wrote about Odysseus. He thought that Homer most likely greatly exaggerated by using poetic license—and most men were blind to it.[56] The depiction of Odysseus in Sophocles' (496—406 BCE) drama *Philotectes* (409 BCE) makes his strategic shrewdness problematic in contrast with the value of straightforwardness as exhibited by Nestor in the *Iliad*, Telemachus in the *Odyssey*, and Neoptolemus in *Philotectes*. Mirroring Plutarch's comments about temperance above, moralizing Aristotle interpreted the character of Neoptolemus in *Philotectes* as the moral example of the temperate man who is appropriately continent.[57]

In my opinion, rather than taking sides, we should be content to see the reality of strategy for what it is—there are no absolutes in the metaphor of life lived as game. All of the subsequent strategic masters agree that strategic advantage is at least partially constructed on the integration of opportunism, timing, patience, experience, and adaptability. The same strategic values expressed through the exemplars of strategic virtuosos were expressed aphoristically by the most famous of their Mediterranean heirs, Guicciardini,

Machiavelli, and Gracián. Although the past can be instructive, the master Guicciardini saw that "judging based on previous examples is faulty. It does not work unless the two are entirely the same. The slightest variation causes the greatest of effects, and one needs clear-sighted vision to discriminate the nuances."[58] Machiavelli agreed, noting that every action needs to be "adapted to the times."[59] Gracián recommended that one develop great reflexes—good impulses spring from a readiness of spirit.[60] "Recognize where things are in transformation in order to take advantage of them. All works of nature reach for completion in perfection, first waxing, then waning."[61] He gave similar advice to people; "discern temperaments—don't show the same face to everyone equally, and apply minimal energy to the situation."[62]

WWMD? WWZD? WWOD? The answer to all of these questions is surprisingly similar—they all use Strategic Intelligence. It is what makes them heroic and enables them to achieve their aims. What remains after filtering out the narratological particularities of each story is a common world view, a kingly way which is a strategic orientation in the world that prescribes the means by which the human species can assign kingly significance, heroic meaning, and power in a reality that is antagonistic to or ambivalent about its existence. Strategic Intelligence is a powerful form of hope.

NOTES

1. Bill Peet, Wolfgang Reitherman, and T. H. White, *The Sword in the Stone* (Burbank, CA: Walt Disney Home Video, 1963).

2. Peet, *Sword*.

3. Ernest Becker, *The Denial of Death* (New York: Free Press Paperbacks/Simon & Schuster, 1973).

4. Søren Kierkegaard, *Fear and Trembling*, trans. Alastair Hannay, (Penguin Classics; Reprint edition January 7, 1986).

5. Isaiah 24:17 KJV.

6. In contrast to Johan Huizinga, I highlight the competitive gaming aspect in lieu of the play aspect of *homo ludens*. See Johan Huizinga, *Homo Ludens: A Study of the Play-Element in Culture (*Boston: Beacon Press, 1955), 105.

7. Alfred Adler, *The Science of Living*, ed. Heinz L. Ansbacher (New York: Anchor Books, 1969), 1.

8. That which is suffered is learned: τα παθηματα μαθηματα.

9. Plato, *Letters*, 2.310e, Perseus Digital Library, Tufts University, accessed 26 April 2017, http://perseus.uchicago.edu/perseus-cgi/citequery3.pl?dbname=GreekFeb2 011&getid=1&query=Pl.%20Ep.%20310d. πέφυκε συνιέναι εἰς ταὐτὸν φρόνησίς τε καὶ δύναμις μεγάλη, καὶ ταῦτ' ἄλληλα ἀεὶ διώκει καὶ ζητεῖ καὶ συγγίγνεται.

10. John 1:1.

11. *Book of History Shàngshū* 尚書, the *Book of Rituals Lǐjì* 禮記, the *Master of Demon Valley Guǐgǔzi* 鬼谷子, and the *Exemplary Transmission of the Arts of Plastromancy and*

yarrow cleromancy Guīcè Lièzhuàn 龜策列傳 Sīmǎ Qiān 司馬遷 in the Annals *Records of the Grand Historian Shǐjì* 史記, accused 27 January 2019, https://ctext.org/shiji/gui-ce-lie-zhuan. Original texts at Chinese Text Project, https://ctext.org/shiji.

12. Hesiod. *Theogony*, and *Works and Days*, in *The Homeric Hymns and Homerica*, trans. Hugh G. Evelyn-White (Cambridge, MA: Harvard University Press), 1914. *Theogony, Works and Days*, Perseus Digital Library, Tufts University, accessed 17 January 2019, http://www.perseus.tufts.edu/hopper/text?doc=Perseus:text:1999.01.0129.

13. μῆτις; I have generally tried to avoid philological and philosophical terms of art. For a more precise study of these terms, such as *"mētic* intelligence," please refer to Marcel Detienne and Jean-Pierre Vernant, *Cunning Intelligence in Greek Culture and Society*, trans. Janet Lloyd (New Jersey: Humanities Press, 1978), and Jeffrey Barnouw, *Odysseus, Hero of Practical Intelligence* Boulder: Lanham: 2004); for a cross-cultural comparison, see Lisa Raphals, *Knowing Words: Wisdom and Cunning in the Classical Traditions of China and Greece* (Ithaca: Cornell University Press, 1992).

14. Ambition *thumos* θυμός; Strategic Intelligence μῆτις.

15. *Crooked-wise* ἀγκυλομήτης Prometheus who tries to trick him ἐξαπάτησε.

16. Crafty ποικίλον αἰολόμητιν. Ἰαπετιονίδη, πάντων πέρι μήδεα εἰδώς, ὦ πέπον, οὐκ ἄρα πω δολίης ἐπιλήθεο τέχνης.

17. Farsighted εὐρύοπα, forever seeing through machinations μήδεα εἰδώς, *dolophrone* δολόφρονε, trap-wise.

18. Snares δολον. Hesiod, *Theogony*, 520–550.

19. ἔρις. *Works*, lines 1–40.

20. Plato, *Republic*, Book 7.

21. Polybius, *Histories*, 12:27, trans. Evelyn S. Shuckburgh (London, New York: Macmillan, 1889), Perseus Digital Library, Tufts University, accessed 17 January 2019, http://www.perseus.tufts.edu/hopper/text?doc=Perseus:text:1999.01.0234:book=12:chapter=27&highlight=needs%2Chistorian.

22. Hesiod, *Theogony, Works and Days*, lines 25–30.

23. Rock of ruse *omphalos* ὀμφαλός. Hesiod, *Theogony, Works and Days*, 499.

24. οὗ τὸ μαντεῖόν ἐστι τὸ ἐν Δελφοῖς, οὔτε λέγει οὔτε κρύπτει ἀλλὰ σημαίνει.

25. For a philological analysis of the *Odyssey*, see Jeffrey Barnouw, *Odysseus, Hero of Practical Intelligence* (Boulder: Lanham: 2004), and Silvia Montiglio, *From Villain to Hero: Odysseus in Ancient Thought* (Ann Arbor: University of Michigan Press, 2011).

26. Hans Blumenberg, *Shipwreck with Spectator: Paradigm of a Metaphor for Existence*, trans. Steven Rendeall (Cambridge, MA: MIT Press, 1997).

27. *Quid aliud est vita, (o) quàm peregrinatio quædam, totundique casibus objecta & petita? cui nulla hora non imminet finis, qui potest levissimis de causis accidere.* Juan Luis Vives, *Introductio Ad Sapientiam Introduction to Wisdom*, 36: *Introductio Ad Sapientiam Introduction to Wisdom*, ed. John Georgi Cottæ. 1704, Biblioteca Nazionale Centrale di Firenze (National Central Library of Florence), accessed 12 January 2019, https://archive.org/details/bub_gb_UwWuXbKXKY4C/page/n35.

28. Silvia Montiglio, *Wandering in Ancient Greek Culture* (Chicago: University of Chicago Press, 2005).

29. Jeffrey Barnouw, *Odysseus, Hero of Practical Intelligence* (Boulder: Lanham: 2004).

30. Epictetus, *Fragments*, Perseus Digital Library, Tufts University, accessed 26 April 2017, http://perseus.uchicago.edu/cgi-bin/philologic/getobject.pl?c.132:4.GreekFeb2011.
31. Niccolò Machiavelli, *Discorsi*, 3.31.
32. κλέος.
33. Barnouw, *Odysseus*.
34. Psalms 52:2–3.
35. *Phronesis,* Aristotle, *Nicomachean Ethics* 2.9. Homer, *Odyssey* 12.219.
36. πολυμηχανος.
37. φρόνιμος. Plutarch, *De Pythiae Oraculis* 22, in *Plutarch. Moralia,* trans. Frank Cole Babbitt (Cambridge, MA. Harvard University Press, 1928), Perseus Digital Library, Tufts University, accessed 17 January 2019, http://www.perseus.tufts.edu/hopper/text?doc=Perseus:text:2008.01.0247:section=22&highlight=odysseus.
38. Homer, *Odyssey,* 6:105.
39. Homer, *Odyssey,* 6:130–134.
40. Homer, *Odyssey,* 6.229–235.
41. Homer, *Odyssey,* 6:186–189.
42. Heraclitus Fragment B112.
43. Homer, *Odyssey,* 13: 285–300.
44. δῖος Ὀδυσσεύς.
45. Polybius, *Histories,* "A Historian Needs Practical Experience" 12.27. Perseus Digital Library, Tufts University, accessed 26 April 2017.
46. Xenophon, *Symposium,* in *Xenophon in Seven Volumes,* Vol. 4 (Cambridge, MA; Harvard University Press, 1979), Perseus Digital Library, Tufts University, accessed 26 April 2017.
47. Xenophon, *Memorabilia* 1.3.7–11, in *Xenophon in Seven Volumes,* Vol. 4, trans. Todd, O. J. Loeb Classical Library (Cambridge, MA: Harvard University Press, 1923), *Perseus Digital Library, Tufts University,* accessed 26 April 2017, http://data.perseus.org/citations/urn:cts:greekLit:tlg0032.tlg002.perseus-eng1:3.11.
48. Plutarch, *Moralia, Conjugalia Praecepta,* in *Plutarch. Moralia,* trans. Frank Cole Babbitt (Cambridge, MA. Harvard University Press, 1928), Perseus Digital Library, Tufts University, accessed 17 January 2019, http://www.perseus.tufts.edu/hopper/text?doc=Perseus:text:2008.01.0181:section=5&highlight=discretion.
49. Plutarch, *Moralia, De garrulitate* 8, in *Plutarch. Moralia,* trans. W. C. Helmbold (Cambridge, MA. Harvard University Press, 1939), Perseus Digital Library, Tufts University, accessed 17 January 2019, http://www.perseus.tufts.edu/hopper/text?doc=Perseus:text:2008.01.0287:section=8&highlight=odysseus.
50. *Etiam mala, quæ dicuntur corporis, vel fortunæ, licebit in bonum vertere, si patìenter feras. & tanto sis ad virtutem promotor, quo minus tibi in illis succedit, ac proinde es expeditor.* Juan Luis Vives, *Introductio ad Sapientiam,* 79.
51. *Vivir a la ocasion. Es gobernar, el discurrir, toda ha da ser al casio. Querer quando se purede, que la sazon, y el temp a nadie aguardan.* Baltasar Gracián, *Oracle,* 288. Hathi Trust Digital Library, accessed 17 January 2019, https://babel.hathitrust.org/cgi/pt?id=ucm.5316526610;view=2up;seq=522;size=175, 510.

52. *Come conviene variare co' tempi volendo sempre avere buona fortuna. Io ho considerato più volte come la cagione della trista e della buona fortuna degli uomini è riscontrare il modo del procedere suo con i tempi: perché e' si vede che gli uomini nelle opere loro procedono, alcuni con impeto, alcuni con rispetto e con cauzione.* Niccolò Machiavelli, *Discorsi*, 3.9.

53. *E quanta pazzia è giuocare a uno giuoco che si possa perdere più sanza comparazione che guadagnare; e quello che non importa forse manco, mutato che sia lo stato, ti obblighi a uno perpetuo tormento d'avere sempre a temere di nuova mutazione.* Francesco Guicciardini, *Ricordi Politici E Civili*, in *Opere inedite di Francesco Guicciardini*, ed. Piero Luigi Guicciardini (Firenze: Barbèra, Bianchi e comp., 1857–1867), Hathi Trust Digital Library, accessed 17 January 2019, https://babel.hathitrust.org/cgi/pt?id=uc1.$b502397;view=2up;seq=148;size=150.

54. *Sarebbe periculoso proverbio, se non fussi bene inteso, quello che si dice: el savio debbe godere el beneficio del tempo; perché quando ti viene quello che tu desideri, chi perde la occasione non la ritruova a sua posta, e anche in molte cose è necessaria la celeritá del risolversi e del fare; ma quando sei in partiti difficili, o in cose che ti sono moleste, allunga e aspetta tempo quanto puoi, perché quello spesso ti illumina o ti libera. Usando cosí questo proverbio, è sempre salutifero; ma inteso altrimenti, sarebbe pernizioso.* Guicciardini, *Ricordi*, accessed 17 January 2019, https://babel.hathitrust.org/cgi/pt?id=uc1.$b502397;view=2up;seq=158;size=150, 114.

55. Plato, *Lesser Hippias*.

56. ἔλπομαι λόγον Ὀδυσσέος ἢ πάθαν διὰ τὸν ἀδυεπῆ γενέσθ᾽ Ὅμηρον· ἐπεὶ ψεύδεσί οἱ ποτανᾷ τε μαχανᾷ σεμνὸν ἔπεστί τι· σοφία δὲ κλέπτει παράγοισα μύθοις· τυφλὸν δ᾽ ἔχει ἦτορ ὅμιλος ἀνδρῶν ὁ πλεῖστος. Pindar, *Nemean* "ΣΩΓΕΝΕΙ ΑΙΓΙΝΗΤΗ, ΠΑΙΔΙ ΠΕΝΤΑΘΛΩ," 7:20–25, *The Odes of Pindar including the Principal Fragments with an Introduction and an English Translation*, trans. Sir John Sandys (Cambridge, MA: Harvard University Press, 1937), Perseus Digital Library, Tufts University, accessed 27 January 2019, http://www.perseus.tufts.edu/hopper/text?doc=Perseus:text 1999.01.0162:book=N.:poem=7&highlight=odysseus.

57. Aristotle, *Nicomachean Ethics* 7:9, 1151–1152. By "moralizing," I point out that Aristotle in his *Nicomachean Ethics* tried to tame the value of expediency that is articulated in the *phronesis* of earlier texts by integrating it with his conception of the morally good.

58. *E fallissimo il giudicare per gli esempli; perchè se non sono simili in tutto e per tutto, non servono; con ciò sia che ogni minima varietà nel caso può essere tanto causa di grandissima variazione nello effetto; e il discernere queste varietà, quando sono piccole, vuole buono e perspicace occhio.* Guicciardini, *Ricordi*, Hathi Digital Library, accessed 17 January 2019, https://babel.hathitrust.org/cgi/pt?id=uc1.$b502397;view=2up;seq=172;size=200, 128.

59. *L'altra (che è quasi quel medesimo che la prima), che gli uomini nel procedere loro, è tanto più nelle azioni grandi, debbono considerare i tempi, e accommodarsi a quegli.* Machiavelli, *Discorsi*, 3.8.

60. *Tener buenos repentes.* Nacen de una prontitud feliz. No ai aprietos ni acasos para ella, en fe de su vivacidad y despejo. Baltasar Gracián, *Oracle*, 56. https://babel.hathitrust.org/cgi/pt?id=ucm.5316526610;view=2up;seq=472;size=150.

61. Gracián, 39. *Conocer las cosas en su punto, en su saço, y saberlas lograr. Las obras de la naturaleza, todas llegan al copletameto de su perfección; hasta allí fueron ganado, desde allí perdiedo,* accessed 19 January 2019, https://babel.hathitrust.org/cgi/pt?id=ucm.5316526610;view=2up;seq=468;size=150

62. Gracián, 58. *Saberse atemperar: No se ha de mostrar igualmente entendido con todos; ni se han de emplear mas fuerças de las que son menester,* accessed 19 January 2019, https://babel.hathitrust.org/cgi/pt?id=ucm.5316526610;view=2up;seq=472;size=150.

Chapter 3

Greco-Roman Strategic Intelligence
Beasts and Philosophers

> Our soul has escaped like a bird
> out of the fowler's snare.
> The snare is broken, and we have escaped.[1]

What do *Looney Tunes, Hunger Games, Game of Thrones, Theogony, Odyssey, Zootopia, Peter Rabbit,* and Disney's *Sword and the Stone* have in common?[2] It is not only that these are immensely popular stories of Strategic Intelligence—what links them together is the underlying model of life lived as a game, that life *is* game. In other words, life is the story of the contest between the hunters and the hunted, of the necessary stressful relationship of predators and their prey, that humans are paradoxically both hunter and quarry. In this chapter, I demonstrate that the hunt is a type of game of strategy that reveals the underlying world view and paradoxical metaphorological paradigm of Strategic Intelligence in the culturally foundational texts of Western civilization. This chapter incorporates insights from the ancient masters of strategy who shared their insights on the divine hunt, including Homer's *Odyssey*, Oppian's *The Hunt* and *Fishing*, various texts composed by Xenophon, and Aesop's *Fables*.[3]

I have alluded to the life of the hunt and life as hunt repeatedly through the preceding pages, especially in the episodes of Merlin and Mim, and Nausicaa and Odysseus. I pointed out that Homer depicted Princess Nausicaa of the Phaeacians as a composite figure that integrated the Strategic Intelligence of both Athena and the divine Huntress Artemis.[4] The double meaning of game is encoded in this scene—not only did Homer depict Odysseus and Nausicaa through the motif of predator and game since he is described as a wild lion compelled to the hunt by insatiable hunger, they also met while she was literally playing a game with her handmaidens.[5] Homer fleshed out the metaphor of the hunt in various ways—for example, Odysseus was scarred as a youth during a bear hunt, a sign by which his wet nurse revealed his identity years later. The neglected hunting hound Argos who dies on the dung heap is a metonymic device for Odysseus himself, as is the description of his cloak, on which was depicted a hound pinning down a dappled fawn as it writhed, by which he proved his identity to his wife Queen Penelope, who offers yet another exemplar of feminine Strategic Intelligence.[6] In Sophocles' drama *Ajax*, finding Odysseus on the prowl after his quarry Ajax, Athena remarked that "your course leads you well to your goal, like that of a keen-scenting Laconian hound," which was also a phrase used often in Platonic corpora.[7]

The trope of the hound of hunt is a feature that reflects the metaphor of the heroic hunt in the strategic world view, and has been used in the domains of war and the cultivation of strategic intellect. For example, Homer in the *Iliad* portrayed the Trojan hero Hector as a hound—

> "Amid the foremost went Hector exulting in his might. And even as a hound pursueth with swift feet after a wild boar or a lion, and snatcheth at him from behind either at flank or buttock, and watcheth for him as he wheeleth; even so Hector pressed upon the long-haired Achaeans, ever slaying the hindmost; and they were driven in rout."[8]

Plato in the *Republic* extended the metaphor of the hunting hound to describe a type of spirit required for the guardians,

> "Do you think," said I, "that there is any difference between the nature of a well-bred hound for this watch-dog's work and of a well-born lad?" "What point have you in mind?" "I mean that each of them must be keen of perception, quick in pursuit of what it has apprehended, and strong too if it has to fight it out with its captive." "Why, yes," said he, "there is need of all these qualities." "And it must, further, be brave if it is to fight well." "Of course." "And will a creature be ready to be brave that is not high-spirited, whether horse or dog or anything else? Have you never observed what an irresistible and invincible thing is spirit, the presence of which makes every soul in the face of everything fearless and unconquerable?" "I have." "The physical qualities of the guardian, then, are obvious." "Yes." "And also those of his soul, namely that he must be of high spirit."[9]

In *Parmenides*, Plato, through the voice of Zeno, describes Socrates as a hound that "follows the arguments with a scent as keen as a Laconian hound's."[10] But for the soldier-philosopher Xenophon, the hunt is a divine legacy from the gods themselves, and the strategic means by which the greatest excellence, as articulated by the figures of the Greek hero-founders, is cultivated. He thought that the hunt was passed as a legacy from the deities Apollo, patron of seers and prophets, and his sister Artemis the Goddess of the Hunt, through the Satyr Chiron to a long list of Greek cultural heroes that, not surprisingly, includes Odysseus. "Therefore," said Xenophon,

I charge the young not to despise hunting or any other schooling. For these are the means by which men become good in war and in all things out of which must come excellence in thought and word and deed.... For among the ancients the companions of Chiron to whom I referred, learnt many noble lessons in their youth, beginning with hunting; from these lessons there sprang in them great virtue, for which they are admired even today. That all desire virtue is obvious, but because they must toil if they are to gain her, the many fall away. For the achievement of her is hidden in obscurity, whereas the toils inseparable from her are manifest.[11]

The poet Oppian in *The Hunt* concurs with Xenophon about the hunt as a divine legacy. We can excavate the underlying strategic values expressed by the poem by examining more closely the particular images that he used. What is fascinating about the *Hunt* and *Fishing* is that the terms he uses to characterize predators and prey, including "wily," "tricky," "resourceful," and "strategically planning," are also the very royal attributes of the kings of gods and men that I discussed previously, including Cronos, Zeus, Odysseus, and his wife Queen Penelope. These terms gesture to the presence of a metaphorological paradigm that highlights existential threat.

"Sing" commanded the Divine Huntress Artemis to her poet, "of the glory of the hunt,"[12] and "the battles of wild beasts and hunting men; sing of the breeds of hounds and the varied tribes of horses; the quickly devised strategic plans and the deeds of skillful tracking."[13] The "mysteries" of Artemis, full of artful plotting, rival the mysteries of the cult of Bacchus, the epics of warriors and journeyers, and the intrigues of Aphrodite.[14] The sacred song of the goddess Artemis, for Oppian, is a celebration of the excellent competition of hunters and prey, to whom "God hath given strength, courage and wits, not far inferior to the hunters themselves."[15] The competition, Artemis proclaims, is one of "valiant might, resourceful strategic planning, and of heart-minds full of strategic craftiness and traps."[16]

In the schema of life lived as hunt, the successful hunter must interpret the threats and weaknesses of opponents. But the strategic resources of each opponent, Oppian revealed, varied widely across species. Some were small, yet wise and rascally; others were physically strong but "weak in strategic planning."[17] The enlightened hunter needed to know the strengths and weaknesses of each—the bull uses its horns whereas the stag flees; the lion's teeth are its weapon, whereas the teeth of the Oryx are harmless. The hare's feet are its armor in a way that the rhinoceros' are not. The leopard is deadly with its claws, the ram with its forehead, and the boar with its tusks. The villainous apes, mimics of humanity, are full of strategic plotting.[18] Horses exceed all creatures in that nature has bestowed on them an artful resourcefulness, an attribute closely shared with the tiger's cunningly artful nature.[19] The porcupine is an especially wickedly wrought[20] foe:

There is nothing in the shady wood more terrible to behold nor aught more deadly. Their size is like that of the bloody wolves; short, small, and strong is their body, but their hide bristles all about with rough and shaggy quills, such as those with which the cunning tribes of hedgehogs are armed. But when far mightier beasts pursue it, then it uses this strategy.

Strategic Intelligence is even apparent in the behavior of the various creatures of the watery depths. The oceans are a domain that lacks justice and order, and strife is rampant.[21] Just like humankind, all opponents differ in skill. In lieu of brawn or physical weapons, God has armed some fish with a crafty mind which is a weapon they use to beguile and even destroy the predators that seek to devour them. Many are wily and have their own traps—for example, although weak and slow, the family of rays practice the art of paralyzing their prey.[22] The largest, though physically weak, can even ensnare and overcome sly men through strategy, "for he greatly delights to banquet upon man, and human flesh above all is to him pleasing and a welcome food."[23] Crabs and starfish both are characterized by Strategic Intelligence, and even urchins have wits. Cuttle-fish are *snare-crafty* (δολόμητις), and prawns are deadly because they destroy by being destroyed, by killing their predator only after being swallowed—achieving ultimate victory like the famous Trojan horse that enabled the Greeks to figuratively swallow their enemies after the Trojans first swallowed them.[24] Interestingly, King Gōujiàn of Yuè of ancient Chinese civilization similarly swallowed the feces of his lord-captor in order to destroy him (chapter 6). The image of the snare-crafty (δολόμητις), will express itself again in latter Western cultural evolution through Ransom theory, which emphasized the narrative that Christ destroyed by himself being destroyed, and which served as a theory of salvation that was dominant for the first millennium of Christianity (chapter 4).

Other marine animals live through the art of deception. The octopus strategically molds itself to the shapes of rocks, avoiding notice, but it is deadly when prey approach. Likewise, the fishing frog, though soft and sluggish, feeds itself through the use of strategy; it sets a trap by hiding in the mud and uses its own flesh as bait for prey.[25] This is not unlike the schemes of the wily fox:

A like device, I have heard, the cunning fox contrives. When she sees a dense flight of birds, she lies down on her side and stretches out her swift limbs and closes her eyes and shuts fast her mouth. Seeing her you would say that she was deep asleep or even lying quite dead: so breathless she lies stretched out, contriving guile. The birds, beholding, rush straightway upon her in a crowd and tear her fur with their feet, as if in mockery. But when they come nigh her teeth, then she opens the doors of guile and suddenly seizes them, and with wide gape cunningly catches her prey, even all that she takes at a swoop.[26]

Although some animals are fearful and weak, others derive their strategic advantage from integrating strategy, strength, and agility. For example, the mongoose is a master of wiles and artifice who can overcome the asymmetric threat posed by two far bigger and deadlier opponents, snakes and crocodiles.[27] The mongoose does this through strategic ensnarement, entrapment, and wickedly wrought strategic plans.[28] "O Mongoose," the poet praised, "great wonder, greatly valiant and of wily strategic planning, who is able to advance to the very jaws of death and overcome his foes! He is worthy to be praised!"[29]

Evidence from many of the world's cultures shows that there is but one paragon of strategic perfection, that is the fox. For Oppian, the fox was the most strategically intelligent of all the animal masters of ruse. Cunning and resourceful, the fox

> dwells in remotest lair, with seven-gated openings to her house and tunneled earths far from one another, lest hunters set an ambush about her doors and lead her captive with snares.[30] Terrible is she to fight with her teeth against stronger wild beasts and hunting dogs. And when chilly winter comes and she lacks food, and the vines show bare of grapes, then she weaves a deadly device for hunting, to capture by craft birds and the young of hares.[31]

The fox's mind is incredibly alert as it is sensitive to the possibility of entrapment.[32] And for this reason, the fox outwits its predators—this stratagem-enlightened master avoids capture through resourcefulness, and it can also set its own traps when needed. Because it sees through stratagem, the fox is a generalissimo of strategic positioning and rapidly adaptive orienteering.[33]

These sources all demonstrate that the true masters of life are those who are ruse-minded. This includes hunters who capture Libyan lions by trickery, crafty fishermen who fish at night, hunters whose machinations lure jackals to their death in pits, and leopards to entrapment by the "love of wine," or through whose "wise foresight" flush hares downhill so that they cannot take advantage of their strong forepaws.[34] What is fascinating is that the terms used to depict heroic ruse-minded animals are equally applicable to the strategic deities and heroic humans discussed earlier. For example, King Odysseus' wife Queen Penelope, a devotee of Athena, who is "wise and makes good counsel in her mind," also "wove her web of wiles."[35] Penelope here is foil for Clytemnestra who is "snare-strategied."[36] Zeus and Cronos are both described as masters of strategic plans and traps (chapter 2). And Odysseus famously hubristically boasted of his fame: "I am Odysseus, son of Laertes, who for all my tricks am known to men, and my glory reaches heaven."[37]

Eternal glory is achieved by ruse-minded, foxy masters of strategy who, through an acute awareness of changing reality, are able to achieve their single-minded purpose.[38] In the motif of the hunt, ruse and stratagem, artifice and machination, denial and deception, and resourcefulness all define the contest of wits. This profound truth has been captured nowhere as simply and precisely as in the texts associated with the Archmage of Strategic Intelligence himself, Aesop. Strategic values have via Cultural Cryptology, been hidden in plain sight in the form of the Aesopic tradition for over two millennium, cited almost continuously by both literati and philosophers, including Aristophanes, Aristotle, and Plato. The following parable is just one of many examples of this tradition.

> A lion had grown old and weak. He pretended to be sick, which was just a ruse to make the other animals come and pay their respects so that he could eat them all up, one by one. The fox also came to see the lion, but she greeted him from outside the cave. The lion asked the fox why she didn't come in. The fox replied, "Because I see the tracks of those going in, but none coming out."[39]

The fox in the fable is the master of strategy who, being ruse-minded, evades the trap because it can see through it using strategic vision. The fox interprets the indicators properly because it is sensitive to the parameters of the threat environment and can therefore rapidly adapt and appropriately react, which results in strategic advantage.

In this short fable, there are three beneficiaries—the fox as the master of Strategic Intelligence, the reader/listener of the text who is sensitized to the reality of ruse vicariously, and the man of culture who must speak during times of political deliberation. The political nature of the example above is clear; the rhetorical technique of expressing values and arguments indirectly through an imaginary story such as Aesop's fables is what the philosopher Aristotle referred to as one aspect of an *enthymeme*, which he defended as a type of exemplary political discourse.[40] The strategic aspect of the fables that Aristotle refers to in order to explain the effectiveness of the *enthymeme* is interesting for the manner in which it resonates with the leitmotif of entrapment and escape discussed throughout this book.

> A fable, to give an example, is that of Stesichorus concerning Phalaris, or that of Aesop on behalf of the demagogue. For Stesichorus, when the people of Himera had chosen Phalaris dictator and were on the point of giving him a body-guard, after many arguments related a fable to them: "A horse was in sole occupation of a meadow. A stag having come and done much damage to the pasture, the horse, wishing to avenge himself on the stag, asked a man whether he could help him to punish the stag. The man consented, on condition that the horse submitted to the bit and allowed him to mount him javelins in hand. The horse agreed to the terms and the man mounted him, but instead of obtaining vengeance on the stag, the horse from that time became the man's slave. So then," said he,

"do you take care lest, in your desire to avenge yourselves on the enemy, you be treated like the horse. You already have the bit, since you have chosen a dictator; if you give him a body-guard and allow him to mount you, you will at once be the slaves of Phalaris.⁴¹

Thus, this art of indirect speech, known in classical Rhetoric as *ductus obliquus*, is a mode of discourse appropriate to the free man who wields Strategic Intelligence.

"Fables are suitable for addresses to popular assemblies," noted Aristotle, "and they have one advantage—they are easy to invent . . . all you require is the power of thinking out your analogy, a power developed by intellectual training."⁴² For those who share a view of the European dark ages as a period of cultural sluggishness, it may come as a surprise that *Aesops' Fables* was enormously influential in the medieval world, functioning exactly as that type of primer of intellectual training that sharpened the mind in preparation for the game of life, a fact reflected in many of the medieval sources I will examine in chapter 5.⁴³

The cultural evidence that I provided in this chapter demonstrates that underneath these stories of strategically heroic and kingly gods, humans, and animals, lie the values of the age-old strategic world view, a form of pragmatic wisdom that teaches humanity the means of dealing with unanticipated threat and insecurity. The answer to "WWFD?" *What Would Fox Do?* is crystal clear—fox avoids entrapment because it foresees it; it foresees it because it saw it personally in the past, and that experience has taught it to be resourceful. Its resourcefulness is the outcome of the proper interpretation of the threat features of its ambivalent and antagonistic environment. The strategic vision of the fox is providential, and it is a form of hope by which it can escape the trap of finitude, and the trauma of lost identity. For fox, for the readers of *Aesop's Fables* throughout the aeons, and for the voyeurs of *Looney Tunes, Game of Thrones, Odyssey, Zootopia, Peter Rabbit*, and Disney's *Sword and the Stone* who imbibe strategic values vicariously, *forewarned is forearmed.*

PRAEMONITUS, PRAEMUNITUS: FOREWARNED IS FOREARMED

There is a popular saying in Spanish, *a man forewarned is a man forearmed, the worth of two, and ready to fight.*⁴⁴ In the preceding pages, I argued that Greco-Roman Strategic Intelligence gestured to a way of life that seamlessly integrated the strategic with the heroic in a framework that valorized appropriate interpretation and adaptability. In this chapter, I explore this theme by demonstrating the importance of vision in the strategic world view; strategic vision is the common denominator and ultimate goal of multiple cultural domains, including, but not limited to, the religious, the philosophical, the martial, and the literary. Masters who achieve strategic vision, including mystics, generals, seers, prophets, satirists, and strategists, are thaumaturges—wonder workers who wield power over fate and fortune.

What immediately stands out about strategic vision is its utilitarian and instrumental associations. Strategic vision is *good at* because it helps us to achieve one's objectives, rather than being inherently good or evil in itself. Resuming the preceding section about master fox, Oppian wrote that foxy masters are "mighty," of "strategic planning," and a "great wonder," who are able to escape insecurity and death. In other words, the fox is like King Zeus, the "immortal master of schemes."[45] By describing foxy Strategic Intelligence as a "great wonder," Oppian pointed out that strategic vision is a particularly potent tool or weapon, which resonates with other examples of wondrous weapons in ancient Greek sources. For example, Hesiod described both Herakles' famous shield and Zeus' famous rock of ruse which became the foundation of the oracle at Delphi as "great wonders."[46] This description in epic was picked up by philosophy—the philosopher Aristotle wrote that philosophy was born out of human wonder and puzzlement about reality. "Even the lover of myth is in a sense a lover of Wisdom," wrote Aristotle, "for the myth is composed of wonders." Notably, following Plato, who advocated for an escape from ignorance and illusion in the cave to insight to eternal forms, Philosophy, from Aristotle's perspective, is a wondrous thing that enables *escape* from the trap of ignorance.[47]

Common to all of these stories of Strategic Intelligence is the emphasis placed on strategic vision as a wondrously potent weapon. The Greek root *thauma* "wonder" itself is semantically related to terms for vision, which in turn have generated a host of terms, including theory, theorem, and theater—all three of which describe reality through a demonstration by vision.[48] The intellectual battle of wits formed the agonistic venue in which one could expose to view the excellence of wonderful Strategic Intelligence—this explains both the contest between Zeus and Prometheus in *Theogony*, and the contest of wits between Merlin and Mim two millennia later.

In ancient Greek culture, the *theoros* was an emissary sent by a community to consult an oracle, observe a (wonderful) religious feast, or view a wondrous vision (*thea*).[49] Plato and the Pythagoreans were fascinated with mathematical theorems and arguments in their philosophical texts, which were the intellectual means that revealed the concealed. Most importantly for my purpose here, is that according to many Greek etymological dictionaries, the term *to behold* (θεάομαι) is related to *wonder* (θώϋμἄ), and to the military action of reconnoitering (θέσιν), as used by Thucydides in *The*

Peloponnesian War (5.7).[50] Plato even makes this point through the voice of Socrates in his exploration of courage in *Laches:*

> Socrates: It seems to your friend and me that, to take the various subjects of knowledge, there is not one knowledge of how a thing has happened in the past, another of how things are happening in the present, and another of how a thing that has not yet happened might or will happen most favorably in the future, but it is the same knowledge throughout. For example, in the case of health, it is medicine always and alone that surveys present, past, and future processes alike; and farming is in the same position as regards the productions of the earth. *And in matters of war; I am sure you yourselves will bear me out when I say that here generalship makes the best forecasts on the whole, and particularly of future results, and is the mistress rather than the servant of the seer's art, because it knows better what is happening or about to happen* in the operations of war; whence the law ordains that the general shall give orders to the seer, and not the seer to the general.[51] (italic added for emphasis)

We can extrapolate and generalize from this—a world view that emphasizes agonism and conflict more highly values the way of knowing of generalship (*stratego*). As a master contender (στρατεύομαι/*strateuomai*) for meaning and significance, the figure of the heroic general demonstrates the strategic aspect of Strategic Intelligence. As seen by the examples provided by figures who are both kings and generals, such as Zeus, Odysseus, fox (metaphorically), and Socrates (as philosopher-king below), weaponizing sight as insight, and becoming *snare-aware* through foresight, mitigates injustice and disorder (*Ἀδικία*) and enables strategic advantage, in terms of life, dignity, power, and position.

In addition to linking the divine sight of the religious seer to the more highly valued strategic vision of the general, both Oppian and Xenophon emphasized the role of providential strategic vision in the motif of the hunt. For example, Oppian wrote:

> Many are the modes of glorious and profitable hunting: modes innumerable, suited to the various beasts and tribes and glens. Who with his single *mind* should *comprehend* them all and tell of them in order with euphonious song? Who could *behold* them all? Who could *behold* so much, being mortal? Only the Gods easily *see* all things. But I shall tell what I have *seen* with my own *eyes* when following in the woods the chase, splendid of boons, and whatever cunning mysteries of all manner of mysterious craft I have learned from them whose business it is.[52] (italics added for emphasis)

Seeing with one's own eyes articulates an understanding of enlightenment that is authoritative because it is grounded in the criteria of personal experience. Personal experience is the critical feature that enables one to see reality as it truly is, to see both the revealed and the concealed.

Strategic vision, with its emphasis on the change of perspective required when dealing with the overt and the covert, is a major motif in Xenophon's *On Hunting*. In that text, Xenophon clarifies that hunting is a form of education that leads to heroic virtue that is "wondrous."[53] The hunt hones the artfulness, reason and battle skills of the most heroic of Greek warriors.[54] Most importantly, the hunt is the wondrous means by which hidden virtuosity is revealed.[55]

> It may be that, if the body of excellence were *visible*, men would be less careless of virtue, *knowing* that she *sees* them as *clearly* as they *see* her. For when he is *seen* by his beloved every man rises above himself and shrinks from what is ugly and evil in word or deed, for fear of being *seen* by him. . . . But in the presence of Virtue men do many evil and ugly things, supposing that they are not *regarded* by her because they do not *see* her. Yet she is present everywhere because she is immortal, and she honors those who are good to her, but casts off the bad. Therefore, if men knew that she is *watching* them, they would be impatient to undergo the toils and the discipline by which she is hardly to be captured, and would achieve her.[56] (italics added for emphasis)

Xenophon's *Memorabilia* often links Strategic Intelligence with strategic vision. His depiction of Socrates binds the Strategic Intelligence of a general with discrimination of noble and base men, the appropriate reaction to which results in strategic advantage. In addition to other duties, the generalissimo must be "resourceful, active, careful, hardy and quick-witted; she must be both gentle and brutal, at once straightforward and designing, capable of both caution and surprise, lavish and rapacious, generous and mean, skillful in defense and attack."[57] "Oh youth," Socrates exclaims, "just as a general needs to know the right and wrong disposition of his forces in different situations, he must also be able to discern the noble from the base."[58] In other words, the strategic vision of the military domain is analogous to the strategic vision required in threats rising in the social domain. Both are related to the appropriate deployment of force effectuated by strategic discernment.

The human mind is the most potent of weapons.[59] When it sets out to expose social and political traps and vice, it can deliver the paralyzing sting of the stingray, as in the case of the genre of satire, which compels vision through the subtle attack of exposé. The following two examples from Xenophon and Horace both compel insight by exposing the social entrapment of miscreants.

Xenophon's story about Socrates and the beauty Theodote is an interesting example of the manner in which a master of strategy compelled strategic vision through satirical exposure, linking the motif of the hunt with the development of strategic insight for the naïve reader.[60] On hearing of the legendary beauty of Theodote, Socrates rushed over to examine her closely as he could "learn more from seeing than hearsay."[61] There she was, *a sight to behold*, having her portrait painted. After watching for a while, Socrates asked: as for we the viewers (θέα) and her the viewed, who has the greater advantage?[62] Socrates very quickly surmised that Theodote had the more to gain because all who saw her pined for her.[63] Examining her even more closely, Socrates realized that Theodote's life was actually sustained by gentleman callers in the same way that spiders lured flies to their web. Theodote was a huntress who lived through artifice—she fed on anyone who got stuck in her web.[64] Her life was sustained just in the same way that hounds pursued their prey, except she had a pimp in lieu of hounds, and she used her body as a net to ensnare her prey. Xenophon thus integrates vision with the agonistic conflict of life and death, a theme that echoes in the Platonic corpora. For example, Socrates' pilgrimage to view Theodote puts him in the role of the *theoros*-pilgrim just in the same way as he functions in the *Phaedrus*. The motif of the viewer is also prominent in the *Symposium* and in the *Republic* once we recall that the text begins with a trip down to Piraeus to view the religious spectacle, that the section about Plato's cave is essentially a trip that enables the reader to vicariously escape ignorance by lodging in the secure domain of eternal forms.

The Roman satirical poet Horace, like Xenophon, also sought to compel strategic insight by satirically exposing legacy hunters on the prowl for a sugar daddy.[65] In response to the ravages of fortune, Ulysses (Odysseus) asked the ghost of the blind prophet and "master of cunning" ('*iamne doloso*) Tiresias by what arts (*artibus*) and means (*modis*) could he restore his wealth? Tiresias encouraged Ulysses to use his famous mastery of deception to prey on vulnerable old men and to worm himself both into their affections and their final will and testament. To do so, the ghost recommended that he take their sides at all times, make himself irreplaceable as a second son, and slavishly adapt to the old man's every need and desire. Tiresias encouraged Ulysses to adapt to all situations—if the old man is a poet, praise his poetry, and if he is a lecher, give him your woman. Practice dissimulation—make sure you say some nice things and shed a tear to show your sadness when the old man passes, for "it is fit to disguise your countenance (*est gaudia prodentem vultum celare*) which [otherwise] would betray your joy." This is the way to "live well and prosper!" (*vive valeque*)

These satirical exposés from Xenophon and Horace and are just two examples of satire that compel strategic vision through the exposure of vice. These literary forms are direct descendants of earlier dramatic texts—many ancient Greek tragedies and comedies exposed reality as a spectacle for those voyeurs in the place of seeing, the theater. Aristophanes' *Knights*, *Wasps* and *Lysistrata,* for example, all exposed the horror of war in an entertaining way. From this vantage point, strategic vision and proper interpretation were important features and cultural dominants of Greco-Roman culture. Strategic vision and proper interpretation of external reality marked the difference between being free (πόρε) or bewildered (απορια); quite simply, strategic vision, and proper interpretation were an expression of power and life potential.

PHILOSOPHY AS STRATEGY

I end this chapter with my interpretation of the figure of Socrates as a master of strategy. Reading against the grain of philosophers who have usurped the identity of Socrates for over two thousand years, I want to reclaim his identity as a hybrid prophet-warrior, a type of diviner of the Cultural Cryptologic tradition who vanquished his princely foes through the virtuosic wielding of the strategic weapons of dialogue and clear-sightedness. What the figure of Socrates reveals to us in the Platonic corpora is a vision of the love of wisdom *(philo + sophia)* that is largely synonymous with Strategic Intelligence. As opposed to many philosophers who have focused their studies on the arguments in the Platonic dialogues themselves, in this last section I will proceed by examining *how* the figure of Socrates maneuvers in the dialogues agonistically and polemically, and contemplate why he was depicted as dangerous. I pay more attention to what Plato shows us about Socrates in terms of his dramatic role rather than what he has Socrates tell us. I conclude that Plato uses the figure of Socrates in the dialogues to dramatically demonstrate to his readers a novel form of heroism constructed on the combination of the prophetic and the martial, which utilizes a pedagogy of deception *(elenchus/ aporia).*

To recap, the general of ten thousand warriors who directly studied under Socrates, Xenophon, portrayed his master as a spell master and peddler of love potions and jinxes.[66] Socrates himself in the *Symposium* confesses to learning from the prophetess of the erotic, Diotima, and he claims in the *Menexenus* to have studied the arts of Rhetoric with the *strategos* (general) Pericles' consort, the remarkable Aspasia. Meno called him a sorcerer who entrapped and bewitched with spells and incantations that stunned his prey like a ray, a curious description that reminds us of Oppian's *Fishing* and Sophocles' *Odysseus Wounded*, a lost source in which Odysseus' son kills his father with the spike of a stingray. In Plato's *Republic*, Socrates is a mischievous quibbler who intends to overpower his foes by laying traps, and he is depicted as a snake charmer.[67] Socrates agrees with Meno—his prey are stunned to the degree that he is also stunned by the bewilderment of *aporia*, of seeing no way out of the trap.⁶⁸ And in the *Lesser Hippias*, Socrates' stunning conclusion, discussed below, causes both himself and his listener to be lost in his own mind.⁶⁹

Socrates is a ruse-minded seer like the fox, a master of many-means like Odysseus, and on the "road of many forks and crossroads" like the Hebrew prophets.⁷⁰ In the *Epistles*, Plato even depicts himself as Odysseus caught in political wrangling, which he depicts in terms of entrapment between Scylla and Charybdis.⁷¹ Socrates follows the scent of reality like a hound at hunt and paralyzes his listeners like a manta ray. In the *Republic* he is like a "hunter surrounding a bush . . . take care that justice nowhere escapes us and disappear from our view. . . . Here I caught a glimpse . . . Glaucon, here is something that looks like a track, and I believe the game will not altogether escape us"⁷²

Rather than as a well-meaning but irksome gadfly biting the hind side of the state, which is the metaphor utilized to describe Socrates in the *Apology*, these various descriptions depict Socrates as dangerous—deadly dangerous. Dangerous enough to warrant the death penalty. The question arises, though, why is he dangerous? To whom is he a threat, and how does he threaten?

Plato's *Republic* provides a clue to how Socrates does battle, and to the polemical undertones of the dialogues. The text begins by framing Socratic/Platonic dialogue as a type of competition akin to the athletic games celebrated during the festival of the Huntress Goddesses Bendis and Artemis, of Thrace and Athens respectively, and the conflict begins immediately when Socrates is trapped from leaving the scene, after being provoked by mighty princes to "show yourself stronger." The human excellence exhibited through the competition of the chariot race is subjected to the greater spectacle and excellence of Platonic discourse, for Socrates' weapon of choice is clear—like the Chinese strategic hero Liú Bèi discussed in chapters 6–8 who preferred to vie with cunning wits against his brawny foe, Socrates, whose name means something like *salvific power* (σώζ- κράτος *sos-kratos*), contends in the discursive domain of dialogue and dialectic. The agonism of the *Republic* is not only the conflict between two worlds of value, heroic meaning and identity, it is an agonism that is an abstraction from war and *eros*. That is to say that the body that desires to be free is actually the master of mind which goes to war on its behalf. The path to meaning is opened through the agonism of verbal contest in dialogue and dialectic—she who wins the laurel overcomes the deficiency of body with the armor of mind, and transcends it.

Not only is the Thracian goddess Bendis and the chariot races in her honor a novelty, the type of hero that is Socrates is also innovative. In fact, I argue that Plato presents Socrates in his oeuvre as a heroic warrior whose power is actuated by a Strategic Intelligence that is informed by Greek divination practices. What is salient in the dialogues presented in the Platonic corpora is the manner in which Socrates battles for meaning, by attacking the relative strength of opponents' views as articulated by newly exposed value-standards that putatively make those views authoritative, legitimate and valid. Socrates seems to gesture to the possibility of subverting cultural hegemony by means of the question, and the questioning dialogue, while always strategically concealing his own position through the ironic assertion of ignorance.

Socrates, the philosopher Aristotle tells us, is an example of the rhetorical strategy of understatement or dissimulation, now known as Socratic irony, in order to make one's discourse more appealing rather than making it appear as if offered for gain or attention.[73] I would go one step further: Socratic irony was a strategy that he used to undermine his opponents. Just like the switchblade scene in *Twelve Angry Men* (1957), Socrates of the Platonic dialogues, like Henry Fonda, plays the long game—strategically setting the stage so that he can dramatically undermine his cocksure combatants.[74] Although he denigrates sophistry, rhetoric, and oratory in the *Gorgias*, like the Chinese persuaders explored in the latter half of this book, the figure of Socrates in Plato's *Republic* strategically probes each speaker about his views, and then cleverly adapts his approach to each.[75] In order to get a handle on each of his opponents, Socrates appears to use the strategy that one ancient Chinese primer characterized as "plumbing the depths," in which one should constantly elicit answers in order to acquire sufficient data to manipulate a target's internal world.[76] For example, the manner in which Socrates questions the elder Cephalus, the cautious Adeimantus, the creative Glaucon, the notorious Alcibiades, and the ambitious Meno varies widely, as does his response to each. It is significant that the strategic philosopher-king Socrates tames through speech the wild Thrasymachus who begins his role by terrifying, startling, striking dumb and terrorizing Socrates as "a beast sprang up like he would tear us to pieces."[77] It perhaps is no surprise to learn that the Rhetoricians Thrasymachus and Gorgias were some of Socrates' main competitors in the marketplace of ideas.

Socrates objected in the text *Hippias Minor* to Hippias' contention that the moral integrity represented by the figure of Achilles is superior to the Strategic Intelligence articulated through the figure of wily Odysseus. By comparing and contrasting these values in the figures of Achilles and Odysseus, Socrates surprisingly persuaded Hippias that only the virtuosic man was capable of artifice because he knew how to adapt his technique for strategic advantage. "It is, then, in the nature of the good man to do injustice voluntarily, and of the bad man to do it involuntarily, that is, if the good man has a good soul . . . then he who voluntarily errs and does disgraceful and unjust acts, Hippias, if there be such a man, would be no other than the good man."[78] Therefore, Odysseus and Achilles can both be said to be both true and false, and more alike than opposed.[79]

I get the distinct impression that Plato/Socrates too is engaged in playing with his competitors and his readers some type of game of entrapment, a veritable wizard's duel of bewilderment. The point made by the famous political philosopher Leo Strauss that many philosophers historically obscured their more heterodox ideas in their writings because of a fear of persecution resonates here. My analysis, influenced by my analysis of the heroic figures of Chinese Strategic Intelligence discussed in the latter portion of this book, concludes that Plato may have strategically used a poetics of misdirection.[80] Rather than serving up his ideas in the epic poetry of his forebears, Plato maintains a sense of theatricality, strategically dramatizing often shocking ideas via third party dialogues, while simultaneously concealing his own intent and amusing readers by goading his opponents.[81] After all, one might be considered blameless if one asserts ignorance. And his opponents are not just vanquished: they are forever belittled for their ignorance.

Although Socratic philosophical analysis is often conventionally opposed to the conventions of myth and epic poetry that preceded it, I see that the philosopher king that is Socrates continues the lineage of his forebears, the heroically strategic Kings Odysseus and Zeus.[82] Just as Kings Odysseus and Zeus did battle with strategy and wits in the game of entrapment (chapter 2), philosopher king Socrates coerces his foes to see the trap that they are in, to submit, and to silence via the weapon of dialogue. The famous Socratic method, what philosophers refer to as *elenchus*, most often leads listeners into the trap of bewilderment (*aporia*), a term that literally means *no path*.[83] The point of this method seems not to be a solidification of truth or an expansion of knowing, but rather an accentuation of uncertainty and insecurity—to epistemological defeat. And Socrates is always the victor: he consistently confounds the assertions of his opponents while losing little—since he rarely proposes a definitive answer.

Thus, in the figure of Socrates we see another example of the strategic hero, both the virtuoso of strategy who battles with intellect and discourse, and the general of extraordinary insight who contends by virtuosically setting intellectual snares, schooling the city's princelings, and vanquishing his competitors. Socrates' power is enabled by unmatched insight, which is described as a type of divination. In the same way that Greek priests and priestesses divined the meaning of oracles, Socrates interpreted people and arguments. And he was exemplary at it—the testimony of Hermogenes that was relayed in Xenophon's *Apology* identifies Socrates in the Apollonic seer tradition, noting that the oracle at Delphi revealed that the god Apollo himself claimed that Socrates was the most free, the most just, and the most prudent of all humans.[84] In other words, being honored of Heaven, the hero that is Socrates is effective and prudent because he is free, temperate, and just. In the *Phaedo*, Socrates claims to have prophetic vision equivalent to the priestesses at Delphi, and that he has received the gift of prophecy equal to the swans who are consecrated to the Gods.[85] Socrates' heroism is potent because he integrates in his person the power of the divine and the warrior.

Socrates claims access to a higher, divine authority as a prophet and interpreter of portents, which enables him to speak to power authoritatively. This claim also appears to transform the authority of divination from an exoteric and public mode to an esoteric and private mode. Socrates' ability was not unique—many, including poets, soothsayers, prophets, seers, and even statesmen received the sign or the voice, but most could not interpret what the message portended—with regards to interpretation, they were all in a state of bewilderment (*aporia*).[86] For Socrates, the proof is in the pudding—appropriate interpretation is proven in time, and Socrates never erred.[87]

Book seven of Plato's *Republic* makes this prophetic view of Socrates especially clear—the ascent that Socrates describes in the allegory of the cave is an "escape from fetters," not because it provides sight, but because it redirects sight to an appropriate place of insight. The ethereal world of knowledge provides the possibility of imagination, which can be barely glimpsed, but which when seen, can be used to create progress in the world of Becoming. In fact, the world of imagination informs the virtue of Strategic Intelligence which Plato refers to as this-worldly prudence.[88] This is the quintessence of Strategic Intelligence—"the virtue of prudence," especially the type of prudence that I call Strategic Intelligence, can be both useful and useless, beneficial or malicious depending on the adaptability of sight in different domains.[89] The guardians too can escape from snares and turned to strategic insight, and thus their "souls will become keen-sighted for such pursuits."

Thus, in the Socratic battle for meaning, which is a war of insight, war is waged between masters whose power is enabled by rapid adaptation to both light and dark, and by intellectually blinding their opponents. *Elenchetic* dialogue and dialectic constitute yet another agonistic arena—the athletic body that is Socrates articulates the highest value—he is a place of divinity, power, and a symbolic exposure of the virtuosic wielding and rapid adaptability of Strategic Intelligence as reoriented to the higher and lower, the brighter and the dimmer. The Socratic body enacts the potentiality of the philosophical in the political, which are by necessity mutually informing. The great one is she who not only escapes both the double bewilderment of light and dark through the rapidly adaptive power of the turning of sight to insight, but she is also the hero that can strategically incite blindness in her opponent.[90]

Socrates demonstrates practically a pedagogy of deception and trickery, a strategy of power, and the polemical nature of discourse. Awareness of one's blindness via *aporia* is a necessary prerequisite for the *turning* of insight. By claiming to have no answers to the questions posed, the figure of Socrates uses a rhetorical strategy remarkably similar to some ancient

Chinese strategists, who rendered their opponent impotent during verbal sparring by strategically attacking from a place a place of concealment (chapter 6). By strategically lodging himself in the question to conceal his own view, Socrates wields the question as a weapon of refutation by which he traps his foes in *aporia*, undermines authority and legitimacy, tames the rash and vulgar like Thrasymachus, and coerces elites, such as Alcibiades, Protagoras, Gorgias, and Callicles to listen and learn. At times, Socrates' reasoning in the dialogues is so convoluted that he appears to exemplify what the ancient Chinese text *Guǐgǔzi* (chapter 6) describes as the technique of *pouncing and pinning,* used to bait one's adversary.

> As for using the technique of pounce and pin, be unpredictable. If you cannot win, sometimes attack him, and then hold him down and exhaust him; sometimes hold him down in order to tire him, and then make him submit. Sometimes pin him down and exhaust him in order to overcome him; and sometimes use the possibility of submission as the means to weigh him down and exhaust him.[91]

The identity of the heroic philosopher-king in Plato's *Republic* is made paradigmatic by the figure of Socrates. Socrates' excellence is enabled by his Strategic Intelligence, a form of snare-aware (δολόφρονες) prowess that conceals itself in the question while coercing his opponent to reveal himself. Through the power of insight and the divination of his opponent's interior world, Socrates adapted his approach like King Odysseus, the adaptable (π ολυτρόπως) man of machinations (πολυμηχανος), and led his listener to Socrates' desired end state. He not only schooled the powerful elites of his time, but like Zeus, he also escaped the cave figuratively to the eternal realm of forms, and ascended from death to life, from ignorance to wisdom, from impotency to the greatest potency, from weakness to "showing himself stronger." But the term "stronger" gestures not to brawn. Rather, Socrates is the exemplar of the strategic hero that imparts the message that nature favors the strategically wise. Whereas nobody now remembers all of the great princes of the city with whom Socrates engaged in verbal sparring, the strategically heroic figure of Socrates in the Platonic dialogues has shown himself stronger than all of the princelings who have "suffered" him for more than 2,000 years in Philosophy 101 classes.

These chapters focused on Greco-Roman Strategic Intelligence have demonstrated that Strategic Intelligence and Strategic Culture are but modern instantiations of a very ancient strategic world view, which cultural genealogy can be tracked into pre-history. For over two and half millennia, societies have formalized their life strategies that achieve success in the game of life in cultural narratives and culturally validated heroic identities that double as memories and models that can be recycled to interpret new features of reality. Many masters of Strategic Intelligence have embedded strategic vision in cultural products since culture is itself a repository of strategic values that humans can tap into in order to overcome unanticipated threats. What is common to many stories in the Greco-Roman cultural legacy are a constellation of features that mark the existence of these underlying strategic values. To reiterate, these features emphasize that personal experience is the means of sensitization to surrounding threats, that sensitivity develops strategic vision, which then enables appropriate adaptation, reaction, and subsequent strategic advantage.

I perceive a linkage between the strategic and Liberal Arts, or the Arts of the Free, as a set of strategies that enable *homo ludens* to win the game of life, a game which seemingly has few consistently stable rules. Greco-Roman narratives, such as Hesiod's *Theogony*, Homer's *Odyssey*, various tales of the hunt, and narratives that detail a special emphasis on strategic vision, demonstrate that the values of Strategic Intelligence were delivered historically in cultural products such as myth, epic, drama, satire, and philosophical treatise. Practitioners of Strategic Intelligence in government, security and business communities will all benefit from the vast repository of Strategic Intelligence embedded in the cultural products of the past—these narratives are not irrelevant to our current environment because they are dead artifacts of a by-gone age. They are rather lived memories and an interpretive framework through which entire civilizations showed the means to success in an insecure, threat-ridden and mutable reality. Strategic Intelligence is an approach to the game life that has been culturally authorized, legitimated, justified and validated by the necessity of life itself. What should be salient to the practitioner of strategy by now is that the key to strategic advantage that is understood in terms of domination of meaning in the human terrain is intimately linked to the agonistic contest. Although meaning and values may be obscure, they can be nevertheless exposed and leveraged.

The Western genealogy of Strategic Intelligence does not end here. Enabling both hope through escape and the acquisition of ambition, the soteriological aspects of Strategic Intelligence synthesized with elements present in subsequent cultural evolution, philosophical and religious. In particular, the strategic values of Hellenistic, Latin, and Semitic cultural lineages were preserved and transmitted to posterity through Roman Christianity.

NOTES

1. Psalms 124:7. All citations from the Bible are from the *World English Bible*. Bible Hub. https://biblehub.com.

2. *Looney Tunes*, Suzanne Collins, *Hunger Games Trilogy* (Scholastic Press, 2014) and Francis Lawrence, Dir. *The Hunger Games* (Lionsgate 2012); George R. R. Martin, *A Game of Thrones* (*Song of Ice and Fire*) (Bantam, 1996) and *Game of*

Thrones (TV Series) David Benioff, D.B. Weiss, creators (HBO 2011–2019); *Zootopia*, Dirs., Byron Howard, Rich Moore, Jared Bush (Walt Disney Pictures, 2016); *Peter Rabbit*, Dir. Will Gluck (Columbia Pictures 2018).

3. Translation, with some tweaks, based on Oppian, *Cynegetica, The Hunt* (Κυνηγετικά) and *Fishing* (Ἁλιευτικά *Halieutica*), trans. A. W. Mair, Loeb Classical Library (London: W. Heinemann, 1928).

4. Homer, *Odyssey*, 105.

5. Homer, *Odyssey*, 130–134.

6. Homer, *Odyssey* 17:315, 19:435.

7. Sophocles, *Ajax* 10, trans., Sir Richard Jebb, *Sophocles, the Plays and Fragments with Critical Notes, Commentary, and Translation in English*, Part 7, *Ajax* (Cambridge: University Press, 1896), Perseus Digital Library, Tufts University, accessed 4 May 2017, http://perseus.uchicago.edu/perseus-cgi/citequery3.pl?dbname=GreekFeb2011&getid=1&query=Soph.%20Aj.%201.

8. Homer, *Iliad*, Perseus Digital Library, Tufts University, accessed 4 May 2017, http://data.perseus.org/citations/urn:cts:greekLit:tlg0012.tlg001.perseus-eng2:8.253-8.343.

9. Plato, *Republic*, in *Plato in Twelve Volumes: with an English Translation, Republic, Vols 5–6*, trans. Paul Shorey (Cambridge, MA: Harvard university press, 1935), Perseus Digital Library, Tufts University, accessed 4 May 2017, http://www.perseus.tufts.edu/hopper/text?doc=Perseus%3Atext%3A1999.01.0168%3Abook%3D2%3Asection%3D375b.

10. Plato, *Parmenides* 128B. *Plato in Twelve Volumes: with an English Translation, Cratylus, Parmenides, Greater Hippias, Lesser Hippias*, trans. Harold North Fowler (Cambridge, MA: Harvard University Press, 1926), Perseus Digital Library, Tufts University, accessed 4 May 2017, http://perseus.uchicago.edu/perseus-cgi/citequery3.pl?dbname=GreekFeb2011&getid=1&query=Pl.%20Prm.%20128b.

11. Xenophon, *Memorabilia*, in *Xenophon in Seven Volumes*, Vol 4, trans. Todd, O. J. Loeb Classical Library (Cambridge, MA: Harvard University Press, 1923), *Perseus Digital Library, Tufts University*, accessed 26 April 2017, http://data.perseus.org/citations/urn:cts:greekLit:tlg0032.tlg002.perseus-eng1:3.11.

12. θήρης κλυτὰ δήνε'.

13. Strategic plans: βουλὰς ὠκυνόους; skillful tracking: στιβίης εὐκερδέος ἔργα.

14. Mysteries: μυστήρια; artful: τέχνης; αἰόλα.

15. Wits: φρένας.

16. Strategic planning: ἐπίφρονα βουλήν; strategic craftiness and traps: κέρδεά τ' αἰολόβουλα πολυφράστοις τε δόλοισι. Oppian, *The Hunt*, Book 4.

17. πόρε.

18. αἰολόβουλον.

19. Artful resourcefulness,τεχνήεσσα ἵπποις γὰρ περίαλλα φύσις πόρε τεχνήεσσα. Cunningly artful natureφύσις ὤπασε τεχνήεσσα.

20. ἐμήσατο.

21. δίκη.

22. Mightier fish: τοῖς δ' ἐκ φρενὸς ὅπλον ἔφυσε βουλὴν κερδαλέην, πολυμήχανον, οἵ τε δόλοισι πολλάκι καὶ κρατερόν καὶ ὑπέρτερον ὤλεσαν ἰχθύν. wily:

κερδαλέοι; traps: δόλος; rays (stun/put to sleep): νάρκη; art: τεχνάζεται. Oppian, *Fishing Halieutica.*

23. Oppian, *Fishing Halieutica*; ἐν δέ οἱ εἰσὶν ἀείδελοι ἔνδον ὀδόντες βαιοί τ' οὐ κρατεροί τε· βίῃ δέ κεν οὔτι δαμάσσαι,ἀλλὰ δόλῳ καὶ φῶτας ἐπίφρονας εἷλε πεδήσας·δαιτὶ γὰρ ἀνδρομέῃ ἐπιτέρπεται, ἔξοχα δ' αὐτῷ ἀνθρώπων κρέα τερπνὰ καὶ εὐάντητος ἐδωδή.

24. Strategic Intelligence: μῆτις; wits: ὀξυκόμοισι νόος; snare-strategied, δολόμητις; deadly: δόλοισι.

25. Art of deception:τέχνης; deadly:δόλοιο; strategy:μῆτις; trap: δόλον/κρυπτὸν δόλον.

26. Oppian, *The Hunt* (*Κυνηγετικῶν*) Book 4.

27. Wiles: κέρδεσσι; shifty strategies: αἰόλον.

28. Ensnarement: αἰόλον ἕρκος; entrapment:δολίην; wickedly wrought strategies: ἐδαμάσσατο βουλαῖς.

29. Great wonder μέγα θαῦμα; greatly valiant: μεγασθενές; shifty strategic planning: αἰολόβουλε; worthy to be praised: μεγάλοισιν ὁμοίως μέλπεσθαι.

30. Strategically intelligent: αἰολόβουλος; resourceful: πραπίδεσσι καὶ πινυτὴ.

31. Deadly: δόλοισιν; craft: τέκνα.

32. Alert mind: ἐπιφροσύνῃσι νοῆσαι: sensitive to traps: πυκινοῖσι δόλοισιν.

33. Stratagem-enlightened: δολόφρων; strategically prepared στρατοπεδευόντων.

34. Ruse-minded: δολόφρονες; trickery: δόλον; machinations δόλοισι; entrapment: ἐμήσατο; wise foresight: σοφῇσι προμηθείῃσιν.

35. λίην γὰρ πινυτή τε καὶ εὖ φρεσὶ μήδεα οἶδε, 11.445. As a devotee of the Divine Deceiver Athena, who endowed her heart with wiles (116 τὰ φρονέουσ᾽ ἀνὰ θυμόν, ὅ οἱ πέρι δῶκεν Ἀθήνη | 117 ἔργα τ᾽ ἐπίστασθαι περικαλλέα καὶ φρένας ἐσθλὰς | 118 κέρδεά θ᾽. Homer, *Odyssey*, 19.137–158: οἱ δὲ γάμον σπεύδουσιν· ἐγὼ δὲ δόλους τολυπεύω.

36. δολόμητις, 11.422.

37. δόλοισιν, κλέος ix 19–20.

38. Ruse-minded: δολόφρονες.

39. *Aesop's Fables: A New Translation by Laura Gibbs*, trans. Laura Gibbs (Oxford: Oxford University Press, 2002), 12. (Laura Gibbs, *Aesop's Fables* (Oxford University Press) Reproduced with permission of the Licensor through PLSclear.)

40. Aristotle, *Rhetoric* 2: 20, trans. Henry John Freese, in *The Art of Rhetoric,* Loeb Classical Library (London: W. Heinemann, 1926), Perseus Digital Library, Tufts University, accessed 17 January 2019, http://www.perseus.tufts.edu/hopper/text?doc=Perseus:text:1999.01.0060:book=2:chapter=20&highlight=himera.

41. Aristotle, *Rhetoric* 2: 20.

42. Aristotle, *Rhetoric* 2: 20.

43. David G. Hale, "Aesop in Renaissance England," *The Library*, Vol. 5–XXVII (2), 1 June 1972: 116–125. Edward Wheatley, *Mastering Aesop: Medieval Education, Chaucer, and His Followers* (Gainesville: University Press of Florida, 2000). Jacqueline de Weever, *Aesop and the Imprint of Medieval Thought: a Study of Six Fables as Translated at the End of the Middle Ages* (Jefferson: McFarland & Co, 2011). "Fable," *Routledge Revivals: Medieval France, An Encyclopedia,* ed. William W. Kibler, Grover A. Zinn (Milton Park: Routledge , 1995/2016), 331.

44. *Hombre prevenido es hombre armado, vale por dos, y ya está armado para la lucha.*
45. Strategic planning: αἰολόβουλε. "Great wonder" μέγα θαῦμα. Ζεὺς ἄφθιτα μήδεα εἰδώς. Hesiod, *Theogony, Works* and *Days*, line 561.
46. "Great wonder to behold" θαῦμα ἰδέσθαι. Rock of ruse: ὀμφαλός. Hesiod, *Theogony, Works and Days*, line 499. τὸν μὲν Ζεὺς στήριξε κατὰ χθονὸς εὐρυοδείης Πυθοῖ ἐν ἠγαθέῃ γυάλοις ὕπο Παρνησοῖο σῆμ' ἔμεν ἐξοπίσω, θαῦμα θνητοῖσι βροτοῖσιν.
47. Escape φεύγειν. διὸ καὶ ὁ φιλόμυθος φιλόσοφός πώς ἐστιν: ὁ γὰρ μῦθος σύγκειται ἐκ θαυμασίων: ὥστ' εἴπερ διὰ [20] τὸ φεύγειν τὴν ἄγνοιαν ἐφιλοσόφησαν. Aristotle *Metaphysics* 982B, in *Aristotle in Twenty-three Volumes*, trans. Cyril Armstrong (London: W. Heinemann, 1933), Perseus Digital Library, Tufts University, accessed 17 January 2019, http://www.perseus.tufts.edu/hopper/text?doc=Perseus%3Atext%3A1999.01.0052%3Abook%3D1%3Asection%3D982b
48. Vision, θέα, θεάομαι.
49. *The Cambridge History of Literary Criticism*: *Classical Criticism,* ed. George A. Kennedy, Vol.1 (Cambridge: Cambridge University Press, 1989), 24–29.
50. Vision: θεάομαι. generals στράτευμα. " θ. τὸ στράτευμα *to review* it." Henry George Liddell, Robert Scott, *A Greek-English Lexicon* Perseus Digital Library, Tufts University, accessed 27 April 2017, http://www.perseus.tufts.edu/hopper/morph?l=qea%2Fomai&la=greek&can=qea%2Fomai0#lexicon.
51. Plato, *Laches*, 198e. *Plato, in Twelve Volumes,* Loeb Classical Library, Volume 2, ed. and trans. Walter Lamb (Cambridge, MA: W. Heinemann/Harvard University, 1967. Perseus Digital Library, Tufts University, accessed 4 May 2017, http://perseus.uchicago.edu/perseus-cgi/citequery3.pl?dbname=GreekFeb2011&getid=1&query=Pl.%20La.%20198e.
52. Single mind φρενί. See: ὀρόωσιν. Seen: ὀφθαλμοῖσι. My own eyes ἐμοῖς ἴδον. Cunning αἰόλα. Mysterious craft: μυστήρια τέχνης. Oppian, *The Hunt Cynegetica*, Book 4, accessed 27 April, 2017, http://penelope.uchicago.edu/Thayer/E/Roman/Texts/Oppian/Cynegetica/4*.html.
53. ἐθαυμάσθησαν.
54. τέχνας καὶ λόγους καὶ πολέμους ἀγαθοί.
55. Hidden "excellence μεγάλη ἀρετή. Revealed: φανεροί.
56. Xenophon's *On Hunting Κυνηγετικός,* in *Xenophon's Minor Works*, trans. John Watson (London: George Bell & Sons, 1878), Perseus Digital Library, Tufts University, accessed 27 April 2017, http://data.perseus.org/citations/urn:cts:greekLit:tlg0032.tlg014.perseus-eng1:1.
57. Xenophon's *On Hunting Κυνηγετικός,* ἀλλὰ μήν, ἔφη ὁ Σωκράτης, τοῦτό γε πολλοστὸν μέρος ἐστὶ στρατηγίας. καὶ γὰρ παρασκευαστικὸν τῶν εἰς τὸν πόλεμον τὸν στρατηγὸν εἶναι χρή, καὶ ποριστικὸν τῶν ἐπιτηδείων τοῖς στρατιώταις, καὶ μηχανικὸν καὶ ἐργαστικὸν καὶ ἐπιμελῆ καὶ καρτερικὸν καὶ ἀγχίνουν, καὶ φιλόφρονά τε καὶ ὠμόν, καὶ ἁπλοῦν τε καὶ ἐπίβουλον, καὶ φυλακτικόν τε καὶ κλέπτην, καὶ προετικὸν καὶ ἅρπαγα καὶ φιλόδωρον καὶ πλεονέκτην καὶ ἀσφαλῆ καὶ ἐπιθετικόν, καὶ ἄλλα πολλὰ καὶ φύσει καὶ ἐπιστήμῃ δεῖ τὸν εὖ στρατηγήσοντα ἔχειν.
58. ἀγαθοὺς καὶ τοὺς κακούς.
59. φρενὸς ὅπλον ἔφυσε βουλὴν κερδαλέην.

60. Xenophon, *Memorabilia*, 3.11 Perseus Digital Library, Tufts University, accessed 26 April 2017, http://data.perseus.org/citations/urn:cts:greekLit:tlg0032.tlg002.perseus-eng1:3.11.

61. καταμαθεῖν.

62. A sight to behold θεασομένους; exhibitionist: ἐπέδειξεν; ὠφελιμωτέρα.

63. κερδαίνει.

64. There is a clever implicit pun in the text: *biós*, Homeric word for bow puns with *bíos*, life. φάλαγξ, Phalanx is both military maneuvering and a reference for spiders. Artifice: μηχανᾷ. ἀράχνια γὰρ δήπου λεπτὰ ὑφηνάαρμεναι, ὅ τι ἂν ἐνταῦθα ἐμπέσῃ, τούτῳ τροφῇ χρῶνται.

65. *Hereditatum captatores quibus artibus uterentur faceto Ulyssem inter et Tiresiam dialogo exponit."* In a humorous dialogue between Ulysses and Tiresias, he exposes those arts which the fortune hunters make use of, in order to be appointed the heirs of rich old men." Horace, *Satyrarum Libri, Works of Horace, Satyrarum Libri,* Perseus Digital Library, Tufts University, accessed 26 April 2017, http://data.perseus.org/citations/urn:cts:latinLit:phi0893.phi004.perseus-lat1:2.5.

66. φίλτρων τε καὶ ἐπῳδῶν καὶ ἰύγγων ἐστί. Xenophon *Memorabilia*, 3.11 Perseus Digital Library, Tufts University, accessed 27 April 2017, http://www.perseus.tufts.edu/hopper/text?doc=Perseus:text:1999.01.0208:book=3:chapter=11&highlight=wheel.

67. Plato, *Republic*:, 341:a-b: intent of laying a trap, overpower people intelligence, sight and health values for their own sake and for their results, 357: Thrasymachus yielded like a snake to Socrates charm 358b.

68. ναρκῶμαι.

69. πλανῶμαι. Plato, *Lesser Hippias,* 376C, in *Plato in Twelve Volumes: with an English Translation, Cratylus, Parmenides, Greater Hippias, Lesser Hippias,* trans. Harold North Fowler (Cambridge, MA: Harvard University Press, 1926), Perseus Digital Library, Tufts University, accessed 17 January 2019, http://www.perseus.tufts.edu/hopper/text?doc=urn:cts:greekLit:tlg0059.tlg026.perseus-eng1:376c.

70. Ruse-minded δολόφρονες. Many-means πολυτρόπως. Hebrews 1:1. "Forks and crossroads," Plato, *Phaedo,* 108A, 242b8–c8. *Five Dialogues: Euthyphro, Apology, Crito, Meno, Phaedo,* trans. G. M. A. Grube, ed. John M. Cooper, 2nd Ed. (Indianapolis: Hackett, 2002).

71. Plato, *Letters* 7.345d, in *Plato in twelve Volumes: with an English Translation, Plato: Timaeus, Critias, Cleitophon, Menexenus [and] Epistles,* trans. Robert Gregg Bury (Cambridge, MA: Harvard University Press, 1929), accessed 17 January 2019, Perseus Digital Library, Tufts University, accessed 4 May 2017, http://www.perseus.tufts.edu/hopper/text?doc=Plat.%20L.%207.345e&lang=original.

72. Plato, *Republic* 4:432d.

73. Aristotle, *Nichomachean Ethics,* 4.7.

74. *Twelve Angry Men,* MGM Studios, Sidney Lumet, Director. 1957.

75. Leo Strauss, *The City and Man* (Chicago: University of Chicago, 1964).

76. *Guǐgǔzi* 鬼谷子, *Plumb the depths Chuāipiān* 揣篇, 故常必以其見者而知其隱者，此所謂測深揣情., accessed 5 January 2019, https://ctext.org/gui-gu-zi.

77. Plato, *Republic,* 1:336.

78. Plato, *Lesser Hippias*, 376B.
79. Plato, *Lesser Hippias*, 369b.
80. Leo Strauss, *Persecution and the Art of Writing* (Chicago: University of Chicago Press, 1952/1988).
81. Strauss, *City*.
82. Socrates is associated with dissembling in Aristophanes *Clouds*, and the figures Alcibiades (*Symposion*, 216e), Thrasymachus (*Republic*, 337a), and Callicles (*Gorgias*, 489e) accuse him of it as well.
83. ἀπορία.
84. Χαιρεφῶντος γάρ ποτε ἐπερωτῶντος ἐν Δελφοῖς περὶ ἐμοῦ πολλῶν παρόντων ἀνεῖλεν ὁ Ἀπόλλων μηδένα εἶναι ἀνθρώπων ἐμοῦ μήτε ἐλευθεριώτερον μήτε δικαιότερον μήτε σωφρονέστερον. Xenophon, *Apology*, 14, in *Xenophon in Seven Volumes*, Vol. 4 (Cambridge, MA; Harvard University Press, 1979), Perseus Digital Library, Tufts University, accessed 17 January 2019, http://www.perseus.tufts.edu/hopper/text?doc=Perseus%3Atext%3A1999.01.0211%3Atext%3DApol.%3Asection%3D14.
85. Plato, *Phaedo* 85b. Xenophon, *Apology* 13.
86. Plato, *Meno* 99C.
87. Xenophon, *Apology*.
88. Plato, *Republic* 7: 517.
89. Plato, *Republic* 7:518–519.
90. Plato, *Republic* 358b, 7:518–519.
91. *Guǐgǔzi* 鬼谷子, *Fēiqián* 飛箝. I translate 'fly and grasp' as "pounce and pin." 引鉤箝之辭，飛而箝之。鉤箝之語，其說辭也，乍同乍異。其不可善者，或先徵之，而後重累；或先重以累，而後毀之；或以重累為毀；或以毀為重累。

Chapter 4

The Legacy of Judeo-Christian Strategic Intelligence

> Discretion will watch over you.
> Understanding will keep you,[1]
>
> He takes the wise in their own craftiness;
> the counsel of the cunning is carried headlong.[2]
>
> A prudent man keeps his knowledge,
> but the hearts of fools proclaim foolishness.[3]
>
> A simple man believes everything,
> but the prudent man carefully considers his ways.[4]

Strategic Intelligence is a mode of wisdom also highly valued by Abrahamic faith traditions. I document in this chapter the cultural genealogy of strategic values in Western civilization by excavating the presence of strategic heroes in Jewish and Christian cultural products, which I define as cultural products that recognize as authoritative features such as divine revelation, hierarchy, scripture, and religious tradition. Strategic values in modern Western cultures have a dual heritage—authoritative Greek and Jewish strategic values synthesized in Latin Christianity, and enshrined the strategic as a cultural dynamic for the next two millennia. In contrast to previous assertions, the evidence from the religious patrimony shows that Christian culture was also a bearer of Strategic Intelligence.[5] Like the Enlightenment philosopher Immanuel Kant who thought that the Christian religion bore morality, I explore in the next two chapters the manner in which Jewish and Christian religious cultural products transmitted the heroic values of Strategic Intelligence.[6] Not only did religious cultural products simultaneously serve as strategic models of living and cultural memory, but holy Strategic Intelligence was invested with the authority and legitimacy deemed critical by Jewish and Christian religious traditions. Holy Strategic Intelligence was validated as universal, cosmological, scriptural, traditional, divinely revealed, ancient, and wise. Holy Strategic Intelligence was a preeminent means that enabled and threatened human freedom and dignity.

JEWISH STRATEGIC INTELLIGENCE

The marriage of Greek and Jewish strategic lineages in the great synthesis of Roman Christianity bequeathed to Europe an incredibly rich patrimony of resources that articulated Strategic Intelligence as a superior means to achieve strategic advantage. The Old Testament alone offers a surprising quantity of stories about heroic Strategic Intelligence, proffering lessons peopled with a devious deity, probing patriarchs, gaming generals, cunning kings, witty women, and prudent prophets.

Similar to Hesiod's depiction of the ambivalence of the gods toward humanity in *Theogony* (chapter 2), the first five books of the Old Testament, referred as the Torah or the Pentateuch, similarly reveal that strategic deception is a primary experience of human reality. The story of the serpent in Genesis memorialized that cunning was the impetus that led humankind into enlightened maturity, a postlapsarian state in which humans realized that they were divine, self-aware, and tragically finite—that enlightenment to reality is paradoxically enabled by crafty deception. A close reading of the text shows that God is not necessarily angry at the ambiguous language used by the serpent, but rather that the serpent aided Adam and Eve in disobeying. In the myth of the Garden of Eden, divine deception is cosmological and universal—without the machination of the serpent, Jesus could not ultimately trick the trickster, enslaving the devil while liberating humanity—the central premise of one of Christianity's earliest and most enduring soteriological doctrines. This insight appears to be evidenced in the story of Cain and Abel as well—whereas the deity is angered at the murder, he nowhere condemns Cain's dissembling. Despoiling one's political masters also appears to be divinely authorized—the Old Testament provides evidence that Yahweh commanded the enslaved Hebrews to righteously steal from their Egyptian overlords, "But every woman shall ask of her neighbor, and of her who visits her house, jewels of silver, jewels of gold, and clothing; and you shall put them on your sons, and on your daughters. You shall plunder the Egyptians."[7]

Most shocking perhaps to many modern, literalist Christians are three scriptural texts that indicate that the Hebrew God depicted in the Old Testament, the Tetragrammaton Yahweh, may be more like the Greek gods than what is generally assumed. For example, certain passages in the Old Testament such as the following from 1 Kings, when taken literally, seem to indicate that Yahweh himself summons and dispatches the spirits of deceit into the world of man,

> Yahweh said, "Who shall entice Ahab, that he may go up and fall at Ramoth Gilead?" One said one thing; and another said another. A spirit came out and stood before Yahweh, and said, "I will entice him." Yahweh said to him, "How?" He said, "I will go out and will be a lying spirit in the mouth of all his prophets." He said, "You will entice him, and will also prevail. Go out and do so." Now therefore, behold, Yahweh has put a lying spirit in the mouth of all these your prophets; and Yahweh has spoken evil concerning you.[8]

Ezekiel echoes this, "If the prophet is deceived and speak a word, I, Yahweh, have deceived that prophet, and I will stretch out my hand on him, and will destroy him from the midst of my people Israel."[9] The fact that *2 Chronicles* in the New Testament copies the text from 1 Kings indicates that early Christians may have shared the same view that the deity sends forth deception into the world.[10]

The existential contest for life is a zero-sum game, and Strategic Intelligence at times includes the necessity of ruthlessness. The wizard's duel between the Hebrew and Egyptian mages and their deities that is detailed in the *Exodus* is a contest that demonstrates the ultimate virtuosity of the concealed God *who yet sees*—a God whose power is revealed strategically by increasing ruthlessness and yet apparently just means.[11] The ten plagues not only overcome Pharaoh's deception, but they do so in a strategic way—Pharaoh is ultimately devastated only after God repeatedly *hardens his heart*, ensuring a thorough and devastating victory. And it is an ultimate victory—the battle for freedom from enslavement is won only by the ruthless massacre of the innocents at the denouement.[12] Can a holocaust of the innocent really be godly? The murder of the innocents is a gift of death that not only enables the escape that we now know as the exodus, but it was memorialized in the Jewish and Christian faiths as passover, and the yearly and eternal sacrifice of the innocent messiah at Easter, reminding us of the paradoxical metaphorological paradigm that life *is* death, that life and death set the conditions for each other, and that freedom is predicated on death. When we recall that stories of deities often inform the model of *good* human behavior, we must pause and ask the rhetorical question—in light of the above evidence, *WWGD?*

Strategic Intelligence is also one of the key characteristics of many of the Jewish patriarchs. In Genesis chapters 12 and 20, Abram passed off his wife Sarai as his sister twice, and his son Isaac created a similar artifice with his wife Rebekah.[13] Isaac's son Jacob was perhaps the greatest of all of the Jewish masters of Strategic Intelligence—in fact his name puns with the Hebrew word for betrayal.[14] Like Odysseus with his matron Athena, Jacob in chapter

27 cozened his old blind father's blessing over Esau the firstborn with his mum's help, and then he out-schemed his scheming uncle Laban. After Laban the Aramean, a place name which puns with "deceiver" and "trickster," tricked Jacob into marrying his spinster daughter Leah, Jacob labored for another seven years to marry the bride whom he desired.[15] Through his discerning use of selective breeding of the herd, Jacob enriched his father-in-law's family and himself, with the result that he aroused the envy of his brothers-in-law. Like fox in chapter 3, Jacob needed a way out, so his wife Rachel stole the clan's fetishes and they escaped. Laban pursued them for seven days before making peace, but not before Rachel tricked Laban again—she blocked him from searching her tent on the pretext that she was menstruating. In essence, the deceiving Aramean was himself deceived by a cleverer deceiver, which offers us yet another example of a heroic mistress of Strategic Intelligence.

Jacob's strategic inclinations were evidently passed on to his sons. After their sister Dinah was raped by Shechem the Hivite, they agreed to wed her to him if he and his kin were first circumcised. Two of Jacob's sons enacted their revenge through chicanery during the recovery period relayed in Genesis 38 by murdering all of the men in the town in order to avenge her honor. One did not have to be literate in order to learn the message of the Rape of Dinah—the lesson was forever memorialized and sanctified in a sacred space. The strategic values of this story were articulated visually in the fifth-century mosaic of the *Rape of Dinah*, which one can still view in the nave of the Basilica of Santa Maria Maggiore in Rome. One thousand years later, artists such as sixteenth-century painter Giuliano Bugiardini also re-articulated the same values—his *Rape of Dinah*, still hangs in the Kunsthistorisches Museum in Vienna.[16] The lesson is clear—Strategic deception in support of vengeance is righteous and just, and worth replicating in culture.

Referring back to Judah, the prophet Jeremiah later described the Judahites in terms of this archetype of brotherly deception, "Take heed everyone of his neighbor, and don't trust in any brother; for every brother will utterly supplant, and every neighbor will go about with slanders."[17] This judgment should make us wonder about other asymmetric social relationships as well—was the second son Abel's sacrifice a kind of righteous trick that aided the underdog? Is the masterful utilization of Strategic Intelligence "owned" by the younger religion of Christianity as opposed to its older sibling Judaism? Regardless of the answer, the legacy of Strategic Intelligence was transmitted through Jacob to the patriarch Judah, although he was not as exemplary as his father.

Patriarch Judah thought he was clever, but in the end he was deceived by another mistress of Strategic Intelligence, Tamar. Tamar was first wed to Judah's evil first son Er, who subsequently died without heir. Judah's second son Onan attempted to deceive her and God through the now famous sin that carries his name—that resulted in his death. Tamar successfully outmaneuvered the old man after he tried to dodge her by not marrying her to his third son Shelah. Judah himself then unknowingly impregnated Tamar when she lured him into a boudoir with a clever ruse by disguising herself as a temple prostitute, and holding onto a token that she would later use to her advantage. Tamar passed down the strategic DNA to another generation when she birthed twins. Her son Perez was a wily strategist even in the womb! Even though his brother Zerah stuck his hand out of the womb first, Perez raced ahead when Zerah pulled his arm back in—yielding to Perez the birthright. It is through Perez that we can trace the royal line that produced Kings Solomon, David, and Jesus.[18]

The heroic aspect of Tamar's Strategic Intelligence was apparently highly valued even by the early Christians, to a degree that may be shocking to contemporary Christians. In his *Hymns on the Nativity*, the fourth-century Saint Ephraem wrote, "For holy was the adultery of Tamar for Your sake. You it was she thirsted after, O pure Fountain. Judah defrauded her of drinking You. The thirsty womb stole a dew-draught of You from the spring thereof."[19] The New Testament Gospel of Matthew traces Jesus' lineage straight back to Perez through King David[20]; with a pedigree that includes cozening women and hustler kings, one sympathizes with the righteous Nathaniel, who asked of Jesus: "Can any good thing come out of Nazareth?"[21] Tamar's righteous trick became a favorite theme of later European Christian visual culture—an image query on the internet quickly reveals hundreds of examples, such as the mid-seventeenth-century rendition *Judah and Tamar*, produced by a painter associated with Rembrandt, and which still hangs in the Residenzgalerie in Salzburg, Austria.[22]

Both the Old Testament patriarchs Moses and Joseph serve as figures of heroic patriarchal Strategic Intelligence. Jochebed, Moses' mother, tricked the Egyptians by having him adopted by Pharaoh's own daughter, and Moses duped the Egyptians through the power of the Hebrew God, such as when Aaron's staff transformed into a snake which consumed the snakes of the Egyptian court sorcerers. The *Qur'ān* especially makes it clear that Moses was a strategic trickster who revealed the deception of the Egyptian wise men,[23] and frames the story as a plot intended to achieve genocide.[24] In the Old Testament, the patriarch Joseph also betrayed the betrayers—after his brothers exiled Joseph into slavery, he got the last laugh. First he accused them of being spies and imprisoned them for three days. And then he set them up by hiding a silver chalice in his brothers' sack and accused them of theft.[25] The integration of the heroic and the strategic in the lessons of duplicitous patriarchs also informs the answer to the question—*WWPD? What Would the Patriarchs Do?*

In addition to deceptive deities and cunning patriarchs, heroic Strategic Intelligence is also an attribute of kings and warriors in the Old Testament. Joshua destroyed the Kingdom of Ai through subterfuge.[26] In *Judges*, God explicitly told Gideon to spy on his enemies, and he intentionally reduced the number of Gideon's soldiers in order to emphasize both the subtlety and power of God. Gideon was victorious through ruse—his small regiment blew horns and smashed empty pots to confuse their foe.[27] Conversely, the Gibeonites tricked Joshua into making a treaty with them.[28] The con of the Gileadites enabled them to slaughter 42,000 Ephramites because of their shibboleth.[29] The righteous King Jehu destroyed all of the priests of Baal after strategically tricking them—he made it publicly known that he was more pious than Ahab and then murdered in cold blood all of the pagan priests after they assembled in their temple.[30] The judge Ehud assassinated the Moabite King Eglon through treachery when Ehud used a concealed dagger to penetrate Eglon's abdomen. Locking the door and escaping, the Israelites killed 10,000 Moabites that day.[31] King Saul lied to the witch of Endor, who in turn saw through his "snare." King David lied to the priest Ahimelech, to his liege lord Achish, and feigned insanity.

> David laid up these words in his heart, and was very afraid of Achish the king of Gath. He changed his behavior before them, and pretended to be mad in their hands, and scrabbled on the doors of the gate, and let his spittle fall down on his beard. Then Achish said to his servants, "Look, you see the man is mad. Why then have you brought him to me? Do I lack madmen, that you have brought this fellow to play the madman in my presence? Shall this fellow come into my house?"[32]

Apparently, this episode made a big impact on later Christian values—there is a wonderful image of it in the twelfth-century Bible de Saint Etienne Harding, entitled "David Feins Lunacy before Achish king of Gath."[33]

1 Samuel describes David in Hebrew and Latin as insidious or crafty—he lies in ambush for King Saul and opportunistically takes advantage of the situation while Saul relieves himself in a cave.[34] Later, David used a female spy who hid Ahimaaz and Jonathan in a well, lying to Absolam's officials.[35] This story was picked up a few centuries later by one of the most famous of the early church fathers, St. John Chrysostom who, to add scriptural authority to his views on honorable deception, cited two scenes from the Old Testament—*1 Samuel* which depicted how David's wife Michal tricked Saul's soldiers in order to help her husband David escape, and Jonathan's lie to Saul about David's whereabouts.[36]

In addition to the plethora of examples of heroic Strategic Intelligence in the figures of deities, kings, and warriors, Old Testament prophets and witting women also exemplify its merits. Ancient Jewish holy men and prophets were no strangers to Strategic Intelligence, as evidenced by the stories of Elisha, Samuel and Daniel. Through God's power, Elisha tricked the enemy by blinding them and trapping them in Samaria. Later he tricked the enemies of the Israelites into retreating because they thought that they heard a great din of hostile forces.[37] Samuel fooled the Bethlehemites through divine inspiration—although they thought that Samuel had come to sacrifice, his real mission was to identify King Saul's successor, a man outside of the royal bloodline (but inside the royal line of Strategic Intelligence), David.[38] In the apocryphal text *Bel and the Dragon*, the prophet Daniel exposes the treachery of the priests of Bel by spreading ashes over the floor and exposing their secret. And in the episode about Susanna and the Elders in the *Daniel*, Daniel used his Strategic Intelligence to ferret out the truth of the situation, saving Susanna's honor.

Like the stories of Rachel and Rebecca, figures of wily women abound in the Old Testament, including Judith, Esther, Jael, and Rahab. As early as the *Exodus*, heroic Hebrew mid-wives Shiphrah and Puah lie to the Pharaoh in order to save the Hebrew babies, thus righteously beguiling the beguiler, a heroic act visualized in the fourteenth-century Catalan illuminated manuscript, the Golden Haggadah in the British Museum.[39] Judith beheaded the Assyrian general Holofernes after getting him soused. Esther saved the Hebrew nation through artifice when she tricked the king and the evil councilor Haman at a banquet.[40] Offering respite to the enemy combatant Sisera, Jael stabbed him through the head with a tent stake after he fell asleep.[41] And Rahab lied to the enemy who had come to ferret out the Hebrew spies.[42]

Righteously strategic Hebrew femme fatales made a lasting impression on subsequent cultural production. In the Old Testament, lying, cheating, stealing, and tricking are apparently sometimes legitimate, just, and righteous. And it mattered little that medievals and early moderns were mostly illiterate—artists depicted these themes in Christian religious art displayed in church and religious texts for thousands of year. A query on the internet about any of the heroines mentioned above provides an astonishing quantity of visual cultural products that transmitted these strategic values. In addition to Lucas Cranach the Elder's sixteenth-century *Judith with the Head of Holofernes* in figure 4.1, I encourage the interested reader to seek out Jacopo Amigoni's eighteenth-century painting *Jael and Sisera*. Visual cultural production points us to the answer for *What Would Rachel, Rebecca, Judith, Esther, Jael, and Rahab Do?*

The many lessons of heroic Strategic Intelligence from the Jewish sacred heritage enriched the legacy of Greco-Roman thought. Sacred Strategic Intelligence captured the imagination of medieval and Renaissance Europeans,

Figure 4.1 Judith and Holofernes. Lucas Cranach the Elder (German, Kronach 1472–1553 Weimar) 1530. Rogers Fund, 1911.

and was memorialized in the visual cultural products of Roman Christianity as that which was worth remembering. For example, Donatello's statue *Judith and Holofernes*, commissioned by Cosimo de' Medici, was displayed in front of the Palazzo della Signoria along with Donatello's *David*. Both became enduring symbols of anti-Medici sentiment. *Judith and Holofernes* is especially interesting as a figure that links Strategic Intelligence as a form of hope with salvation and popular determination because it was installed after the expulsion of the Medici, and accompanied by the phrase "*exemplum salutis publicae cives posuere*" (erected by the citizens as an exemplar of public salvation).⁴³

The values of Strategic Intelligence articulated through heroic strategic figures in the Jewish tradition again demonstrate the potency of the strategic as a form of hope in light of existential threat. The strategic is common to both the ethical and the juridical dimensions of analysis, and to moral philosophy and political theory, explicitly providing answers to questions about what one *should* do, and what one is *authorized* to do. The Jewish tradition bequeathed to Christianity the strategic as a form of hope that is authoritative and legitimate in culture because; in addition to being divine, kingly, prophetic, wise, and salvational, it is holy, just, revealed, and traditional.

CHRISTIAN STRATEGIC INTELLIGENCE

> Behold, I send you out as sheep in the midst of wolves.
> Therefore be wise as serpents, and harmless as doves.⁴⁴

> *Circumdederunt me gemitus mortis:*
> *Doloris inferni circumdederunt me.*
> Wailing of death encircled me:
> The woes of hell enclosed me.
>
> Cristóbal de Morales (1500–1553 CE)

> Be sober and self-controlled. Be watchful.
> Your adversary, the devil,
> walks around like a roaring lion,
> seeking whom he may devour.⁴⁵

Strategic values from the Greeks and the Jews, both of which were the beneficiaries of even more ancient Mediterranean and Near Eastern cultures, were subsequently synthesized in the pan-mediterranean Christian synthesis of the common era, forming the patrimony and foundation on which subsequent generations of masters would articulate strategic values. This section excavates the descent of strategic values and worldview in Roman-Byzantine Christianity, as evidenced by features in the New Testament and patristic corpora, its underlying presence in the Ransom Theory in theological circles, the depiction of strategic saints in holy tradition, and some more contemporary examples.

Although at first glance there appears to be far fewer references to heroic strategic rationality in the New Testament than the Old Testament, a careful examination of the cultural data reveals that strategic values can be found both explicitly and implicitly in various passages. Strategic rationality appears to be a part of Jesus' royal DNA—the first chapter of the Gospel of Matthew traces Jesus' genealogy in a line of descent from the most famous of Hebrew strategists, including Jacob, Judas, Solomon, and David. This chapter indicates that, like the classical Greek texts discussed above, Jesus' Strategic Intelligence was also born in trickery and strife—like Zeus, Jesus is saved from infanticide only after Herod is thwarted by the deception of the wizard-like magi.[46]

Perhaps the most revealing aspect of stories about the life of Christ that relates to strategic rationality is the game of entrapment played by Jesus and the Pharisees. *Dolophron*-like entrapment was not unknown in the Hebrew tradition, as shown by this passage from Job 5: "He frustrates the devices of the crafty, So that their hands can't perform their enterprise. He takes the wise in their own craftiness; the counsel of the cunning is carried headlong."[47] With the exception of the Gospel of John, the other Gospels point out that the Pharisees were trying to trap Jesus, and the parables that Jesus uses were in fact strategic rhetorical weapons that intended to expose "the leaven of the Pharisees, which is hypocrisy."[48]

The manner in which Jesus entraps the trapper is analogous to the snare-aware *dolophron* theme in Greco-Roman culture, discussed in previous chapters. The word used throughout the synoptic gospels for *temptation* πειραζόμενος can also be translated as *testing*—as in the agonistic competition of contenders. For example, Jesus immediately saw through the Pharisees' trap when they goaded him into answering the question

> "Is it lawful for us to pay taxes to Caesar, or not?" But Jesus perceived their craftiness, and said to them, "Why do you test me? Show me a denarius. Whose image and inscription are on it?" They answered, "Caesar's." He said to them, "Then give to Caesar the things that are Caesar's, and to God the things that are God's." They weren't able to trap him in his words before the people. They marveled at his answer, and were silent.[49]

Almost humorously, the scriptures point out that the pharisees realized the trap—"They reasoned with themselves, saying, "If we say, 'From heaven,' he will say, 'Why didn't you believe him?' But if we say, 'From men,' all the people will stone us, for they are persuaded that John was a prophet."[50] Jesus himself set snares for the pharisees elsewhere, such as when he asked them whether it was lawful to heal on the sabbath.[51] If it were lawful, then it exposes the moral bankruptcy of the Pharisees since they were not helping the less fortunate; if it were not lawful, then their practice of the law is exposed for its inhumanity. Often he left them in a state in which "they didn't dare to ask him any more questions."[52]

In Luke 4, like the verbal sparring of Socrates and the competition between Merlin and Mim described earlier, Jesus enters the agonistic arena with the devil himself for a forty-day contest of wits. Jesus demonstrates his virtuosity and freedom from the temptation of the devil through Strategic Intelligence. By trapping his foes, Jesus strategically beguiles the beguiler, as Paul wrote, "For the wisdom of this world is foolishness with God. For it is written, 'He has taken the wise in their craftiness.'"[53] "Taken the wise," renders the Greek word for the one who *traps* the trapper, and is exactly the same word used to describe what Shechem did to Dinah in Genesis 34![54]

Jesus' parables of the wily steward and the ten virgins, which point to the values of foresight and strategic preparedness, are among the more explicit articulations of the positive valuation of strategic rationality. Luke 16 relays the story of the crooked steward who is about to be fired because he wasted his lord's goods. Knowing that he was not well liked by the many debtors he had to collect from on behalf of the lord, the crafty steward made the best of a bad situation by cleverly cutting in half the debt that was owed. This resulted in a feeling of gratitude toward him, rather than the lord, and provided the crafty steward with an escape route. "His lord commended the dishonest manager because he had done wisely, for the children of this world are, in their own generation, wiser than the children of the light."[55] And Jesus taught, "I say to you, make friends for yourselves by means of the wealth of unrighteousness, so that when it fails, they will receive you into the eternal dwellings."[56] This parable, spoken by the son of God himself, legitimates, and authorizes crafty deception.

Relayed by Jesus, the parable of the ten virgins who waited for the arrival of the bridegroom in the Gospel of Matthew 25 also points to the strategic values of foresight and resourcefulness enabled by memory and preparation. Like Oppian's description of the resourceful and strategically planning fox discussed in chapter 3, the five wise virgins were resourceful in that they all remembered to bring extra oil along with their oil lamps. Even though they all fell asleep while the bridegroom tarried, the five wise virgins were well prepared for the bridegroom's midnight arrival. The result? The wise virgins went to the party and the foolish ones were locked out. The Eastern Churches have triumphantly memorialized this parable of Strategic Intelligence by incorporating it into the Bridegroom Matins during the first four nights of Holy Week: "Behold the Bridegroom comes at midnight, and blessed is the servant whom he shall find watching, and unworthy is the servant whom he shall find heedless. Beware, therefore, oh my soul. Do not be weighed down with sleep, lest you be given up to death, and lest you be shut out of the kingdom."

Jesus' positive valuation of strategic rationality is further conveyed in the parable of the man who built his house on a great rock: "He is like a man building a house, who dug and went deep, and laid a foundation on the rock. When a flood arose, the stream broke against that house, and could not shake it, because it was founded on the rock."[57] Strategic foresight appears to have been highly valued by the early Christian apostles and disciples as well—the strategic value of foresight is explicitly called out in both Acts of the Apostles and Hebrews.[58]

In addition to functioning like the snare-aware (*dolophron*), the life of Jesus related in the New Testament also depicts him dissimulating. Jesus in the *Gospel of John* attended a feast in secret after telling others that he would not attend.[59] In the Gospel of *Matthew* Jesus denies a non-Jewish Canaanite woman who is begging for his assistance, most likely as a ruse to save her after an explicit assertion of belief.[60] Similarly, the apostle Peter villainously denied that he knew Jesus in Mark 14, and Paul criticized Peter for hypocritical dissimulation (*simulatio*) that pandered to the Jewish Christians.[61] This irony is further accentuated in Acts 16 where we witness Paul circumcising Timothy, an act designed to cater to the prominent Jewish Christians, an example cited by the Archbishop of Constantinople St. John Chrysostom a few centuries later. Paul followed up on this in 2 Corinthians in which he claimed, "But, being crafty, I caught you with deception."[62] Paul even admits to an extreme adaptability to achieve his strategic aims:

> For though I was free from all, I brought myself under bondage to all, that I might gain the more. To the Jews I became as a Jew, that I might gain Jews; to those who are under the law, as under the law, that I might gain those who are under the law; to those who are without law, as without law (not being without law toward God, but under law toward Christ), that I might win those who are without law. To the weak I became as weak, that I might gain the weak. I have become all things to all men, that I may by all means save some.[63]

The apostles also taught that Christians should be strategic by being forearmed with foresight. Christian adepts were warned against those who are "full of all deceit and all cunning . . . son of the devil . . . enemy of all righteousness . . . full of deceit and fraud" so that they "may no longer be children, tossed back and forth and carried about with every wind of doctrine, by the trickery of men, in craftiness, after the wiles of error," and that Christians would not be taken advantage of because they have been enlightened to devilish scheming.[64] These lessons of Christian Strategic Intelligence from the son of God himself and his first-generation disciples certainly informs the questions, *WWJD?* and *WWAD? What Would the Apostles Do?*

Scriptural authority for Holy Strategic Intelligence was soon adopted into the nascent holy tradition that was being informed by the patristic corpora created by the Church fathers. In time, holy tradition would itself become a source of authority that mirrored the legitimacy of holy scripture. We can trace a continuous genealogy of Holy Strategic Intelligence in the writings of the saints as well, including St. Clement of Alexandria (~150–215 CE), Origen (185–254 CE), St. Jerome (347–420 CE), St. Augustine (354–430 CE), St. John Cassian (360–435 CE), St. John Chrysostom (349–407 CE), St. Gregory of Nyssa (335–395 CE), St. John of Damascus (675–749 CE), Bishop Theodulf of Orléans (~750–821 CE), and Bernard of Clairvaux (1090–1153 CE). Since all of these have been studied in depth from the perspective of Church history and theology, and because my goal here is to trace the cultural genealogy of Strategic Intelligence through the ages, this section will aim to relay the more intriguing assertions that demonstrate the manner in which Christian cultures transmitted strategic values.

St. Clement of Alexandria (~150 AD–215 AD) in his *Stromateis* noted Paul's dissimulation and also made allowance for it. He also approved of stratagem, as evidenced in his writings that explore the generalship of Moses. Stratagem for Clement is characterized by security, boldness, speech, and actions, all of which are made possible through "persuasion, violence, injustice in self-defense, justice, deceit, truthfulness, or use of all these simultaneously." Clement interpreted Moses' stratagems in Scripture as exemplars for those who wish to identify advantage, and his surprise attacks were proof of his excellent generalship.[65] This sentiment was amplified 1,000 years later by Machiavelli, who wrote that anyone who can read the Bible cannot but acknowledge that Moses had to kill off his opponents in order to create laws and institutions.[66] Apparently Machiavellianism preceded Machiavelli by centuries.

The fourth-century Bishop of Milan St. Ambrose's (340–397 CE) text *On the Duties of the Clergy* demonstrates the superior potency of Christian belief as a strategy that enables liberation. Belief in God leads to a blessed state through which the believer is liberated from the entrapment of the wheel of fortune. Moses' belief in God was a strategy by which he was able to escape the Egyptians by parting the Red Sea—Aaron's faith enabled him to free the innocent from the wrath of God, and Daniel the prey became invulnerable to ravenous lions.[67] The blessed state is strategic in that it frees the worthy from the empty values of this world. For example, Ambrose transmitted the tradition of the third-century archdeacon-martyr St. Lawrence—during the persecution of Christianity by the Emperor Valerian, Lawrence preemptively gave away all of the wealth of the Church instead of allowing it to be confiscated. When the day of reckoning arrived, Lawrence out-schemed the pagan emperor by handing over the sick and needy, who he claimed were the true treasure of the Church.[68]

In commenting on Galatians, St. Jerome (347–420 CE) made a case for Holy Strategic Intelligence when he explained that both apostles were dissimulating—Peter was really using *good management* (*œconomia/dispensatio*), and Paul was also dissimulating (*simulatio*) because he actually was aware of what Peter was intending to do. St. John Cassian (360–435 CE) believed that he was only transmitting the Strategic Intelligence of the desert fathers—in a chapter entitled "How Even Apostles thought that a Lie was Often Useful and the Truth Injurious," St. Cassian wrote that Paul was not free from dissimulation. Citing the Old Testament tragic hero Samson, Cassian pointed out the irony that Samson was safe when he hid his secret with a lie, and that he caused his own destruction by disclosing the truth.[69] Like St. Jerome, St. Cassian, through the figures of ascetic monks Germanus and Abba Joseph, appealed to "good management" (*œconomia/dispensatio*), citing the Old Testament exemplary models of Rahab and Jacob and New Testament authorities.[70] St. Thomas Aquinas (1225–1274 CE) lays out the same in his *Summa Theologiae* when he cites Jerome and Old Testament stories such as David's feigned insanity and the trickery of the priests of Baal to conclude the validity of dissimulation. But the best expression of strategic values in the early Church occurs, in my opinion, in the ancient source *On Priesthood*, written by the golden-tongued orator of the early Church, the Archbishop of Constantinople St. John Chrysostom (349–407 CE).[71]

In *On Priesthood*, Chrysostom adapted the noble lie of Plato's *Republic* by claiming that deception is permissible and advisable when done in love.[72] After he tricked his friend Basil into accepting the priesthood by "concealing himself," Basil accused him of deceit, treachery and craftiness. Basil's reality is described as a journey, and as a battle amongst snares in a "cruel era" in which "the wily are many," and "true love has been replaced by envy." Understanding that he had been deceived by his own friend, Basil is even more upset. In response to his friend's agitation, the great Bishop Chrysostom "laughs for joy." For Chrysostom, the evil of deception is not absolute, but rather is good or bad according to intention, justifying deception in the ultimate foundation of authority, Christian love. In fact, not only should a loving deceit be heartily welcomed by the one deceived, the well-intentioned deceit delivered opportunistically brings advantages, and not engaging in deceit has even resulted in punishment.

Chrysostom taught that this type of deception is the Strategic Intelligence of generals, whose reputations throughout the annals of history were made through the victories acquired by stratagem rather than violence, victories which entangled their enemies with folly and disaster. There is a need for the deceit of Strategic Intelligence, notes Chrysostom, at all levels of human society, both public (the kingdom), and private (children and parents, friends, husband, and wife). Chrysostom grounded his argument for Holy Strategic Intelligence in both practical wisdom and scripture. For the first, like Plato's *Republic,* in which lies are said to be useful like medicine, Chrysostom described the placebo effect in medicine, in which a patient recovers due to psychological factors.[73] For the second, he cited examples of holy deception in scripture, including the lies of David's wife and friends (1 Samuel), and the story of Paul and the circumcision of Timothy.[74] And like previous saints, Chysostom justified deception with the concept of "good management" (œconomia).

Paraphrasing Chysostom, well-intentioned, righteous deceit devoid of malice is of great value, and should be referred to as œconomia, which is a type of cunning that strategically finds solutions when the mind is stymied and resources are lacking. And he cites many examples which seem quite strange to our modern sensibility, such as the story of the grandson of the high priest Aaron (brother of Moses) Phineas, who righteously murdered two people in retribution for being ensnared by the surrounding pagans[75]; and to two stories about the prophet Elijah—in the first, through heavenly fires he righteously burned alive 100 innocent soldiers sent to fetch him[76], and in the second he righteously murdered 450 pagan priests.[77] In the name of righteousness and justice, many conventional sins appear to be heroic, including the attempted infanticide of Isaac,[78] and the despoilment of the Egyptians during the Egyptian holocaust.[79] The perpetrators of these acts are blameless and admirable because the acts were done in righteousness, in response to God's command, and for a good purpose. Thus, deception is a tool that enables great advantage—much more advantage in fact than what might be achieved through a straightforward approach.

Subsequent bishops after Chrysostom followed in the same vein. The Carolingian Bishop Theodulf of Orléans (~750–821 CE) in his *The Lost Horse* (*De Equo Perdito*) extolled the cunning of the soldier who attempted to recover his horse which had been stolen by a thief, noting that Strategic Intelligence enables the weak to overcome asymmetry in social relations.[80] The tenth-century poem *Heriger* in the *Cambridge Songs* depicts Bishop Heriger as a man of Strategic Intelligence who catches a thief in his own lie, and then cleverly punishes him for something that he actually did not do. Similarly, the story of the *Priest and the Wolf* (*Sacerdos et Lupus*) that is preserved in the same collection shows the instrumentality and two-way potency of *ars*, strategic craftiness.[81] After the priest created a ruse to trap his foe the wolf, the poet praised the genius of human Strategic Intelligence.[82] But the priest is surprised when the wolf uses *ars* to escape the trap by using the priest's back as a spring board. Der Stricker's thirteenth-century narrative depicts the hero Amis as a strategic priest who outwits a jealous bishop. *WWCFD? What Would the Church Fathers Do?*

The strategic bishops of this world are mirrored by strategic saints from the next. The eleventh-century Bernard of Angers' hagiography of St. Foy *Liber Miraculorum Sancte Fidis* states that the miracles performed by St. Foy were called tricks (*joca*). One legend relates that rather than donating his late wife's golden ring to the Church as promised, a castellan used it to marry his second wife. The new wife was compelled to come to the shrine after St. Foy enflamed her finger.[83] Here then is another case of the trickster being tricked. The question *WWSD? What Would the Saints Do?* gestures to a similar answer.

I conclude this chapter with evidence that the strategic world view not only informed Christian scripture and Holy Tradition, but that it also functioned as the foundation for the most important theological doctrine of the Church for more than 1,500 years. Known as Ransom Theory, or the theory of *Christus Victor*, this soteriological understanding is remarkably similar to the stories of cosmological duping in Hesiod's *Theogony* (chapter 2). Ransom Theory posits that Satan, the great deceiver of humanity in the *Genesis*, was cosmologically duped by God through the sacrifice of Jesus. In other words, in the great competition between God and Satan for human souls, Satan was outwitted through the strategic trickery of Jesus, and humanity was rescued from the ensnarement of the devil.

This soteriological tradition was grounded in an interpretation of sacred scripture that was shared and developed successively by Bishop Iraneaus of Lyon (–202 CE), Origen, St. Gregory of Nyssa and St. Ambrose of Milan (340–397 CE).[84] For example, St. Augustine wrote: "The Redeemer came and the deceiver was overcome. What did our Redeemer do to our Captor? In payment for us He *set the trap,* His Cross, with His blood *for bait.* He [Satan] could indeed shed that blood; but he deserved not to drink it. By shedding the blood of One who was not his debtor, he was forced to *release* his debtors."[85] (italics added for emphasis)

Agreeing, St. Gregory of Nyssa wrote that "in order to secure that the ransom on our behalf might be easily accepted by him who required it, the Deity was hidden under the veil of our nature, so that as is done by greedy fish, the hook of the Deity might be gulped down along with the bait of flesh."[86] St. John of Damascus in *On the Orthodox Faith* echoed this:

> And since the enemy snared man by the hope of Godhead, he himself is snared in turn by the guise of flesh."[87] "Wherefore death approaches, and swallowing up the body as a bait is transfixed on the hook of divinity, and after tasting of a sinless and life-giving body, perishes, and brings up again all whom of old he swallowed up. For just as darkness disappears on the introduction of life, so is death repulsed before the assault of life, and brings life to all, but death to the destroyer."[88]

The monk Rufinus of Aquileia (~344–411 CE) in his *Commentary on the Apostles' Creed* noted that the cosmic baiting was the very mystery of the Incarnation:

> For the object of that mystery of the Incarnation which we expounded just now was that the divine virtue of the Son of God, as though it were a hook concealed

beneath the form and fashion of human flesh (He being, as the Apostle Paul says, *"found in fashion as a man"*), might lure on the Prince of this world to a conflict, to whom offering His flesh as a bait, His divinity underneath might catch him and hold him fast with its hook, through the shedding of His immaculate blood. For He alone who knows no stain of sin has destroyed the sins of all, of those, at least, who have marked the door-posts of their faith with His blood. As, therefore, If a fish seizes a baited hook, it not only does not take the bait off the hook, but is drawn out of the water to be itself food for others, so He who had the power of death seized the body of Jesus in death, not being aware of the hook of Divinity inclosed within it, but having swallowed it he was caught immediately, and the bars of hell being burst asunder, he was drawn forth as it were from the abyss to become food for others. Which result the Prophet Ezekiel long ago foretold under this same figure, saying, *"I will draw you out with My hook, and stretch you out upon the earth: the plains shall be filled with you, and I will set all the fowls of the air over you, and I will satiate all the beasts of the earth with you.*[89]

This complex metaphor certainly disrupts other interpretations of the Christian *ichthys* (ἰχθύς) fish symbol—Jesus is actually *Prey*-Pantocrator who redeems the universe. Christian strategic deception is holy, righteous, just, virtuous, and cosmological.

The strategic world view enables us to see that the body of Christ in Ransom theory is a type of Trojan horse, the very means by which the deceiver is deceived, a theme amplified visually by the medieval depiction of the harrowing of hell, a Christian belief that Jesus traveled to Hell to liberate the dead from the Satan's gullet. (Figure 4.2) Not only is Christ's flesh deadly to Satan, Christ is snare-enlightened like the prawn in Oppian's *Fishing* that "destroys by being destroyed."[90] Christ's body compelled Satan to vomit up his captives just like Cronos was forced to vomit up Zeus' siblings in earlier Greek myth (chapter 2).

St. Augustine went one step further when he stated that the cross was in fact the "mousetrap for the devil."[91] This vision of the cosmological dupe echoed through the centuries, in martyrdom stories in which martyrs were depicted as cosmological warriors who defeated the devil through their death;[92] in sacred art such as the fifteenth-century Mérode altar triptych which shows the earthly father of Jesus St. Joseph carving a mousetrap, which one may find at the Cloisters in the Metropolitan Museum of Art in New York City; in the sermons of St. Leo (400–461 CE); the *Moralia* of St. Gregory the Great (540–604 CE); and the teachings of Bernard of Clairvaux, who affirmed that Satan had indeed had rights (*ius*) and dominion over humanity. For example, Bernard preached that Christ was a godly deceiver who redeemed the innocent who had been ensnared by devilish strategy. The messiah's holy trick enabled freedom, and Jesus' Jewish critics indeed were right in claiming that

Figure 4.2 Harrowing of Hell. This image in the twelfth-century Psalter of Henry of Blois which shows Christ liberating souls from Satan's snare is reminiscent of the manner in which Zeus also freed his siblings from the bowels of his father. Image provided and reprinted courtesy of © The British Library Board. (The Harrowing of Hell (BL Cotton Nero C IV, f. 24r). 'Winchester Psalter' or 'Psalter of Henry of Blois,' Mid-twelfth century 2nd half of the thirteenth century.

he was a deceiver, but he was righteous deceiver rather than a sinful one.[93] Two texts of the fourteenth century, *Piers Plowman* and *The Lily*, one English and one Icelandic, both pick up this theme—in *Piers Plowman* the conqueror taunts that Lucifer was beguiled by the beguiler, and *Lily* points out that the great worm was baited, and destroyed by the use of a clever decoy.[94]

The patrimony of the modern West includes a vision of Holy Strategic Intelligence that stretches as far back as Greco-Roman and Judaic pre-history, and as far forward as the twenty-first century. The trope of cosmological consumption and the strategic emetic mirrors Hesiod's *Theogony*, in which the most ancient of gods were tricked and castrated. In lieu of the mousetrap, the Swedish Bishop Gustaf Aulén (1879–1977) in his treatise *Christus Victor*, picked up the metaphor of the cross as a fishhook from scripture,[95] through Origen, St. Gregory of Nyssa, and St. John of Damascus.[96] Aulén's soteriology emphasized the competitive agonism between the Godhead and the devil—just like a fish that is baited, the devil was deceived by the Godhead who cleverly hid himself in human flesh, reversing the predator with the prey.[97]

This strategic world view is still perceivable in the various liturgies of the Eastern Orthodox Churches. For example, the theme of *beguiling the beguiler* is reflected as the "capture of hell," and as "destroying death by death" in the Paschal Sermon by St. John Chrysostom, which is traditionally read aloud from the pulpit every year on Easter morning.

> Let no one fear death, for the Savior's death has set us free. He that was held prisoner of it has annihilated it. By descending into Hell, He made Hell captive. He embittered it when it tasted of His flesh. And Isaiah, foretelling this, did cry: Hell, said he, was embittered, when it encountered Thee in the lower regions. It was embittered, for it was abolished. It was embittered, for it was mocked. It was embittered, for it was slain. It was embittered, for it was overthrown. It was embittered, for it was fettered in chains. It took a body, and met God face to face. It took earth, and encountered Heaven. It took that which was seen, and fell upon the unseen. O Death, where is your sting? O Hell, where is your victory? Christ is risen, and you are overthrown. Christ is risen, and the demons are fallen. Christ is risen, and the angels rejoice. Christ is risen, and life reigns. Christ is risen, and not one dead remains in the grave. For Christ, being risen from the dead, is become the first fruits of those who have fallen asleep. To Him be glory and dominion unto ages of ages. Amen.

The Paschal Troparion (hymn) echoes this: "Christ is risen from the dead, trampling down death by death, and upon those in the tombs, bestowing life!"[98] The celebration described transmits strategic values descended in culture from the Old Testament: "He has swallowed up death forever! The Lord Yahweh will wipe away tears from off all faces. He will take the reproach of his people away from off all the earth, for Yahweh has spoken it."[99]

The worldview informed by Holy Strategic Intelligence continues in the twenty-first-century Western Church as well. Pope Francis at the 2014 Feast of the Holy Epiphany intimately linked the birth of the savior of humanity with a Strategic Intelligence articulated through the figures of the Magi. "The Magi," the Pope taught, "teach us how not to fall into the snares of darkness and how to defend ourselves from the shadows which seek to envelop our life." Holy cunning for the pope "is a spiritual shrewdness which enables us to recognize danger and to avoid it." Like the magi, we need to "safeguard the faith with holy cunning, guard it from that darkness which, many times, is also disguised as light," he said. "Spiritual cunning" enables the faithful to see through the "deception of appearances."[100] Pope Francis has also preached about shrewdness as an aspect of Strategic Intelligence expressed through the figure of Paul, who was "inspired by the Holy Spirit."[101] He wrote in his catechesis on Christian hope that "A Christian travels along his road in this world with the essentials for the journey, but with his heart full of love. The true defeat for him or her is to fall into the temptation of revenge and violence, by responding to evil with evil. Jesus tells us: "I am sending you out as lambs among wolves."[102] Therefore, without jaws, without claws, without weapons. Instead, the Christian has to be prudent, and sometimes shrewd: these are the virtues accepted by the logic of the Gospel."[103]

Elsewhere, he extols Christian shrewdness over worldly fraud.

> The fraudster is a man who has no faith, ... The Gospel tells us about him in the parable of the dishonest manager. How did this manager arrive at the point of defrauding and stealing from his master? From one day to the next? No. Bit by bit. Perhaps one day he gave a tip here, a bribe there, and gradually, step by step he arrived at the point of corruption. In the parable, the master praises the manager for his shrewdness. But this is an entirely worldly and sinful shrewdness, which does great harm. There exists, instead, a Christian shrewdness, of doing this in an astute way, but not in a worldly spirit: doing things honestly. And this is good. It is what Jesus says when He invites us to be wise as serpents and harmless as doves: putting these two dimensions together is a grace of the Holy Spirit, a grace we must ask. Today too there are many of these corrupt fraudsters . . . . I am struck by how corruption is widespread everywhere.[104]

In conclusion, the evidence from the Western religious patrimony shows that Christian culture itself was a bearer of Strategic Intelligence. Not only did its cultural products simultaneously serve as models of living and cultural memory, but holy strategy was invested with the authority and legitimacy deemed critical by Christendom—it was validated as universal and cosmological, scriptural, traditional, ancient, patriarchal, apostolic, saintly, and wise. In short, it was a form of hope and preeminent means that enabled human freedom, dignity, and transcendence. Strategic Intelligence is simply divine.

NOTES

1. Proverbs 2:11 World English Bible (WEB), Bible Hub, https://biblehub.com.
2. Job 5:13 WEB, Bible Hub, https://biblehub.com.
3. Proverbs 12:23 WEB, Bible Hub, https://biblehub.com.
4. Proverbs 14:15 WEB, Bible Hub, https://biblehub.com.
5. I disagree with Detienne and Vernant's assumption that *mêtic* intelligence was devalued by Christianity. "In studies of the Greeks pursued by scholars who claim to be their heirs, there has been a prolonged silence on the subject of the intelligence of cunning. The fundamental reasons for this have been two-fold. The first is

perhaps that, from a Christian point of view, it was inevitable that the gulf separating men from animals should be increasingly emphasized and that human reason should appear even more clearly separated from animal behavior than it was for the ancient Greeks. The second and even more powerful reason is surely that the concept of Platonic Truth, which has overshadowed a whole area of intelligence with its own kinds of understanding, has never really ceased to haunt Western metaphysical thought." Marcel Detienne and Jean-Pierre Vernant, *Cunning Intelligence in Greek Culture and Society*, trans. Janet Lloyd (New Jersey: Humanities Press, 1978).

    6. Immanuel Kant, *Religion Within the Limits of Reason Alone*, trans. Theodore M. Greene and Hoyt Y. Hudson (New York: Harper, 1934).

    7. Exodus 3:22 WEB, Bible Hub, https://biblehub.com.

    8. 1 Kings 22:20–23 WEB, Bible Hub, https://biblehub.com.

    9. Ezekiel 14:9 WEB, Bible Hub, https://biblehub.com.

    10. 2 Chronicles 18:19–21 WEB, Bible Hub, https://biblehub.com.

    11. The God who sees (*el roi* ראי אל) is one of the names of God in the Torah. Genesis 16:13.

    12. Deceit ἐξαπατῆσαι Exodus 8:29.

    13. Genensis 26:7 WEB, Bible Hub, https://biblehub.com.

    14. Betrayal (יַעְקֹב deceit *yacqob*).

    15. Deceiver' *rama'i;* trickster עָרֵם.

    16. Giuliano Bugiardini (1531) "The Rape of Dinah," Entführung der Dina, Kunsthistorisches Museum Vienna, accessed 4 January 2019, https://www.khm.at/objectdb/detail/368/.

    17. Hebrew *çaqob yacqob* Jer 9:4 WEB, Bible Hub, https://biblehub.com.

    18. Genesis 38: 27–30 WEB, Bible Hub, https://biblehub.com.

    19. "Hymns on the Nativity," Hymn 7, Catholic Encyclopedia, New Advent, accessed 13 October 2018, http://www.newadvent.org/fathers/3703.htm.

    20. Matthew 1:1–3.

    21. John 1:46 WEB, Bible Hub, https://biblehub.com.

    22. "Judah and Tamar," 1650–1660, School of Rembrandt, Residenzgalerie, Wikimedia Commons, https://commons.wikimedia.org/wiki/File:Rembrandt%27s_school_Tamar.JPG.

    23. *Qur'ān* 7.118.

    24. *Qur'ān* 7.123.

    25. Genesis 44:2 WEB, Bible Hub, https://biblehub.com.

    26. Joshua 8:1–29 WEB, Bible Hub, https://biblehub.com.

    27. Judges 7:20 WEB, Bible Hub, https://biblehub.com.

    28. Joshua 9.

    29. Judges 12 WEB, Bible Hub, https://biblehub.com.

    30. 2 Kings 10:18–31 WEB, Bible Hub, https://biblehub.com.

    31. Judges 3:15–25 WEB, Bible Hub, https://biblehub.com.

    32. 1 Samuel 21: 12–15 WEB, Bible Hub, https://biblehub.com.

    33. "David Feins Lunacy before Achish king of Gath," *David simulant la folie devant Akish,* Bible de Saint Etienne Harding, Cîteaux, abbaye Notre-Dame, Bourgogne, France, 1109–1111 CE,—ms. 0014, f 013. http://www.enluminures.culture

.fr/public/mistral/enlumine_fr?ACTION=CHERCHER&FIELD_98=REF&VALUE_98=D-002984.

34. 1 Samuel 23–24 Insidier יַעְרִם/ ya'rim WEB, Bible Hub, https://biblehub.com.
35. 2 Samuel 17 WEB, Bible Hub, https://biblehub.com.
36. 1 Samuel 19–20 WEB, Bible Hub, https://biblehub.com. Paul J. Griffiths, *Lying: An Augustinian Theology of Duplicity* (Grand Rapids: Brazos Press, 2004), 139.
37. 2 Kings 7:6–7 WEB, Bible Hub, https://biblehub.com.
38. 1 Samuel 16:1–3 WEB, Bible Hub, https://biblehub.com.
39. Exodus 1:10, 1:15–22 and 3:22 WEB, Bible Hub, https://biblehub.com. Pharaoh and the Hebrew Mid-wives, the Golden Haggadah, Catalonia, 14th century. British Library.
40. Esther 5:1–8; 6:14–9:17 WEB, Bible Hub, https://biblehub.com.
41. Judges 4–5 WEB, Bible Hub, https://biblehub.com.
42. Joshua 2:1–7 WEB, Bible Hub, https://biblehub.com.
43. Edward Hutton, *Florence* (London: Hollis and Carter, 1952), 53–54.
44. Matthew 10:16 WEB, Bible Hub, https://biblehub.com.
45. 1 Peter 5:8 WEB, Bible Hub, https://biblehub.com.
46. Mathew 2:16 WEB, Bible Hub, https://biblehub.com.
47. Job 5:12–13 WEB, Bible Hub, https://biblehub.com.
48. Luke 12:1. Entrapment: Matthew 22:15–18, Mark 12:13, Luke 20:20, Matthew 26:3, Mark 14, Luke 22, WEB, Bible Hub, https://biblehub.com.
49. Luke 20 WEB, Bible Hub, https://biblehub.com.
50. Luke 20:5–6 WEB, Bible Hub, https://biblehub.com.
51. Matthew 12:10, Luke 14:3 WEB, Bible Hub, https://biblehub.com.
52. Luke 20:40 WEB, Bible Hub, https://biblehub.com.
53. 1 Corinthians 3:19. WEB, Bible Hub, https://biblehub.com. The Greek word is πανουργια.
54. Justly traps δρασσόμενος.
55. Luke 16:8 WEB, Bible Hub, https://biblehub.com.
56. Luke 16:9 WEB, Bible Hub, https://biblehub.com.
57. Luke 6:48, Matthew 7:24 WEB, Bible Hub, https://biblehub.com.
58. Acts 2: 24:2–3, 31; Heb. 12:15. προϊδὼν, προνοίας, *providens*.
59. John 7 WEB, Bible Hub, https://biblehub.com.
60. Matthew 15:21–28 WEB, Bible Hub, https://biblehub.com.
61. Galatians 2. Paul J. Griffiths, *Lying: An Augustinian Theology of Duplicity* (Grand Rapids: Brazos Press, 2004), 146.
62. 2 Corinthians 12:16 WEB, Bible Hub, https://biblehub.com.
63. 1 Corinthians 9:19–23 WEB, Bible Hub, https://biblehub.com.
64. Acts 13:10. Ephesians. 4:14. 2 Corinthians 2:11 WEB, Bible Hub, https://biblehub.com.
65. Clement of Alexandria, *Stromateis* 1.24 (160–161) and 7.9.53, in *The Fathers of the Church: a New Translation*, trans. John Ferguson (Washington DC: The Catholic University of America Press, 1991), Vol. 85, 140–144. In Everett L. Wheeler, *Stratagem and the Vocabulary of Military Trickery* (Leiden: E.J Brill, 1988), 22–23. ἀρετή του στρατηγικου; εμπειρίας γαρ και στρατηγίας.

66. Machiavelli, *Discorsi*, 3.30. *E chi legge la Bibbia sensatamente, vedrà Moisè essere stato forzato, a volere che le sue leggi e che i suoi ordini andassero innanzi, ad ammazzare infiniti uomini, i quali, non mossi da altro che dalla invidia, si opponevano a' disegni suoi.*

67. Numbers 16:48. Book 2:4.

68. St. Ambrose, *On the Duties of the Clergy De Officiis Ministrorum*, 2.28, Catholic Encyclopedia, accessed 2 February 2019, New Advent, http://www.newadvent.org/fathers/34012.htm.

69. St. John Cassian, The Second Conference of Abbot Joseph, Chapter 20. Full translation at C. S. Gibson. From Nicene and Post-Nicene Fathers, Second Series, Vol. 11, ed. Philip Schaff and Henry Wace (Buffalo, NY: Christian Literature Publishing Co., 1894.) Revised and edited for New Advent by Kevin Knight, Catholic Encyclopedia, New Advent, accessed 4 January 2019, http://www.newadvent.org/fathers/350817.htm.

70. 1 Corinthians 9 WEB, Bible Hub, https://biblehub.com.

71. St. John Chrysostom Ἰωάννης ὁ Χρυσόστομος, *On the Priesthood*. Various Translations exist, including New Advent, trans. W.R.W. Stephens, ed. Philip Schaff, *Nicene and Post-Nicene Fathers,* First Series, Vol. 9 (Buffalo, NY: Christian Literature Publishing Co., 1889). Revised and edited for New Advent by Kevin Knight, accessed 4 January 2019, http://www.newadvent.org/fathers/1922.htm. Also, in B. Harris Cowper, trans. S. John *Chrysostom, On the Priesthood in Six Books* (London: Williams and Norgate, 1866), accessed 17 January 2019, https://books.google.com/books?id=Kt4TAAAAYAAJ&pg=PR3&source=kp_read_button#v=onepage&q&f=false. Paul J. Griffiths, *Lying: An Augustinian Theology of Duplicity* (Grand Rapids: Brazos Press, 2004), 136.

72. Noble lie γενναῖον ψεῦδος, *gennaion pseudos*.

73. Chrysostom, *Priesthood*, 382d.

74. Acts 21, Galatians 5 WEB, Bible Hub, https://biblehub.com. Timothy had a Jewish mother and a Greek father. Although Paul preached that circumcision was unnecessary, he still circumcised Timothy.

75. Numbers 25:7 WEB, Bible Hub, https://biblehub.com.

76. 2 Kings 1:9–12 WEB, Bible Hub, https://biblehub.com.

77. 1 Kings 18 WEB, Bible Hub, https://biblehub.com.

78. Genesis 22:3 WEB, Bible Hub, https://biblehub.com.

79. Exodus 11:2 WEB, Bible Hub, https://biblehub.com.

80. Marc Wolterbeek, *Comic Tales of the Middle Ages: An Anthology and Commentary* (New York: Greenwood Press, 1991), 47–48.

81. Wolterbeek, *Comic*, 22.

82. Wolterbeek, *Comic*, 21–24.

83. Kathleen M. Ashley and Pamela Sheingorn, *Writing Faith: Text, Sign & History in the Miracles of Sainte Foy* (Chicago: University of Chicago Press, 1999), 139.

84. Jeffrey Burton Russell, *Satan: The Early Christian Tradition* (Ithaca: Cornell University Press, 1981), 83, 140, Note 91.

85. St. Augustine, Sermon 80, "On the New Testament," trans. R.G. MacMullen. From *Nicene and Post-Nicene Fathers, First Series,* Vol. 6, ed. Philip Schaff (Buffalo, NY: Christian Literature Publishing Co., 1888). Revised and edited for New

Advent by Kevin Knight, accessed 2 February 2019, http://www.newadvent.org/fathers/160380.htm. "Doctrine of the Atonement," *Catholic Encyclopedia* (Denver: New Advent, 2000).

86. St. Gregory of Nyssa, *Nicene and Post-Nicene Fathers*, Second Series, Volume V, edited by Philip Schaff. See chapter 24, 494.

87. ἐπειδὴ θεότητος ἐλπίδι ὁ ἐχθρὸς δελεάζει τὸν ἄνθρωπον, σαρκὸς προβλήμα τι δελεάζεται). St. John of Damascus, *On the Orthodox Faith* Ἔκδοσις ἀκριβὴς τῆς ὀρθοδόξου πίστεως "Concerning the Divine Œconomy and God's care over us, and concerning our salvation. ΚΕΦΑΛΑΙΟΝ 45. Περὶ τῆς θείας οἰκονομίας καὶ περὶ τῆς δι' ἡμᾶς κηδεμονίας καὶ τῆς ἡμῶν σωτηρίας. Book 3,1:45, accessed 4 January 2019, https://babel.hathitrust.org/cgi/pt?id=njp.32101063614737;view=1up;seq=419.

88. St. John, *Orthodox*, trans. Henry Wace and Philip Schaff (New York: The Christian Literature Company; 1890–1900), 72. Also, *A Select Library of Nicene and Post-Nicene Fathers of the Christian Church*, Second series, accessed 4 January 2019, https://babel.hathitrust.org/cgi/pt?id=njp.32101063614737;view=1up;seq=446.

89. Rufinus of Aquileia, "*Commentary on the Apostles' Creed,*" *Catholic Encyclopedia* (Denver: New Advent, 2000), 16. Translated by W.H. Fremantle. From *Nicene and Post-Nicene Fathers, Second Series*, Vol. 3, ed. Philip Schaff and Henry Wace (Buffalo, NY: Christian Literature Publishing Co., 1892), Revised and edited for New Advent by Kevin Knight, accessed 14 January 2019, http://www.newadvent.org/fathers/2711.htm.

90. Deadly (δόλοισι); snare-enlightened δολόφρονες.

91. *Crux muscipula diaboli*. Mortis avidus diabolos fuit, mortis avarus diabolos fuit. Crux Christi muscipula fuit: mors Christi, immo caro mortales Christi tamquam esca in muscipula fuit. Augustine's *Sermon* CCLXV (d). Cited in ed. G. Morin, *Sancti Augustini Sermones post Maurinos reperti. Miscellenea Agostiniana* 1 (Rome, 1930), p. 662 (cf. PLS 2, col. 707). *Sermones* CXXX. Extensive literature review in Paul G. Remley, "*Muscipula Diaboli* and medieval English Antifeminism," *English Studies*, 70:1 (1989), notes 1 & 2.

92. Candida R. Moss, *The Other Christs: Imitating Jesus in Ancient Christian Ideologies of Martyrdom* (Oxford: Oxford University Press, 2010), 87–102.

93. Matthew 27.63 WEB, Bible Hub, https://biblehub.com. Anthony N. S. Lane, *Bernard of Clairvaux: Theologian of the Cross* (Collegeville: Liturgical Press, 2013), 160–170.

94. Piers Plowman, 18.356. 18.78–86. Lawrence Warner, *The Myth of Piers Plowman: Constructing a Medieval Literary Archive* (Cambridge: Cambridge University Press, 2014), 31. Eiríkr Magnússon and Eysteinn Ásgrímsson, *Lilja* (*The Lily*) *an Icelandic Religious Poem of the Fourteenth Century*, (Ulan Press, 2012), 60, 61.

95. Revelations 12:9 and Job 41:1–2 WEB, Bible Hub, https://biblehub.com.

96. Jeffrey Burton Russell, *Satan: The Early Christian Tradition* (Ithaca: Cornell University Press, 1981), 131 note 60; 193.

97. Gustaf Aulén, *Christus Victor: an Historical Study of the Three Main Types of the Idea of the Atonement*, trans., A. G. Hebert (London, S.P.C.K., 1970).

98. Χριστὸς ἀνέστη ἐκ νεκρῶν, θανάτῳ θάνατον πατήσας, καὶ τοῖς ἐν τοῖς μνήμασι, ζωὴν χαρισάμενος!

99. Isaiah 25:8 WEB, Bible Hub, https://biblehub.com.

100. "Guard faith with 'spiritual cunning,' says pope," *The Catholic Sun*, 6 January 2014, accessed 18 January 2018, http://www.catholicsun.org/2014/01/06/guard-faith-with-spiritual-cunning-says-pope/.

101. "The Shrewdness of St. Paul," Holy See Press Office, Daily Bulletin, Pope Francis Morning Meditation in the Chapel of the Domus Sanctae Marthae, Thursday, 1 June, accessed 4 January 2019, https://w2.vatican.va/content/francesco/en/cotidie/2017/documents/papa-francesco-cotidie_20170601_shrewdness-of-saint-paul.html.

102. Matthew 10:16 WEB, Bible Hub, https://biblehub.com.

103. Pope Francis General Audience, Holy See Press Office, St. Peter's Square, Wednesday, 28 June 2017, accessed 4 January 2019, https://w2.vatican.va/content/francesco/en/audiences/2017/documents/papa-francesco_20170628_udienza-generale.html.

104. "Mass for the 200th anniversary of the Vatican Gendarmerie: the Poor Pay the Price of Fraud and Corruption," Holy See Press Office, 18 September 2016, accessed 4 January 2019, https://press.vatican.va/content/salastampa/en/bollettino/pubblico/2016/09/18/160918a.html. See also https://aleteia.org/2017/06/28/pope-francis-christians-love-but-they-are-not-always-loved/.

Chapter 5

The Patrimony of Medieval & Renaissance Strategic Intelligence

Aut aliquis latet error: equo ne credite, Teucri.
Some tricks lie hidden: trust not the horse, Trojans.

Virgil (70–19 BCE)

Ill is it to trust to Fortune's fickle bounty.

Boethius (480–524 CE)

Strategic Intelligence has always been invested with the highest forms of authority. In contrast to earlier periods in which authority in strategy was grounded in metaphysical justifications and through divine revelation, subsequent ages authorized it from the perspective of philosophical, societal, and interpersonal necessity. In modern times, Strategic Intelligence is known through one of its greatest masters, Niccolò Machiavelli, although it should be clear by now that he was merely tapping into a much older tradition. For example, Machiavelli in his *Discourses on Livy* alludes to the authority of history with regards to the need for the strategic type of intelligence that enables freedom and strength—for him it was clear that Roman Strategic Intelligence enabled the Romans to transform themselves from insignificance to eternal glory. In fact, the more hidden the deceit, the less blameworthy they were.[1] But regardless of how the underlying justifications for Strategic Intelligence evolved over time, the strategic values that informed many genres remained intact.

The existence and necessity of deceit in public life was already explored by Plato in his *Republic* as early as the fourth century BCE, by Aristophanes in *The Birds*, and to some degree Rome itself was founded on deceit. In addition to the betrayal of brotherly love in the mythological founders of

Rome, Romulus and Remus, the myth of the rape of the Sabine women again clarifies the connection of strategic thought, power and the acquisition of aim (*eros*) seen in the various rapes of Zeus (Metis, Hera, Antiope, Danae, Europa, Leda, Callisto, Ganymede, Helen). Writing about the eighth century BCE myth of the founding of Rome, the Roman historian Titus Livius Patavinus, also known simply as Livy (~64 BCE–17 CE), relayed that the Romans set up the games (*ludi*) as a pretext to abduct the Sabine women. This deceit was memorialized yearly in the *Consualia Ludi*, a public festival that integrated the themes of war with agricultural and family fertility, and which mode of piety was celebrated with the spectacle of races, hunts, and theatrical performances.

Strategic values are reflected in Roman military history, and in Virgil's epic Roman genealogy, the *Aeneid*. For example, strategic virtuosity is on display in the Roman historian Appian's (95–165 CE) description of the war between Masinissa and Carthage,

> Masinissa was an example in all doing and enduring and had only cavalry, no pack animals and no provisions. Thus he was able the more easily to retreat, to attack, and to take refuge in strongholds. Often, when surrounded, he divided his forces so that they might scatter as best they could, concealing himself with a handful until they should all come together again, by day or by night, at an appointed rendezvous. Once he was one of three who lay concealed in a cave around which his enemies were encamped. He never had any fixed camping-place. His generalship consisted especially in concealing his position. Thus his enemies never could make a regular assault upon him, but were always warding off his attacks. His provisions were obtained each day from whatever place he came upon toward evening, whether village or city. He seized and carried off everything and divided the plunder with his men, for which reason many Numidians flocked to him, although he did not give regular pay, for the sake of the booty, which was better.[2]

Virgil's (70–19 BC) epic *Aeneid* continued the exploration of strategic piety, a term that sounds rather strange to modern sensibilities. This epic depicts the circuitous and *Odyssey*-like journey of *pious* exile Aeneas from the fall of Troy to the founding of Rome. However, Aeneas' *pietas* was only possible because of a strategically intelligent deceitfulness. In lieu of the Strategic Intelligence of the martial deities Athena or Diana, Venus served as the matron of Aeneas—she was a formidable mistress of strategy who enabled devotees to achieve their life aims (*eros*).

Evidence from the *Aeneid* demonstrates that heroic strategic values were just as foundational to Roman as they were to Greek culture.[3] For example, deception is a key feature of theophany—like in the *Odyssey* when Odysseus met his mother Athena, Aeneas also met his matron Venus on the Libyan coast. In this episode in which Venus oddly disguised herself as Artemis, a Greek huntress out of place on African soil, Aeneas called her out after seeing right through her ruse, asking why she was so blatantly lying to him.[4] Later in the narrative when Aeneas is on his way to meet Dido in Carthage, Venus first conceals him in a cloud that enables him to benefit from the advantage of unobserved observation. And just like the scene in the *Odyssey* in which Athena glamored Odysseus to make him appear god-like to Nausicaa, Venus also enhances Aeneas' characteristics, giving him the aura of a god.[5]

Divine deception is a leitmotif in the *Aeneid*—in fact, divine deception is necessary to flesh out the tragedy of Dido. First, Venus sends Love in disguise to bewitch Dido to fall for Aeneas, and then she schemes with Juno to consummate the union, which the poet reveals was both the first sorrow and what led to death.[6] This conniving led to Dido's downfall. She lost her freedom by accepting Aeneas as master and lost both her integrity and reputation.[7] To add insult to injury, Aeneas uses deception once again when he schemes to leave Carthage in secret. Dido also lies to her sister about the pyre, and Venus strategically deceives Dido with Aeneas' son Ascanius.[8] There is also the scene in which the god Somnus, disguised as Phorbas, appears to the helmsman Palinurus and tries to make him lose focus by lulling him to sleep.[9] Finally, I recall the fascinating episode of Turnus and the Fury Allecto. Whereas Odysseus came under the heal of Calypso, a nymph whose name means "the concealed," Turnus encountered the Fury Allecto, disguised as an old woman named Calybe, a name derived from the same etymology as that which is concealed.[10]

The leitmotif of deceit in the *Aeneid* was not lost on the medieval moralist Dante Alighieri (1265–1321 CE)—who imagines that Virgil resides in the pleasant first circle of the underworld. In Canto XVII *Inferno* of the *Divine Comedy*, Dante described how the monster Geryon, a figure of fraud, responded to Virgil's beckoning, and bore the two down to the abyss of the Circle of Fraud, the famous Malebolge, where they meet ancient heroes, including Ulysses (Odysseus).

BOETHIUS' THE CONSOLATION OF PHILOSOPHY

Anicius Manlius Severinus Boëthius' (hereafter Boethius') (480–524 CE) *Consolation of Philosophy* is a foundational text of late Roman antiquity, and it was highly influential and widely read throughout the Middle Ages. *Consolation* is an artifact of political intrigue and a type of philosophical martyrology—the quintessentially Roman politician and philosopher Boethius was executed by the Ostrogothic King Theodoric in 524 on charges of conspiracy to overthrow the regime.

We hear an echo of Platonic Strategic Intelligence in this late Roman philosophical text that depicts the tragedy of the hero who is enslaved in this world because he lost the power of his internal harmonization. *Consolation* opens with a depiction of Boethius enslaved to the illusion of worldly value, which fortune ravished.

> To pleasant songs my work was erstwhile given, and bright were all my labours then; but now in tears to sad refrains am I compelled to turn. Thus my maimed Muses guide my pen, and gloomy songs make no feigned tears bedew my face . . . . Ill is it to trust to Fortune's fickle bounty, and while yet she smiled upon me, the hour of gloom had well-nigh overwhelmed my head. Now has the cloud put off its alluring face, wherefore without scruple my life drags out its wearying delays.[11]

Boethius claims that he has been deceived. Originally inspired by Plato's vision of the heroic philosopher-king, Boethius returned to the chaotic world of change, only to be brought low by Fortune's fickle bounty. But, the goddess Philosophy points out, this is (self) deception—the only deception involved is the deception of true values. Recalling Hesiod's description of the ambiguity of the muses in *Theogony* and Plato's exiling of poets in the *Republic*, the goddess accuses the muses of enslaving his mind: "they free not the minds of men from disease, but accustom them thereto." Like the Sirens in the *Odyssey*, they are "seductive unto destruction!" This ensnarement is accentuated by Philosophy when she notes ironically that previously Boethius was a devotee of philosophy, having studied the eleatics and the academics: "This man has been free to the open heaven: his habit has it been to wander into the paths of the sky: his to watch the light of the bright sun, his to inquire into the brightness of the chilly moon; he, like a conqueror, held fast bound in its order every star that makes its wandering circle, turning its peculiar course."

Conversely, unlike the truly free philosophers, Boethius had enslaved himself to the false values of this world, of fame, power, and reputation rather than truth and justice: "Now he lies there; extinct his reason's light, his neck in heavy chains thrust down, his countenance with grievous weight downcast; ah! the brute earth is all he can behold."[12] In his worldly concerns, Boethius is more like a beast than the image of God:

> In what different shapes do living beings move upon the earth! Some make flat their bodies, sweeping through the dust and using their strength to make therein a furrow without break; some flit here and there upon light wings which beat the breeze, and they float through vast tracks of air in their easy flight. "Tis others" wont to plant their footsteps on the ground, and pass with their paces over green fields or under trees. Though all these thou seest move in different

shapes, yet all have their faces downward along the ground, and this doth draw downward and dull their senses. Alone of all, the human race lifts up its head on high, and stands in easy balance with the body upright, and so looks down to spurn the earth. If thou art not too earthly by an evil folly, this poses as a lesson. Thy glance is upward, and thou dost carry high thy head, and thus thy search is heavenward: then lead thy soul too upward, lest while the body is higher raised, the mind sink lower to the earth.

Philosophy then provides Boethius with the therapy that restores him to the true sight, and divine *foreknowledge* by which the hero can evade the entrapments of the world and the contingency of the wheel of Fortune.

Let us therefore raise ourselves, if so be that we can, to that height of the loftiest intelligence. For there reason will see what it cannot of itself perceive, and that is to know how even such things as have uncertain results are perceived definitely and for certain by foreknowledge; and such foreknowledge will not be mere opinion, but rather the single and direct form of the highest knowledge unlimited by any finite bounds.

The moral of *Consolation* is that true philosophy is that which enables one to escape from the trap of empty values—philosophy is what makes one snare-aware and immune to time's trap. The values of this world, whether fame, glory, or riches, are bound to the realm of time, and therefore not everlasting. Seeing through the trap, one can then align oneself with eternal values. Boethius' *Consolation* is informed by Strategic Intelligence—it is a strategy of escape, in which snare-awareness leads to the unbound infinity of human dignity, empowerment, and liberty.

STRATEGIC INTELLIGENCE IN MEDIEVAL ISLAM

Although the culture of late Roman antiquity came to an end around the time of the execution of Boethius by the Germanic King Theodoric in 524 CE, it by no means marked the end of strategic values. Rather, they emigrated as the Germanic and Islamic capitals north and south of the Roman-Byzantine center increasingly came to dominate their respective cultural and political ecosystems.

The depiction of Odysseus/Ulysses as a beggar king in the *Odyssey* was quite powerful for the Latin West because the figure of noble indigence articulated a complex set of concepts that centered on very similar Latin roots for "mind," "lie," and "need" (*mens*, *ment*, and *mend*). These themes combined in interesting ways to explore necessity and contingency, poverty and wealth, fortune and freedom, and often informed the depictions of mendicant wanderers, including philosophers, beggars, and saints. Regardless of the cultural influences that led to it, from the perspective of the strategic, it is quite easy to observe a genealogical link between Odysseus, Badi' al-Zamān al-Hamadāni's (hereafter, al-Hamadhāni) figure Abū al-Fath al-Iskandari created in the ninth century CE, and the picaresque novels of Renaissance Spain.[13] Recalling that North Africa formed the southern terminus of Greco-Roman culture, we should not be surprised that Northern African and Arabic cultural influences synthesized with those from Germanic and Hispano-Roman societies when the Umayyads defeated the Visigothic kingdom in eighth-century Spain.

The character Abū al-Fath al-Iskandari, whose name means "Father the Victorious Alexandrian," is a great example of strategic thought in the medieval Islamic world. Reminiscent of the legendary exploits of Alexander the Great that circulated around the Mediterranean world for centuries, the heroic and noble stratagems of al-Iskandari and his contemporary Abū Zayd are intimately linked to the *maqāmāt* literary genre, a collection of stories of the *Banū Sāsān* or society of trickster-strategists.[14] The *maqāmā* genre made salient the problem of contingency and focused attention on human dignity amidst the dire consequences of an ever rotating wheel of fortune. These stories revealed the gamut of predatory strategists who cloaked their means in Islamic piety.[15] Most importantly for our purposes here is that these heroic figures also functioned as a medium that transmitted strategic values to subsequent epochs.

Al-Iskandari and Abū Zayd are masters of strategy whose special talent lie in shapeshifting—throughout the stories they pose in various guises, including beggar, blind and maimed, male and female elderly, mendicant sufi, young poet, refugee, exiled princely gentleman, lunatic, and sheik, in order to opportunistically exploit the unique conditions of various situations. Both of these heroes adapt themselves to the opportunities of the present, overcoming the trap of hardship with clever ingenuity and appropriate speech. Like the mendacious mendicant Odysseus, Al-Iskandari is a composite character on a journey against hardship, which enables his virtuosic ability to appropriately interpret the threat, respond opportunistically to the parameters of any situation, rapidly adapt, and heroically deceive when necessary.

Al-Iskandari in the *Maqāmā of Kufa* and *Poetry* highlights the theme of the alienation of the exiled mendicant which has been caused by a threatening environment. Posing as a wandering Sufi, Al-Iskandari waxes poetic as a gentleman subjected to the turn of the wheel of fortune, exiled, enslaved by night, and made prey to hunger.[16] The *Maqāmā of Poetry* echoes this beautifully—suffering the fate of misfortune and thinning clothes, he is vulnerable to the cold of night and the heat of day.[17] The *Maqāmā of Jurjan* complements this with the image of the Odyssean wanderer exiled to roam the deserts.[18] The *Maqāmā of Adharbayján* reveals him as a beggar wandering over horizons as the plaything of time.[19] And the *Maqāmā of Al-Fazara* reveals that Al-Iskandari's power of strategic adaptation models the patterns of adaptability in nature itself. He is an opportunist, becoming a counsellor or an orator as the situation requires. In the denouement of each poem, Al-Iskandari is again revealed to be a master of the craft in the form of a beggar.[20] Strategic deception is the highest form of that masterly art, as exemplified in the *Maqāmās* of the *Date*, the *Lion*, and *Isfahan*.[21] In *Lion*, for example, the reader observes the manner in which a fashionable young man dupes travelers by means of his good looks and earnest service, only to be tricked by them in turn.[22] And in *Isfahan*, Al-Iskandari panders to the hyper-pious by adapting to them—he cons the faithful by selling in front of the mosque perfumed slips of paper on which he had written the contents of a vision of the prophet that he supposedly saw while sleeping. In response to questioning by the narrator as to what compelled Al-Iskandari to this life of graft, Al-Iskandari justified his fraud with the argument that men are fools, tools, and resources that one should tap.[23]

MEDIEVAL EUROPE

In addition to migrating south and east to find expression in the highly urbane and sophisticated Islamic world, to include that of the cultural splendor of the medieval Islamic kingdoms of the Iberian peninsula, strategic values emigrated north as northern European capitals increasingly dominated the political and cultural landscape. Hints of the northern emigration of strategic values can be glimpsed in stories originating from folklore and legend associated with the various Germanic and Celtic peoples who participated in the multi-century *völkerwanderung,* in *fabliaux*, and in the courtly literature at the turn of the first millennium, such as in the *nugae* "trifles" and *ridicula* genres.

Heroic strategists are everywhere in Germanic and Celtic heroic epics, sagas, and lays. As in earlier periods explored, I perceive that the judgment of the utility of Strategic Intelligence depends on the values held by the author and the surrounding cultural context—it is magical when it reverses asymmetric relationships, and treacherous when the high and mighty fall due to it. It is what defines in Machiavelli's words *chi vuole acquistare o chi vuole mantenere*, what we refer in English as the *haves and the have-nots*.[24] As in earlier periods, Strategic Intelligence is often a tool that empowers the disenfranchised, including youth and women. But one also detects an increasing resentment on the part of male writers toward the treachery of strategic deception, especially by women in the domain of the boudoir in the practice of the arts of love (*ars amatoria*), a criticism made canonical by the Roman poet Ovid (~43 BCE) when he wrote "cheaters cheat: on the whole, they are godless. Let them fall into the traps of their own devising."[25]

As opposed to the majority of the male figures in the old Irish heroic saga *Táin bó Cúailnge* of the Ulster Cycle, which roots may go as far back as the eighth century CE, Queen Medb is a figure that expresses strategic values.[26] Medb's special talent is a knack for *savoir-faire*, and she is a force to be reckoned with. In order to prod her warriors to enter into what is essentially fratricide, Medb first dulls their wits through alcohol, and then goads them with promises of land, riches, and sex. To Ferdia, the foster brother of the hero Cú Chulainn who he now opposes, she offers her own daughter Finnabair. When he refuses, she contrives a story that makes Ferdia believe that Cú Chulainn had offended honor. The tragic hero Fergus, who is the foster father to his now opponent Cú Chulainn, is also not without strategy—in order to avoid killing his own foster son and offending the cultural value of honor, Fergus shrewdly balances the tension between loyalty to kin and fealty to liege, and maintains his vow of killing three warriors by symbolically lopping off the tops of three mountains.[27] In another example, Medb uses her own daughter as bait—she tricks her daughter's beloved by allowing him to return home after sleeping with her daughter. The next day, seven hundred of his warriors died while seeking revenge for the ruse. Medb attempted a similar stratagem with the hero Cú Chulainn, but the deceiver was outwitted—he saw through the ruse of the disguised jester, and promptly killed him on the spot.

There are almost too many examples of strategic deception and trickery in medieval texts to cite here, but I will briefly cite the better known. Beowulf defeated Grendl by trickery when he feigned sleep.[28] *Énide* showed her *savoir faire* and saved her love Érec via the noble lie in Chrétian de Troyes' twelfth-century Arthurian romance *Érec et Énide*. After being duped by Gawain, Érec complained, "Ah! Gawain, your shrewdness has outwitted me. By your great cunning you have kept me here."[29] In Gerbert de Montreuil's *Continuation to the Conte du Graal*, after a night of bliss with Gawain, Boiesine deceived her family through a lie, and saved Gawain's life.[30] Geoffrey of Monmouth's twelfth-century *Historia Regum Britanniae* (*History of the Kings of Britain*) relays the story of Arthur's conception through the trope of the bed trick—Merlin glamored Uthor as Gorlois, the husband of Igerna. Disguised Uthor seduces Igerna who subsequently conceives Arthur, a legendary Christian king so intriguing that his name would be taken up again in the twentieth-century animated movie *The Sword in the Stone* that I discussed in chapter 2. In the thirteenth-century Icelandic *Laxdœla saga,* the character Brynhildr is deceived into marrying Sigurðr's sworn-brother Gunnarr, just as Guðrún is deceived by Bolli into marrying him.[31] The fifteenth-century *Sigrgarðs Saga Frækna* continues similar themes—when three princesses are cursed by their father's concubine, a royal suitor must demonstrate the *bona fides* of Strategic Intelligence associated with the kingly way by continually disguising himself in order to break the spell and win their hearts. One observes similar types of deception, noble and base, in the *Nibelungenlied* (9–11 CE), *Völsunga saga*, and the *Prose* and *Poetic Edda*. This Germanic strain of Strategic Intelligence indubitably influenced the Disney animated film *Frozen* (2013), in which the protagonist Anna is deceived by her paramour Hans.[32]

Although history has documented the slick intrigue utilized by King Charlemagne in aligning himself with Muslim powers such as Ummayad Shiekh Haroun al Rashid against Byzantium in the ninth century, *La Chanson de Roland* offers an alternative history in which the Saracens are associated with trickery rather than the straightforward military prowess of Roland. Loyalty, fealty, honor, and dignity are problematically intertwined in a period in which religious confraternity did not exactly match political gerrymandering. Charlemagne's allies made for strange bedfellows—he allied with Muslim states in the Iberian peninsula as opposed to the Basques, who ultimately routed him in the Battle of Roncevaux Pass in 778 CE. In the world of *Chanson*, however, the royal uncle Ganelon is scapegoated. Ganelon, whose very name like the Hebrew "Jacob" means "deceiver," betrays his own people by colluding with Muslims in response to an apparent maneuver by Roland in which Ganelon is *voluntold* to go on a dangerous mission.[33] The ambush at Roncevaux Pass would turn out to be Charlemagne's only defeat, and subsequent ages would not forget the deception. In fact, Dante banished Ganelon to the second round of the ninth circle of hell in the *Inferno*.[34]

Both the Bishop John of Salisbury (~1115 CE) and the courtier Walter Map (~1130–1210 CE) made salient the primacy of deception in life, and both of these masters of strategy produced didactic texts that aimed to expose the illusions of the political life of the times. John of Salisbury observed that the possibility of great fortune creates the conditions for an extremely dangerous situation that often blinds men, and his source *Policraticus* is a type of strategic primer that transmits strategic values as a form of hope that mitigates human weakness in a dark era in which the standards of order and justice in civilization (law, faith, and language) had been lost.[35] The courtier Map in his *Courtier's Trifles* wrote about a variety of pranks, tricks, and cons for the purpose of making people aware of the deception vicariously through the means of storytelling. *Trifles* is also a type of primer that grounds itself in expediency which aims at opening one's eyes and ears for the dangerous game of life. In fact, it is a source of strategy that enables the blind to see the past, present, and future clearly in order to make better decisions about the way forward.[36]

Borrowing a line from the Roman dramaturge Terence's play *Andria*, *fallacia alia aliam trudit* (trick follows trick), Salisbury's text enlightens through the systematic exposure of deception at court.³⁷ This includes delegitimizing hunting, gaming, entertainers, and various types of practitioners of legerdemain and *praestigium,* such as magicians, soothsayers, prophets, astrologers, mantic artists, enchanters, dream interpreters, augurs, and interpreters of various signs and omens, supernatural and natural. The courtier Walter Map agreed—he humorously depicted antagonistic reality as the royal court itself, which was comparable with hell, bound to the visible world of insecurity and instability. Map humorously begins his text by comparing the dangers of court life with mutable time itself, quoting St. Augustine, "I exist in time, and I speak of time, but of what it is I know not." Map is "bewildered . . . I exist at court and speak of the court, but Lord knows what the court is. But like time it is mutable and alienating, demonic and predatory like a hundred-handed giant or the hydra of many heads. It is only constant in inconstancy."³⁸

Trickery and deception are everywhere in Map's *Trifles,* which appears to be an encyclopedia of deception. In the story of King Herla, the good king is tricked by the fairy folk who invite him to a banquet. Upon returning, he discovers to his horror that he has been gone for ages, and he and his band become phantom wanderers.³⁹ The King of Portugal, lured into a "snare," murders his loving wife, who was a "second Susanna."⁴⁰ Monastics are suspect—like hawks on larks, they are predators who lure knights into their abby, despoiling the Egyptians on behalf of the Hebrews.⁴¹ Map's Third and Fourth distinctions seem to be especially set on developing snare-enlightenment in the reader. The noble lie is played out in the exemplary friendship of Sadius and Galo, in which one disguised friend sacrifices himself for another.⁴² This is contrasted by the deplorable and treacherous possibilities between friends, frenemies and enemies, as demonstrated through the story of Parius and Lausus. After successfully secretly poisoning his rival, the scheming chamberlain Parius is then entrusted with his rival's son for rearing. Envious of the king's affection for the boy, Parius creates a creative scheme to sow enmity between the two—he tells the boy that he has halitosis, and that the king is disgusted by it. Horrified, the boy quickly distances himself so as not to offend the king, who then grieves over losing the love of the boy.⁴³ Interestingly enough, this same story is almost exactly mirrored in the ancient third century BCE Chinese primer of strategy, appropriately named *Strategies of the Warring States,* except in that story the victim loses her nose.⁴⁴

In Map's story about the merchants Sceva and Ollo, the envious Sceva connives with a whole village in an elaborate con designed to disenfranchise the naïve and gullible Ollo from his home and hearth, which results in his insanity and exile.⁴⁵ The perfidy and unfaithfulness of Raso's Christian wife is contemplated when she absconds through deception with her Muslim lover.⁴⁶ The imprudent lad Eudo is tricked three times, which results in the very loss of his soul. His wealth is claimed by predatory neighbors after his wealthy knight-father passes. Then, Satan himself helps the boy by disguising himself as Eudo, thus enabling the real Eudo to escape. After Satan raises his fortune, Eudo ultimately falls again into a nadir of existence when the Christian bishop refuses to receive his repentance.[47]

The didactic value of relating these stories of strategic trickery even made its way into medieval primers of rhetoric. Imagine if our middle schoolers learned how to write an essay from a primer that demonstrated the introduction, body, and conclusion of an essay by citing stories of deception! What exactly might that say about the values in our culture? Geoffrey of Vinsauf's thirteenth-century *Poetria Nova* provides an example of the rhetorical technique of abbreviation by showing how a cuckolded father outwits his adulterous wife through deceit. In response to her lie that she conceived a snow child, he sells the child off and then lies that the child melted in the hot sun.[48] What might a story like this reveal about the importance of strategic values in medieval European culture?

In addition to these trifles, the genre of comic tales known as *ridicula* is also chock full of didactic stories that relay the importance of the strategic worldview. In his study *Comic Tales of the Middle Ages*, Marc Wolterbeek characterized the medieval genre of *ridicula* as primers about fraud. This medieval literary genre obsessed with deception makes salient the primacy of fraud in life, most often unmasking the deceiver at the denouement of the story, who is often humorously trapped by his or her own lie or trap. The hero in the genre is the master of strategy, which in this era was called *ars*, the *arts of craftiness*, who is celebrated for his virtuosity.[49]

In his illuminating study, Wolterbeek provides a plethora of examples that demonstrate that this genre also functioned as medium that transmitted strategic values. There is a whole genre of songs, the *mendosa cantilena,* that celebrate lying, and lies are at the center of many narratives.[50] In one anonymous twelfth-century epigram, the philosopher Aristotle saves Athens by tricking Alexander the Great.[51] The eleventh-century author Egbert of Liège relayed a story of fraud between hunters, concluding that the deceiver who cannot deceive covertly does so overtly.[52] The story of Unibos, a medieval master of strategy parodies Christian hymnody even as it explores the theme of human manipulation. Unibos outwits social superiors and others intent on his murder, usually by identifying and leveraging his opponents' vices for his own strategic advantage. Unibos overcomes antagonistic reality and escapes poverty because he is a master of stratagem—he is the greatest of all deceivers (*magis seducens*), and deadly (*dolosus*).[53]

The figure of Unibos is but one of many that expressed strategic values in European cultures. Other notable figures include Sly Peter of the Balkans, the German rogue Till Eulenspiegel, the Priest Amis in various Germanic cultures, Reynart the Fox, and many other characters in medieval French fabliaux. These stories that express strategic values are ubiquitous in late medieval and early modern culture—and the strategic figures derived from *fabliaux* were again transmitted to subsequent literary sources. For example, Giovanni Boccaccio's (1313–1375 CE) *Decameron* includes many stories that express the strategic in a fun way—such as the strategic heroine Francesca in one story dupes two suitors by having one simulate a corpse, and she forces the other to retrieve him. Boccaccio even included the story *Gombert et les deus Clers,* originally derived from *fabliaux*, and which was subsequently reworked in Geoffrey Chaucer's (1343–1400 CE) *The Reeve's Tale* included in *The Canterbury Tales*, a story in which a miller who figuratively screws everyone over literally gets screwed in return via the bed trick.

Oriented at the fulcrum between tension and release, *la grande vie* and *la petite mort*, potency and impotency, *eros* and *thanatos*, and the potentiality of both self-esteem and meaning, what better way to articulate strategic values than through the frame of the agonistic conflict of procreation? To screw and to screw over are ultimately acts of power, attempts to win self-worth. The fact that these stories were presented as culture, in terms of storytelling, entertainment, and as jokes and trifles, should not obscure their strategic intent. These stories functioned as primers of strategy that sensitized the young and innocent to the snares of the world. Interpreting any given hostile situation, the young could ultimately beguile the beguiler through clarity of vision and sharpness of wit.[54] And the development of the strategic worldview in the cultural texts of the European Middle Ages further solidified the foundation on which early modern masters of strategy produced their stunning masterpieces.

RENAISSANCE STRATEGIC INTELLIGENCE

Mankind only does good when forced by need.[55]
Men are more prone to evil than to good.[56]

Niccolò Machiavelli

From the perspective of the cultural genealogy of Strategic Intelligence, it is crystal clear that the synthesis of classical Mediterranean and Germanic cultures directly resulted in the efflorescence of strategic thought in the cultures of early modern Europe, especially those of Golden Age Spain and Renaissance Italy. These cultures validated the need for strategy as adherents continued to face the antagonistic and ambivalent environments of their times. As with the previous chapter which was scoped to demonstrating the strategic values articulated through the foundational texts of their times, in this chapter I focus on providing cultural evidence for strategic values expressed in the most important and accessible (in translation) sources of the Renaissance. This chapter finishes our exploration of the cultural genealogy of strategic values in Western European culture by interpreting six preeminent primers of strategy, including three perverse picaresque novels from Golden Age Spain, and three dazzling dramas of intrigue from Renaissance Italy. These titles include the anonymous *La Vida de Lazarillo de Tormes* (~1553 hereafter *Life*),[57] Francisco de Quevedo's (1580–1645 CE) *El Buscón* (hereafter *Wanderer*),[58] Mateo Alemán's (1547–1615 CE) *Guzmán de Alfarache* (hereafter *Guzmán*),[59] Niccolò Machiavelli's *Mandragola,* Ludovico Ariosto's (1474–1533) *The Procuress* (*La Lena* 1538 CE),[60] and Gl'Intronati Literary Society of Siena's *Gl'Ingannati* (*The Deceived* 1538 CE).[61]

RENAISSANCE: STRATEGIC INTELLIGENCE IN SPANISH PICARESQUE

The three novels of the Spanish Golden Age are extraordinary for the way in which they re-articulate the strategic values identified in Greco-Roman culture discussed earlier. Not only does the figure of the *pícaro* (rogue) explore the intersection of the false (mendacious) through the journey (mendicant), the emerging genre of the picaresque anticipates the *bildungsroman,* a coming of age narrative in which the protagonist's maturity is developed through personal experience. This observation nicely dovetails with the features of strategic thought identified in earlier chapters, which I reiterate, as (1) personal experience as a means of sensitization to the threat and opportunity features of any given antagonistic reality; (2) this sensitization to the threat features leads to strategic vision, which is the capacity to interpret the nuances of any new environment; and (3) proper interpretation then enables appropriate adaptation and reaction, which leads to strategic advantage. The success of the *pícaro* in overcoming social asymmetries is directly tied to his virtuosic wielding of the tools of the strategist, and his ability to negotiate with ingenuity the sociocultural values of nobility, dignity, honor, and familial lineage. The voyeur is enriched vicariously through the *pícaro's* successes and failures. The lesson of the figure of the *pícaro* is that during times of disorder, chaos and injustice, kings are those who pursue the kingly way—every prince can become a king if he virtuosically thinks and acts strategically.

The author and narrators of *Vida* and *Guzmán* explicitly call out the strategic tradition by centering the narrative on the theme of seeing through and on contingency. Like the example provided by Walter Map that I discussed previously, the narrator of *Vida* claims that he is writing a trifle through which he hopes to reveal phenomena which should not have been forgotten. What the narrator seeks to bring to light is simply himself. The battle for meaning and power is made explicit—this story of Strategic Intelligence is, he tells us, comparable to the act of the first soldier to leap into battle—he does not do so because he wishes to die, but rather because he wishes to live with self-esteem, and for the sake of honor. The issue at hand is that of value and meaning, of agency and subjectivity. The figure of the *pícaro* is not only of the Odyssean exile afloat during hard times—it also depicts a person who is attempting to assert meaning and dignity in an antagonistic social reality that denies both.

There is a clear thematic link between Odysseus in the *Odyssey,* strategic Islamic beggar-kings like Abū Fath al-Iskandari, and the *pícaro*—king, beggar, and rogue are all different figures which point to the metaphorological paradigm of the strategic. King Odysseus, a character who linked the concepts of lineage, royalty, honor, dignity, nobility, freedom, necessity, contingency, mutability, indigence, and cunning, captured the imagination of Mediterranean-influenced cultures for thousands of years—and provided one model that articulated strategic heroism. But the model of the indigent king was probably less relevant to new non-aristocratic classes that emerged in early modernity than were the heroic down-and-out underdogs. The heroic rising of the underdog represents the most classical of all journeys, the journey of descent that sets the condition for ascent, which literary pedigree derives from Odysseus' descent into Hades, Socrates' *katabasis* (descent) to the Piraeus in the opening line of the *Republic* (and the ascent from the cave), and Jesus' harrowing of hell. When we subtract the feature of royalty from the above list, we realize that WWPD? *What Would the Pícaro Do?* is as comparably informative as *WWOD?*

The figure of the heroic *pícaro* in the three novels of the Spanish Renaissance is a bearer of Strategic Intelligence because the rogue both orients us to an ambivalent or antagonistic social reality and the heroically strategic means to overcome it. In fact, the anonymous author of *Life* hopes that the tales of the *pícaro* will enlighten the elite to the possibility of the greater internal nobility and heroism of the *pícaro* as opposed to the putative virtue and excellence (*ariste*) of the aristocrat who inherited nobility. The scions of aristocracy inherited good fortune rather than earning it, and they are therefore inappropriate protagonists to play the role of heroic strategists such as Odysseus who, through strength and wits when beset by misfortune, made it home to safety.[62] This sentiment is paralleled in an aphorism memorialized by another master of strategy, the Italian statesman and historian Guicciardini, who wrote that it is not possible in this world to elect the class into which one is born, nor the circumstance in which to live. In judging, look not at the circumstance of birth, but rather to the response to it. Like in comedy and tragedy, rather than respecting the role of the master or king, we pay more attention to the quality of the performer's acting of a part, rather than the identity of the role itself.⁶³

The cultural identity of the *pícaro* imparts the message that Strategic Intelligence is a preeminent means to overcome the alienation caused by societal exclusion, enabling meaning and power when it is systematically denied. The strategic identity of the *pícaro* offers a form of hope, and is an assertion of value grounded in personal agency over and above the legitimacy provided by external social structures. The Spanish strategic master Vives in his *Introduction to Wisdom* added that nobility today is but a chance birth in privilege and an empty value of the ignorant masses. "How can the undignified be called dignified, or the dishonorable be called honorable when their honor is acquired through deceit, ambition, avarice, and evil ruse?"⁶⁴ Machiavelli amplified this sentiment in Book two of his *Discorsi*, noting that deceit is actually a "necessity," and that on the whole men climb the social ladder through the use of fraud than of force.⁶⁵ This concept clearly threatens the authority and legitimacy of claims of superiority justified by the arbitrary value of lineage. If the athlete born with a silver spoon in her mouth heroically finishes the marathon, how much more heroic is it then when those handicapped by low-station also cross that finish line?—for they have run much further!

The image of the *pícaro* enacts the theme of the snare-aware, and functions as a literary and philosophical means by which minds can be sensitized to the threats of the world. In de Quevedo's words, *Guzmán* forms part of a curriculum that seeks to enlighten his prince to worldly risk. The figure of the *pícaro* is a revelation both of the maturation of young men and their endeavors, and how "though their eye-sight be clear, they will not see."⁶⁶ In Mabbe's English rendition of the dedication to the prince Don Francisco De Roias, de Quevedo sought to inoculate his prince from naivety of the snares of society. For him, falsity in the form of serpentine "evil intention" and "secret malice" are like skillful hunters that lie in wait—one discovers the mortal wound without knowing how it was even incurred. Since they are like basilisks, the strategy to defeat these terrible monsters is enabled by knowing them preemptively and vicariously through stories. Therefore, by exposing the prince vicariously to what *hispanohablantes* call *estafas de socaliñas* (impostrous graft), *artimañas* (artifices), *trucas* (tricks), and *engaños* (scams), the prudent prince can protect the commonwealth against "knaves of innocence" and "despoilers of virtue." For these types of men are "predators," from whose "subtle snares (as death traps) no person lives secure."⁶⁷

There are three features of the *pícaro* that clarify that this figure is a bearer of Strategic Intelligence. These features include a common characterization of antagonistic reality and social asymmetry, a common educational process of sensitization to the realities of the world through experience, and the mastery of strategic adaptation as a means of achieving goals. Whereas the ancient world marveled at royal and noble mendicants like Odysseus who lost all through the sudden turn of the wheel of fortune, the early modern world explored the possibility of dignity and freedom from the starting line of misfortune. What the three *pícaros* of these stories share in common is psychosocial anxiety about a threat to the very mission of meaning in life—these greenhorns are handicapped from the start by their problematically mixed pedigree. They are trapped by blood, humble birth, and base minds.[68] In lieu of the threat of treacherous and deceptive gods and monsters of unknown lands from stories handed down from classical times, early modern texts highlighted the danger of the journey amongst the world's most dangerous predators—one's kith, kin, and neighbors. As the Italian scholar Leon Battista Alberti (1404–1472 CE) proclaimed in his farcical novel about the Greek god of deception *Momus*, "man is the ultimate trauma that man must endure. Man is the pest of man"![69] The seventeenth-century Jesuit master of strategy Baltasar Gracián agreed, famously writing that human life on earth is a "militia against *malicia*," a war against human antagonism fought with stratagems and sagacity.[70]

For example, Lazarillo's father was a cheat, and his widowed mother gave birth to an illegitimate boy of mixed heritage after she took up with a dark man. In order to maintain his family, the new beau stole from the lord, and the family was ruined after the simpleton Lazarillo naively spilled the beans to the authorities. In *Wanderer*, Don Pablos' father was a scam artist who posed as a barber—his seven-year-old son pick-pocketed clients as they were shaved.[71] His mother hid her Jewish or Moorish ancestry under a respectable old Christian name, but she was a witch, a procuress, and a loose woman, a point of great shame for Pablos.[72] Although Guzmán did not suffer from a base lineage per se, his father was a crafty merchant and his mother a two-timing cozening woman.

In order to overcome social asymmetry and achieve a meaningful life of dignity, each of these young protagonists began a journey with various teachers who *habituated* their pupils to the ways of the world. Lazarillo studied with a series of masters, progressing from a blind beggar, a priest, and an impoverished but well-attired dissimulating squire who put on airs, a pardoner, a tambourine maker, a chaplain, a constable, and a lawman. Each is more morally bankrupt than the one preceding, with the most excellently bankrupt standing at the apogee of society. Although he was difficult and poor, the blind beggar is described as the "craftiest of all men." He ironically most enabled the innocent protagonist to survive when he served the penniless squire.[73] Close to death from starvation, Lazarillo leveraged the insight given to him by the blind beggar to find food. The Master Pardoner he described as a master strategist of cunning ruse.[74]

Hunger was the real master during his internships with the priest and the squire, and Lazarillo, like Odysseus, faced the existential threat of finitude through the accursed belly, which the *Odyssey* relayed "many evils to men gives." Lazarillo concurs, but interestingly suggests that intelligence is coerced by the necessity of the body, because hunger makes the wits grow keener. The young *pícaro* engaged in a life and death contest of wits with the priest, which is depicted by reference to another classical mistress of Strategic Intelligence, Queen Penelope, who by day wove and by night secretly loosed her tapestry in order to thwart her predatory suitors.[75] In the end, Lazarillo outwitted the priest due to God and wits, and slowly climbed the social ladder as he became more sensitized to the snares of the world, and developed his capacity to adapt.[76]

From the penniless yet elegantly attired squire, he learned about the reality of false appearances and of those who put on pretenses. The irony is that the penniless squire was a fancy man who appeared to all as a gentleman, but in reality he had not eaten in more than a week.[77] Not only is the episode of the squire entertaining, it is also enlightening—the effort to keep up appearances was ironically killing him. The squire's great ambition, his *summum bonum*, was to become a sycophantic private secretary to a gentleman so that he could obtain the good life. In a decadent age, the virtuous are gadflies who are unwelcome in the homes of the so-called honored and ennobled.[78] This depiction of the moral and intellectual depravity of the aristocratic classes is simultaneously an attack on the legitimacy of its philosophical foundations. This harsh critique both of the legitimacy and authority of the political order and the so-called excellence (virtue) of the gentlemanly classes gestures to the requirement for a conception of virtue-as-virtuosity rather than the older idea articulated through classical Aristotelian virtue ethics, in which virtue was understood as a good in and of itself, achieved through cultivation (habituation) for the sake of moral character, resulting in magnanimity and the civic spirit that aims for the common good.

The didactic goal of the text as a primer is also highlighted by Alfarache's English translator, who commented on the innocence of youth: "but it is, and ever will be the fashion of young fellowes, to cast themselves away headlong, upon their present pleasures, without having an eye, or any regard in the world to their future hurt; or the harme that will follow after."[79] Like Lazarillo, Guzmán also learns from masters, including a poet, a mendicant hermit-friar, a sexton, and a hidalgo who exposed the ways of the world to him, inspiring him to choose a life of roguery.[80] Wit, made sharp through the suffering made all of the difference in the world—in fact, it was a "philosopher's stone" that turned everything into gold.[81] Strategic rationality is both "liberal" and salvational—and freedom is described as the evasion of punishment.[82] The mention of the word "liberal" here is humorous as a jab at Aristotelian virtue ethics that recommended a program of liberal education that habituated the student to good character. Instead of building good character, the philosophy of the picaresque body enables the pícaro to heroically escape physical pain. Guzmán is educated strategically—he learns to adapt by serving the scion of a rich lord, and he ultimately transforms into an exemplary prankster, an eminent rogue among rogues who is almost able to pass as anybody he wishes to be.[83]

Most importantly, habitual sensitization to the threat features of any given antagonistic reality results in the ability to overcome through awareness and adaptation. This ability to be sensitive is what makes one human. The linkage of practical knowledge (*savoir vivre*), sensitivity, and enlightenment is underscored in the following passage in which Guzmán is the only one who realizes that what the crafty innkeeper offered them was donkey meat, not veal—an example of "coozening tricks which hosts put upon poor travelers."

> For my Companion, there was no care to be taken for him, all meates were alike to him; for he was borne amongst Savage people, and bred up by brutish Parents, whose palate was seasoned from the cradle with a clove of Garlicke; and your rude rusticall Clownes (as a thing not belonging to their either goodnesse, or cleanliness) in matter of taste can seldome distinguish ill from good. To most of them there is a want of perfection in their Senses; and albeit they see, yet do they not see that, which they ought to see: and though they heare, yet do they not heare that which they ought to heare . . . . But these kindes of unnurtured people are like unto Dogs.[84]

Strategic Intelligence here is transformed into a *savior faire* capacity of superior common sense and discerning aesthetic taste.

All three of our roguish heroes of Strategic Intelligence are able to shift their identities nearly as easily as one changes socks, through the virtue of adaptability. Don Pablos, for example, flourishes as a servant, an actor, a professor and a gentleman caller of the lower gentry before he became the "rabbi of ruffians," which he describes as a way of life better than any he had known previously.[85] Similarly, Lazarillo apprentices and masters the trades of beggar, acolyte, page, and water-peddler. He reckons that he makes it big time when gets the government jobs of man of justice, and town-crier.

One certainly may draw the moral lesson that strategic sneakiness always ends badly. For example, Lazarillo ends up as a husband cuckolded by an archpriest who has married Lazarillo to his own maid. One can imagine how seventeenth-century elite Spaniards, with their highly exclusive cultural values of honor and lineage, would have mocked Lazarillo. But Lazarillo appears perfectly content: what is the value of honor when honor is exposed as false? As the preface explains, honor is empty when separated from truth.

There is in this threat a subtle expression of social anxiety on the part of the elite—one can not entirely account neither for the honor or the pure lineage of one's ancestors, nor for the purity of one's own birth. Honor derived from lineage is a shaky foundation on which to build a cultural myth that justifies social superiority. When we remember that Don Pablos was nearly successful in marrying into the elite class, we recall another feature of why adaptability is so threatening—if one can appear the same and sound the same as the elite through sheer effort or trickery, then there is no ultimate foundation on which to ground a system of exclusion. The system is revealed to be arbitrary, illegitimate, unjust, and invalid.

WWPD? Should the fact that Don Pablos ultimately ends up as the "rabbi of the ruffians" and the best of scalawags compel us to conclude that Strategic Intelligence has led him along the wrong path? I would say no. Strategic Intelligence is both a framework and a tool for discerning action—it always defies the simple binary classification of good or bad, of hero or villain. The quality of Strategic Intelligence can only be discerned in how well it is used. Like all arts, it must be continually practiced until one absorbs its quintessence, as will be clarified in the masterpieces of Strategic Intelligence from the Italian Renaissance.

STRATEGIC INTELLIGENCE IN ITALIAN RENAISSANCE DRAMA

Vivere . . . militare est.
To live is to fight.[86]

Seneca (4 BCE–65 CE)

It matters then little to a general along which road
he travels, provided he has virtuosity.[87]

Niccolò Machiavelli

Nothing becomes a general more than
to anticipate the enemy's plans.[88]

Niccolò Machiavelli

Enosh hu shinnujim vekammah tebhaoth haf
Man is a living creature of varied, multiform and ever
changing nature.

Pico Della Mirandola (1463–1494 CE)

The virtuosic strategist always wins the prize in the three sixteenth-century Italian Renaissance dramas surveyed here, Machiavelli's (1469–1527 CE) *Mandragola*,[89] Ludovico Ariosto's (1474–1533 CE) *The Procuress* (*La Lena* 1538 CE),[90] and Gl'Intronati Literary Society of Siena's *The Deceived* (*Gl'Ingannati*, 1538 CE).[91] Rather than analyzing these texts as others have previously, as social satire, political allegory, or as stories that extol libertinism, important clues in the texts show that these stories are also primers of Strategic Intelligence. I do not think it an exaggeration to characterize these stories, which focus on underdog generalissimos of the strategic arts, as a celebration of human ingenuity and hope. And because they take as their primary theme Strategic Intelligence in the realm of day-to-day life, the student of Strategic Intelligence is benefitted more quickly than through perusing the conventional and tedious treatises of Strategic Intelligence one finds in the domains of military strategy and political theory.

What these stories articulate is the gospel of Strategic Intelligence—subtle stratagems enable the practitioner to achieve her heart's desire, against all odds. These primers dramatize the ancient worldview of Strategic Intelligence through the cunning deeds (*solaria durum facta*) of strategic generalissimos who utilize planning (*consilium*), foresight (*providentia*), and timing (*occasio*).[92] The generalissimo of Strategic Intelligence is one who orchestrates and outmaneuvers by interpreting the social landscape and leveraging the vulnerabilities of his co-gamers. His or her prowess, what Machiavelli calls *virtù*, is directly proportional to his or her ability to, what the Chinese refer to as *fāhuī* (發揮), "to orchestrate, to put into force, or to bring to bear," what one ancient called the "first wisdom," that is to say, victory without the use of force.[93]

The plots of all three dramas are indebted to models provided by ancient Roman comedy. However, to excavate the Strategic Intelligence from the texts, we must both acknowledge the meaning of the model in Renaissance Italian society and move beyond it to what is really being displayed on stage. The bed trick was still just as relevant to patriarchal Italy as it was to Spain because it challenged the authority and legitimacy of familial lineage and honor. The trope of the bed trick threatened the status quo—the possibility of reversing one's fortune by getting one's cock in a greater man's henhouse, figuratively speaking, delegitimized this system of cultural authority. Shifting weight to prowess (*virtù*) held important ramifications for self-esteem as young underdogs could still be heroic even if they had not been blessed by *fortuna* and lineage.[94] The laws and conventions (*νόμος/nomos*) undergirding the political order were defenseless against the Strategic Intelligence enabled by the strategic nature of bodily concern (*φύσις/physis*). Machiavelli accentuates this theme in *Mandragola* by juxtaposing fortune and nature in a zero-sum game through the mouth of the slick (*inganno*) servant Ligurio who describes the elder noble Nicia as an absolute idiot who has been blessed by fortune.[95] And Callimacho calls him a simpleton, and pointed out that his idiocy was the vulnerability that provided hope.[96] In essence, the trope of the bed trick framed reproduction as an ultimately agonistic arena in which one's excellence, *qualità*, and prowess could be manifest. And Ligurio the grifter "restores" Callimacho "to life," and gives him "too much hope," a type of hope that he wishes is not "evanescent like smoke."[97]

The idea that one could undermine the legitimacy and authority of the patriarchy through imposture was apparently very titillating, but it was hardly novel. The basic plot synopsis of each of these love stories is actually quite boring, and largely interchangeable with the next—boy desires girl, boy and girl desire each other, girl desires boy. I argue that the love story provides the conventional backdrop against which the drama of exemplary, innovative, and sophisticated stratagems were shown off. For example, the young noble Callimaco in *Mandragola* schemes to obtain the wife of the patriarch Nicia, Flavio and Licinia both contrive against her father in *La Lena*, and Lelia outwits both her father and her elderly intended in *The Deceived*. What is really fascinating about young love in these stories is the juxtaposition of *virtù*, *necessità* and *fortuna*—that is to say, the heroic capacity (*virtù*) to do what is necessary (*necessità*) to bend antagonistic reality to one's will (*fortuna*), for *fortune favors the brave*.[98] To achieve their aim, which is depicted as a life-or-death proposition, they must (*necessità*) employ the full range of strategic concepts inherited from the classical Latin past, including plans (*consilium*), tricks (*dolus*), deceit (*fraus*), calculations (*ratio*), and craftiness (*artificium*).[99] The lesson of these stories is that hope for erotic, ambitious acquisition, figured in the narratives as "young love," lies in ingenuity.

Hope is threaded through these narratives, explicitly and implicitly. The highest form of hope (*speranza*) is a good ruse which enables protagonists to escape the trap of despair. For example, the idiocy of Nicia gives Callimacho grounds for hope in *Mandragola,* and he is desperate for release from want and desire (*la voglia, et il desiderio*), a state of life that is worse than death.[100] However, despair not, Machiavelli tells us through his characters, "for there is always hope when there is machination."[101] To understand the mechanics of stratagem-as-hope in these stories, one must understand the strategic competition of two stock character types, the *pater familias* (*senex*) and the sly servant (*calliditas*), for Callimacho's hope lies in taking advantage of the information that he has on them, which leads to strategic advantage.

Hope for the underdog is made possible by the vulnerability of the *pater familias*, who can be manipulated if the strategist can clearly see his weakness. Nicia, Ilario, Fazio, Gherardo, and Virginio all function as the image of authority, legitimacy, and power, but in name only since they lack prowess (*virtù*). They are described variously in the texts as foolish, silly, imprudent, stingy, stupid, inexperienced, book-smart, insensible, gullible, naïve, and obsessed with honor; such men must be lured in and ensnared by means of deception.[102] To do so, one must strategically discern how to manipulate them. As the strategic master Gracián pointed out, "Understand the nature of those you treat with in order to divine their intentions. . . ."[103] The discerning man is master over objects and not subject to them. He delves deep into profundity, and knows to make an anatomy of another's capability—he knows them through and through as soon as he meets them . . . . With rare powers of observation he decrypts their interior. He watches carefully, understands subtleties, and reasons with discernment—he discovers, notices, grasps and understands all . . . ."[104] Find the leverage point of each—it is the art of moving wills."[105]

Nicias in *Mandragola* is the best example of this—the sly servant Ligurio uses the patriarch Nicia's desperation to have a child as the leverage point that compels Nicia to willingly cuckold himself and whore out his pious wife.[106] Friars too are strategically induced to follow the strategist's will, but carefully since "friars are cunning and astute, which is reasonable since they know all of our sins and their own. Someone who isn't familiar with them could be deceived by them, and would not be able to induce them along the intended way."[107] Friar Timoteo is astute enough to see through the ruse, realizing the strategic advantage of the great deception, and that Ligurio approached him with a test case to see how he would respond before exposing the true stratagem. And although deceived, he realizes that the deception is still to his advantage since he has been bribed.[108]

Very similar to the mention of *œconomia* of deception by St. John Chrysostom that I discussed in chapter 4, Fra Timoteo uses his power of suasion (*persuadere*) to move (*conducete*) the innocent Lucrezia along his desired path, to sleep with a stranger who will supposedly die on the morrow. He persuades her that by getting pregnant she will contribute to the "greater good" by bringing a Christian soul into the world, maintaining marital bliss, and paving the way to paradise.[109] And it is not a sin, since "it is the will that sins, not the body."[110] The master of suasion went on to say that "the Bible teaches that the daughters of Lot believed that they were the last women in the world, and therefore lay with their father. And because their intention was good, they did not sin."[111]

The true strategic masters in these Renaissance stories are not the progeny of the nobility who hope to get laid.[112] Rather, the slick servants of each of the three dramas, Ligurio, Corbolo, and Clemenzia, are the exemplary generalissimos of Strategic Intelligence who orchestrate and implement the strategic plan, outmaneuvering their opponents through sophisticated ruses. This is called out explicitly by the servant Corbolo in *La Lena:* "What's needed is that type of cunning servant I've seen in comedies, who through deceit and ruse knows how to take advantage of the codger. I may not be a Davo nor a Sosia, nor born amongst the Getae or Syrians, but couldn't I have some wiles of my own? Can't I devise a fiendish snare that aligns with Fortune, since it is supposed to favor the brave?"[113] These dramas are actually *battles* of wits—this is made explicit by Ligurio who humorously juxtaposes cuckoldry (horns, st. Coucou) with warfare: "Let's waste no more time—I'll be the captain providing the daily battle orders. Callimaco will man the right horn, and I'll be on the left. Siro will guard the rear, to fetch the fallen. The password is St. Coucou . . . come, let's set the ambush."[114] The cunning servant Corbolo in *La Lena* echoes this military strategy—"On guard! You stand guard here so that you can quickly react if they pass. You guard over there. Now that's an artillery deployed on the flanks. My forces of deceit were retreating from battle, defeated and broken. And now the hunted is the hunter of Ilario. Here he comes. Victory is all but assured if my tactics endure . . . ."[115] The army of deceits most dangerous and the many travails will ultimately be victorious in the end, in spite of Fortune, which defended Ilario's purse."[116]

All of the stealthy servants are master tacticians who orchestrate multi-pronged strategic campaigns. The generalissimos of *Mandragola* dramatize the strategic arts of generalship that Machiavelli described in his *Discorsi*—the master of strategy analyzes the details of the circumstances just like a virtuosic general who knows both the "lay of the land," and the "nature of the country," a skill which is honed through hunting, the most warlike activity.[117] Ligurio entraps Nicias by enlisting the help of Nicias' mother-in-law Sostrata, who ironically becomes a procuress, and the confessor of Nicias' wife, Fra Timoteo. Ligurio traps Fra Timoteo by opportunistically leveraging the friar's greediness, and greed similarly characterizes Lena's weakness in *La Lena*. Sly servants practice all of the strategic arts, and they even defraud each other—for example, by lying about the handsome men at a certain inn, the strategic servant manipulates the pedant by appealing to his homosexual inclinations, coercing him to go to one inn over another.[118] The furtive servant Pasquella in *The Deceived* even prays a special prayer of strategic trickery to ward off an unwanted suitor: "Demon, demon, haunting me night and day, erect you came, and erect still you'll go away. Sad, so sad, the timing was bad, you sought to pick me, but you've been had. Amen."[119]

What is most extraordinary about these stories of heroic strategy is that each resolves itself cathartically with a scene of requited love. In *Mandragola*, Callimacho obtains the object of his desire, his beloved benefits from the prowess of younger lover, and Nicias the elder presumably gets an heir. In *Lena*, the young lovers successfully get together, and the vengeful procuress Lena is reconciled to her lover Fazio. In *The Deceived*, the brother and sister pair both turn trysts into a respectable marriage. And here the voyeur is again confronted with the paradox—the best hope that humanity has to offer, its ingenuity, is also the nadir of human behavior. Strategic Intelligence can be quite simply despicable. Paradoxically, human ingenuity as hope is both comic and tragic—we are compelled to laugh, cry, and rage.

Although I discontinue excavating the cultural genealogy of Strategic Intelligence in Western Civilization at this point in the seventeenth century, it by no means disappeared, as evidenced by my discussion of the twentieth-century *The Sword and the Stone* in chapter 2. Rather, strategic values have been transmitted in every cultural domain up to the present time. Strategic Intelligence is present in Pico Della Mirandela's famous fifteenth-century humanistic essay *On the Dignity of Man*, when he describes the great trick to be akin to "Circe's wiles" and man's metamorphosis into beastliness rather than deification.

> Who will look not admire our chameleon? Or, who will more admire another? Because of man's ability to transform himself, Asclepius of Athens correctly said that man's mutability was symbolized by the figure of Proteus in the mysteries . . . and which the Pythagoreans transform criminals into brutes . . . whence the Chaldean saying *Enosh hu shinnujim vekammah tebhaoth haf*— "man is a living creature of varied, multiform and ever-changing nature."[120]

The Political Philosopher Thomas Hobbes (1588–1679 CE) in his seventeenth-century classic *Leviathon* claimed that equality is only possible because Nature has neutralized stronger bodies with quicker minds, and the weak can overcome the strong through secret machination.[121] John Milton (1607–1674 CE) in *Paradise Lost* "attributes intelligence of the highest order to the devil."[122] We must discuss elsewhere Cartesian anxiety and skepticism at the base of Western foundationalism, which was figured through Rene Descartes' (1596–1650 CE) evil genius who is *quantumvis potens*, *quantumvis callidus*, and *summe potens* and *callidus* (ultimately powerful and cunning).[123] The Dutch philosopher Baruch Spinoza (1632–1677 CE) wrote that "fish are naturally conditioned to swim in water, the greater devour the lesser; therefore, sovereign natural right is that which enables the life of fish, and the greater to consume the lesser . . . . The right and ordinance of nature" (*Jus et Institutum naturae*) . . . "does not forbid contention, hatred, wrath, nor cunning deceit."[124] The famous philosopher of liberty Jean-Jacques Rousseau (1712–1778 CE) wrote that *L'homme est né libre, et partout il est dans les fers* (mankind is free, but everywhere shackled), and that civil society itself was founded on deceit when simpletons believed the first man to claim ownership.[125]

Immanuel Kant demonized the illegitimate deception of tradition that he referred to as a religion of priestcraft which was the most ancient fiction.[126] Friedrich Nietzsche thought that moderns had been deceived historically by a transvaluation of moral values motivated by the *ressentiment* of prey.[127] Martin Heidegger (1889–1976 CE) constructed a philosophical grand narrative based on the withdrawal and self-concealment of Being. Ludwig Wittgenstein thought that philosophy was the domain in which flies might be liberated from the self-imposed trap of the fly-bottle. Jean-Paul Sartre and the existentialists articulated the possibility of self-deception as "bad faith" (*mal fides/mauvaise foi*), and absurdists like Albert Camus (1913–1960 CE) thought that we should be happy like Sisyphus in our heroic striving for meaning even though we are trapped in absurd meaninglessness.

Sigmund Freud (1856–1939 CE) and the psychoanalytic tradition contended that the human is often deceived by irrational impulses arising from the subterranean realm of the psyche, and the twentieth-century North American Psychoanalyst Ernest Becker asserted that our most meaningful heroic roles which were culturally validated were actually vital lies. The postmodern deconstructionist Jacques Derrida (1930–2004 CE), re-interpreting the Biblical story of the sacrifice of Isaac after reading the existentialist religionist Søren Kierkegaard (1813–1855 CE), traced social responsibility to the religious trap of the *mysterium tremendum*, a frightful double secret of fear and trembling that requires silence and secrecy—which the American philosopher Francis Ambrosio beautifully characterized as the "encrypted secret buried in the tomb of the dissimulation of the Gift of Death figured as sacrifice."[128] Perhaps nowhere has the cultural model of the snare-aware been so clarified as in the French Sociologist of Knowledge Michel Foucault's analysis of Immanuel Kant's eighteenth-century essay *What is Enlightenment*? (*Was ist Aufklärung?*)—for Foucault and Kant, enlightenment (*aufklärung/Lumières*) is *ausgang* and *sortie*, "an *exit* or *escape* from immaturity."[129] Kant's famous charge *sapere aude*! (dare to know) is then, also a moral imperative of escape—it is the reworked soteriology of the snare-aware.

Strategic Intelligence refuses to be boxed in: it always insists on hope. As the most notorious modern strategic master Machiavelli pointed out, "I well affirm that people can subordinate, but not oppose fortune, and that they can weave, not break its warp. No matter what happens, one must never despair because there is always hope."[130] For the enlightened snare-aware, hope is a continuous and radical opening of possibility. These values and worldview are so compelling that Strategic Intelligence has been transmitted in Western Civilization continuously since the dawn of history, and has been invested with the highest forms of authority and legitimacy. No matter to what degree culture, language, and ways of life have evolved, strategic values have been embedded in cultural products. Although Strategic Intelligence itself is cunningly deceptive, often presenting itself as mere shallow entertainment, it is, in fact, a philosophically informed worldview and way of life guided by strategic values, and a general approach to the threat of any given antagonistic reality.

NOTES

1. *Che si viene di bassa a gran fortuna più con la fraude; che con la forza. Vedesi pertanto i Romani ne' primi augumneti loro non essere mancati etiam della fraude; la quale fu sempre necessaria a usare a coloro che di piccoli principii vogliono a sublimi gradi salire: la quale è meno vituperabile quanto è più coperta, come fu quest de' Romani.* Machiavelli, *Discorsi Sopra la Prima Deca di Tito Livio*, *Discourses on the First Decade of Titus Livy,* 2.13.

2. Appian, *The Punic Wars*, 2:12. Appian. *The Foreign Wars,* trans. Horace White (New York: Macmillan, 1899), Perseus Digital Library, Tufts University, accessed 27 April 2017, http://perseus.uchicago.edu/perseus-cgi/citequery3.pl?dbname=GreekFeb2011&getid=1&query=App.%20Pun.%2014.

3. Everett L. Wheeler, *Stratagem and the Vocabulary of Military Trickery* (Leiden: E. J Brill, 1988).

4. *Aeneid*: 1.573–582. *Virgil's Aeneid* (Boston, Ginn, 1923), trans. J. B. Greenough, Perseus Digital Library, Tufts University, accessed 17 January 2019, http://www.perseus.tufts.edu/hopper/text?doc=Perseus%3atext%3a1999.02.0055 see also Riggs Alden Smith, *The Primacy of Vision in Virgil's Aeneid* (Austin: University of Texas Press, 2005), 28.

5. Homer, *Odyssey,* 6.229–235, *Aeneid*: 1.825–832, Smith, *Primacy,* 30.

6. Virgil, *Aeneid.*

7. Virgil, *Aeneid.*

8. Virgil, *Aeneid*, 1.990–996.

9. Virgil, *Aeneid*, 5.1126–1132. Smith, *Primacy*, 33–36.

10. Virgil, *Aeneid*, 7.312–7.605. Smith, *Primacy*, 36–39.

11. Boethius, *The Consolation of Philosophy*, trans. W. V. Cooper, 1908. Ex-classics Project, *The Consolation of Philosophy by Anicius Manlius Severinus Boethius*, 2009, accessed 9 February 2018, https://www.exclassics.com/consol/consol.pdf.

12. Boethius, *Consolation.*

13. J. Horovitz, "Traces of the Greek Mimes in the Orient" in Clifford Edmund Bosworth, *The Mediaeval Islamic Underworld: The Banū Sāsān in Arabic Society and Literature* (Leiden: E. J. Brill, 1976), 19, 96.

14. Clifford Edmund Bosworth, *The Mediaeval Islamic Underworld: the Banū Sāsān in Arabic Society and Literature* (Leiden: E.J. Brill, 1976), 20.

15. Bosworth, *Mediaeval*, 20, ix, 96.

16. Badí Al-Zamán Al-Hamadhání, Maqámát, *The Maqámát of Badí Al-Zamán Al-Hamadhání*, trans. W. J. Prendergast (London: Curzon Press, 1973), 38–40.

17. Al-Hamadhání, *Maqámát*, 29.

18. Al-Hamadhání, *Maqámát*, 53–58.

19. Al-Hamadhání, *Maqámát*, 50–53.

20. Al-Hamadhání, *Maqámát*, 67–68.

21. Al-Hamadhání, *Maqámát*, 32.

22. Al-Hamadhání, *Maqámát*, 40–46.

23. Al-Hamadhání, *Maqámát*, 58.

24. Machiavelli, *Discorsi,* 1.5.

25. *Fallite fallentes: ex magna parte profanum sunt genus: in laqueos quos posuere, cadant.* Ovid, *Ars Amatoria,* 1.645–46.

26. Garret Olmsted, "The Earliest Narrative Version of the Táin: Seventh-Century poetic references to the Táin bó Cúailnge," *Emania* 10 (1992), 5–17.

27. Philip O'Leary, "Choice and Consequence in Irish Heroic Literature," *Cambrian Mediaeval Studies* 27 (Summer 1994), 49. Philip O'Leary, "Magnanimous Conduct in Irish Heroic Literature," *Eigse* 25 (1991), 28–44.59. Philip O'Leary, "Verbal deceit in the Ulster cycle," *Éigse* 21 (1986), 16–26.

28. *Beowulf,* trans. David Wright (New York: Penguin Books, 1957), 44.

29. *Ahi ! Gauvains, fait il, ahi! Vostre granz sens m'a esbahi ; Par grant sens m'avez retenu.* Chrétien de Troyes. *Erec et Enide.* vv. 4143–45.42.

30. Marco Prost, "Female Cunning on the Edges of Chivalry in Gerbert de Montreuil's Continuation to the Conte du Graal," Selected Proceedings from "On the Edge," March 2015, University of Reading, accessed 7 February 2018, http://blogs.reading.ac.uk/trm/.

31. Margaret Clunies Ross, *The Cambridge Introduction to The Old Norse-Icelandic Saga* (Cambridge: Cambridge University Press, 2010), 130.

32. Chris Buck, Jennifer Lee, Dirs, *Frozen,* Walt Disney Studios, 2013.

33. From Italian *inganno.*

34. In Canto XXXII of the *Inferno* (*Divine Comedy*), Dante banished Ganelon (*Ganellone*) to Cocytus in the depths of hell as punishment for his betrayal to his country.

35. John of Salisbury, *Policraticus,* in *Frivolities of Courtiers and Footprints of Philosophers: Being a Translation of the First, Second and Third Books and Selections from the Seventh and Eighth Books of the Policraticus of John of Salisbury,* trans., Joseph B. Pike (Minneapolis: University of Minnesota Press, 1938), Book 1, chapter 1, 11.

36. Walter Map, *De Nugis Curialium: Courtier's Trifles,* ed. & trans. M.R. James (Oxford: Clarendon Press, 1983), 4.1, 279.

37. Map, *Nugis, Book 2, 136.* From Terence *Andria* line 752.

38. Map, *Nugis,* 3.

39. Map, *Nugis,* 1.11, 27–31.

40. Map, *Nugis,* 1.12, 31–37.

41. Map, *Nugis,* 1.25, 85.

42. Map, *Nugis,* 2, 211–247.

43. Map, *Nugis,* 3.3, 247–263.

44. A translation of this can be found at Paul Rakita Goldin, "*Miching Mallecho:* The Zhanguo ce and Classical Rhetoric," *Sino-Platonic Papers,* No. 41 (1993), 23–24, accessed 26 January 2018, http://sino-platonic.org/complete/spp041_zhanguoce_intrigues.pdf. From 5.23bf.; 17.815f.; 200.

45. Map, *Nugis,* 4.16, 393–403. Compare this with the honorable deceit in the American movie *Doc Hollywood* (1991), the Disney/Pixar animated film *Cars,* and *The Grand Seduction* (2013).

46. Map, *Nugis,* 3.4, 263–271.

47. Map, *Nugis,* 4.6, 315–341.

48. Marc Wolterbeek, *Comic Tales of the Middle Ages: an Anthology and Commentary* (New York: Greenwood Press, 1991), 44. Known in French as *L'enfant de neige*.

49. Wolterbeek, *Comic*, 1.

50. Wolterbeek, *Comic*, 13.

51. Wolterbeek, *Comic*, 68–69.

52. Wolterbeek, *Comic*, 52.

53. Master of stratagem (*artificem versutiae*). Cleverness (*calliditas*). Wolterbeek, *Comic*, xiii. 33.

54. Beguile the beguiler (*sic fraud framed vicerat*) through the sharpness of wit (*quia suo ingenio decepti fuerunt*). Wolterbeek, *Comic*, 52.

55. Che gli uomini non operono mai nulla bene, se non per necessità. Machiavelli, *Discorsi*, 1.3.

56. Perché sendo gli uomini più proni al male che al bene. Machiavelli, *Discorsi*, 1.9.

57. *La Vida de Lazarillo de Tormes*, ed. H. J. Chaytor (Manchester: The University Press, 1922), Hathi Trust Digital Library, accessed 16 January 2019, https://babel.hathitrust.org/cgi/pt?id=uc1.$b256846;view=2up;seq=8. All following citations (*Rogue, Lazarillo*), refer to the page of translation in David Frye, trans., *Lazarillo de Tormes & The Grifter: Two Novels of the Low Life in Golden Age Spain* (Indianapolis: Hackett: 2015).

58. Francisco de Quevedo, *El Buscón*, In *Vida del Buscón* (Madrid: Ediciones de "La Lectura," 1911). Based on the Zaragoza 1626 edition. Hathi Trust Digital Library, accessed 16 January 2019, https://babel.hathitrust.org/cgi/pt?id=mdp.39015067208168;view=2up;seq=8.

59. Mateo Alemán, *Guzmán de Alfarache*, Edited and transcribed by Julio Cejador (Madrid: Renacimiento, 1913). Reprint of Coimbra, edition published in 1600. Hathi Trust Digital Library, access 16 January 2019, https://catalog.hathitrust.org/Record/006137328. Translation at James Mabbe (1623), *The Rogue or the Life of Guzman de Alfarache* (New York: AMS Press, 1967).

60. Ludovico Ariosto, *La Lena, Comedia*. Stampata in Vinegia: Per maestro Bernardino Vinitiano de Vitali (1535), Hathi Trust Digital Library, accessed 2 February, 2019, https://babel.hathitrust.org/cgi/pt?id=gri.ark:/13960/t3qv9vv2p;view=2up;seq=8.

61. Translations of which can be found in *Five Italian Renaissance Comedies*, ed. Bruce Penman (Harmondsworth: Penguin Books, 1978).

62. *Lazarillo*, 4.

63. Non si può in questo mondo eleggere el grado in che l'uomo ha a nascere, non le faccende e la sorte con che l'uomo ha a vivere; però a laudare o riprendere gli uomini s'ha a guardare non la fortuna in che sono, ma come vi si maneggiano drento, perché la laude o biasimo degli uomini ha a nascere da' comportamenti loro, non dallo stato in che si truovano; come in una commedia o tragedia non è più in prezzo chi porta la persona del padrone e del re, che chi porta quella di uno servo, ma solamente si attende chi la porta meglio. Francesco Guicciardini, *Ricordi Politici E Civili*, in *Opere inedite di Francesco Guicciardini*, edited by Piero Luigi Guicciardini (Firenze: Barbèra, Bianchi e comp., 1857–67), Hathi Trust Digital Library, accessed

17 January 2019, https://babel.hathitrust.org/cgi/pt?id=uc1.$b502397;view=2up;seq=208;size=150, 164.

64. *Iam nobilitas quid est aliud, quàm nascendi sors, & opinio à populi stultitia inducta? ut quæ sæpenumero latrociniis quæritur. Vera, & folida noblitas à virtute nascitur, stultumque est gloriari te parentem habuisse bonum, quum sis ipse malus, & turpitudine tua dedecori sis pulchritudini generis.* 54: *Dignitates quis potest sic appellare, quum indignissimis quoque hominibus contingant? nempe fraude, ambitione,præmiis, pessimis artibux quæsitæ.* Juan Luis Vives, *Introductio* 47–48.

65. *Che si viene di bassa a gran fortuna più con la fraude; che con la forza.* Machiavelli, *Discorsi*, 2.13.

66. *Rogue*, 20.

67. *Rogue*, 11.

68. *Rogue*, 9.

69. *Homo hominid aerumnarum ultima? Pestis est homo homini!* Leon Battista Alberti, *Momus*, trans. Sarah Knight (Cambridge, MA: Harvard University Press, 2003), Book 2, paragraph 102, 185.

70. *Milicia es la vida del hombre contra la malicia del hombre, pelea la sagazidad con estratagemas de intencion.* Baltasar Gracián, *Oráculo Manual y Arte de Prudencia*, in *Obras de Lorenzo Gracian: Tomo Primero, que contiene El Criticon, Primera, Segunda y Tercera Partes, El Oraculo, y El Heroe* (Madrid: Universidad Complutense de Madrid, 1664. Hathitrust), accessed 14 January 2019, HathiTrust https://babel.hathitrust.org/cgi/pt?id=ucm.5316526610;view=2up;seq=462;size=150451.

71. *Lazarillo*, 60.

72. *Lazarillo*, 63.

73. *Lazarillo*, 7.

74. *Lazarillo*, 42.

75. *Lazarillo*, 21–22.

76. *Lazarillo*, 17.

77. *Lazarillo*, 31, 35.

78. *Lazarillo*, 39.

79. *Rogue*,106.

80. *Rogue*, 126.

81. *Lazarillo*, 122.

82. *Lazarillo*, 128, 61.

83. *Rogue*, 23, 84–85.

84. *Rogue*, 125–126, 129–130.

85. *Lazarillo*, 179.

86. Seneca, *Epistles Morales*, 96.5.

87. *Importa, pertanto, poco ad uno capitano, per qualunque di queste vie e' si cammini, pure che sia uomo virtuoso, e che quella virtù lo faccia riputato intra gli uomini.* Machiavelli, *Discorsi*, 3.21.

88. *Nessuna cosa è più degna d'uno capitano, che presentire i partiti del nimico.* Machiavelli, *Discorsi*, 3.18.

89. Machiavelli, *La Mandragola The Mandrake*, in *La Mandragola: Comedia di Niccolò, Macchiavelli Fiorentino* (Venetia: Per Plinio Pietrasanta, 1554). Hathi Trust

Digital Library, accessed 14 January 2019, https://babel.hathitrust.org/cgi/pt?id=gri.ark:/13960/t3908r537;view=2up;seq=6.

90. Lodovico Ariosto, *La Lena: Comedia* (Stampata in Vinegia: Per maestro Bernardino Vinitiano de Vitali, 1535), Hathi Trust Digital Library, accessed 16 January 2019, https://catalog.hathitrust.org/Record/102217675.

91. Accademici Intronati di Siena, *Gl'Ingannati the Deceived*, In *Commedie del Cinquecento*, ed. Ireneo Sanesi (Bari: G. Laterza, 1912), Hathi Trust Digital Library, accessed 16 January 2019, https://babel.hathitrust.org/cgi/pt?id=uc1.$b732928;view=2up;seq=320.

92. Everett L. Wheeler, *Stratagem and the Vocabulary of Military Trickery* (Leiden: E. J. Brill, 1988), 1.

93. First wisdom (πρώτη σοφία), Wheeler, 7.

94. For a fuller treatment of intergenerational conflict of the times as represented in drama, see Anthony Ellis, *Old Age, Masculinity, and Early Modern Drama: Comic Elders on the Italian and Shakesperean Stage* (Farnham: Ashgate, 1988), 63–115.

95. Machiavelli, *Mandragola*, Act 4.

96. *La semplicità di Messer Nicia mi fa sperare.* Machiavelli, *Mandragola* Act 4:1.

97. *Tu mi resusciti, questa è troppo gran promessa , pascimi di troppo grande speranza! d'una speranza, che io temo non se ne vada in fumo.* Machiavelli, *Mandragola*, Act 1.

98. Machiavelli, *Discorsi*.

99. Wheeler, *Stratagem*, 56.

100. *Io non credo che sia nel mondo il più sciocco uomo di costui, quanto la Fortuna l'ha favorito. E gli ricco, egli bella Donna . . . che Callimaco ha che sperare.. meglio è morire che viver così.* Act 1.

101. *E' non e mai alcuna cosa sì disperata, che non vi sia qualche uid di poterne sperare; in speranza da qualche partito.* Machiavelli, *Mandragola* Act 1:17.

102. *Lo conducono in qualche luogo, che gli far anno vergogna . . . dove si tenda questo loro inganno.* Machiavelli, *Mandragola* Act 2.

103. *Comprehension de los genios con quien trata. Para conocer los intentos, conocida bien la causa, se conoce el efecto.* Gracián, *Oracle*, Aphorism 273, 154. 507.

104. *Hombre juizioso, y notante. Señoreale el de los objetos dèl. Sonda luego el fondo de la mayor profundidad: sabe hazer anatomía de un caudal con perfección. En viendo un personage, le comprehende, y lo censura por essencia. De raras observaciones, gran descifrador de la mas recatada interioridad. Nota actor concibe futile, infiere, juizioso, todo lo descubre, advierte, alcança, y comprehende.* Gracián, *Oracle*, Aphorism 49, accessed 14 January 2019, https://babel.hathitrust.org/cgi/pt?id=ucm.5316526610;view=2up;seq=470 459.

105. *Hallarle su torcedor a cada uno. Es el arte de mover voluntades.* Gracián, *Oracle*, Aphorism 26, accessed 14 January 2019, https://babel.hathitrust.org/cgi/pt?id=ucm.5316526610;view=2up;seq=466454.

106. Machiavelli, *Mandragola*, 28.

107. *Questi frati son trincati, astuti, è ragionevole, perché sanno i peccati nostri e' loro; chi non è pratico con esi, potrebbe ingannarsi, à non li sa per condurre à suo proposito.* Machiavelli, *Mandragola* Act 3, Scene 2.

108. Chi s'habbia giutato?Que to tristo de Ligurio ne venne à me con quella prima novella per tentarmi, perché se io non glie la consentiva, non mi haurebbe detta questa, per non palesare i disegni loro, senza utile, di quella ch'era falsa non si curavano. Egliè vero, che io ci sono stato giuntato; nondimeno questo giunto e con mio utile. Machiavelli, *Mandragola*, 3.9.

109. Che voi ingraviderete, acquisterete un'anima à Messer Domenedio.

110. La voluntà è quella che pecca, non il corpo.

111. Dice la Bibbia, che le figliole di Lotto credendosi de essere rimase sole nel mondo, usarono col padre;Et perché la loro intenzione fu buona, non peccarono.

112. With the exception of Lelia in *The Deceived* who proactively disguises herself as a page to get the object of her desire. Gl'Intronati, *The Deceived*.

113. *Bisognaria d'un servo, quale fingere Vedut' ho qualche volta in le comedie, Che questa somma con frauds, & fallacia Sapesse de'l boreal del vecchio mungere, Deh se ben io non son Davo, ne Sosia, Se ben non nacqui tra,i, Gets, ne in Siria, Non ho in questa testacea anch'io malitia, Non sbarco ordir un giunt'an ch'io, che tessere, Habbia fortuna poi, lacuali propitia Come si dice, a gl' audaci suol essere.* Ariosto, *La Lena*, 3.

114. *Non perdiam più tempo qui, io voglio essere il capitano, ordinare l'essercito per la giornata, maldestro corno sia proposto Callimaco, al ministro io, intra le due corna starà qui il Dottore, Siro sia retroguardo, per dare sussidio à quella banda che inclinasse. Il nome sia San Cuccù . . . mettiam l'aguato . . .* St. Coucou was the patron saint of adultery. Machiavelli, *Mandragola* Act 4.

115. *Hora fermatevi. Tu qui, e, tien l'occhio, che se la passassino Le carta, in un momento posso correra. E tu à quest' altra via farai la guardia, Post ho l'artegliaria à li canti, facciano Qui testa ormai le bugie, che fuggivano Cacciate, e, rotte, & tornando con impeto Hilario, che l'hanea cacciate, caccino, Ma eccolo uscir fuor, pur ch' elle possano A' questo duro principio resistere, Non temo non tavern poi vitoria . . . .* Ariosto, *Lena*, Act 5.

116. *Ben succede l'impresa, barra l'esercito. De le bugie doppo tanti pericoli, Doppoi tanti travagli al fin vittoria, Mal grado di fortuna, che dessendere Tolt'havea contra me il borsel d' Hilarie . . . .* Ariosto, *Lena*, Act 5.

117. *Che uno capitano debbe essere conoscitore de' siti..e de' paesi." Si acquista più mediante le cacce che per veruno altro esercizio.* Machiavelli, *Discorsi*, 3.39.

118. Gl'Intronati, *Deceived*.

119. *Fantasima, fantasima, che di e notte vai, se a coda ritta ci venisti, a coda ritta te n'andrai. Tristi con tristi, in mal'ora ci venisti e me coglier ci credesti e'ngannato ci remanesti. Amen.* Gl'Intronati, *Deceived*, Act 4.

120. *Quis hunc nostrum chamaeleonta non admiretur? Aut omnino quis aliud quicquam admiretur magis? Quem non immerito Asclepius Atheniensis versipellis huius et se ipsam transformantis naturae argumento per Protheum in mysteriis significari dixit . . . Et Pythagorici scelestos homines in bruta deformant et . . . Hinc illud Chaldeorum idest homo varias ac multiform et dusultoriae naturae animal.* Giovanni Pico Della Mirandola, *De Dignitate Hominis* "Oration on the Dignity of Man."

121. Thomas Hobbes, *Leviathan*, 13.

122. John Erskine, "The Moral Obligation to Be Intelligent," in *The Moral Obligation to Be Intelligent and Other Essays* (Indianapolis: Bobbs-Merrill 1921).

123. René Descartes, *Meditations on First Philosophy. Deus deceptor*, French *dieu trompeur*.

124. *Non contentiones, non odia, non iram, non dolos, nec absolute aliquid, quod appetitus suadet, aversari . . . Pisces a natura determinati sunt ad natandum, magni ad minores comedendum, adeoque pisces summo naturali jure aqua potiuntur, et magni minores comedunt . . . .* Baruch Spinoza, *Tractatus Theologico-Politicus*, 16.

125. *Le premier qui, ayant enclos un terrain, s'avisa de dire: Ceci est a moi, et trouva des gens assez simples pour le croire, fut le vrai fondateur de la sociéte civile.* Jean-Jacques Rousseau, *Discourse on the Origins of Inequality/ Discours sur l'origine de l'inegalite*.

126. Immanuel Kant, *Religion Within the Limits of Reason Alone*, trans. Theodore M. Greene and Hoyt H. Hudson (New York: Harper, 1960), 15.

127. See herd instinct (11), beast of prey (22, 90), lambs and bird of prey (25), Nietzsche, *Genealogy*.

128. Jacques Derrida, *Littérature au secret: une filiation impossible*, in Jacques Derrida, *Donner la mort* (Paris: Galilée, 1999). Francis J. Ambrosio, *Dante and Derrida: Face to Face* (Albany, NY: State University of New York Press, 2007), 226. Kierkegaard, Søren. *Fear and Trembling*. Translated by Alastair Hannay. Penguin Classics; Reprint edition January 7, 1986.

129. Michel Foucault, *"What is Enlightenment?"* in *The Foucault Reader*, ed. Paul Rabinow (New York: Pantheon Books, 1984), 32–50. *Qu'est-ce que les Lumières?*

130. *La fortuna accecca gli animi degli uomini, quando la non vuole che quegli si opponghino a' disegni suoi. "Affermo, bene, di nuovo, questo essere verissimo, secondo che per tutte le istorie si vede, che gli uomini possono secondare la fortuna e non opporsegli; possono tessere gli orditi suoi, e non rompergli. Debbono, bene, non si abbandonare mai; perché, non sapendo il fine suo, e andando quella per vie traverse ed incognite, hanno sempre a sperare, e sperando non si abbandonare, in qualunque fortuna ed in qualunque travaglio si truovino.* Machiavelli, *Discorsi*, 2.29.

Chapter 6

Toward a Cultural Genealogy of Chinese Strategic Intelligence

夫事以密成，語以泄敗.
*From secrecy success,
From disclosure doom.*

Hán Fēizi 韓非子 (280–233 BCE)[1]

弱之肉，强之食
The weak are meat, the strong do eat.

Hán Yù 韩愈 (768–824 CE)[2]

少不讀水滸, 老不讀三國
*Youth should not read Outlaws of the Marsh,
Elders should not read Three Kingdoms.*
Chinese saying

何異虱處裈中乎?
How does (the great man) differ from the louse in the crotch?

Ruǎn Jí 阮籍 (210–263 CE)

    I previously hypothesized that the intellectual foundation of strategic thought derives from the necessity of life itself, and that culture is the medium in which strategic values are memorialized and transmitted. I used the metaphors of the tree of life and cultural genealogy to trace the cultural evidence from prehistoric Mediterranean and Near Eastern cultures that influenced the development of the Western tree, while speculating about an invisible rhizomatic sub-structure that precedes the tree. That rooting, rhizomatic substructure I understand to be the paradoxical metaphorological paradigm of *life is death*. If my hypothesis about Strategic Intelligence is correct, I can again hypothesize that other civilizations may have transmitted strategic values in cultural products to the degree that they have validated the strategic as a form of meaning that is worthy of memorializing. Moreover, I assert that as rhizomatic diffusion puts forward shoots in each generation that encounters new antagonistic and ambivalent environments, these novel cultural, linguistic, and historically conditioned environments will influence the expression of the types of trees the shoots become in the forests of strategic cultures.

This chapter considers the forest that is Strategic Intelligence, that is the degree to which the root metaphor of the strategic might be operating in other cultural patrimonies, the ways that it has been expressed, and the possibility of recovering the global and universal pedigrees of strategic rationality. The questions I explore in the next three chapters are (1) To what degree do the identities of heroic strategists in cultural sources from Chinese civilization exhibit the values of Strategic Intelligence? (2) Is/are Strategic Intelligence(s) as core to the Chinese royal *Way* as it was for Zeus, Athena, Odysseus, Fox, Moses, Tamar, Jesus, and the *pìcaros*?[3] (3) Do Chinese cultural sources also depict an orientation to an antagonistic environment that holds human meaning at risk, and which necessitates the use of Strategic Intelligence? (4) And do Chinese versions of Strategic Intelligence offer hope?

TOWARD A GLOBAL STRATEGIC INTELLIGENCE

Like my depiction of the Western cultural tree which roots lie in various ancient Near Eastern and Mediterranean cultures, modern China's cultural roots are similarly culturally diverse. We cannot rule out the possibility that early middle kingdoms were influenced by neighbors, themselves also heirs to the Middle and Near Eastern cultures that influenced Greco-Roman thought discussed earlier.[4] The influence of South Asia on thought in the middle kingdoms is well documented, as is the influence of North Asian cultural elites who ruled various middle kingdom polities in different periods. A rudimentary survey of the foundational sources of other Eurasian cultures reveals the intriguing existence of heroic Strategic Intelligence that parallels its descent in Western civilization. In the Islamic tradition, Qur'ānic lore often praises divinely heroic Strategic Intelligence as *makir* (ركام) "cunning, planning, foxy, sly, scheming," and which is translated as plans in the following verses:

- Do they feel secure from Allah's devising? No one feels secure from Allah's devising except the people who are losers.[5]

- When the faithless plotted against you to take you captive, or to kill or expel you. They plotted and Allah devised, and Allah is the best of devisers.[6]
- When We let people taste [Our] mercy after a distress that has befallen them, behold, they scheme against Our signs! Say, "Allah is more swift at devising." Indeed Our messengers write down what you scheme.[7]
- Surely those who had gone before them had also plotted; but God's is all the *planning*.[8]

In addition to the stories of al-Iskandari and Abū Zayd in the Arabic middle ages discussed in chapter 5, strategic values were also disseminated over time via the cultural identities of strategic tricksters that populate Islamic cultural sources in Iranian and Turkish forms, indubitably enabled by historical processes of cultural diffusion along cultural networks such as the Silk Road. In Abu 'l-Qasim Firdowsi Tusi's (940–1020 CE) epic poem *Shahnameh (Book of Kings)*, a text that has been described as "the essence of Iranian nationhood," primeval conflict is engendered when the evil Ahriman hatches a plot with his son Khazuran against King Kayumars. Later King Zahhak is repeatedly tricked by devilish plots, and the hero Rostam can only slay the dragon and witches through cunning strategy.[9] This is mirrored by many stories of deception and strategy in the Seljuk vizier Nizam al-Mulk's (1018–1092 CE), *Siyasatnama (Book of Government)*, such as when Nushirwan the Just exposes the religious chicanery of Mazdak.[10] *Arabian Nights* is an extended ruse on the part of the raconteur who continues to tell stories every night in order to stave off execution, and the *Conference of the Birds,* by Farid Ud-Din Attar (1145–1221 CE), is written as a beneficial deception that intends to lead the Sufi neophyte into Enlightenment—the quest for the elusive Simorgh is ultimately a journey toward self.[11]

The figure of the cunning magician functions as another cultural identity that expresses the values of Strategic Intelligence in the cultural products of Islamic Asia, such as the tales of Amir Hamza narrated in the *Hamzanama*, a text which roots have grown out of the cross-fertilization of Iranian and Indian cultural traditions.[12] The sly Amar is the chief of the strategists, the "general" over a 100,000 others. Like the wizards duel in Disney's *Sword and the Stone* discussed in chapter 2, the contest of ingenuity is displayed in the numerous magical competitions, and master strategists compete to outwit their competitors through ever more ingenious snares and traps.

The root metaphor of entrapment/liberation is operative in South Asian religious traditions as well. In Hinduism and Buddhism alike, humans are trapped like Odysseus in the great *wandering* (*saṃsāra*) of appearances (*māyā*), seeking for a strategy of escape (*mokṣa*).[13] The Vedic depiction of the deity Indra provides a metaphysical foundation for deception—Indra is at times portrayed as a trickster god who used a magic net (*indrajala*) to snare his enemies.[14] This net simultaneously refers to darkness, magic, deception, illusion, and sorcery.

What the West commonly refers to the law of the jungle, the South Asians have rendered as the law of fishes (*matsya nyaya*), a description appropriate to the depiction of Strategic Intelligence in the pike scene of *The Sword and the Stone* that I discussed in chapter 2.[15] And like the various Greek examples discussed in chapters 2 and 3, the values of Strategic Intelligence have also been articulated through divine, human, and animal figures. For example, the figures of Krishna in the *Mahabharata* and Hanuman the monkey deity in the *Ramayana* exemplify the godly. Most of the women in the *Mahabharata*, whose Strategic Intelligence is seen in their secret and expedient liaisons with lovers, articulate the human (the character Manthara, the hunchback, is a particularly great example of the female strategist), and many of the animals in Buddhist Jataka stories and in the *Pañcatantra* express Strategic Intelligence in a similar way to the aphoristic *Aesop's Fables*.[16] Translated into English as "Fables of Bidpai," and "The Morall Philosophie of Doni of the auncient sages," sixteenth-century English intellectuals correctly understood that the *Pañcatantra* was a cultural medium that bore the values underlying a cohesive moral and political philosophy.[17]

A secular type of authority underlies the Political Philosophy articulated through Kautīlya's *Arthaśāstra* (fourth century BCE), which made Strategic Intelligence a high art in the employ of the state. Strategic Intelligence is the tool of espionage practiced by messenger diplomats, apostate monks, spying nuns, disguised ascetics, faking farmers, merchants, orphans, poisoners, and double agents.[18] And a religious authority buttresses the strategic rationality conveyed through one of Mahayana Buddhism's most revered scriptures, the *Lotus Sutra*, a text composed in the early centuries of the Common Era. Like the examples of the platonic noble lie and Christian *œconomia* discussed in previous chapters, Buddhism expressed the strategy of benevolent deception and provisional truth as *expedient means* (*upāya*).[19] When utilized by Buddhist masters, it signifies a strategic utilization of contingency and customized adaptation that is intended to result in, and thus legitimated by, strategic advantage in the spiritual domain.

There are two famous parables in the *Lotus Sutra* that legitimate beneficial deception, sometimes referred to as pious fraud. In the parable of the burning house, a rich man is unable to compel his young children to flee from a burning mansion because, deep at play in the innards of the palace, they have no understanding of the threat. In response to the realization that he could not save all of his children because there were too many to carry out of the one gate, he then made use of *expedient means* to enable his sons to escape death—he customized a fib for each son, promising that what each most desired was waiting for him outside of the gate. This strategy worked—the sons ran out of the burning house as fast as they could. The parable finishes with Buddha confirming that the father was not guilty of falsehood because each son in fact gained what they most desired, their own life. The ends justify the means—strategic means enable salvation.

In the parable of the abandoned city in the *Lotus Sutra,* the benevolent deception of *expedient means* is a core attribute of buddhahood itself. Buddha intentionally creates false realities (illusions) that are appropriate for each being in order to offer temporary respite and attainment of the long game. For example, when a group of pilgrims in search of the final treasure become despondent and disheartened while on an arduous trek, the leader strategically conjures up an illusory city in which they can rest. Only after attaining a complete sense of ease and after having been made ready for the next leg of the journey does the leader dissolve the fantasy and urge the pilgrims to continue to the ultimate treasure. Buddha, the parable reveals, is just like the leader who created the temporary fantasy—the temporary illusion was exposed only after the travelers were well-rested and able to proceed to the great treasure.

TOWARD A GENEALOGY OF CHINESE STRATEGIC RATIONALITY

> After dried, 'tho the ocean bed revealed, 海枯終見底,
> In death man's heart lies e'er concealed.人死不知心.
>
> *Romance of the Investiture of the Gods* (seventeenth century CE)[20]

With the historical rise of China over the last thirty years, research into Chinese strategic thought is increasingly garnering interest in academic, business, and national security circles.[21] Although there is a growing interest in the realm of business management, the study of Chinese strategic thought is clearly dominated by researchers who specialize in military and International Relations theory, and whose analyses explore strategic culture and grand strategy derived from sources such as the seven military classics, and especially the famous *Art of War* by the ancient military strategist Sūnzi. One of the key arguments that I make in this book is that many literary and dramatic sources are simply more insightful to students of strategic thought because of the way that strategy is dramatized: literati can and have vivified core strategic values such as *discerning dynamics* (*shì* 勢) in a manner that is unavailable to the theoretical treatise.

A comprehensive genealogy of Strategic Intelligence in Chinese cultural sources still needs to be researched and documented, but for our purposes here it is sufficient to call out some of the more intriguing exemplars of heroic strategists in a preliminary attempt to stitch together cultural evidence that may illuminate a line of cultural descent. Notably, the philosopher Lisa Raphals' monograph *Knowing Words: Wisdom and Cunning in the Classical Traditions of China and Greece* is an instructive exploration of the intellectual foundations of Chinese cunning intelligence, tracing the use of words and attitudes in intellectual and cultural contestation over the long course of Chinese cultural history. Here I build on and complement the extensive evidence provided and interpreted through Raphals' structuralist and epistemological exploration of words as used in classical and Míng dynasty sources. I envision that a cultural genealogy of Strategic Intelligence in Chinese civilization has to take into consideration its articulation in multiple cultural domains, figures, and metaphors. And by querying the cultural data as evidence for underlying values and meaning as opposed to a way of knowing, I may shed light on its importance as a way of hope born out of the necessity of life. My goal in this chapter is to set up the general contour of Strategic Intelligence across the breadth of Chinese cultural evolution in a foundational sort of manner: important questions about the nuances of Strategic Intelligence in a given period or among thought leaders associated with a certain philosophic school, and about the possibility of multiple forms of Chinese Strategic Intelligences, must await future studies.[22]

At this point, I want to make a slight detour to explore the meaningfulness of Chinese Strategic Cultures. In addition to my analysis which focuses on excavating the values associated with Chinese Strategic Intelligence from the meaningful identities of heroic strategists articulated in culture, others have explored in detail the aspects of Chinese strategic rationality expressed in discourse. Recall the discussion in chapter 3 about the strategic and political nature of poetry such as Hesiod's *Theogony* and *Works*, and epic poetry such as Homer's *Iliad* and *Odyssey*, and the theatrical poetics of misdirection that may have been used by Plato in the dialogues. Although they did not use the same words, Western scholars of early Chinese literature have also noticed the strategic aspect of many Chinese texts of the late Zhōu and Warring States period, seeing a connection between the "word-magic of early *fù*" poetry and the prose in the classic text, *Strategies of the Warring States,* and politicized interpretations of the *Classic of Poetry*.[23] More recently, François Jullien's book *Detour and Access: Strategies of Meaning in China and Greece* is an analysis of the logic and history of the Chinese strategy of indirect speech, in which the value of "obliquity recommended in the art of war corresponds to an obliquity in speech."[24] For example, Classical Chinese poetry became a critical component of Chinese political subjectivity because it enabled defensive and offensive capability when mastered. Poetry enabled courtiers to express their intent and ambition, while discretely cloaking both in poetic allusion.[25]

Chinese masters of suasive power enabled a strong defensive position when they encrypted their critique, threat, warning, and remonstrance with citations drawn from the ancient *Classic of Poetry*.[26] This type of culturally coded discourse was a cloaking device, argues Jullien, that enabled the critic to remain invulnerable while rendering his potent attack, and shifted the burden of meaning to the process of decoding intentions, and to the need for, in my view, a mastery of Cultural Cryptology.[27] As many insightful intellectuals have pointed out, cloaking dissent and critique in ambiguous cultural allusions remains a primary feature of Chinese political rhetoric, and one that is little understood by Western analysts.[28] And for this reason culture, a domain that includes contestation at the level of idea, meaning, and value, can be especially charged in contemporary China.[29] Chinese officials have not only attacked opponents using cultural references, but as Jullien points out, cultural references function as indirect signalers of upcoming policy decisions. The threat to the Chinese Communist Party's "fetishism of cultural symbols," as the scholar Jing Wang describes it, explains the *Yellow River Elegy* cultural controversy in the late 1980s, and the Party's antagonistic reaction to artistic expression.[30] The Party response to artist Ài Wèiwèi's *Sunflower Seeds* illustrates this perfectly—Ài was ultimately exiled from China after the Party harassed him and took him into custody in 2011.[31]

Cultural orthodoxy continues to be a top concern of the Party in the twenty-first century, and cultural allusion remains a preferred means of communicating. In an article entitled "Let Heroic Culture Become the Leitmotif of a Great Era," published in the Chinese Communist Journal of theory *Qiushi*, an author employed by the Central Propaganda Ministry under the pseudonym "Affection for the People" integrates heroism, values, culture, the private and the public good in service to a nation precariously balanced at the "critical juncture of life and death,"[32] a nation on the "verge of realizing its historical dream of great revival."[33]

> *The indomitable heroic spirit, awe-inspiring through ages upon ages.* A people who have hope cannot but have heroes, a nation with a bright future cannot but have its vanguard. The transmission of heroic culture is the most important gene that a people can pass down; the promotion of heroic culture is the most powerful expression of a nation's spiritual power: General Secretary Xí Jìnpíng has repeatedly reiterated: "With respect to the heroes of the Chinese people, we must cherish and venerate them, recording and depicting heroes in as evocative a manner as possible, so that the mass circulation of heroes embedded in cultural products will lead the people to establish the correct historical, ethnic, national and cultural world view. We must never engage in the business of blaspheming the ancestors, blaspheming the classics, or blaspheming the heroes."[34] (Italics added for emphasis)

The ideological aspects of these statements can hardly be ignored—the assertion of meaning and power defined in terms of Chinese ethnocentric cultural roots should not be avoided. Heroes are both worthy of emulation and adulation, as are the ways of meaning and power offered by the Chinese cultural legacy itself.[35] The article goes on to note that heroes are the "coordinates" by which people orient themselves;[36] they are a bright sword that guards the Chinese nation against the meaninglessness of cultural nihilism,[37] and provide models to fight existential threat by enabling Chinese people to volunteer, to train to struggle against all odds, and to bravely face death.[38] Not only does the article explicitly suggest that the history of Chinese heroism is equivalent to Chinese cultural history as a whole,[39] but the article masterfully uses the poetics of indirection to signal the type of heroism that the Chinese nation should venerate, which is cloaked in the most sophisticated cultural nuance. Beginning the article by quoting the first verse of a poem written in the ninth century by poet Liú Yǔxī, *"The indomitable heroic spirit, awe-inspiring through ages upon ages,"* the Party-state appears to be valorizing two arch strategists from China's venerable strategic history, Cáo Cāo and Liú Bèi from the Three Kingdoms period, since the term for "indomitable heroes" was directly used by Cáo when speaking to Liú, and which has been reproduced in various cultural sources and genres for 2,000 years.[40] Encrypted in cultural allusion, the possibility of decrypting Chinese Communist Party-state leadership plans and intentions becomes possible to the degree that one can understand the values that these cultural identities articulate.

Ancient Chinese strategists developed the soft power concept of *winning hearts and minds* thousands of years ago.[41] Poetry, in the hand of the Chinese strategist, was also a weapon that enabled offense in the domain of human emotions. Like air, land, sea, space, and cyber, the interior domain is also a terrain of battle, and ancient Chinese discursive offense attacked human sensitivity by delivering effects in the emotional domain of human affectivity. As Jullien pointed out, albeit not in these exact words, Chinese strategists attempted to fāhuī (發揮), "to orchestrate, to put into force, or to bring to bear" their objective through poetry, because poetry is that which "moves people's feelings," and a "subtle means to effect [one's opponent's] emotional disposition." This type of interior strategic movement indicated by the Chinese word gǎn 感 finds a parallel in the English word emotion, which Latin root emoveo signifies movement—the virtuosic utilization of poetry enabled Chinese strategists to move their target away from or toward desired meanings and courses of action by *inciting* desired feelings and inducing the requisite emotional state.[42] Mastery of the human affective domain, in essence, enabled the Chinese strategist to grasp their foe's handle.[43] In other words, as the ancient Chinese mirrors for princes, the *Huáinánzi*, points out, Chinese masters were sensitive to the *dynamic situation*, and their *strategic position* was achieved and maintained by leveraging the appropriate *response*.[44] Using cultural sources to deliver effects in the domain of human emotion-perception, what Jullien describes as the "oblique" approach to conflict is a core feature of Chinese Strategic Intelligence, and resonates in many examples cited in the following two chapters.

Returning now to the cultural genealogy of Chinese Strategic Intelligence, to the long list of strategically intelligent martial heroes that have been valorized throughout the long evolution of Chinese culture, including Jiāng Ziyá (11th BCE), Sūn Wǔ (~500 BCE), Zhūgé Liàng (181–234 CE), Hán Xìn (201–196 BCE), Zhāng Liáng (186 BCE), Xiāo Hé (206–196 BCE), Sīmǎ Yì (179–251 CE), and Cáo Cāo (155–220 CE), we can broaden our understanding of Chinese strategic rationality by recovering the strategic values expressed by strategists in the culturally foundational genres of myth and legend, and in subsequent fiction and drama.[45] Many of the legendary cultural heroes of misty pre-history also gesture to the values of a Chinese strategic rationality. For example, the Lord-god of the Granary is a figuration of the "resourceful hero" who outwitted the trickster Goddess of Salt River.[46] Cháng'é was a deity who stole the drug of immortality from the goddess Queen Mother of the West—in return she was either banished or fled to the moon, where she may also have been transformed into a three-footed toad.[47] This story was included in the Ruist canon since it was associated with Hexagram 54 "Returning Maiden" of the *Book of Changes* (*Yijing*), and revealed by the Zhōu dynasty *Return to the Hidden* divinatory text.[48]

A possible *ressentiment* driving the Strategic Intelligence and worldview of calculating Chinese intellectuals can be excavated from a sensitive reading of the figures of classical founder-heroes of the Chinese legendary past, an insight implicit in Sarah Allan's *The Heir and the Sage: Dynastic Legend in Early China*.[49] Like the texts discussed above in the Western cultural trajectory, as Allan pointed out, the basic human problem of social asymmetry was expressed in ancient Chinese culture in political concerns about legitimate succession. But there is a more fundamental issue at stake that is expressed in the mythopoetic—the conflict between royal blood and merit, between good that is being and good that is doing, and between the virtue and *virtù* (prowess) of the masters of culture (*wén* 文), which is also an exploration of the axiological foundations of governance, justice, and order. This contest was an existential values conflict for meaning itself—by undermining the authority and legitimacy of the concept of hereditary royal succession as a cultural foundation, the calculating class simultaneously enabled the possibility of its own infinite self-actualization. In place of bloodlines, the new foundation was grounded on worth and merit, the worth and merit of the *worthies*, the *sages* of historical Chinese culture.[50]

With the Orthodox tradition grounding its sense of the heroic in the *way of the former kings*, Chinese elites had to deal early on with two different ways of valuing kingship—the *good* and the *good-at* are two ways of valuing that are at odds.[51] By the time of the Ruist philosopher Mencius, at least, kingship characterized the *good* as the moral path of the gentleman-lord (*jūnzi*), the humane king who was effective because of the moral way of *empathy*.[52] Harmony is engendered, the Ruist text *Doctrine of the Mean* tells us, from fostering it in the self, from which it radiates outward through the family, the town, the nation, and the universe.[53] But there is a strategic aspect as well— the *good-at* is gestured at in the *Doctrine* through an apparently Chinese version of the *snare-aware*: "the master said, 'Everyone says I am wise, but when lured into the ruse, they do not know how to escape.'"[54]

The Robber Zhí section in the Daoist masterpiece the *Zhuāngzi* is another example of an agonistic conflict in the domain of discourse between values-combatants and their opposing values-standards, of the morally *good* and the virtuosically *good-at,* of the *humane way* with the *way of the hegemon*. In this story, similar in manner to the way in which Socrates won against Thrasymachus in Plato's *Republic*, Confucius goes head to head with the elite, yet villainous, Robber Zhí. And like the use of figures to articulate positions in the *Republic*, the author expresses the idea of the morally good through the figure of the moralistic would-be courtier Confucius, is who is figuratively trapped by Robber Zhí, who is a figuration of the *good-at*.[55] The scene is evocative and playful because robber (dào 盜) from Zhí's name puns with the term for Way in Chinese. The Chinese phrase "[even] robbery has its way" implies a potential contradiction between moral and pragmatic valuation—gangs of thieves must have some sense of governance and order, or their small polity will collapse.[56] And master thieves can be also be virtuosic and sagely—for example, the ancient text *Huáinánzi*, an ancient syncretistic Chinese mirror for princes, makes explicit the view that *great sages great thieves doth make*.[57] Chewing Confucius out and then sending him on his way crestfallen shows the inadequacy of the Confucian power of suasion in light of this type of kingly power that is ruthlessly aware of, and thus invulnerable to, Confucius' attempt at emotional manipulation through the discursive means of flattery and exhortation.[58]

What exactly do the former kings, that is the kingships of Yáo, Shùn, Yǔ, Shāng, Tāng, Wén, Wǔ, and the Duke of Zhōu, have to tell us about the royal Way?[59]

The Mǎn Gǒudé dialogue in the *Zhuāngzi* has an answer for this question, highlighting the vapidity of Ruist conceptions of kingly virtue in values such as *empathetic response, rightness, trustworthiness, sincerity, credibility*, and family like affection. Mǎn Gǒudé sees that Chinese heroic kingship is only made possible by shamelessness, slavishness, greed, reputation, and self-centeredness, which negates authenticity, integrity, and dignity. For Mǎn, shamelessness and slavishness are the mechanisms of greatest fame and gain—great lords and thieves are two sides of the same coin! "Small thieves get caught and great ones become lords—and that is where one finds the loyal Ruists!" As for the so-called *humane kingly way* of *empathy* enabled by *family affection*, Mǎn pointed out Ruist hypocrisy—Duke Huán murdered his older brother and usurped his wife, and yet the Ruist heroic minister Guǎn Zhòng still became his minister. Tián Chéng committed regicide and seized power, and still Confucius accepted gifts from him. "Ruists criticized them verbally, but only demeaned themselves in their vassalage. This irrational contradiction in their words and behavior reflects the perverse conflict in their own hearts. And thus we are told: Who is good and who is bad? The winner is the head and the loser the tail."

As for family affection, Mǎn asks of the former kings, "Did Yáo and Shùn observe family morality when one killed his eldest son, and the other banished his half-brother? Did Kings Tāng and Wǔ regard the reciprocity of the noble and base when the former deposed Jié and the latter overthrew Zhòu? Did King Jì and the Duke of Zhōu respect their elders when the former took his older brother's place and the latter murdered his?" Mǎn asserts that the way of the former kings was, in all actuality, the way of the hegemon, that critical Ruist moral values are specious.

In actuality, like the strategically heroic figures explored in the first half of this book, the values of Strategic Intelligence can still be glimpsed in the legendary hero-kings of Ruist yesteryear. The legendary rulers, Shùn the Great and Yǔ the Great, beloved heroes in Ruist traditions and foundational to its political philosophies, were legendary hero-rulers from pre-history who may have used a strategic, calculating intelligence to achieve their goals. Both were strategic heroes because they broke the tradition of hereditary succession.[60] As myth, they function as cultural models that express the hope of ultimate self-actualization of the have-nots, those who were not privileged by aristocratic lineage and therefore heroes to the scribal class. Due to his supposed sagacity, although he was a commoner, Shùn became heir to King Yáo and married his two daughters.[61] Although later moralists tried to depict him historically as the icon of filial and brotherly piety, we can recover an earlier mythic depiction of Shùn's Strategic Intelligence—his biological father Blind Man and half-brother Xiàng tried to burn Shùn alive in a granary and bury him alive in a well. In both cases, the tricksters were out-tricked by the exemplary Strategic Intelligence of Shùn's two female consorts, the Xiāng river goddesses É Huáng and Nǚyīng, who saved him with a clever ruse each time.[62]

A similar tradition exists for Yǔ the Great, who, some ancient sources claimed, "desired the throne."[63] In contrast to Ruist moralist interpretations,

Yǔ's Strategic Intelligence can be clearly observed in his reaction to the murder of his father Gǔn by King Yáo. Yáo executed Gǔn because Gǔn was not able to manage the floodwaters, even after he had illicitly snatched the "expanding earth" from the gods.[64] Rather than escaping, Yǔ continued to serve Yáo, even though this can be considered to be a clear violation of filial piety.[65] This invulnerability to shame combined with the capacity to suffer shame for the long game, I conjecture, is the *locus classicus* of the metaphor of *thickened face* discussed in *Theory* (chapters 7 and 8), and resonates in the stories of the conflicts of King Gōujiàn of Yuè and King Wén discussed next.[66] In being universally known in Chinese cultures, both figures resemble the stories of King Arthur in Western cultures. But the resemblance stops there, for, driven by ambition and simmering *ressentiment,* these heroic Chinese strategists make strategic deception their weapon of choice in lieu of excalibur.

When threatened with annihilation by a stronger power, King Gōujiàn of Yuè voluntarily submitted to the shame and humiliation of living as a vassal, strategically biding his time to reverse his fortune and overcome his militarily superior foe. Gōujiàn suffered for three years as a servant to the foreign court, and opportunistically devised a clever ruse to demonstrate his loyalty and affection, even debasing himself to personally taste his captor's feces in order to diagnose his illness (an act meant to give the illusion of intense loyalty to and care for his lord). In his monograph, *Speaking to History: The Story of King Goujian in Twentieth Century China*, the historian Paul Cohen describes how this heroically strategic figure who *ate bitter*, and who "slept on brushwood and tasted gall" in order to transform weakness into strength, has been repeatedly recycled in Chinese culture to articulate Chinese political subjectivity—asserting meaning and power in support of national renewal, China's historic *Rising*, and an indicator, I think, of China's aspiration and historical mission to topple global hegemony.[67]

Cohen correctly acknowledges that the figure of King Gōujiàn is a "root metaphor of the human condition," and thus has been invisible to History as an analytic variable worth exploring, (but not to a Cultural Cryptology that seeks for meaning covertly dispositioned in various media).[68] It is precisely Gōujiàn's Strategic Intelligence that enabled him to move from the humiliation of drinking the great king's urine to eating his heart, and from the shame of tasting his feces to the glory of devouring his liver. By identifying his foe's personal weaknesses, and by strategically and heroically using "deception, trickery, lying, and bribery," Gōujiàn destroyed his enemy by using nine stratagems.[69] The nine stratagems appear to have been slightly adapted for contemporary threats—in testimony delivered during a 2018 US Senate Committee by officials from the Judiciary, the Federal Bureau of Investigation and Homeland Security about Chinese industrial espionage, Senator

John Cornyn described how China "uses any means available" to achieve its objectives, and he even included the "Intelligence Community's so-called wheel of doom," a chart which depicts eleven different cunning strategies of collection.[70]

The lengths that Chinese heroic strategists go to for vengeance can be both breathtaking and extreme. For example, the retainer Yù Ràng attempted to demonstrate his honor and loyalty by avenging his murdered lord. Rather than beautifying himself like a courtesan might do for his or her lord, Yù disfigured his face to vent his *ressentiment*.[71] Using his new disguise as a means to get a job in the palace as a plasterer, Yù was discovered hiding in the royal privy with a sharpened trowel. Later, he transformed himself into a leprous beggar by carefully applying lacquer to his skin which destroyed his face and hair, and he swallowed hot ashes to permanently alter his voice. Failing in his endeavor three times, this heroic and loyal strategist committed suicide.

The eminent Chinese political philosopher of the Warring States period Hán Fēi recognized a basic economy of meaning which he saw in terms of a zero-sum game and the necessity of the strategic arts of governance. He cited King Gōujiàn as an example of a strategist who fostered kindness instrumentally for his own advantage, and noted that many dependents and inferiors, including courtiers and one's own royal family members, stand to gain through one's loss.[72] In the *Five Pests*, Hán rejected an altruistic notion of the public good that is not opposed to personal gain, the confusion about which can only result in calamity.[73] Predating the comments of the medieval European courtier Walter Map by more than a thousand years (chapter 5), Hán noted that the court itself, quoting the Yellow Emperor, was a site of internecine warfare between superiors and inferiors.[74] The ruler had to guard herself against wily and persuasive courtiers who could manipulate the potential fierceness of the kraken because they thoroughly analyzed her interior world and appropriately adapted their rhetoric accordingly.[75] Courtiers were tigers one had to guard against[76] by concealing one's thoughts,[77] and hiding one's power.[78] Ancient sages organized society to mutually spy on each other,[79] and the deception valorized by Strategic Intelligence was honorable when exercised in service to the state.[80] Hán illustrated this example by transmitting the story of Duke Wǔ of Zhèng.

> Once Duke Wǔ of Zhèng married his daughter to the ruler of the state of Hú in order to beguile him with pleasure, precisely because he desired to annex it. He then publicly inquired of his ministers, "I desire to use my militia—which state should I attack"? In response to the recommendation of the grand minister Guān Qísī to attack Hú, Duke Wǔ flew into a rage and had him executed, saying "Hú is a blood ally, how could you suggest something like that"? The Lord of Hú, fooled into thinking that his kingdom was safe because it was related to Zhèng through blood, was blind to the threat. Zhèng easily took it by force.

The *Master of Demon Valley* (*Guǐgǔzi*), believed to be the teacher of the famous strategists of the Three Kingdoms Sū Qín and Zhāng Yí, bequeathed to posterity a remarkable primer of Chinese Strategic Intelligence.[81] Like Plato's *Republic*, the received version of the *Guǐgǔzi* correlates exoteric governance explored in the first twelve chapters to esoteric governance of the interior domain discussed in the later chapters. And like my argument about the evolution of political philosophy from the political practice of divination, the *On Discernment* chapter of *Guǐgǔzi* correlates the strategic counsel of would-be courtiers with the diviners of turtle shells. I speculate that the title *Master of Demon Valley* may be derived from the term for a popular Chinese form of divination by interpreting the patterns on turtle shells—*guǐ* "spirit, demon" puns with *guī* "turtle," and valley *gǔ* is very close in pronunciation to *bǔ* 卜 "divining." Regardless of whether that etymological reconstruction stands up to scrutiny over time or not, the text makes salient that the political counsel of "discerning situations" is *the* critical faculty for resolving the insecurity of all human affairs and implementing results.[82] It is equivalent to the manner in which the kings of old used the means of divining from turtle shells "to divine themselves."[83] In other words, the political strategist who would exercise power at court must also divine the inner world of the ruler in order to enable the good of the kingdom.

Guǐgǔzi is also a remarkable text because it explicitly proselytizes a strategy of emotional manipulation that I think is unparalleled in human civilization—certainly predating Machiavellian machination by millennia. The diviner-persuader-courtier is advised to expose the ruler's internal world via his words, the appropriate and successful interpretation of which will result in the revelation of his emotional response.[84] Using a strategy of ensnarement, the virtuoso of schemes and machinations[85] captures his quarry with the fishhooks of "angling words" and nets,[86] occupies, worms his way in,[87] and strategically leverages his target's emotive world,[88] all of which are the "arts of the *Way*."[89] Dialogue is a battle of wits, and the interior world of the target a unique terrain that must be strategically surveilled and its depths plumbed[90] in order to opportunistically deliver effects which are perfectly timed with schemes and stratagems.[91] She who wishes to orienteer and dominate this interior battlefield coerces her target by manipulating the affective domain of ambitions and intentions, and by divining plans and schemes.[92] Timing is everything—the virtuosic strategist strikes at the critical moment.[93] Sometimes the virtuoso should bait, and sometimes bide her time.[94] The strategist's schemes and plots mark the difference between life and death,[95] and the mouth is her greatest weapon.[96] She is like a puppeteer who camouflages herself, practices extreme adaptability,[97] and channels her target in the desired direction like compelling water through a dike.[98]

Much too can be learned about the cultural history of Chinese Strategic Intelligence from the heroic strategic identities of the two most famous disciples of the Master of Demon Valley, Sū Qín and Zhāng Yí.[99] The American Sinologist James Crump, in his monograph *Legends of the Warring States*, reconstructed the now lost romances of both heroic strategists by combining elements of their stories recorded in the canonical histories and from the pre-Hàn dynasty classic of strategy, *Strategies of the Warring States*.[100] Via a mastery of heroic Strategic Intelligence, both strategists rose from poverty and obscurity to the highest positions in government—legends even record kings bowing at their feet begging for their guidance. But the quest for meaning and power was always fraught with danger—like the examples of the anabasis of Zeus, Jesus, Skywalker, and Potter explored in previous chapters, the Chinese strategic hero must also suffer before he rises again. For example, the heroic strategist Fàn Jū of the kingdom of Wèi, accused of political treachery, was severely beaten and thrown into the privy for all to defecate on him.[101] From such an ignominious turn of the wheel of fortune, Fàn escaped to a competitor state which honored him, entitled him as Marquis, and provided the platform to enact his vengeance by utterly destroying his tormentors and toppling the kingdom.[102] Literary scholars such as Crump have misunderstood the provenance of strategic rationality informing the texts that they study, relegating them to the domains of the literary, the rhetorical and to "ages of sophistry." From the interpretative perspective of Strategic Intelligence which emphasizes political subjectivity in terms of power and meaning, sources such as *Strategies of the Warring States* clearly demonstrate the mythopoetic mode in which the underlying strategic values of power and meaning are transmitted.[103] To gain meaning and power, the heroic strategist must virtuosically master opportunism, timing, forbearance, concealment, and revelation.

The game of "capturing the concealed," that is how the Chinese refer to the game of hide and seek, holds a special place in their culture.[104] In fact, concealing and revealing identity is one of the great leitmotifs of classical Chinese literature, and should be considered as central to Chinese Strategic Intelligence. One of the defining features of the clear-sighted man, as indicated by the phrase used ubiquitously in Chinese vernacular fiction "I have eyes but I did not recognize Mt. Tài," was to see through the external camouflage to the internal prowess of the one viewed.[105] Conversely, the virtuoso of strategic concealment might also aim to worm closer in to the center of influence. For example, the slave-cum-chef-cum-Imperial regent Yī Yǐn posed as a cook in the harem in order to influence the king, and the would-be imperial advisor Bó Lǐxī voluntarily became a slave to attain his goal. The eminent political philosopher Hán Fēi held these two figures up as exemplars who strategically sullied themselves temporarily in order to achieve the long game—noting that it is no *shame* for the *virtuoso* who saves the realm by coercing the ruler to listen.[106] The strategic genius of Jiāng Ziyá was quickly recognized by the legendary King Wén when the king found him posing as a fisherman after he had previously escaped the tyrant's court by feigning madness.[107] A cunning mage who practiced the occult, this reverend master correctly interpreted omens and aided the overthrow of the Shāng dynasty (~1766–1122 BCE).[108] He has since become a saint in East Asian folk religions and a potent avatar in contemporary gaming culture.

The strategic values articulated through all of these cultural models would be manifest again thousands of years later in the "small tradition" of vernacular fiction.[109] For example, the hero Sūn Wùkōng, a magic-egg turned stone-monkey king from the sixteenth-century novel *Journey to the West,* demonstrates the Strategic Intelligence of the kingly way, and gains eternal life through heroic theft, the illicit snatching of the peaches of immortality, jade liquor, and Lǎozi's golden elixir of immortality.[110] And taking up the ancient story of King Wén (1152–1056 BCE) of the Zhōu dynasty, the legendary king gifted with foresight and the originator of the Yìjīng (I Ching) divination hexagrams, the sixteenth-century novel *Romance of the Investiture of the Gods* demonstrates King Wén's inheritance of Strategic Intelligence from the model provided by Yǔ the Great.[111] Although he sees through her wicked plots, Wén's son Bó Yìkǎo is ultimately unable to escape the trickery and predatory web of the fox spirit that possesses the queen's body.[112] Steadfast against her lustful advances, she then responds with a vow to dice him up and serve him to his father Wén in a mince pie.[113] In addition to being a form a revenge designed to "vent her resentment," it is also a display of what the text humorously describes as his majesty's "empathic virtue of not being murderous," and a test of Wén's strategic foresight as he is known to have great ability reading portents.[114] This trap is a moment of identity-defining crisis for Wén, nothing less than his personal heroism is at stake—he is a threat to the tyrant if he foresees the ruse, and his heroic significance is lessoned if he does not.

Being pinned down between the proverbial Scylla and Charybdis, Wén's response is remarkable for the way in which he strategically displays forbearance to insult, provocation, and utter shame in the present in order to obtain long-term strategic advantage. Alerted to the ruse through astounding sensitivity when he perceived a murderous sound emanating from his zither, Wén saves his own life expediently—he knowingly eats three of the flesh pies in order to outwit his enemy and expediently save himself, and only vomits them up after he leaves court so as not to incur more suspicion. The three white rabbits (that was his son) that his vomit transforms into go on to live on the moon with the goddess Cháng'é, where they were believed to mix the elixir of life throughout eternity. By linking these stories to the figure of the moon, the values of heroically strategic cunning, the knack of revealing and concealing, and immortality were all linked mythically and cosmologically to time through the lunar calendar.

This strategy of *covering your light and nursing the dark,* and of *conceal, not reveal* is the quintessence of Chinese strategic rationality.[115] Truly unfathomable is the hidden heart, notes the author of the novel—"tho' he appears loyal on the surface, one can never know the inner heart, as the saying goes, *only after dried is the ocean bed revealed, but in death man's heart lies e'er concealed."*[116] *WWWD? What Would Wén Do?* By strategically seeing through the ruse, accepting short-term shame, willingly losing face, and adapting, the heroic Wén strategically out-tricks the trickster, getting his revenge in the long term by toppling the tyrant and asserting his own meaning and power.

This strategy has been just as relevant to China's rise in the twentieth and twenty-first centuries as it was in the seventeenth century, and the question *WWDD? What would Dèng do?* is just as instructive. *Covering your light* was the bedrock of Chinese foreign affairs under the premiership of Dèng Xiǎopíng (1904–1997 CE), who advised the Chinese state to bide its time until it was in a strategically advantageous position vis-à-vis international predators, or maybe just one hegemon in particular. To what end? China's savvy utilization of covert means to steal US intellectual property over the last thirty years enabled, according to one patriarch of American Strategic Intelligence, "the greatest transfer of wealth in history."[117] In the early twentieth century, the Chinese intellectual Lǐ Zōngwú claimed that the *thick* and *black*, his metaphor for Chinese indigenous Strategic Intelligence (I provide an analysis and translation of *Theory* in chapters 7 and 8), was a secret weapon that Westerners could not understand, and one that would enable China to thwart the strength of the ravenous international predators of his time.[118] Perhaps his prediction came true—the *Summary of the 2018 National Defense Strategy of the United States of America* now characterizes the People's Republic of China as a "strategic competitor using *predatory* economics to intimidate its neighbors"[119] (italics added for emphasis).

In addition to ancient sources of Strategic Intelligence that express court and inter-kingdom intrigue (*Strategies of the Warring States, Commentary* of Zuǒ (*Zuǒzhuàn*), *Spring and Autumn Annals*), fictive and dramatic sources such as *The Orphan of Zhao* and *Snatching Tiger Mountain by Strategy* remind us of other heroically strategic figures that express the values of Chinese Strategic Intelligence.[120] The eighteenth-century masterpiece that features another sentient stone, the *Dream of the Red Chamber/Story of the Stone*, which can be summed up in one of its most famous lines, "when the false is taken for true, then the true is also false," reminds the reader of the primacy of illusion.[121] Countering this elegant novel of manners, Chinese literary history resounds with the adventures of strategically heroic deplorables, such as cunning folk and masters of arts, prognosticators, shamans, fox spirits, and rogues *of the lakes and rivers*.[122] Strategic rationality is just as central to the Robin Hood-type hoodlums in the late Imperial novel *Outlaws of the Marsh* as it is for other lowlifes in late Imperial literature, such as the humble hawker from Míng dynasty author Féng Mènglóng's (1574–1646) story, *The Oil Peddler Alone Claims the Flower Queen*, a morality tale in which the protagonist achieves his life ambition by acquiring a high-class courtesan. Through the *savior faire* strategy of hyper-courteous accommodation, this generalissimo of the social battlefield won the day by strategically inducing a positive emotional response—his virtuosic mastery of human affection heroically exemplified the late Imperial Chinese cultural value of empathy.[123]

The same Machiavellian themes are as ubiquitous in the vernacular short stories of the late Míng dynasty as they were for the roughly contemporaneous stories from the Italian renaissance discussed before in chapter 5. For example, in the story of how the *Nun Intoxicated the Flower* from Líng Méngchū's (1580–1644 CE) collection *Slapping the table in Amazement,* a young official named Téng, enflamed with desire, schemes to win the heart of the virtuous Lady Dí.[124] Like in Machiavelli's play *Mandragola*, when Ligurio enlists the help of a divine, Téng focuses his energy on co-opting the Buddhist abbess Huìchéng associated with the temple that he spies Dí visiting. He begins his strategy by offering Huìchéng a generous *gift*, without making explicit any strings that might be attached. Huìchéng, whose name puns with "will succeed," or "will bring to completion" is depicted as a master strategist. As one of the nine classes of dangerous women, she has a heart full of wiles, with many tricks up her sleeves, and a well-seasoned mind that has seen it all, and because of that she is shrewd and can see right through situations.[125] Women like Huìchéng are depicted as dangerous strategists the equal of the eminent heroes from the Warring States period such as Zhāng Liáng and Chén Píng, and they are more polished than the famous pleaders Suí Hé and Lù Jiǎ.[126] Virtuous women easily fall into their traps and take their bait.[127] In this case, by leveraging Dí's weakness for pearls, Huìchéng merely "laid out the bait, and waited for the fish to bite."[128] Once Dí takes the bait, Téng quickly launches his emotional attack, inciting lasting affection by stimulating her arousal.

Special mention should be made of the seventeenth-century author Zhāng Yìngyú's *Book of Swindles*, selections of which have recently been gifted to the Anglophone world through Christopher Rea and Bruce Ruskin's monograph.[129] This selection is notable because its eighty-four stories of ruses, cons, swindles, and "switcharoos" are actually a precise taxonomy of antagonistic reality—it is an ontology of antagonistic reality in which eighty-four aspects of potential threats are labeled with regard to agent (who), location

Toward a Cultural Genealogy of Chinese Strategic Intelligence   147

(where), and method (how). Like the literature surveyed throughout this book, the *Book of Swindles* is edutainment that is practical, soteriological, heroic, and cosmological. It is practical because it is described as a primer that intends to foil swindles through the authority of personal experience, which enables the reader to vicariously see through treacherous hearts and thieving ways plucked from their hidden recesses exposed to our very eyes.[130] It is soteriological because it is a *precious raft* that assures safe passage in an age beset by storms. It is cosmologically heroic in the sense that the number of stories that it includes, eighty-four, resonates as a Buddhist heroic number that integrates mind's enlightenment to reality across time and space.[131] All in all, the *Book of Swindles* provides another compelling piece of evidence of the manner in which culture bears strategic values, and the translators correctly point out the paradox that Strategic Intelligence, as something that is both excoriated and celebrated, may just be the best and the worst that humanity has to offer.[132]

We should not be tempted to think of these types of deception as just a cultural representation that is not pegged to a real occurrence in the phenomenal world. The scholar Mark McNicholas has demonstrated through his sophisticated reading of Qīng dynasty legal history that fraud was a common form of late imperial Chinese deception that "struck right at the political bedrock," affecting "official authority and prerogatives such as revenue collection, conferring titles and dispensing rations, stipends, and honors."[133] The real-life Strategic Intelligence of the elite class of calculating Chinese mandarins was merely reproduced in the cultural products discussed in subsequent chapters.

Of all of the cultural products produced over the long span of Chinese civilization, the preeminent source which has expressed East Asian strategic rationality, and which has subsequently shaped generations of East Asians, are the stories of the Three Kingdoms period (220–280 CE) which have been almost continuously evolving for more than 2,000 years. Set at the decline of the great Hàn dynasty, Three Kingdoms' narratives detail *ad nauseam* the ruthless intrigues, plots, ruses, and cons of heroic strategists such as Cáo Cāo and Liú Bèi as they respond to the disorder and chaos of the time. The values of the heroically strategic can be found in all aspects of East Asian Three Kingdoms cultural production, in high art, theater, games, videos, movies, contemporary military doctrine, manga, and as one of the four Chinese literary masterworks, the *Romance of the Three Kingdoms*.[134] Since at least the eighteenth century, *Romance of the Three Kingdoms* has transmitted the metaphysical foundation of East Asian strategic thought. Opening the novel with the famous phrase "It's oft been said of the empire—'er split, must merge; 'er merged, must split," the novel brings clarity to its audience about the necessity of navigating a reality that is always in flux.[135] And the Strategic Intelligence of *The Romance of the Three Kingdoms* is a key theme picked up on in Lǐ Zōngwú *Theory of the Thick and Black*, which I discuss in chapters 7 and 8.

While it is easy to recognize heroically strategic values in novels such as *Romance of the Three Kingdoms*, most likely due to a bias for military strategy and political intrigue, to my knowledge nobody has suggested excavating the strategic dimension from other foundational Chinese cultural products. This bias for military strategy has most likely obfuscated our appreciation of the manner in which Chinese cultural products continue to transmit strategic values, albeit conditioned by uniquely Chinese cultural features. In fact, I argue that many of the most famous literary classics can also be read against the grain of the literary historians as sourcebooks of Chinese strategy. In my view, master novels such as the seventeenth-century erotic novel *Plum in the Golden Vase* and the eighteenth-century *Story of the Stone/Dream of the Red Chamber* may just be the modern equivalents of *Strategies of the States* from the Warring States era. Interpreted in the ways that Literary Historians find professionally important and disciplinarily interesting, such as aesthetically as literary masterpieces, structurally in terms the evolution of the genre, and contradictorily in terms of both prurience and a comprehensive moral vision, these erudite interpretations overlook the fact that the plots of these novels focus attention on ambition in daily life, and that the primary narratological structure is an episodic linking of ruses, cons, conflicts, and intrigues. Perhaps this is true because form follows function? What I mean to suggest is that the origin of the episodic form in the oral storytelling tradition is less interesting philosophically, culturally, and cryptologically than the possibility that the literary form appropriately expresses an experience of reality that informs a particular world view. Perhaps what the masterworks reveal to us in their discursive re-presentation of consciousness is that human consciousness' grasp on reality has been systematically experienced in terms of episodic deception, that the *real* is always bookended by or intersected through the *illusory*, and that strategies are critical to (and sometimes ironically impotent against) mitigating a sense of alienation and displacement. The key to interpreting the secret teachings of sources such as *Story of the Stone* may be developed by becoming aware of what is precious to human embodiment, and the strategies utilized to expand life.[136]

I hope that the cultural evidence that I surveyed in this chapter, although cursory, will both sensitize readers to this interpretative framework, as well as tempt future researchers to delve more deeply into the cultural genealogy and evolution of strategic values in Chinese civilization. Like in the Mediterranean and Western European examples that I explored in the first half of this book, Chinese cultural evidence points to a similar experience of antagonistic reality, and the posturing of Strategic Intelligence as a preeminent and kingly form of hope.

NOTES

1. Hán Fēizi 韓非子, *On the Difficulty of Persuasion Shuìnán* 說難.
2. Hán Yù 韩愈, *Composed for Abbot Wén Chàng* 送浮屠文畅师序.
3. The term *Way dào* 道 is the most important metaphor in Chinese philosophy.
4. The Chinese language does not mark for number, and so the word for China, *Zhōngguó* 中國, "central kingdom," can also be translated as middle or central kingdoms.
5. *Qur'ān* 7:99. أَفَأَمِنُوا مَكْرَ اللَّهِ ۚ فَلَا يَأْمَنُ مَكْرَ اللَّهِ إِلَّا الْقَوْمُ الْخَاسِرُونَ *The Quran Online Translation and Commentary*, https://al-quran.info/#8, accessed 17 August 2019.
6. *Qur'ān* 8.30. وَإِذْ يَمْكُرُ بِكَ الَّذِينَ كَفَرُوا لِيُثْبِتُوكَ أَوْ يَقْتُلُوكَ أَوْ يُخْرِجُوكَ ۚ وَيَمْكُرُونَ وَيَمْكُرُ اللَّهُ ۖ وَاللَّهُ خَيْرُ الْمَاكِرِينَ *The Quran Online Translation and Commentary*, https://al-quran.info/#8, accessed 17 August 2019.
7. *Qur'ān* 10.21. وَإِذَا أَذَقْنَا النَّاسَ رَحْمَةً مِنْ بَعْدِ ضَرَّاءَ مَسَّتْهُمْ إِذَا لَهُمْ مَكْرٌ فِي آيَاتِنَا ۚ قُلِ اللَّهُ أَسْرَعُ مَكْرًا ۚ إِنَّ رُسُلَنَا يَكْتُبُونَ مَا تَمْكُرُونَ *The Quran Online Translation and Commentary*, https://al-quran.info/#8, accessed 17 August 2019.
8. *Qur'ān*, 7:99, 8:30, 10:21, 13:42. *The Quran Online Translation and Commentary*, https://al-quran.info/#8, accessed 17 August 2019.
9. Firdawsi, *Shahnameh: The Epic of the Persian Kings*, trans. Admad Sadri (New York: Quantuck Lane Press, 2013).
10. Nizam al-Mulk, *The Book of Government or Rules for Kings* (*The Siyāsatnāma of Siyar al-Mulūk*), trans. Hubert Darke (New Haven: Yale University Press, 1960), chapter 44.
11. Farid ud-din Attar, *The Conference of the Birds* (London: Penguin Books, 1984), 16.
12. Hamid Dabashi, "Introduction," *The Adventures of Amir Hamza, Lord of the Auspicious Planetary Conjunction*, trans. Musharraf Ali Farooqi (New York: The Modern Library, 2007), xvi. Cunning magician *ayar* ऐयार.
13. Great *wandering saṃsāra* संसार; appearances; *māyā* माया; escape *mokṣa* मोक्ष.
14. Magic net *indrajala* इन्द्रजाल.
15. Law of fishes *matsya nyaya* मत्स्य न्याय.
16. Visnu Śarma, *The Pancatantra*, trans. Chandra Rajan (London: Penguin Books), 1995.
17. Sir Thomas North (London: Ballantyne Press 1570), accessed 20 January 2018, HathiTrust Digital Library, https://catalog.hathitrust.org/Record/100654063.
18. Aradhana Parmar, *Techniques of Statecraft: A Study of Kautilya's Arthaśāstra* (Delhi: Atma Ram & Sons, 1987), 231–242.
19. *Expedient means* Sanskrit: *upāya-kaushalya* उपाय- कौशल्य; Chinese: *fāngbiàn* 方便. Noble lie γενναῖον ψεῦδος.
20. 自古人心難測，面從背達，知外而不知內，知內而不知心，正所謂"海枯終見底，人死不知心。Xǔ Zhònglín 許仲琳, *Romance of the Investiture of the Gods Fēngshén Yǎnyì* 封神演義 (Hong Kong: Zhōnghuá Shūjú 中华书局, 1976), chapter 21.
21. Rise of China *zhōngguó juéqí* 中国崛起.
22. A structuralist linguistic analysis of Chinese cunning intelligence born by the character *zhì* 智 is very complicated since the term is polyvalent and polysemous.

For example, it varies in value in various Daoist schools from the Warring States to late antiquity: *zhì*-type machination can be a negative value contrasted with simplicity (*pǔ* 樸), such as for some Six dynasties (220—589 AD) period thinkers. But it is clearly represented as a positive value by eclectic Daoist schools influenced by Huánglǎo黃老 (aka Zhuānglǎo 莊老) and Legalism.

23. Cited in J. I. Crump, Jr, *Strategies: Studies of the Chan-kuo Ts'e* (Anne Arbor: University of Michigan Press, 1964), 76. See Arthur Waley, *The Temple and Other Poems* (London, 1923), 18. Hellmut Wilhelm, "The Scholars Frustration: Notes on a Type of Fu," in *Chinese Thought and Institutions*, ed. John Fairbank (Chicago: University of Chicago Press, 1964), 313. *Classic of Poetry* (*Shījīng* 詩經).

24. François Jullien, *Detour and Access: Strategies of Meaning in China and Greece,* trans. Sophie Hawkes (New York: Zone Books, 2000), 49.

25. Poetry expresses ambition: *Shī yán zhì* 詩言志.

26. *Book of Poetry Shījīng* 詩經.

27. The roaming strategic pleader of cases *yóushuì* 遊說 was seen to be successful to the degree that he could move the affection of the leader *shuōqíng* 說情 he was trying to influence.

28. Regarding China's grand strategy, in his review of RAND corporation analyst Tim Heath's *China's New Governing Party Paradigm: Political Renewal and the Pursuit of National Rejuvenation*, Sinologist Dr. Michael Metcalf wrote "it is likely that the answer has been there under our noses all along, but we chose to dismiss the evidence as merely political rhetoric somewhat akin to an American party platform or a campaign stump speech." Michael K. Metcalf, "Book Review: *China's New Governing Party Paradigm: Political Renewal and the Pursuit of National Rejuvenation*," by Tim R. Heath, *Journal of Strategic Intelligence*, National Intelligence University, Summer 2016: 99, accessed 21 January 2019, http://ni-u.edu/wp/csir/journal-of-state gic-intelligence/chinas-new-governing-party-paradigm-by-timothy-r-heath/. Tim R. Heath, *China's New Governing Party Paradigm: Political Renewal and the Pursuit of National Rejuvenation* (Burlington, VT: Ashgate, 2014). Jullien, *Detour,* 30. Paul Cohen, *Speaking to History: The Story of King Goujian in Twentieth-Century China* (Berkeley: University of California Press, 2010), 177–203.

29. Marxist-inspired intellectuals have produced the best analyses of Chinese cultural contestation over the last thirty years, indubitably because they are attuned to the issue of political subjectivity in culture. For example, see Xudong Zhang, *Postsocialism and Cultural Politics: China in the Last Decade of the Twentieth Century* (Durham: Duke University Press 2008); *Chinese Modernism in the Era of Reforms: Cultural Fever, Avant-Garde Fiction, and the New Chinese Cinema* (Durham: Duke University Press, 1997; and *Whither China? Intellectual Politics in Contemporary China* (Durham: Duke University Press, 2001). Jing Wang, *High Culture Fever: Politics, Aesthetics, and Ideology in Deng's China* (Berkeley: University of California Press, 1996); Liu Kang, *Globalization and Cultural Trends in China* (Honolulu: University of Hawai'i-Press, 2004); and Liu Kang and Xiaobing Tang, eds., *Politics, Ideology and Literary Discourse in Modern China: Theoretical Interventions and Cultural Critique* (Durham: Duke University Press, 1993).

30. Wang, *High Culture*, 118–136.

31. Ài Wèiwèi 艾未未. Chinese Communist authorities were very concerned evidently by the possibility of social disruption in the PRC caused by the Taiwanese Sunflower Student Movement (Tàiyánghuā Xuéyùn 太陽花學運) in Spring 2014.

32. 生死存亡的关键时刻.

33. "让英雄文化成为伟大时代的主旋律" *Qiushi* 求是 12/24/ 2018. Online at QSTHEORY.CN 《求是》 2018/24, accessed 6 February 2019, http://www.qstheory.cn/dukan/qs/2018-12/22/c_1123888093.htm. Also: http://theory.people.com.cn/n1/2018/1224/c40531-30484502.html. 时候都更加接近实现中华民族伟大复兴的目标. Affection for the People Cí'ài mín 慈爱民

34. "天地英雄气，千秋尚凛然。" 一个有希望的民族不能没有英雄，一个有前途的国家不能没有先锋。英雄文化的传承，是民族基因最重要的传承；英雄文化的弘扬，是民族精神力量最有力的迸发。习近平总书记多次强调："对中华民族的英雄，要心怀崇敬，浓墨重彩记录英雄、塑造英雄，让英雄在文艺作品中得到传扬，引导人民树立正确的历史观、民族观、国家观、文化观，绝不做亵渎祖先、亵渎经典、亵渎英雄的事情"。广大文艺工作者必须努力创作更多更优秀的弘扬革命英雄的精品力作，让英雄文化成为伟大时代的主旋律。

35. 一个崇尚英雄的时代.

36. 精神坐标.

37. 坚决向历史虚无主义亮剑.

38. 挺身而出，力挽狂澜，慷慨赴死，奋斗中培育.

39. 一部中国文化史，就是一部中华民族英雄史.

40. "Indomitable heroes" *tiāndì yīngxióng* 天地英雄. Liú Yǔxī 刘禹锡, Shǔ Xiānzǔ Miào 蜀先祖庙.

41. "Winning hearts and minds" has been a strategy common to many counter-insurgency strategies over the last hundred years. The American political scientist Joseph Nye coined the term soft power to signify co-opting in his book *Bound to Lead: The Changing Nature of American Power* (New York: Basic Books, 2013).

42. Incite *xìng* 興.

43. Grasp someone's handle: *zhuāzhù bǎbǐng* 抓住 把柄. Jullien, 142–151.

44. Dynamic situation/ strategic position shì 勢, response yīng 應, dào 道, Liú Ān 劉安, *Huáinánzi* 淮南子: *Way and Responding Dàoyīng* 道應, 12:36, *Chinese Text Project*, accessed 6 February 2019, https://ctext.org/huainanzi. See introduction by Sara A. Queen, in *The Huainanzi: A Guide to the Theory and Practice of Government in Early Han China*, trans. and ed. John S. Major, Sara A. Queen et al. (New York: Columbia University Press, 2010), 429–438.

45. Jiāng Ziyá 姜子牙, Sūn Wǔ 孫武, Zhūgé Liàng 諸葛亮, Hán Xìn 韓信, Zhāng Liáng 張良, Xiāo Hé 蕭何 206–196, Sīmǎ Yì 司馬懿, Cáo Cāo 曹操.

46. Anne Birrell, *China Mythology: An Introduction* (Baltimore: John Hopkins Press, 1993), 179, 204–205.

47. Cháng'é 嫦娥. Birrell, *Mythology*, 11, 144.

48. Edward Shaughnessy, *Unearthing the Changes: Recently Discovered Manuscripts of the Yi Jing (I Ching) and Related Texts* (New York: Columbia University Press: 2014), 141, 154. *Return to the Hidden* 歸藏.

49. Sarah Allan, *The Heir and the Sage: Dynastic Legend in Early China* (Albany: State University of New York Press, 2016).

50. Worthy is usually translated as sage: *xián* 賢.
51. Way of the former kings: *xiānwáng zhī dào* 先王之道.
52. Humane king *rénwáng* 仁王. Empathy *rén* 仁.
53. *Doctrine of the Mean Zhōngyōng* 中庸.
54. *Zhōngyōng*, 7. "Everyone says I am wise, but when lured into the ruse, they do not know how to escape." 子曰：人皆曰：予知；驅而納諸罟擭陷阱之中，而莫之知辟也.
55. *Humane way réndào* 仁道; hegemonic way, *bàdào* 霸道. Robber Zhí 盜跖.
56. Even robbery has its *way Dào yìyǒu dào* 盜亦有道.
57. 跖之徒問跖曰：「盜亦有道乎？」跖曰：「奚適其無道也！夫意而中藏者，聖也；入先者，勇也；出後者，義也；分均者，仁也；知可否者，智也。五者不備，而能成大盜者，天下無之。」由此觀之，盜賊之心，必托聖人之道而後可行。故老子曰：「絕聖棄智，民利百倍。」 Liú Ān 劉安, *Huáinánzi* 淮南子: *Way and Responding Dàoyīng* 道應, 12:36, *Chinese Text Project*, accessed 6 February 2019, https://ctext.org/huainanzi. *The Huainanzi: A Guide to the Theory and Practice of Government in Early Han China*, trans. and ed. John S. Major, Sara A. Queen et al. (New York: Columbia University Press, 2010), 467.
58. For the historical context of this text, see Yuri Pines, *Envisioning Eternal Empire: Chinese Political Thought of the Warring States Era* (Honolulu: University of Hawai'i Press, 2008), 79–80.
59. The former kings include Yáo 尧, Shùn 舜, Yǔ 禹, Shāng 商, Tāng 汤, Wén 文, Wǔ 武, Duke of Zhōu (Zhōugōng) 周公.
60. Shùn the Great 大舜, Yǔ the Great 大禹.
61. King Yáo 尧, commoner *pǐfū* 匹夫.
62. Blind man Gǔsǒu 瞽瞍, Xiàng 象, Xiāng river 湘, É Huáng 娥皇, Nǚyīng 女英. Allan, *Heir*, 43–50; Birrell, *Mythology*, 104.
63. Desired the throne 贪位, Birrell, *Mythology*, 68.
64. Gǔn 鲧, expanding earth 息壤; Birrell, *Mythology*, 80.
65. Yǔ the Great's strategy of "governing the waters" 大禹治水. Birrell, *Mythology*, 146–147; Allan, *Heir*, 69.
66. King Gōu Jiàn of Yuè, 越王勾踐. Thickened face: *hòuliǎn* 厚脸.
67. See Paul Cohen, *Speaking to History: The Story of King Goujian in Twentieth-Century China* (Berkeley: University of California Press, 2010). Eat bitter: *chīkǔ* 吃苦. Slept on brushwood and tasted gall *wòxīnchángdǎn* 臥薪嘗膽.
68. Cohen, *Speaking to History*, XXI.
69. Cohen, *Speaking to History*, 2–33.
70. "Judiciary, FBI and Homeland Officials Testify on Chinese Espionage," December 12, 2018, Aired 12–15 December 2018, accessed 5 January 2019, https://www.c-span.org/video/?455665-1/judiciary-fbi-homeland-officials-testify-chinese-espionage. Program ID: 455665-1. 19:20–20:20.
71. Yù Ràng 豫讓. Crump, *Intrigues,* 79.
72. Hán Fēizi 韓非子, *Guarding Against the Inner [Court]* 備內. strategic arts *shù* 術.
73. Hán Fēizi 韓非子, *Five Pests* 五蠹: 今以為同利者，不察之患也.
74. Hán Fēizi 韓非子, *Wielding Power* 揚權: 黃帝有言曰：「上下一日百戰。」下匿其私，用試其上；

75. Hán Fēizi 韓非子, *Difficulty of Persuasion* 說難: 知所說之心，可以吾說當之。說者能無嬰人主之逆鱗，則幾矣.
76. Hán Fēizi 韓非子, *The Rulers Way* 主道:不固其門，虎乃將存.
77. Hán Fēizi 韓非子, *The Two Handles* 二柄: 故曰：去好去惡，群臣見素。群臣見素，則大君不蔽矣.
78. Hán Fēizi 韓非子, *Wielding Power* 揚權: 權不欲見.
79. Hán Fēizi 韓非子, *Polishing Jade* 和氏: 商君教秦孝公以連什伍，設告坐之過.
80. Hán Fēizi 韓非子, *The Difficulty of Persuasion* 說難:昔者鄭武公欲伐胡，故先以其女妻胡君以娛其意。因問於群臣：「吾欲用兵，誰可伐者？」大夫關其思對曰：「胡可伐。」武公怒而戮之，曰：「胡，兄弟之國也，子言伐之何也？」胡君聞之，以鄭為親己，遂不備鄭，鄭人襲胡，取之。宋有富人，天雨牆壞，其子曰：「不築，必將有盜。」其鄰人之父亦云。暮而果大亡其財，其家甚智其子，而疑鄰人之父。此二人說者皆當矣，厚者為戮，薄者見疑，則非知之難也，處知則難也。故繞朝之言當矣，其為聖人於晉，而為戮於秦也。此不可不察.
81. *Master of Demon Valley Guǐgǔzi* 鬼谷子. Sū Qín 蘇秦 (380–284 BCE), and Zhāng Yí 張儀 (329 BC–309 BCE).
82. In Chinese, the term *qíng* 情 communicates both the external reality of situations and emotional perception of reality in feelings.
83. *Therefore, determining situations and settling insecurity is critical to the myriad affairs of men, used to mitigate disorder and resolve results which are difficult to achieve. Therefore, the former kings used the means of divining from tortoise shells to discern themselves.* 故夫決情定疑，萬事之機，以正治亂，決成敗，難為者。故先王乃用蓍龜者，以自決也。 *Master of Demon Valley Guǐgǔzi* 鬼谷子, *On Discernment* 決篇.
84. *Another's words [signify the possibility of] moving [them]; your taciturness is tranquility. Attend to their words, and listen to their speech. When words do express [the interior], seek more deeply, and the emotive response must emerge.* 人言者，動也；己默者，靜也。因其言，聽其辭。言有不合者，反而求之，其應必出. Emotional response *yìng* 應. *Master of Demon Valley Guǐgǔzi* 鬼谷子.
85. *Master of Demon Valley Guǐgǔzi* 鬼谷子, *Pressing into Cracks* 抵巇. Schemes and machinations 通達計謀.
86. *When phishing matches up with situations, then you may size up a person. It is like setting a snare for animals.* 其釣語合事，得人實也。其猶張罝而取獸也. 反應: *This is the net of phishing people. Always maintain your net and drive them in.* 此釣人之網也。常持其網而驅之. Feeling out: 摩篇, *The virtuosic at feeling catch the big one by dangling the bait on a hook over the deep.* 古之善摩者，如操鉤而臨深淵，餌而投之，必得魚焉. *Acquire his feelings/emotive situation* 得其情. *Master of Demon Valley Guǐgǔzi* 鬼谷子.
87. *Worms his way in* 抵巇. *Master of Demon Valley Guǐgǔzi* 鬼谷子, *Pressing into Cracks dǐ xī*.抵巇.
88. *Obtain his emotional [domain]* 得其情. *Master of Demon Valley Guǐgǔzi* 鬼谷子, Internal Constraints *nèiqián* 內揵.
89. *Pressing into cracks is utilizing the arts of the Way* 抵巇之隙為道術用. *Master of Demon Valley Guǐgǔzi* 鬼谷子.

90. *Therefore one must always expose it to see the interior—this is called evaluating and plumbing feelings* 故常必以其見者而知其隱者，此所謂測深揣情. Unique terrain *xíngshì* 形勢. *Master of Demon Valley Guǐgǔzi* 鬼谷子, *Plumb the Depths Chuāipiān* 揣篇.

91. *Therefore, even though on has the plots of sagely strategic wisdom of the Way of the former kings, it will not be made plain if on does not plumb feelings and the hidden unknown* 故雖有先王之道，聖智之謀，非揣情隱匿，無可索之. 此謀之大本也，而說之法也. 言必時其謀慮. *Master of Demon Valley Guǐgǔzi* 鬼谷子, *Plumb the Depths Chuāipiān* 揣篇.

92. *Coerce through leveraging ambitions and intentions, by knowing his plans and schemes. Discerning advantage and disadvantage is the power of wielding transformation. He who fails to leverage it did not analyze it with due respect.* 動則隨其志意，知其計謀. 勢者，利害之決，權變之威. 勢敗者，不以神肅察也. *Master of Demon Valley Guǐgǔzi* 鬼谷子.

93. 用分威散勢之權，以見其兌威，其機危乃為之決. *Use the power of dividing might and dispersing momentum to see his pleasure. Empower the critical moment and resolve it. Master of Demon Valley Guǐgǔzi* 鬼谷子, *Diminishing and Increasing Pattern the Numinous Yarrow* 損兌法靈蓍.

94. 或量能立勢以鉤之，或伺候見而箝之，其事用抵巇. *Master of Demon Valley Guǐgǔzi* 鬼谷子, *Pounce and Pin Fēiqián* 飛箝.

95. *Plans and schemes are the lever of life and death*, 計謀者，存亡之樞機. *Master of Demon Valley Guǐgǔzi* 鬼谷子.

96. *Therefore, the mouth is the critical means by which to manipulate feelings and ideas.* 故口者，機關也；所以開閉情意也. *Master of Demon Valley Guǐgǔzi* 鬼谷子, *Exigency Quánpiān* 權篇.

97. *The knight who encounters a hostile world and disordered times should adapt to various stimuli to avoid pits, at times adapting one's enabling words for one who would attack and harm, at times adapting to the violent one of dubious virtue, at times adapting to commit crimes for one who represses, at times adapting to one who is smug, at times adapting to one who is dour and self-seeking. Therefore, what counts for the Way is the control of other, and the Way discounts being controlled by others. To control others is to wield power; to be controlled by others is death.* 蓋士遭世異時危，或當因免填坑，或當伐害能言，或當破德為雄，或當抑拘成罪，或當戚戚自善，或當敗敗自立。故道貴制人，不貴制於人也。制人者，握權；制於人者，失命. *Master of Demon Valley Guǐgǔzi* 鬼谷子, *Center Classic zhōngjīng* 中經.

98. *So it is for the master of persuasion, for it is like channeling water through a dike, or rolling a boulder into a deep gorge. Those who can do this, their influence will be no less.* 故善損兌者，譬若決水於千仞之堤，轉圓石於萬仞之谿。而能行此者，形勢不得不然也. *Master of Demon Valley Guǐgǔzi* 鬼谷子.

99. *Master of Demon Valley Guǐgǔzi* 鬼谷子. Sū Qín 蘇秦 (380–284 BCE), and Zhāng Yí 張儀 (329 BC–309 BCE). *Strategies of the Warring States* 戰國策. Canonical histories *Shǐjì* 史記.

100. J. I. Crump, *Legends of the Warring States* (Ann Arbor: University of Michigan, 1998). Canonical histories *Shǐjì* 史記.

101. Fàn Jū 范雎, also known as Fàn Suī 睢.
102. Marquis Yīng 應侯. Wèi 魏.
103. For example, Crump writes "The loss of a Sū Qín to Chinese history "whose political genius and discourses were already highly esteemed by Sīmǎ Qiān . . . and which were admired by 20 centuries of Chinese literati" was not lightly to be borne by the Chinese . . . " *Intrigues*: 29. Also: the Sū Qín legend not only had the amour proper of the literati values, but "the literary value of the Sū Qín legend . . . has won this work its fame for centuries in the face of a continuing *odium theologicum*." (31).
104. Capturing the concealed: *zhuōmícáng* 捉迷藏.
105. Have eyes but did not recognize Mt. Tai: *yǒuyǎn bùshí Tàishān* 有眼不識泰山.
106. *Shame chǐ* 恥. *Virtuoso shì* 仕. Hán Fēizi 韓非 relayed the stories of Yī Yǐn 伊尹 and Bó Lǐxī 百里奚 in *Difficulty of Persuasion Shuìnán* 說難. In Chinese legend, Yī Yǐn 伊尹 started as a slave and became a cook. He would go on to help King Tāng 湯 of the Shāng 商 dynasty overthrow the Xià 夏 dynasty. Starting in poverty, Bó Lǐxī 百里奚 was an eminent strategist that flip-flopped for years between various kingdoms. The king of Qín, who would go on to rule the Hàn empire, found Bó in the kingdom of Chǔ. He redeemed him with five pieces of goat skin, and then had Bó secreted away in a prisoner's cart to elude the King of Chǔ. 皆所以干其上也，此二人者，皆聖人也，然猶不能無役身以進，如此其汙也。今以吾言為宰虜，而可以聽用而振世，此非能仕之所恥也. Jiāng Zǐyá is also known as Preceptor Father Wàng 師尚父 and Tàigōng Wàng 太公望.
107. Grand Duke's Hope Tàigōng Wàng 太公望.
108. Reverend Master 師尚父, Shāng 商 dynasty. Allan, Heir, 98, 107, 153, 167.
109. The term "small tradition" *xiǎoshuō* 小說, is used to mean "fiction."
110. Sūn Wùkōng 孫悟空, *Journey to the West Xīyóujì* 西游记.
111. King Wén 文王 . Xǔ Zhònglín 許仲琳, *Romance of the Investiture of the Gods Fēngshén Yǎnyì* 封神演義 (Hong Kong: Zhōnghuá Shūjú 中华书局, 1976), Chapters 19–23. *Yiching/yìjīng* 易經.
112. Bó Yìkǎo 伯邑考, trickery: *fǎ* 法, web: *luówǎng* 羅網.
113. *Fěngǔsuìshēn* 粉骨碎身.
114. Vent resentment: *xiāo hèn* 消恨. Humane virtue of not being murderous: *bù shā zhī rén* 不殺之仁. Reading portents: *míng huòfú, shànshí yīnyáng* 明禍福, 善識陰陽.
115. *Cover your light and nurse the dark tāoguāngyǎnghuì* 韬光养晦. *Conceal, not reveal yǐncáng bù lù* 隐藏不露.
116. 自古人心難測，面從背達，知外而不知內，知內而不知心，正所謂"海枯終見底，人死不知心。Chapter 21.
117. Comments made by the director of the National Security Agency General Keith B. Alexander during his July 11, 2012, speech at the American Enterprise Institute. American Enterprise Institute, accessed 27 October 2018, https://www.aei.org/events/cybersecurity-and-american-power/.
118. Lǐ Zōngwú 李宗吾, *Collected Sayings on the Thick and Black Hòuhēi Cónghuà* 厚黑叢話.
119. "Summary of the 2018 National Defense Strategy of the United States of America: Sharpening the American Military's Competitive Edge," accessed

11 November 2018, https://dod.defense.gov/Portals/1/Documents/pubs/2018-National-Defense-Strategy-Summary.pdf. Underline added for emphasis.

120. *Strategies of the Warring States Zhànguócè* 戰國策. *Commentary* of *Zuǒ Zuǒzhuàn* 左傳. *Lǔshì Chūnqiū* 呂氏春秋. *The Orphan of Zhao Zhàoshì Gū'ér* 趙氏孤兒. *Snatching Tiger Mountain by Strategy Zhìqǔ Wēihǔshān* 智取威虎山.

121. *Jiǎ zuò zhēn shí, zhēn yì jiǎ* 假作真时真亦假. *Dream of the Red Chamber/Story of the Stone Hónglóumèng / Shítou jì* 紅樓夢/石頭記.

122. Cunning-folk and masters of arts: *fāngshù* 方術/*fāngshì* 方士. Shamans *wū* 巫. Fox spirits: *húlíjīng* 狐狸精. Rogues of the lakes and rivers: *zǒu jiānghú* 走江湖.

123. Positive emotional response *gǎnyìng* 感應. Human feeling 情 *qíng*. *Chronicle of the Water Margin Shuǐhǔ zhuàn* 水滸傳. Courteous accommodation: *bāngchèn* 帮衬. Féng Mènglóng 馮夢龍 *Tales to Awaken the World Xǐngshì Héngyán* 醒世恒言, 卷三, *Màiyóuláng Dúzhàn Huākuí* 卖油郎独占花魁.

124. *Fùrén Díshì* 妇人狄氏. Huìchéng's name "bright & clear" 慧澄 puns with "will succeed" 會成, and Téng's 滕 name puns with "pained" 疼. Líng Méngchū 凌濛初, *Slapping the Table in Amazement* 初刻拍案惊奇, 卷之六:酒下酒赵尼媪迷花机中机贾秀才报怨. See full translation in Chapter 6 "Zhao the Nun Drugs a Beauty into a Stupor," in *Slapping the Table in Amazement: a Ming Dynasty Story Collection*, trans. Shuhui Yang, Yunqin Yang and Robert E Hegel (Seattle: University of Washington Press, 2018), 115–140.

125. 心计又巧，见识又多，路数又熟, 慧澄是个老世事的，一眼瞅去，觉得沉重.

126. Chén Píng 陳平, Lù Jiǎ 陸賈, and Suí Hé 隨何 were all silver-tongued masters of intrigue who helped Liú Bāng 劉邦 (256—195 BCE), founder of the Hàn by persuading new allies to join the cause.

127. 针缝也没有的, 他会千方百计弄出机关, 智赛良、平, 辨同何、贾, 无事诱出有事来. 安排扑鼻香芳饵, 专等鲸鲵来上钩.

128. 原来人心不可有欲, 一有欲心被人窥破, 便要落入圈套.

129. Zhāng Yìngyú, *Book of Swindles* 杜騙新書, in Christopher Rea and Bruce Rusk, trans, *The Book of Swindles: Selections from a Late Ming Collection* (New York: Columbia University Press, 2017).

130. Zhāng, *Book of Swindles*, 211. It has been called a *New Book of Swindles Personally Experienced amidst Rogues* 江湖歷覽杜騙新書.

131. In the same ways that many Christians see the cross as the means of salvation, Buddhists metaphorically refer to the *precious raft bǎofá* 寶筏 Ibid., 212. Eighty-four relates to the number 84,000 and has been used to signify the paths to enlightenment (dharma), as in 84,000 teachings of Buddha, 84,000 mahasiddhas, 84,000 gates 法門 (teachings) to enlightenment, 84,000 Mahakalpa, and 84,000 treasures 法藏.

132. Zhāng, *Book of Swindles*, xii–xx.

133. Mark P. McNicholas, *Forgery and Impersonation in Imperial China: Popular Deceptions and the High Qing State* (Seattle: University of Washington Press, 2015), 6.

134. Four Chinese literary masterworks 四大奇书 the *Romance of the Three Kingdoms Sānguó yǎnyì* 三國演義.

135. It's oft been said of the great affairs of the realm: 'er split, must merge; 'er merged, must split 話說天下大事:分久必合，合久必分.

136. Jiǎ Bǎoyù 賈寶玉, the protagonist of *Story of the Stone* is the reincarnation of a sentient stone. His surname Jiǎ puns with the word *illusory*, and his given name Precious Jade (Bǎoyù) puns with "treasured desires." Thus, the figure Jiǎ Bǎoyù expresses the paradox and contradiction of humanity, and the potential constraints on meaning.

Chapter 7

The Endowment of Chinese Strategic Intelligence
Strategic Officialdom

是以聖人為腹不為目
Thus sages act for the belly, not for the eyes.

Lǎozi, *Dàodéjīng*, 12

In this chapter, I analyze two early twentieth-century Chinese cultural sources that clearly demonstrate Chinese strategic values, Wú Jiǎnrén's (1866–1910 CE) *Uncanny Reality Witnessed over Twenty Years* and Lǐ Zōngwú's *Theory of the Thick and Black.*[1] Like the stories discussed in previous chapters, the values of Chinese Strategic Intelligence expressed through these narratives teach a philosophy of hope in an environment that would deny human ambition. Most importantly for Western students of Chinese Strategic thought, this chapter depicts some examples of Chinese Strategic Intelligence from an internal perspective that is not easily available to the outsider.

One of the constant features of Chinese literary culture since the beginning of Chinese writing is a preoccupation with the affairs of the most eminent in society, men who have been labelled over the long course of Chinese cultural history in various eras as scribe and knight, literatus, mandarin, master, scholar, gentry-scholar, official, and cadre, and who sometimes make the philosophical and religious heroic ranks of sage and worthy, lord and gentleman, the accomplished one, and the authentic man.[2] In fact, one of the most consistent structural divisions in all Chinese societies throughout history has been the clear binary separation between the commoners and the eminent—and the Chinese critique the cultural hegemony, power, and value system of their upper classes in various ways, some of which easily translate into English, and some of which do not. The ways of the mighty have been described as *mandarinism, officialism, bureaucratism,* and *redtape-ism.*[3] In more contemporary times, the Chinese also refer to an authoritarian and oppressive ideology and value system known as *official-foundationalism thought*, *commandism*, *officious-ism*, and to a Communist Party culture that promotes the value of the party elite over the common people, a culture which may be corrupted by the traditional aim to *become an official and get rich*.[4] All of the Chairmen of the Chinese Communist Party-state have railed against it: most recently General Secretary Xí Jìnpíng footstomped the threat of official privilege at the eighteenth National Congress held in November 2012:[5] "Careerism and officialism are totally incompatible both with the spirit and ethos of our Party—they are the great enemy of our Party, the great enemy of the people."[6]

The structural division between the elite and the people has long offered a fertile domain of cultural contestation, and the Chinese have developed a sub-genre of political fiction that they refer to as Officialdom literature.[7] Much of the late Imperial Chinese sub-genre of officialdom literature has been interpreted by Chinese literary historians sociopolitically, structurally, historically, and aesthetically for its condemning social critique, modernism and reportage-like realism, and in terms of being low-brow and reflecting *fin de siècle* decadence.[8] Although it obsesses with the injustice of official corruption, I argue that this genre should also be interpreted philosophically and axiologically as a sustained exploration of human power, meaning, and values, particularly in terms of a form of meaning that is shaped by the paradoxical metaphorological paradigm that *life is death*. Chinese officialdom literature is notable because it depicts a specific orientation in the world, and often surprisingly invokes a celebratory tone to describe *ad nauseam* the heroic human strategies that are necessary for survival in an unjust, chaotic, and disordered polity. After thousands of years of political evolution, there is certainly nothing novel about Chinese political corruption—what is new about these stories is the incredible ingenuity and creative strategies of heroic and villainous officials who seek to survive a predatory environment. Chinese officialdom literature provides excellent cultural evidence about Chinese strategic rationality—that is Strategic Intelligence that is historically, linguistically, and culturally conditioned. Most importantly for researchers of Chinese strategy who are often forced to the *bird-eye* view of the outsider, officialdom literature provides an intimate and detailed source of cultural evidence that documents how the Chinese value strategy.

The traditional Chinese world view was socially intensive to a degree hardly imaginable to those raised in the nuclear families of the late twentieth century and after. Traditional Chinese identity, informed by Ruism (conventionally known as Confucianism), was formed in a great network of extended relationships mediated by family and clan. Family and clan provided the primary orientation in the world, and a strong sense of security in a harmonious universe.[9] They also contributed to a fluid identity (or a hologrammatic identity as the eminent scholar of Chinese Philosophy Roger Ames used to characterize it)—one's identity constantly shifted depending on the particular social interaction, which required sensitivity to navigate hierarchy. The ideal performance of father-son interaction differed from the performance of other roles, such as husband to wife, or lord to vassal. Every interaction was theoretically reciprocal and reinforcing—in theory, ritual interaction enabled dignity through interpersonal relating. In a hierarchically ordered society that emphasized sociopolitical harmony, a clear conception of one's identity enabled dignity, respect, and honor through appropriate and reciprocal interpersonal relationships. In essence, both one's social status and self-esteem, and the self-esteem of the other are both ritually enabled and implicated through the affection conveyed via courtesy, deference, accommodation, and self-control. One was morally responsible to behave with propriety both toward superiors and inferiors—both sides theoretically could *lose face* in any given interaction, which resulted in shame. Undergirding the whole enterprise was the existence of emotions such as affection, love, and sincerity. This type of theoretical ethical behavior articulated in classical Ruist texts is sometimes now referred to in popular culture in praxis as *face* behaviors.

This socially intensive milieu set the condition for the set of values and behaviors that came to be codified as the core doctrine of the *three guides* and *five constants* associated with the moral philosophy known variously as the *Teaching of Names*, as *ritual deportment*, and otherwise known as *Ruism*.[10] It also developed a language to articulate these values, Chinese philosophical and cultural terms of art that are operative in both popular and high culture, and they gave rise to the metaphorical schema that shaped Chinese social reality. Important terms to recognize include *resource relationships, face, human feeling, induced favor, empathetic response, appropriate reciprocity, decorum, filial piety,* and *brotherly love*.[11] Affective emotions made life meaningful because they provided human dignity primarily through reciprocal *resource relationships,* which included relationships with the invisible, departed, and still potent ancestors.

But there was a dark side too—as discussed in the previous chapter with regards to the classical texts *Master of Demon Valley (Guǐgǔzi)* and the Hán Fēizi, the threat to Ruist moral-social order came from socially ambitious practitioners who could instrumentally leverage the system, by strategically inducing good feeling in the other, increasing social capital by creating social indebtedness and obligations that could be leveraged in the present and future, and cashing out when needed by *calling in favors*.[12]

Social networks and *face* are Chinese cultural metaphors that express both values and the means of practical living—author Wenshan Jia even suggested that the metaphor of *face* may define the true nature of Chinese communication, culture, and character.[13] As the famous Chinese intellectual Lǔ Xùn pointed out in his 1934 essay *On Face, face* behavior as a form of self-respect is incredibly complex because dignity, social status, and shame are entangled with social relation-based perspectives, and the maintenance of self-esteem is constructed on top of sensitivity to a cultural ecosystem composed of complex social hierarchies. Lǔ noted that a poor laborer was held to different behavioral face standards than a rich man, and he also pointed out that it was conventionally believed that one's status could be raised by leveraging the charismatic power of someone with a higher face status. For example, Lǔ recounted the irony of face-raising—rather than feeling like his self-esteem was lowered when the rich man told the beggar to get lost, the beggar proudly boasted of his newly raised social status, which was a result of the interaction with someone with higher face status.[14]

This idealized Ruist worldview of warm reciprocity and intimate family feeling provides the backdrop to much officialdom literature, explains the necessity for the strategic mastery of managing social relations, and informs expectations about what the idealized Ruist official should be—an exemplar of human empathy. But, cultural sources of the late Qīng dynasty have described the era as an "age of terror," with urban life having devolved from the "simple purity" of a generation ago to a "bandit's lair of instability, sinister, and deceitful."[15] Many cultural products concur, as can be inferred from the titles of many of the era's novels: *Sea of Regret* (1906), a *History of Pain* (1903–1906), *The Last Days of the World*, *World of Folly* (1906), *Bamboozled* (1904), *Flower in a Sea of Sin*, *The Despicable History of Recent Society* (1909–1910), *After the Holocaust* (1907), and *Living Hell* (1904–1906), to name just a few.[16] The culturally validated role of heroic officialdom was now depicted, after Darwin, in terms of survival, of the necessary strife between predator and prey. Mandarins, the heroic exemplars of political Ruism, were now paradoxically both the consumers and the consumed. Officialdom was akin to a jungle, full of "voracious tigers, rapacious raptors" and sadistic hell demons spreading terror and torture among the populace. In place of the Daoist "joy of fish swimming freely" was a Darwinian realm of species-conflict in which "big fish eat small fish and small fish eat the shrimp."[17] And why shouldn't officials skim off the top? One author wondered. It is only natural that one would "eat off the mountain when on the mountain and drink from the water when near the stream."[18]

Officialdom, meaning the sociopolitical environment in which officials lived, scared people to death, even the officials themselves. Emerging from his shamanistic nightmare, one fictive official in a famous novel reported that he had been haunted in his dream by officials that appeared as rapacious and wild demon-animals on a mountaintop who would swallow prey as quickly as they were spotted. The only thing he could do to avoid their violence was close his eyes and hide:

> Hiding in the woods, the beasts could not see me, but I could see them distinctly and crystal clear, with the so-called discerning eyes. The mountain was not just

inhabited by all kinds of wolves, jackals, tigers and leopards: there were also innumerable other types, including cats, dogs, rats, monkeys and weasels, pigs, goats, and bulls. How could such a world of beasts tolerate humanity in it? The rats were expert drillers boring holes throughout the mountain. They bore wherever possible and will bore ever more obsessively if it hits a patch of impenetrable rock. The dog bit anything it saw, except the tiger: it would pathetically lower its head and wag its tail when it saw the the tiger. The worst was the cat, that would jump up into the tree when it saw a tiger or leopard and return when they left. The monkey does "monkey see—monkey do." The weasel neglects its rear for its front: it merely farts when being chased and escapes. In addition, there are foxes disguised as beautiful women that dally on the mountain seducing men to death. The pigs and goats were by far the most useless. Though the bull was large, but only in appearance.[19]

Empty-hearted *officials* were a "Shànghǎi specialty," engaged in all types of unprecedented intrigue, deception, and trickery.[20] Even political reformers were suspected of actually only being in the game of getting rich—they were "dog-come-monkeymen" without a sense of "human dignity" in a rapidly shifting era in which officials secretly saw reform as an "elixir of immortality."[21] With the demise of the meritocratic imperial exams, Ruist aspirants to officialdom lost their agency and cosmological meaning—they could no longer be described as a majestic *crane amongst chickens,* a phrase traditionally used to celebrate the victor of the imperial exams, or like the ancient paragon of the righteous, politically-alienated courtier Qū Yuán, as a *raptor that does not flock like common birds.* The path to eternal glory was erased—their names would no longer be presented to the ancestors in the Ruist temples.[22] They were now the prey, having been reduced to mere survival. Characters in late Qīng novels have names like *Escaped Alive.*[23] In one, the character named *Nine Lives* informs his reader:

> I'm a good person—my whole life I've never suffered calamity or great obstacles, and no one has ever put out funds as a reward to capture me. So why do I hide my good name and call myself Nine Lives? Because in the last twenty years of scraping by, I reckon that I've only met three kinds of things: the first is snakes, bugs, rats and ants; the second is wolves, wildcats, tigers and panthers; and the third are goblins, trolls, ghouls and bogies. I lived amongst them for twenty years and have never been nibbled by the first, gobbled by the second, or captured by the third. So, I'm Nine Lives by virtue of having evaded them my whole life and this name is a commemoration of myself.[24]

There is much to lament and much to excoriate, but what is curious is a celebratory tone in the genre that has gone unnoticed by many literary historians. Few have read the genre as a means of re-establishing human dignity, meaning, and freedom in an era exposed to be deprived of humane values and the empathy signified by the term *feelings*.[25] Author Wú Jiǎnrén's (1866–1910 CE) novel Uncanny Reality Witnessed over Twenty Years (hereafter Uncanny) for example, in addition to being an exposure of official corruption, is also a systematic playbook that details the heroic and villainous techniques used by Chinese masters of strategy who display what the Chinese refer to as zhìmóu 智谋, a shortened form of Strategic Intelligence composed of the terms for talent (cáizhì 才智) and calculating machination (jìmóu 计谋).[26] The classical etymology of the terms refer to a type of calculating discrimination, and modern definitions point to its valorization of strategic advantage.[27]

An external world of violence, deception, and trickery informed the values of a world view characterized by naturalism and Darwinian conflict, and set the condition for strategic hope. Just like the manner in which the Táng dynasty poet Dù Fǔ's (杜甫 712–770 AD) famous line points to a higher level of hope amidst political decline (The kingdom smashed, the hills and waters remain 國破山河在)—the Qīng imperial order might have given way, but the kingly way of Strategic Intelligence clearly lived on for Wú.[28] *Uncanny's* narrative structure consists of episodes that compel strategic vision in neophytes by detailing in exquisite detail swindles, plots, ruses, graft, bribery, and deception. In a way, *Uncanny* is a primer that intends to "teach man the means of winning" via a cultivated art (*kungfu*), and functions as a strategic response to a newly exposed reality that is antagonistic to or ambivalent about human ambition.[29]

Uncanny provides a great example of the justified, legitimate and heroic use of Strategic Intelligence to achieve one's end, and offers an in depth depiction of a Strategic Intelligence that is conditioned by Chinese culture. In these chapters, Wú presents a sympathetic and celebratory view of a heroic *official* who maintains social harmony through virtuosic strategic manipulation, provides unique insight into Chinese strategic thought, and complicates conventional thinking on the functioning of corruption in Chinese society. Moreover, this literary source offers a deeper observation of Chinese strategic thought that is much more nuanced and evocative than what is available in most Chinese military and political treatises.

Uncanny exposes the network of life, constituted of the five cardinal relationships undergirded by the Ruist values of *empathetic response* and *just reciprocity*, as a spider web in which the self could be devoured by one's kin and kith.[30] The epigraph of chapter 18 "Revealing the Strange Reality of an Intemperate Clan" forewarns that the familial cannot erase social disorder because they are the very source of the pathology.[31] In these chapters, the reader follows the story of the maturing official who frees himself through his virtuosic display of social manipulation. In the story, the protagonist quickly returns to his ancestral village after receiving a cryptic telegram from his mother asking him to return home because she had taken ill. Upon returning home ten days later, he discovered to his great surprise both a healthy mother at odds with the clan leaders, and that the telegram was a ruse to lure him back. The intra-clan conflict was a result of the mother's refusal to pay a fee levied on all clan families by the clan-head in order to repair the ancestral temple that had been damaged. Thinking that her son was a rich official, the clan-head tried to extort her by levying an exorbitant sum. When his mother informed the clan-head that she would not pay without her son's input, knowing full-well that he would not return from the big city anytime soon, if at all, the clan-head sent the deceptive telegram to lure him home. This subterfuge worked: the filial son was emotionally moved by the summons, and returned home quickly.

Although the protagonist is just a gofer employed under the patronage of his friend in the big city, the clan-mates and neighbors of his hometown believe that he has inherited a large sum of money from his recently departed father, and they see him as financial opportunity that needs to be squeezed. He therefore faced the threat of being taken advantage of from the clan-head, the clan-mates, and neighbors who either have designs on his land or who want to profit as middlemen from the sale of his property. He and his mother are trapped. Through the art of strategic manipulation however, our protagonist is able to out-deceive the deceivers while maintaining social harmony, liquidating his assets, and moving his family to safety in another city. He is successful because of the manner in which he strategically used the narcissistic *self-interest* of his opponents as a means to navigate the various threats that he faced, while maintaining the Chinese values of empathy and social harmony. In essence, our hero strategically outscrews his kin who had hoped to screw him over—and his virtuosity in *orchestrating* and *inducing positive feelings* humorously results in them feeling good about it.[32]

First, to soften up the clan-head and make him agree to negotiate a just sum, the protagonist obligated the clan-head, manipulating the old man's self-esteem and sense of *face* by ritually offering him a small token as an "expression of his respect," a euphemism for bribery.[33] Through the act of gift-giving and gift-receiving, both sides entered into a relationship of mutual fellow-feeling and obligation. Not only was the clan-head's social status (*face*) acknowledged, but he was also indebted to the protagonist to identify a more advantageous solution, which he quickly accomplished.

Second, when the voracious hoard of kin learned that the protagonist had returned to their hometown, they quickly plotted to attack in force to find a means to extort him, creating a ruckus so big that he would be *mopped up*.[34] Seeing through their machinations, the protagonist opportunistically redirected their narcissistic self-interest and greed to an even greater future prize—he politely invited his adversaries to stay and enjoy a banquet together, and then utilized the time together to strategically manipulate them. *Seeing through* their covert plan to sponge off a successful relative as privileged official's family members thus enabled him to use this vulnerability to his advantage, what the ancient texts refer to as *grasping their handle*.[35] He lied to them by telling them that he had used all of his capital to procure an even better professional opportunity, and redirected their self-centered greed to a bigger pay-off in the future.

Because the protagonist was exceedingly courteous in hosting the banquet, through what my mother calls "killing them with kindness," he concurrently indebted his guests and mitigated their threat. In light of both his perceived kindness and of future reward, his relatives were too shamed to press him for money, and they subsequently let him off the hook.[36] In other words, through the righteous and legitimate utilization of strategy, via deceptive techniques of social manipulation, bribery, lying, and the preemptive induction of *positive emotional response*, the protagonist maintained both social harmony and the primacy of empathy while creating strategic advantage for himself by indebting them to him through the gift of hosting. He expediently escaped from their trap through a clever scheme, and turned the tables by playing their emotions.[37]

Last, in response to a neighbor who hoped to strong-arm him into selling his property at a loss in order to make a few bucks off of the sale for himself, the protagonist used a ruse to counter him. What is interesting here is the utilization of language that supports my suggestion that these stories are actually an exploration of ways and means one must use in order to live a life of dignity, self-mastery, and freedom. For example, this neighbor is accused of trying to frighten the protagonist as if he were still a naive little boy. Rather than behaving ritually as a *godfather*, this neighbor is accused both of social cannibalism, and of "disregarding *empathetic response* in order to get rich," which is ironically an accusation of impropriety in Ruist terms that shamed the neighbor and made him *lose face*.[38] The protagonist, like Prince Arthur in chapter 2, proves his strategic virtuosity with regards to would-be predators.

It was only through the artifice of strategic manipulation that our protagonist and his mother were able to avoid threat and leave the village. In an age of cannibalistic capitalism when one "only has *face* if one has wealth," this chapter implies that corruption, as an expression of an antagonistic reality, lies in social reality, not in the individual himself.[39] The cultural metaphor of family turns out to be ambivalent with respect to human flourishing—rather, family is diagnosed as sick and cannibalistic. It is the slick, authentic sage who maintains health, wealth, worth, and life by both playing at and winning the agonistic game of life, a game which rules start with, as the ancient text the *Hán Fēizi* taught, identifying the reality and necessity of *self-interest* as a driver in all human relations.

This chapter also exemplifies many of the theoretical aspects of eclectic Daoistic agency, extolled by classical texts such as Lǎozǐ's *Dàodéjīng*, the *Master of Demon Valley (Guǐgǔzi)*, and *Hán Fēi's* reiteration of preserving one's intactness. While not explicit, the protagonist displays the Daoist virtues of *yielding softness, accommodation, humility, contentedness,* and *perceiving subtlety*.[40] And his *techniques of the Way* exemplify much of the principles laid out in the text *Master of Demon Valley (Guǐgǔzi)*—our protagonist is a *virtuoso* of *schemes and machinations*,[41] and a master practitioner of all of the "arts of the Way"[42]; he divines his clan mates' intentions, and implements the appropriate *emotional response*.[43] He surveilled their interior terrain[44] and plumbed the depths of their ambitions[45] in order to opportunistically deliver effects which are perfectly timed with his schemes and stratagems.[46] He used a strategy of ensnarement in which he captured his quarry with the fishhooks of "angling words" and nets,[47] strategically occupied his target's emotive world[48] and *wormed his way*[49] into their affections with a banquet. Because every maneuver happened at the critical moment,[50] he was able to channel his targets toward his desired goal like forcing water through a dike.[51] In such a terrorizing and meaningless world devoid of Ruist *empathetic response* and *loving family-like relationships* that extend into the cosmos, these chapters from *Uncanny* resonate with insights in Lǐ's Zōngwú's *Theory of the Thick and Black* as a type of pragmatic wisdom manual that offers hope in the form of an art or spiritual practice (*kungfu/gōngfu* 功夫) of social manipulation.

THEORY OF THE THICK AND BLACK

There are few authors in Chinese history whose cynicism was so blatant or notoriety so scandalous that the mere mention of their product in conversation causes polite company to blush, giggle nervously, and even exhort the speaker to caution. In addition to the mention of the erotic strategist Pān Jīnlían from the seventeenth-century master novel *Plum in the Golden Vase*, discussing Lǐ Zōngwú's *Theory of the Thick and Black* (hereafter *Theory*) in public venues such as academic conferences has led many sensitive Chinese listeners in my audiences to urge me to be careful because *Theory* exposes uncomfortable truths about Chinese culture and power.[52] Discussing morality and sex on one hand, and morality and power on the other are both *parties honteuses* that some feel should continue to be hidden from view. Lǐ's *Theory* is as scandalous in the first decades of the twenty-first century as it was in the first decades of the twentieth century at the fall of the Qīng dynasty (1911) and during the Republican period when it caused an uproar. In fact, conflicting interpretations of *Theory* have galvanized Chinese culture in the last thirty years, with some judging *thickblackology* as an extreme social pathology, and others as a chicken-soup-for-the-soul self-help manual.[53] Perhaps it is both. China may not have a *House of Cards*, as China's premier Xí Jìnpíng joked during his 2015 press brief in Seattle, but it has the *thick* and *black* in spades.

Lǐ's *Theory* is a cultural exemplar that expresses the strategic world view, and his cultural analyses in sources such as his *Collected Sayings on the Thick and Black* (hereafter *Rambles*) is extraordinarily bold and breathtaking. *Rambles*, for example, is strategic in political theory like Machiavelli in his *Discorsi* and *Principi*, devastating in cultural critique and moral philosophical analysis akin to Nietzsche's *A Genealogy of Morality,* and bold in humanistic and philosophical spirit like Immanuel Kant's famous article *What is Enlightenment?*[54] More importantly, it is an excellent example of Chinese Strategic Intelligence for the way in which it cloaks dissent, however thinly, in cultural allusion, a rhetorical strategy that the French Sinologist François Jullian referred to as the oblique approach.[55] I anticipate that future readers will identify Lǐ the "crazy patriarch" as the latest in a millennia-old Chinese counter-cultural lineage of dissenters, the most eminent of whom I refer to as the five devilish Lǐs, a group of culture mavens that includes Lǐ Lǎozi, Lǐ Bái, Lǐ Hè, and Lǐ Zhì.[56] I predict that Lǐ Zōngwú will ultimately go down in history as one of the most brilliant, provocative and instructive thinkers in Chinese cultural history, and as a father of the twentieth-century Chinese Renaissance.

Theory is notable for three reasons. First, it serves as evidence about the existence of a shared, perhaps even universal, metaphorical, and paradoxical paradigm that *life is death* because it directly links a vision of cultural heroism constructed on ruthlessly cunning strategy as a potent form of hope necessitated by an antagonistic, amoral environment. Second, *Theory* provides evidence about the strategic in terms of values, meaning, worldview, and cultural identity, through an interpretative approach that constructs a cultural genealogy in order to re-interpret authoritative and historical heroic identities produced over the long arc of Chinese cultural history. By attending to different metaphors, values, and forms of meanings, Lǐ compels his reader to reinterpret legacy cultural values and heroic human meaning by exposing his reader to a newly revealed aspect of reality, resulting in a new orientation, and a return to an older path of meaning. By re-orienting the human to a primarily amoral and antagonistic universe, Lǐ enables his compatriots to face their alienation through a sense of human agency empowered by the strategic—the weak become strong when the concealed is revealed—the weak are emboldened when they harness their embodied power. Third, Lǐ's explicit exposure of kung fu-like tactics of social strategy offers the outsider a unique perspective into one account of Chinese strategic thought.

I invite my reader to imagine the wonder they might feel in discovering, upon browsing the shelves of a given bookstore, more than a thousand books written in the last fifteen years that include the term *übermensch* in their title.⁵⁷ Quickly glancing across the shelves in our imaginary bookstore, one finds titles such as *The Übermensch of Sex: Transcending Limits, The Übermensch of Raising Children: Master or Slave?, Be an Übermensch! Making a Killing in Business, Übermensch and the Art of War*, and even *Übermensch in the White House: Secrets the Republicans Don't Want You to Know*.⁵⁸ Many will vaguely recall the Nietzschean figure of the *übermensch* and her *will to power*, and this recollection may lead one to wonder about the extension and popularization of this critical term in titles spanning multiple domains—literature, politics, culture, psychology, relationships, childhood education, and even business management and entrepreneurship. The sensitive consumer may wonder what is it about the metaphorical figure of the *übermensch* that has captured so much of the cultural marketplace? And, in extending its insights to a plethora of self-help strategies, what makes it so compelling? How has it become a form of hope that one book title describes as a *way of success for a chaotic world*?⁵⁹

With this analogy to the *übermensch*, I hope to both contextualize the phenomenon of thickblackology (厚黑学 hòuhēixué) in contemporary China which has galvanized the cultural scene since the 1990s, and introduce the source from which it comes, Lǐ Zōngwú's (1879–1943 CE) satirical masterpiece *Theory*. For our purposes here, we can understand Theory as an interpretative frame which makes salient the most important questions about any form of meaning, including what makes a given form of meaning ultimately authoritative, and to what degree are its claims of legitimacy validated by culture.

Written during the fall of the Qīng dynasty (1644–1911 CE) and expanded in the Republican period (1912–1949), the Sichuanese intellectual Lǐ Zōngwú's *Theory* is a marvelous example of Chinese strategic rationality, and it has been compared to Machiavellianism. Outside of a few short references, *Theory* and the self-help philosophy of *thickblackology* that it spawned have gone unnoticed by many Western scholars of Chinese culture.⁶⁰ In the Sinophone world, the *thick* and *black* is pervasive in culture—it seems as if everyone has heard of the *thick* and *black,* but I have yet to come across someone who actually confesses to having read *Theory*.

New big data capabilities exist that enable us to quantitatively track the proliferation of the concepts of the *thick* and *black* across disparate cultural domains, to at least anecdotally evaluate its significance in Chinese culture. Interest in *Theory* in contemporary China is clearly growing, as evidenced from my quantitative analysis of the data presented here. Based on a metadata analysis of co-referenced terms from data in the China National Knowledge Infrastructure's (CNKI) China Knowledge Resource Integrated Database, and a keyword search in WorldCat, I discovered more than 6,959 articles in which Lǐ's concepts occurred, and around 1,500 related monographs respectively.[61] As figure one shows, when tagged by academic domain, we can track the proliferation of debates about the *thick* and *black* in time across the cultural ecosystem.

In addition to academic publishing, in an intriguing twist in which the *thick* and *black* have become synonymous with the means of acquiring strategic advantage in life, hundreds of self-help books with the the words *thick-black* in their title have been published in the Sinophone world. Topics run the gamut from success in dating, child-rearing, and careers, to political, military, and business strategy. These include Liú Qīnglèi's *Theory of the Thick and Black of Love: Love Actually is Just a Type of Deception,* Yú Bīn's "Children's Theory of the Thick and Black," Zhōu Yōugēn's *Thick and Black Art of War: the Way of Success for a Troubled World,* Chén Pòkōng's *Zhōngnánhǎi Theory of the Thick and Black: Secrets the Chinese Communist Party Won't Reveal,* Chén Yún's *Trump Theory of the Thick and Black,* and Wáng Zhāo's *Thick Black Diary of an Old Fox,* which is subtitled *Thick-black Survival Principles that you can't Afford not to Know!* Chu Chin-Ning and Huáng Wéiyù even published *The New Theory of the Thick and Black Sunzi Art of War,* and Chu also published in English *Thick Face Black Heart: The Path to Thriving, Winning and Succeeding.*[62] The eminent Australian scholar of modern Chinese culture Geremie Barmé relayed that the People's Republic of China's Central Party School, the primary training school for Chinese Communist political commissars, was ironically also the leading

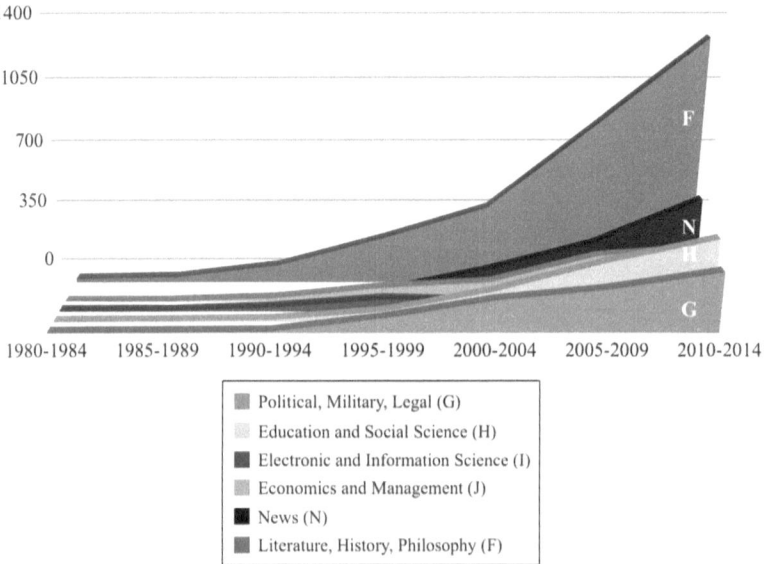

Figure 7.1 Hòuhēi in the PRC Intellectual Ecosystem. Author created.

publisher of *Theory*, having sold 400,000 copies by 1993.⁶³ *Thickblackology* has galvanized the cultural scene in contemporary China, reframing an ancient dialogue about the foundations of cultural legitimacy and authority, heroism, values and corruption, interpersonal strife and harmony, the possibility of organizing a just and fair society, and human meaning itself.

What type of hope is *thickblackology* exactly, and to what does the *thick* and *black* refer?

Lǐ describes *thickblackology* in *Rambling* as a historical world view, a philosophy, and as technique.⁶⁴ As a worldview, *thickblackology* is interpretative and intentionally paradigm-shifting in the same way as Marxism or Darwinism are. As philosophy, *thickblackology* is revelatory and spiritually potent in exposing to view the often ugly truth both about human nature itself, and society.⁶⁵ And as praxis, it is a cultivation regime, a technique shù 術 that results in strategic advantage when wielded with virtuosic mastery. In short, *thickblackology* as a form of hope is a theoretical foundation that intends "to strengthen the weak to resist the strong."⁶⁶

Lǐ offers *Theory* as a cultural genealogy that intends to help the reader identify with the heroic strategists of Imperial China, and the strategic values that these figures express. To do so, he draws both from history, particularly the histories of the Warring States period (475–221 BCE) and eclectic Daoist philosophy. Lǐ depicts Chinese history in terms of a 2,500-year-old cultural war between the Daoist values of *forbearance* (rěn 忍) and the Ruist value of *empathetic response* (rén 仁). Expressed in Chinese yīn-yáng terms, the yáng side of Daoist rěn signifies long sufferance and generous patience with oneself, as expressed in words such as *endurance, toleration, forbearance* (rěnshòu 忍受). The yīn aspect of Daoist rěn, as indicated by its Japanese pronunciation nin as in ninja, signifies deadly potency with others when necessary. The first can also be referred to as *thick* and the second as *black*.⁶⁷ Lǐ understands himself as the patriarch and founder of *thickblackology* in the same way that an excavator might happen upon gold while digging—it is not that the gold is new, it is just that the presence of gold which has been there all along has now been brought to light. Inspired by the utilization of metaphor and allegory in the Daoist text *Zhuāngzi*, Lǐ too exposes his gold, as *thick* and *black,* to sight by naming the phenomenon metaphorically. What was previously culturally ubiquitous and yet theoretically under-articulated now has a name.

The *thick* of *thickblackology* corresponds to the requirement to be *thick-faced*, a metaphorical concept that goes far beyond the invulnerability to insult and criticism implied in the Anglophone world's use of the term *thick-skinned*. In many ways, the idealized Ruist social reality that Lǐ is reacting to can be metaphorically conceptualized as a type of partner dance, rather than as competition. The specific dance, such as waltz, tango, or salsa, is akin to ceremony and *ritual*, which provides a social form to the dancers.⁶⁸ Partners derive their identity from the role they adopt, such as the follower or leader in a partner dance, and deference to other roles leads to dignity, grace, elegance, and social harmony. As all dancers know, the dance is a type of ritual that is aesthetic and emotional, not a rote set of steps that are devoid of feeling. And the dance is not about power *per se*—the identities of follower and leader are mutually reinforcing, and deferential, and the dance as art itself is both the means and the ends, resulting in harmonious beauty when performed well. With this conceptual background, we can begin to understand the Chinese cultural metaphor of *face* in terms of relational identity, deference, reciprocity, and social harmony. In light of this background, a proposal to develop *thick-facedness* signifies a shockingly asocial yet conscious insensitivity to others.

The *black* of *thickblackology* refers to being *black-hearted*. Lǐ presented *black-heartedness* in *Theory* as a type of Nietzchean will-to-power grounded in natural *self-interest*.[69] *Heart* is the metaphor that articulates emotional affection as the grounds of Classical Ruist moral theory, and Ruist philosophy oriented the human in an integrating cosmos that is sympathetic with human concerns (*tiānrén héyī* 天人合一). The value of *black-heartedness* is antithetical to the primary classical Ruist values of *empathetic response, rightness, sincerity,* and *brotherly* and *filial affection*.[70] Like Lǎozi, Zhuāngzi, Machiavelli and Nietzsche before him, Lǐ disrupted the traditional authority and moral grounds of conventional, Orthodox Ruist religious and political theories. In light of the reality and pervasiveness of political corruption devoid of any semblance of empathy, Lǐ's *Theory* both seeks a new grounding for modern life, a means for personal and national survival, and functions for many as a primer for strategic advantage in a reality experienced as antagonistic.

For Lǐ, and other authors of the late Imperial and Republic-era sub-genre of officialdom literature, late Qīng and early Republican mandarins were paradoxical heroes—they were ironically both the greatest exemplars of political Ruism and the most successful of predators located at the top of the food chain, an aspect of reality introduced by Darwinian evolution, and a conceptual metaphor at odds with the analogy of the lead dancer in the example discussed above.[71] At the risk of introducing a metaphorical conceit, Qīng dynasty mandarins and Republican officials were now wolves who strategically chose to dance with sheep, and the new form of the dance was competitive, more like the highly choreographed kung fu fights in Chinese martial art films. The justification for Ruist political heroism derived from familial empathy was exposed by Lǐ as a pretense and a lie— the kungfu routine was actually a means to an end—constructed of *means* and *techniques*.[72] Due to this prevalent experience of antagonistic reality and dissonance, a new genealogy of the heroic was clearly required—in this view, *thickblackology* ironically functions as a *rectification of names*, a term that Chinese philosophical texts use to describe the nexus of social responsibility and political power in light of the values of ritual and family obligation.[73]

Lǐ's *rectification of names* that is *thickblackology* is grounded in Daoist-inspired values, a strategic and eclectic Daoist interpretation of cultural history, and in the authority, validity, and legitimacy of the human body itself. Like Nietzsche who in his polemic *A Genealogy of Morality* looked for hope in the figures of the pre-Socratic aristocratic and noble warrior-heroes of ancient Greece, Lǐ grounded hope in the figures from China's venerable strategic tradition.[74] The forebears of his era's wily officials were the terrible and heroic exemplars of strategic intelligence from pre-Qín dynasty culture, not the moral paragons from an imaginary Ruist past. The roots of the *thick* and *black* can be found in the Daoistic strategists of the pre-Qín dynasty Hundred Schools, including luminaries such as Wén Zhōng, Fàn Lí, Zhāng Liàng, Chén Píng, Yī Yǐn, Sū Qín and his student Kuǎi Tōng, King Gōujiàn of Yuè, and Jiāng Ziyá.[75] According to Lǐ, the esoteric teachings of Lǎozi and Hán Fēi mark the culmination and cultural apogee of this heroic lineage.

Although these masters did not use the terms *thick* and *black*, they were nevertheless masters of it—Lǐ wrote that "Lǎozi presented the theory of *thickblackology*, and Hán Fēi showed us how to practically wield it."[76] The power aspect of Lǎozi's classic text has been captured in various English translations, such as in Arthur Waley's *The Way and Its Power: Lao Tzu's Tao Te Ching and Its Place in Chinese Thought,* and as a masterpiece that *makes this life significant.*[77] From Master Hán Fēi of the Warring States, Lǐ re-articulates the existential threat that lies concealed at the core of power and ambition, and evokes the theme of internecine struggle between the "clear-sighted lord" of the "way of the ruler" and his courtiers who represent various interest groups.[78] For example, Hán Fēi wrote,

> "Daily battles are the norm between the higher and lower," said the Yellow Emperor. Concealing their interests, those below attempt to influence above, and those above divide below through constraint. Therefore, the setting of constraints is the jewel of rulership. The tool of forming alliances is the jewel of ministers. Ministers cannot murder their lord if they are not equipped. When an inch is lost from above, an inch is gained below. The lord of a kingdom does not expand secondary cities, and the minister of the *Way* is not partial to his clan. The Lord of the *Way* is not partial to his minister.[79]

This depiction of agonistic competition at court is akin to, in my view, the competition between Zeus and Prometheus discussed in chapter 3, and Walter Map's depiction of hellish medieval European court life. (Chapter 5) The enlightened lord is free from the "wiles and machinations" of his ministers, impervious to emotional manipulation, and invulnerable to the emotional effects of their virtuosic suasion, and his freedom enables him to avoid harm and retain potency.[80] For Lǐ, texts produced by the masters of the Warring States are the "true classics," and *thickblackology* can help the disciple learn how to unlock the inner teaching.[81] Daoist *rén* is like water; it is generously *thick* in relation to self when flowing to its natural end—and it is ruthlessly *black*, bursting forth and destroying all in its path when it is blocked.[82] The use of the metaphor of water to express Daoist agency, articulated first in Lǎozi's *Dàodéjīng,* was also picked up by the famous martial artist Bruce Lee, who famously advocated to "be formless, shapeless, like water. Now you put water into a cup, it becomes the cup. You put water into a bottle, it becomes the bottle. You put it in a teapot, it becomes the teapot. Now water can flow or it can crash. Be water, my friend."[83]

Like many of the cultural sources discussed throughout this book, *Theory* frames its discussion as a revelation of the concealed. The esoteric truth of the Way (*Dào* 道) was suddenly revealed as *satori*-enlightenment as Lǐ meditated on the many successes of the most eminent heroes in the *Three Kingdoms.* The age-old secret of their success, the one thread that runs through the *Annals* is nothing other than *thickening and blackening.*[84] In *Theory*, the primary antagonists of the *Three Kingdoms*, Cáo Cāo and Liú Bèi, were heroic paragons worthy of emulation because of their ruthless Strategic Intelligence. As Lǐ pointed out,

> Of the heroes of the Three Kingdoms, the exemplar is Cáo Cāo, whose excellence consisted of *heart blackening*. After killing Lǚ Bóshē, Kǒng Róng, Yáng Xiū, Dǒng Chéng, and Fú Wán, he then murdered the empress and the prince. He then boldly pronounced, "Better to strike first than be struck!" As for *blackened hearts*, truly his had reached the highest pinnacle. With such a capacity, of course he is hailed as the greatest hero of the age. The next to be considered is Liú Bèi, whose excellence totally consisted of *facial thickening*: he depended on Cáo Cāo, Lǚ Bù, Liú Biǎo, Sūn Quán, and Yuán Shào, scuttling all over the place living under their patronage with no sense of shame. He was adept at crying—whoever wrote *Romance of the Kingdoms* really described him well, like when he cried himself out of a hairy situation and transformed failure into success. And so the saying goes, *Liú Bèi's lands were won through tears.* He is also an example of a hero with great capacity.[85]

In contrast to Orthodox Ruist traditions that grounded political action in metaphors of family feeling and deference, Lǐ exposed the true roots of political action as a will-to-power grounded in agonistic conflict, albeit articulated in uniquely Chinese cultural metaphors.

> Zōngwú said, "The *thick* and the *black* are not extrinsic to me, but intrinsic. Nature produces people with the *thick* and the *black*, and it is what they like.

This can be verified—go ahead and find a mother who is eating while coddling her child. That child will try to grab the bowl from the mother's hands and the bowl will be broken if one is not careful. He will also try to grab the cake from the mother's hand. He stretches out his arm to grasp it as soon as he sees it and he will pop it in his own mouth. If the mother does not give it to him, he will stretch out his arms and try to snatch it out of her mouth to put it in his own. Or, a child being breastfed or fed while in his mother's arms will push and hit his older brother when he sees him coming towards him. All of these are examples of unlearned behaviors that occur before thought and therefore are examples of innate knowledge and behavior. Those who can leverage and expand this type of innate knowledge and behavior can accomplish great things. Emperor Tàizōng killed his older brother Jiànchéng and his younger brother Yuánjí, and then murdered their sons and usurped their concubines. He also forced his own father to yield the realm to him. These behaviors were nothing more than leveraging and expanding on childlike innate knowledge and behaviors, such as snatching the cake from the mother's mouth, or pushing away or hitting his older brother. While ordinary people have this type of innate knowledge and behavior, they do not leverage and expand on it like Táng Tàizōng did, and so he became the world's greatest hero.[86]

Students of historical Chinese thought are sure to hear in this ancient echoes of the debates between the various schools that explored power and agency in the Warring States (475–221 BCE) period (Yangism, Hán Fēizi, *Master of Demon Valley Guǐgǔzi*) reverberating through the centuries, and philosophers will indubitably recall the subversion of Ruist moral philosophy in famous episodes in Chinese cultural history, such as the Robber Zhí and Mǎn Gǒudé dialogues in the Zhuāngzi (Chapter 6); the beginning of Hán Fēi's famous interpretation of Daoist thought that identifies power with personal intactness; passages from Lǎozi's *Dàodéjīng* that identify the *root* and *Way* of humanity in the belly, and the strategy of returning to the purity of the child without stain who "understands her white while preserving her black"; and metaphors in the *Zhuāngzi* that extol the *master of nourishing life* who protects and preserves his *intactness and integrity,* and the excellence of a human naturalness that is instrumentally useless.[87] Lǐ's theory is an updated, modern foundation for *nurturing life force* that is, however, ironically grounded in interpersonal violence.[88]

In a sense, *thickblackology* is a repackaging of old strategic values in a new way, and a re-articulation of an ancient critique of the legitimacy of Orthodox moral order and governance. For example, one of the famous Seven Sages of the Bamboo Grove, the infamous Ruǎn Jí (210–263 AD), criticized the revered political hero of the Orthodox schools as a flea that lives in the crotch of one's trousers.[89] "Motivated by graft, they con the simple and deceive the innocent, enslave and exhaust the people by binding them to rites and conventions, and conceal their cunning intelligence and moral corruption behind the veil of majesty."[90] In like fashion, Lǐ's particular interpretation is an excellent example of the "blaspheming" of Orthodox cultural heroes that might make General Secretary of the Chinese Communist Party Xí Jìnpíng shudder because it can be read as an ironic and thinly veiled form of cultural contestation that undermines the Party-state propaganda machine when an analogy is established between the ruthless strategists of the three kingdoms and the genealogical lineage that constitutes contemporary Chinese Communist Party-state cadres.

In this regard, *Theory* is provocative and galvanizing: it poses a threat that Chinese Communist Party ideologues would characterize as cultural nihilism, and it threatens Chinese Communist Party-state narratives of righteous self-sacrifice when the analogy is drawn by undermining the root motives (noble, and righteous self-sacrifice) of the ancestors of the Party-state.[91] This threat also indubitably accounts for the popularity of *Theory* across Chinese society. Lǐ wrote in elegant classical Chinese about Chinese political heroism, "Sagedom and the *thick* and *black,* one in the same and the same in one"; and quoting Zhuāngzi, *"as long as the sages live, the robbers will not cease."*[92] Inspired by Warring States stylistics in texts such as *Strategies of the Warring States*, the terseness of which he understood as morally ambiguous, Lǐ posited that the dynamics of human nature and of the *thick* and *black* are amoral and paradoxical. "One cannot discern if human nature is good or bad just like one cannot say for sure that water and fire are good or bad." "What do good and evil have to do with *rěn* 忍," asked Lǐ?[93] This is analogically similar to an evaluation of the value of the *thick* and *black*—it is good when used for good, and bad when used for bad—it is all in the eye of the beholder.[94]

By emphasizing bodily necessity as the *root* of self-expansion, Lǐ Zōngwú, the self-proclaimed patriarch of the cult of self who even took the reign title *veneration* (*zōng* 宗) of *self* (*wú* 吾), seems to be channeling the spirit of another historical proponent of individual authenticity from the radical Tàizhōu sect of Ruism, the contrarian late Míng dynasty literatus Lǐ Zhì (1527–1602 CE), self-styled Lǐ Zhuówú (Outstanding Self 卓吾), whose defense of sincerity, spontaneity and authenticity in his theory of the *childlike heart*, among other heterodox views, led to his imprisonment and suicide 300 years earlier.[95] In the passage cited above, Lǐ evokes the existential frame in the metaphor of consumption, holistically linking the bodily necessity of eating with violence, self-interest, self-expansion, and finitude. The mind is not the master of the soul, which is the master of the body, as Plato taught in the *Republic*—in *Theory* mind is the weapon of the soul, which is the servant of the body for whom it fights.

The existential contest for meaning sets the condition for the strategic, and integrates moral philosophy with political theory—it is just as relevant in personal, interpersonal, national, and international contests. Lǐ noted that although he articulated the technique of the *thick* and *black* in *Theory* through the figures of Cāo and Líu, the "secret knack of the *thick* and *black*" is just as relevant to the international rivalry of political giants such as King Gōujiàn of Yuè and General George Washington, and to the weak Qīng dynasty and Republican era governments beset by predatory colonizing powers.[96] It will be difficult for Western powers to understand the *thick* and *black*, wrote Lǐ, but they may just lay off once they understand China's secret weapon.

Lǐ Zōngwú preached that the seeds of heroism are intrinsic to our humanity, to our very existence as embodied beings—we all can be heroic if we allow ourselves to develop as natural human beings and follow the categorical imperative of the *will to power*—if we all snatch what we naturally desire. Human greatness is inherent, but it still must be nurtured. Humorously, satirically and sacrilegiously inverting a famous passage from the Ruist philosopher Mencius, Lǐ preached that self-actualization was denuded of possibility by the repression compelled by moralism.

> He who ravages his *thickness* and *blackness* is just like the lumberjack to the trees. Cutting it down day by day, his *thickening* and *blackening* will not survive, and it will therefore be insufficient to become a hero. This results in people thinking that they cannot be heroic because they had the *thick* and the *black*: but can this be reckoned as their original propensity? So, the *thick* and *black* will flourish if you cultivate it and wither if you do not.[97]

In essence, Lǐ reworked Robber Zhí's famous judgement in the Zhuāngzi, "Get behind me Confucius! Those who cannot release ambition and intent and nourish their lot are off the *Way* (*Dào* 道)!"[98]

Now that we understand the origins of the *thick* and *black* and why it is necessary, the question that arises is how does one use this theory. Lǐ's *Theory* is a clear example of strategic rationality at work in culture. Expressed through uniquely Chinese cultural metaphors, Lǐ presents the strategic as a process of *kung fu*-like cultivation in which the adept progresses in three degrees from being *black as coal* to *glossy blackness,* and to ultimate invisibility as *insubstantial thickness* and *hueless blackness*. Since at least the time of the classic of covert martial craft, *The Six Sheaths* (~500–200 BCE), conventionally believed to be the masterwork of the legendary master of Strategic Intelligence Jiāng Ziyá, this strategy of cunning concealment has been valorized in culture as *tāolüè*.[99] As Lǐ preached,

> This ultimate mastery is an attribute of the most exemplary *great sages and worthies of the past*. Ruist and Buddhist texts both claim that the mark of mastery is invisibility: some people ask, "how can this type of learning be so profound"? I reply, "the Ruist text *Doctrine of the Mean* (*Zhōngyōng*) teaches

that one cannot exhaust the way until one understands the *soundless and the odorless*.[100] Buddhists must understand that *there is no wisdom tree, nor a stand of mirror bright' before they can attain the buddha nature.'* How much more so for the arts of the *thick* and *black* which are the occult secrets to success of the ancients! Clearly the final stage cannot be attained without achieving *formlessness* and *odorlessness*.

Lǐ thought that the greatest of all Chinese paragons throughout history were actually able to strategically hide their expanded self-interest rather than repress it through moral restraints, through the heroic cultivation of bodily life-force rather than through self-cultivation:

> Some people ask, 'how can this type of learning be so profound'? I reply, the Ruist text *Doctrine of the Mean* (*Zhōngyōng*) teaches that one cannot exhaust the way until one understands the *soundless and the odorless*.[101] Buddhists must understand *there is no wisdom tree, nor a stand of mirror bright* before they can attain the buddha nature.[102] How much more so for the arts of the *thick* and *black* which are occult secrets to success passed down from the ancients! Clearly the final stage cannot be attained without achieving *formlessness and odorlessness*.[103]

If concealment is the *root* (*běn* 本) of life and the primary dynamic of social life, then she who strategically conceals her true intentions and capacity is best postured to attain strategic advantage. So, "cover your face with a layer of whatever suits those folks at any given time and place," suggested Lǐ. "Even if you do not wish to practice the *thick* and *black*, you still must know it in order to protect yourself against others who would use it against you." Not only did moralists hide profit and benefit (*lìyì* 利益) under the Ruist moral homonyms (*lǐyí* 禮儀) *ritual deportment* and *rightness*, Lǐ cynically encouraged disciples of the *thick* and *black* to adapt themselves to their audience instrumentally rather than through feeling.

> When you meet friends who discuss love and sexuality, there is no point in bringing up the Ruist morals of *empathetic response* and *rightness* with them, will that not but invite their disinterest? Instead, you should cover it with the words *sacred love*. If you meet a with Marxist, cover it with *class struggle* and the *dictatorship of the proletariat* and he may even call you comrade.

Lastly, similar to the manner in which Machiavelli revealed the expedient and exigent in his *Discorsi* and the *Principi*, *Theory* should be of interest to students of Chinese strategic thought because it offers a frank discussion of the tools of the strategist's trade, which he characterizes as a kungfu-like cultivational regime of social manipulation. Like the martial arts, neophytes of the *thick-black* strategic arts become virtuosic as they master the three degrees of increasing invisibility—the most sublime are those masters who appear totally virtuous. Lǐ's two mantras, the *Six Words for Seeking Officialdom* and *Six Words for Being an Official*, and his *Two Marvelous Arts for Taking Care of Business*, expose a strategically instrumentalist logic of social manipulation that is learned through the cultivational arts.

To understand Lǐ's regime of cultivation, one should imagine that the cultivation of the art of social manipulation is akin to the cultivation of kungfu techniques. For example, leisure (*kōng* 空), worming in (*gòng* 貢), bragging (*chōng* 沖), flattering (*pěng* 捧), threatening (*kǒng* 恐), and bribing (*sòng* 送) are all weapons that one may utilize to gain strategic advantage. These esoteric techniques must be wielded with sensitivity and tact if one is to be successful. Knowing how and when to use them is a sign of one's interpretation of the particular dynamics of any given situation.

> The mastery of threatening (*kǒng* 恐) is especially subtle, and tricky to wield .... This means to intimidate ... the principle of this word is very profound, so I will say something about it. Official position is a priceless thing, how can one lightly give it away? Some people totally focus on *pěng* to no avail—and this is because they lack the art of *kǒng*. All important officials have a soft spot; if you can identify and lightly press on the vital spot, then he will become alarmed and an official position will be conferred. The disciple should know that *kǒng* and *pěng* are used together. For *kǒng* adepts, even *pěng* is imbued with *kǒng*: for example, although bystanders think one is toadying up in front of leadership, he actually is secretly pushing the vital spot, and the senior official will break out in a cold sweat when he hears him speak. *Pěng* adepts use a *pěng* imbued with *kǒng*. While bystanders see an unyielding spirit criticizing their superiors, actually the superior is so pleased that he goes weak in the knees. Seekers of office must carefully experience this, as the sayings attest: *Investigate it yourself before you can* and *the master craftsman can only transmit the technique, not the ability*. Most importantly, *kǒng* must be appropriately used. If it is overused, then people's shame will flare up into anger and opposition; is that not contrary to the aims of the office-seeker? So, why bother? Do not lightly use *kǒng* unless you are have no other recourse.

Although Lǐ meant to provide a sardonic critique, what is unnerving is that these practices of strategic social manipulation are not just theoretical—many of us have experienced similar situations in China. In fact, the anthropologist Mayfair Mei-hui Yang in her monograph *Gifts, Favors, and Banquets: The Art of Social Relationships in China* documented just these types of behaviors during her field research in the People's Republic of China.[104] It is just as Lǐ predicted, "we must use the *thick* and *black* historical worldview to see society, to see society in the nude, in order to make its true form visible."[105]

Many Chinese nationals have pushed back on me when I have discussed this aspect of Chinese culture at academic conferences. But they inevitably become quiet when I ask to what degree have they ever bestowed *a small token of appreciation,* strategically induced a positive response, or extracted social benefits by *lālā guānxì* (pulling strings, calling in favors).[106] These social strategies mirror, to some extent, the strategies used by the generalissimos in Sūnzi's *Art of War,* who induce success strategically by adapting their plans to contingency and particular circumstances.[107]

In fact, Lǐ thought that the *thickblack* worldview, philosophy, and practical utilization were the theoretical equivalent of an *Art of War*, and that exemplars of Chinese Strategic Intelligence such as Hán Xìn and King Gōujiàn of Yuè taught, like Sūnzi, that you should proactively seek a place from which you cannot be defeated, biding your time for a ripe opportunity, even if that includes temporary suffering, humiliation, and shame.[108] This message is clearly resonating again in contemporary China—in order to get ahead in a cut throat competitive environment, many Chinese college graduates are now studying Lǐ's *thickblack* techniques, and this explains the surge of self help books that I discussed earlier in this chapter.[109] *Theory* is a primer for life that enables strategic advantage through insight—as one edition notes, it is an "authentically true scripture which enables one to see through to the uglier aspects of human nature in society."[110] And this should not, I think, be simply perceived as nefarious—the English adage "you catch more flies with honey than you do with vinegar" also gestures to a gentler and culturally acceptable social strategy of emotional manipulation.

I conclude this exploration of the strategic values expressed through a cultural product that is uniquely conditioned by Chinese history, language and philosophy, Lǐ Zōngwú's *Theory of the Thick and Black*. It is relevant to my theory of Strategic Intelligence because of the way that it focuses attention on the necessity of life in the face of finitude. This *Way* of Strategic Intelligence both orients us to the fundamentally antagonistic aspect of social reality and gestures to a type of human hope the nurturing of which can be both heroic and virtuosic even as it is paradoxically comically brutish and tragically beautiful. In other words, the human encounter with the mystery of death and the traumatizing possibility of no identity has been crystalized paradigmatically in the metaphorical paradox that *life is death,* and sets the condition by which meaning is made possible. Lǐ's *Theory* is a philosophical means of revealing this heretofore concealed aspect of reality, providing vicariously a mode of preparatory training for the contestants in the zero-sum game of life.

NOTES

1. Wú Jiǎnrén 吳趼人, *Uncanny Reality Witnessed over Twenty Years Èrshínián Mùdǔ zhī Guài Xiànzhuàng* 二十年目睹之怪現狀 (Běijīng: Rénmín Chūbǎnshè: Xīnhuá Shūdiàn Běijīng fāxíngsuǒ fāxíng, 1959). Lǐ Zōngwú 李宗吾, *Theory of the Thick and Black Hòuhēixué* 厚黑學. In *Hòuhēixué Dàquán* 厚黑學大全 (Hongkong: Shànghǎi Túshū Gōngsī, year unknown).

2. Scribe and Knight *shì* 士; literati *wénrén* 文人; mandarin *guānliáo*; master *shīfu* 師傅; scholar *rú* 儒; gentry-scholar *shēnshì* 紳士; official *shì* 仕; cadre *gānbù*; sage and worthy *shèng* 聖; lord and gentleman *jūnzi* 君子; accomplished one *zhìrén* 至人; authentic man *zhēnrén* 真人.

3. Mandarinism, officialism, bureaucratism *guānliáozhǔyì* 官僚主義; redtape-ism *wéndúzhǔyì* 文牘主義.

4. Official-foundationalism thought *guānběnwèi sīxiǎng* 官本位思想; command-ism *mìnglìngzhǔyì* 命令主義; officious-ism *shìwùzhǔyì* 事務主義; Communist Party culture that promotes the value of the party elite over the common people *Dǎngshàng mínxià* 當上民下; become an official and get rich *shēngguānfācái* 升官發財.

5. For example: Máo Zédōng 毛泽东 (x–1979), in *Must Focus on Economic Work* 必须注意经济工作, "Second, the manner of mobilizing the masses should not be *a la* officialism." "第二，动员群众的方式，不应该是官僚主义的。" Dèng Xiǎopíng 邓小平 (x—x), 哪怕是辛辛苦苦的～也好，哪怕是艰苦奋斗的命令主义也好，都在反对之列。 In *Report from the Xīnán area News work Conference* 在西南区新闻工作会议上的报告, Cited in "Mandarinism" 官僚主义, 新闻中心-中国网 news.china.com.cn, 4 December 2012, accessed 17 May 2019, http://news.china.com.cn/politics/2012-12/04/content_27303554.htm. Jiāng Zémín 江泽民 (x–x): "Comrade Jiāng Zémín also said, "Some comrades have not formed the appropriate view on power, a major cause of which is complicated by the residue of official-foundationalism which is a leftover from feudalist thought. Every rank of leadership cadre must be clear: as Communists we are determined to do great things, not determined to be great officials. We must by all means prevent our personal life goal focused on getting rich and becoming an official." 江泽民同志又说：一些同志没有树立正确的权力观，一个重要原因是"官本位"的封建残余思想在作怪。"各级领导干部必须明白，我们是共产党人，要立志做大事，不要立志当大官，千万要防止把升官发财作为自己的人生目的。" Wáng Wěi 王伟, "On Jiāng Zémín's Thought about Ethical Leadership: Rule by Virtue (3): the Experience of Studying *Jiāng Zémín's Anthology*." "论江泽民的德治思想：以德治国 (3) ——————学习《江泽民文选》的体会" *Chinese Community Party News, Theory, Party Construction Politics* 中国共产党新闻>>理论>>党建政治>>政治, accessed 17 May 2019, http://theory.people.com.cn/GB/41038/4826096.html.

6. "形式主义、官僚主义同我们党的性质宗旨和优良作风格格不入，是我们党的大敌、人民的大敌。" 30 September 2018, 15:05:40 Jīng Yì 精益, "Firmly Rectify Careerism and Officialism" 坚决整治形式主义、官僚主义 *Qiúshí* 求是, accessed 17 May 2019, http://www.qstheory.cn/wp/2018-09/30/c_1123509631.htm.

7. Officialdom literature *guānchǎng wénxué* 官场文学.

8. David Wang, "Abject Carnival: Grotesque Exposés," in *Fin-de-siècle Splendor: Repressed Modernities of Late Qīng Fiction, 1849–1911* (Stanford: Stanford University Press, 1997), *et passim*. Lǔ Xùn 魯迅, *A Brief History of Chinese Fiction*, trans. Hsien-yi and Gladys Yang (Beijing: Foreign Language Press, 1976). *A Brief History of Chinese Fiction Zhōngguó Xiǎoshuō Shǐlüè* 中國小說史略, reprinted (Hong Kong: Qingwen Shuwu, 1972). Liu, Ts'un-yan, "Introduction: 'Middlebrow' in Perspective," in Ts'un-yan Liu, ed. *Chinese Middlebrow Fiction: From the Ch'ing and the Early Republican Eras* (Hong Kong: The Chinese University Press, 1984), 1–40. Doleželová-Velingerová, Milena, ed. *The Chinese Novel at the Turn of the Century* (Toronto: University of Toronto Press), 1980. Patrick Hanan, *Chinese Fiction of the Nineteenth & Early Twentieth Centuries* (New York: Columbia University Press, 2004); Yáng Chūmíng 杨出明, *Late Qīng Fiction and Socioeconomic Transformation Wǎnqīng Wénxué yǔ Shèhuì Jīngjì Zhuǎnxíng* 晚清文學與社會經濟轉型 (Shànghǎi: Dōngfāng Chūbǎn Zhōngxīn 东方出版中心), 2005.

9. For an account of the emotive resonance of Chinese literati and the universe, please refer to "Between Emotion and Landscape: The World is Not an Object of Representation," in Jullien, *Detour*, 141–164.

10. *Three guides and five constants* (*sāngāng wǔcháng* 三綱五常), Teaching of Names (*míng jiào* 名教), ritual deportment (*lǐjiào* 禮教), *Rú* or Confucianism (*rújiā* 儒家).

11. Resource relationships *guānxì* 關係, face *miànzi* 面子, human feeling *rénqíng* 人情, induced favor *gǎnyìng* 感應, empathetic response 仁, appropriate reciprocity 義, decorum 礼, filial piety 孝, and brotherly love *tì* 悌.

12. Calling in favors *lālā guānxì* 拉拉關係.

13. Wenshan Jia, *The Remaking of the Chinese Character and Identity in the 21st Century: The Chinese Face Practices* (London: Ablex Publishing, 2001), 2.

14. Lǔ Xùn 魯迅, "On Face," *Shuō Miànzi* 說面子, 1934, accessed 20 April 2016, http://www.saohua.com/shuku/luxun/qjtz/017.htm.

15. Wú Jiǎnrén 吳趼人, *Uncanny Reality Witnessed over Twenty Years Èrshínián Mùdǔ zhī Guài Xiànzhuàng* 二十年目睹之怪現狀 (Běijīng: Rénmín Chūbǎnshè: Xīnhuá Shūdiàn Běijīng fāxíngsuǒ fāxíng, 1959), 1–6.

16. Wú Jiǎnrén 吳趼人, *Sea of Regret Hènhǎi* 恨海, in *Compendium of Modern Chinese Fiction Zhōngguó Jìndài Xiǎoshuō Dàxì* 中國近代小說大系 (Nánchāng: Jiāngxī Rénmín Chūbǎnshè: Jīngxiāo Jiāngxīshěng Xīnhuá Shūdiàn 南昌市: 江西人民出版社:經銷江西省新華書店 1988), 1–88. *The Sea of Regret: Two Turn of the Century Chinese Romantic Novels*, trans., Patrick Hanan (Honolulu: University of Hawai'i Press, 1995), 101–205. Wú Jiǎnrén 吳趼人, *History of Pain Tòngshǐ* 痛史, in *Compendium of Modern Chinese Fiction Zhōngguó Jìndài Xiǎoshuō Dàxì* 中國近代小說大系 (Nánchāng: Jiāngxī Rénmín Chūbǎnshè: Jīngxiāo Jiāngxīshěng Xīnhuá Shūdiàn 南昌: 江西人民出版社:經銷江西省新華書店 1988), 7–264. Bāo Tiānxiào 包天笑, *The Last Days of the World Shìjiè Mòrìjì* 世界末日纪, in *Compendium of Late Qīng Fiction Wǎnqīng Xiǎoshuō Dàxì* 晚清小說大系 (Táiběi: Guāngyǎ Chūbǎn Yǒuxiàn Gōngsī 光雅出版有限公司), Vol. 14:1–8. Wú Jiǎnrén 吳趼人, *World of Folly Hútú Shìjiè* 糊涂世界, in *Compendium of Modern Chinese Fiction Zhōngguó Jìndài Xiǎoshuō Dàxì* 中國近代小說大系

(Nánchāng: Jiāngxī Rénmín Chūbǎnshè: Jīngxiāo Jiāngxīshěng Xīnhuá Shūdiàn 南昌: 江西人民出版社:經銷江西省新華書店 1988), 411–561. Wú Jiǎnrén 吳趼人, *Bamboozled Xiāpiàn Qíwén* 瞎騙奇聞, in *Compendium of Modern Chinese Fiction Zhōngguó Jìndài Xiǎoshuō Dàxì* 中國近代小說大系 (Nánchāng: Jiāngxī Rénmín Chūbǎnshè: Jīngxiāo Jiāngxīshěng Xīnhuá Shūdiàn 南昌: 江西人民出版社:經銷江西省新華書店 1988), 411–478. *Flower in a Sea of Sin (Nièhǎihuā* 孽海花 1904). Wú Jiǎnrén 吳趼人, *The Despicable History of Recent Society Zuìjìn Shèhuì Wòchuòshǐ* 最近社會齷齪史, also called 近十年之怪現狀 in *Compendium of Modern Chinese Fiction Zhōngguó Jìndài Xiǎoshuō Dàxì* 中國近代小說大系 (Nánchāng: Jiāngxī Rénmín Chūbǎnshè: Jīngxiāo Jiāngxīshěng Xīnhuá Shūdiàn 南昌: 江西人民出版社:经销江西省 新华书店) 1988), 5–138. Wú Jiǎnrén 吳趼人, *After the Holocaust Jiéyúhuī* 劫餘灰, in *Compendium of Modern Chinese Fiction Zhōngguó Jìndài Xiǎoshuō Dàxì* 中國近代小說大系 (Nánchāng: Jiāngxī Rénmín Chūbǎnshè: Jīngxiāo Jiāngxīshěng Xīnhuá Shūdiàn 南昌市: 江西人民出版社:經銷江西省新華書店 1988), 89–222. Wú Jiǎnrén 吳趼人, *Living Hell Huó Dìyù* 活地狱, in *Compendium of Modern Chinese Fiction Zhōngguó Jìndài Xiǎoshuō Dàxì* 中國近代小說大系 (Nánchāng: Jiāngxī Rénmín Chūbǎnshè: Jīngxiāo Jiāngxīshěng Xīnhuá Shūdiàn 南昌: 江西人民出版社:經銷江西省新華書店 1988), 315–572.

17. *Dàyú chī xiǎoyú, xiǎoyú chī xiāzi.* 大魚吃小魚，小魚吃蝦子.
18. Lǐ Bóyuán 李伯元, *Living Hell* 活地獄 *Huó Dìyù*, in *Compendium of Modern Chinese Fiction* (*Zhōngguó Jìndài Xiǎoshuō Dàxì* 中國近代小說大系 (Nánchāng: Jiāngxī Rénmín Chūbǎnshè: Jīngxiāo Jiāngxīshěng Xīnhuá Shūdiàn 南昌: 江西人民出版社:經銷 江西省新華書店, 1989). 1. "Joy of fish" *zhīyúzhīlè* 知魚之樂: "The fish swim about so freely—such is the happiness of fish!" *Tiáoyú chūyóu cóngróng, shì yúzhīlèyě* 知魚之樂:儵魚出遊從容，是魚之樂也.
19. Lǐ Bóyuán, *The Record of the Revealing (of the Reality) of Officialdom* 官場現形記: *Guānchǎng Xiànxíngjì* (Nánchāng: Jiāngxī Rénmín Chūbǎnshè: Jīngxiāo Jiāngxīshěng Xīnhuá Shūdiàn 南昌: 江西人民出版社 : 經銷 江西省新華書店, 1989), 1106–1112. Another translation at *Officialdom Unmasked*, trans. T.L. Yang (Hong Kong: Hong Kong University Press, 2001), 620–634.
20. Lǐ, *Record* 民風淳樸的地方,變了個輕浮險詐的遭逃藪. 手頭空泛的, 空著心兒，也要充作大老官 . . . 空心老大官.
21. Elixir: *xùmìngdān* 續命丹. Human dignity: *réngé* 人格.*Rén shì hóuzi biànchéngde, hóuzi shì gǒu biànchéngde* 人是猴子變成的，猴子是狗變成的. *Record of Officialdom Reformed Guānchǎng Wéixīnjì* 官場維新紀, in *Chinese Popular Fiction Masterpieces Zhōngguó Tōngsú Xiǎoshuō Míngzhù* 中國通俗小說名著/世界文庫，四部刊登 *Shìjiè wénkù*. Sìbùkānyào (Táiběi: Shìjiè Shūjú 臺北 : 世界書局), 1–69.
22. Crane amongst chickens: *hèlìjīqún* 鶴立雞群. Raptor that does not flock like common birds: *zhìniǎo zhībùqúnxī* 鷙鳥之不群兮, from Qū Yuán's *Lí Sāo* 離騷.
23. Escaped Alive: *Sǐlǐ Táoshēng* 死里逃生.
24. *Nine Lives Jiǔsǐyīshēng* 九死一生. Wú Jiǎnrén 吳趼人, Uncanny, 1–6.
25. *Rénqíng* 人情.
26. Wú Jiǎnrén 吳趼人, *Uncanny*.

27. Discrimination: "The wise discriminate between yin and yang." 智者知阴阳. "智," *Baidu,* https://baike.baidu.com/item/智/2003331. "To gain as much advantage as possible" 尽可能取得最大利益." "智谋," *Baidu* https://baike.baidu.com/item/智谋/1003329: accessed 10 May 2019.

28. To make the metaphor explicit, the phrase "hills and rivers" gestures to a level of natural order higher than the political, and functions analogically as a type of *yin yang* binary (associated with *zhìmóu* 智谋 strategic intelligence) that refers to the flow and flux of reality, an environment in which a protagonist might still exercise intelligent discrimination.

29. Simone de Beauvoir: "The characteristic feature of all ethics is to consider human life as a game that can be won or lost and to teach man the means of winning."

30. Five cardinal relationships 五倫 *wǔlún*.

31. "Revealing the Strange Reality of an Intemperate Clan" (*zìfēngkuáng jiātíng xiànguàizhuàng* 恣瘋狂家庭現怪狀. Pathology *yàng* 恙.

32. Orchestrate *fāhuī* 發揮. Induce positive feelings *gǎnyìng* 感應. Incite/induce *Xìng* 興。

33. Expression of his respect *jìngyì* 敬意.

34. Means *fǎzi* 法子. Mopped up *Nǎodé gè 'luòhuāliúshuǐ* 惱得個'落花流水.

35. Seeing through *kànchuān* 看穿; official's family members *zuò guānqīn* 做官親. Grasp handle.

36. Embarrassed *bùhǎoyìsi* 不好意思.

37. *Positive emotional response gǎnyìng* 感應.

38. *Godfather* 父執. This term implies the intimacy of a father's life-long buddy, who the modern Chinese would refer to as *uncle*, a type of fictive kinship relationship ritualized in the *Book of Rituals* 禮記: (父執 *fùzhí*) 曲礼上: "見父之執, 不謂之進, 不敢進; 不謂之退, 不敢退; 不問, 不敢對。"(為富不仁 *wéifùbùrén*) Mencius《孟子·滕文公上》:" 為富不仁矣, 為仁不富矣. "Social cannibalism *píngbái dì qù chī rén* 平白地去吃人. Disregarding *empathetic response* in order to get rich" *wéifùbùrén*為富不仁, *lose face liǎn zhǎngde fēihóng* 臉漲的緋紅.

39. "Only has *face* if one has wealth" 此刻世界上, 有了銀子, 就有面子. Wú Jiǎnrén 吳趼人 *Uncanny,*139.

40. *Yielding softness: nuòruò* 懦弱; *accommodation: kuānróng* 寬容; *humility: qiānxià* 謙下; *contentedness: zhīzú* 知足; and *perceiving subtlety: jiànwēi*見微. Values discussed at length in Kung-chuan Hsiao, *A History of Chinese Political Thought*, Vol 1: From the Beginnings to the Sixth Century A.D., Trans. F. W. Mote (Princeton: Princeton University Press, 1979): 285–291.

41. Virtuoso (仕) of schemes and machinations 通達計謀. *Master of Demon Valley Guǐgǔzi* 鬼谷子, *Pressing into Cracks* 抵巇.

42. *Pressing into cracks is utilizing the arts of the Way* 抵巇之隙為道術用。 *Master of Demon Valley Guǐgǔzi* 鬼谷子.

43. Another's words [signify the possibility of] moving [them]; your tacitness is tranquility. Attend to their words, and listen to their speech. When words do express [the interior], seek more deeply, and the emotive response must emerge. 人言者, 動也; 己默者, 靜也. 因其言, 聽其辭. 言有不合者, 反而求之, 其應必出. *Master of Demon Valley Guǐgǔzi* 鬼谷子. *Emotional response yìng* 應.

44. Terrain: *xíngshì* 形勢.
45. Therefore one must always expose it to see the interior—this is called evaluating and plumbing feelings 故常必以其見者而知其隱者，此所謂測深揣情. *Guǐgǔzi* 鬼谷子, Plumb the Depths 揣篇.
46. Therefore, even though one has the plots of sagely strategic wisdom of the Way of the former kings, it will not be made plain if on does not plumb feelings and the hidden unknown 故雖有先王之道，聖智之謀，非揣情隱匿，無可索之。此謀之大本也，而說之法也. 言必時其謀慮. *Guǐgǔzi* 鬼谷子, Plumb the Depths 揣篇.
47. When phishing matches up with situations, then you may size up a person. It is like setting a snare for animals. 其釣語合事，得人實也。其猶張罝而取獸也。反應: This is the net of phishing people. Always maintain your net and drive them in. 此釣人之網也。常持其網而驅之。 *Feeling out* 摩篇: The virtuosic at feeling catch the big one by dangling the bait on a hook over the deep. 古之善摩者，如操鉤而臨深淵，餌而投之，必得魚焉. Acquire his feelings/emotive situation 得其情. *Master of Demon Valley Guǐgǔzi* 鬼谷子.
48. *Master of Demon Valley Guǐgǔzi* 鬼谷子, *Internal Constraints* 內揵.
49. *Master of Demon Valley Guǐgǔzi* 鬼谷子, *Pressing into Cracks* 抵巇.
50. 用分威散勢之權，以見其兌威，其機危乃為之決. Use the power of dividing might and dispersing momentum to see his pleasure. give power to the critical moment and resolve it. *Master of Demon Valley Guǐgǔzi* 鬼谷子, *Diminishing and Increasing Pattern the Numinous Yarrow* 損兌法靈蓍.
51. So it is for the master of persuasion, for it is like channeling water through a dike, or rolling a boulder into a deep gorge. Those who can do this, their influence will be no less. 故善損兌者，譬若決水於千仞之堤，轉圓石於萬仞之谿。而能行此者，形勢不得不然也。 *Master of Demon Valley Guǐgǔzi* 鬼谷子.
52. Pān Jīnlían is erotic both in the sexual and the Platonic sense of the term as a driving, ambitious, acquisitive force. *Plum in the Golden Vase* Jīnpíngméi Cíhuà 金瓶梅詞話. *Plum in the Golden Vase* Jīnpíngméi Cíhuà 金瓶梅詞話.*The Plum in the Golden Vase or, Chin P'ing Mei,* Five volumes, trans., David Tod Roy, (Princeton: Princeton University Press, 1997–2015).
53. Extreme social pathology (*jíduān bìngtài* 极端病态 and chicken-soup-for-the soul *xīnlíng jītāng* 心靈雞湯.
54. *Hòuhēi Cónghuà* 厚黑叢話.
55. François Jullien, *Detour and Access: Strategies of Meaning in China and Greece,* trans. Sophie Hawkes (New York: Zone Books, 2000).
56. The Five devilish Lǐs *guǐcái wǔlǐ* 鬼才五李. The term for the five Lǐs *wǔ Lǐ* has the added bonus of punning with the term irrational *wúlǐ* 無理. Lǎozi 老子, one of the two main patriarchs of Daoism, is traditionally believed to have been surnamed Lǐ. Lǐ Bái 李白 and Lǐ Hè 李賀 are famous poets from the Tāng Dynasty, still studied in Sinophone cultures. Lǐ Zhì 李贄 was an influential seventeenth-century thinker. Lǐ Zōngwú refers to himself in his *oeuvre* as patriarch 教主, founder 發明, and as being bonkers 老瘋子.
57. *Übermensch:* superman, or the man who transcends.

58. All titles are meant to be suggestive.

59. Zhōu Yōugēn 周優根, *Thick and Black Art of War: the Way of Success for a Troubled World Hēi Bīngfǎ: Luànshì Chénggōng zhī Dào* 厚黑兵法：亂世成功之道 (Táiběi: Sānchóngshì Sìzhītáng Shūfáng Chūbǎn), 2000.

60. Notable exceptions include Xuezhi Guo, *The Ideal Chinese Political Leader: A Historical and Cultural Perspective* (Connecticut: Praeger, 2002), 134–135; Mayfair Mei-hui Yang, *Gifts, Favors, and Banquets: The Art of Social Relationships in China* (Ithaca: Cornell University Press, 1994), 109; Geremie R. Barmé, *In the Red: On Contemporary Chinese Culture* (New York: Columbia University Press, 1999); and "The Greying of Chinese Culture," *China Review*, 13 (1992), 1–52. Tony Fang, "Negotiation: The Chinese Style," *The Journal of Business and Industrial Marketing*, 21: 1 (2006), 50–60. Wenshan Jia, *The Remaking of the Chinese Character and Identity in the 21st Century: the Chinese Face Practices* (Westport: Ablex Publishing, 2001). Wolfgang Bauer, "The Problem of Individualism and Egoism in Chinese Thought," in *Studia Sino-Mungulica: Festschrift fur Herbert Franke*, ed. Wolfgang Bauer (Wiesbaden: Franz Steiner, 1979), 427–442. Brian Moloughney, "From Biographical History to Historical Biography: a Transformation in Chinese Historical Writing," in *East Asian History, The Continuation of Papers on Far Eastern History*, ed. Geremie Barmé (Institute of Advanced Studies Australian National University, December 1992), #4, accessed 9 February 2019, http://www.eastasianhistory.org/sites/default/files/article-content/04/EAH04_01.pdf.

61. China National Knowledge Infrastructure, "China Academic Journals Full-text Database," http://eng.oversea.cnki.net/kns55/brief/result.aspx?dbPrefix=CJFD, accessed November–December 2015. The database, which consists of over 9,305 full-text journals, purportedly accounting for ~90% of China's journals, holds 53,709,243 records in total, some holdings reaching back to 1949 and 1915. In particular, I performed a lexical co-location query for a syndrome of terms that can only be derived from Lǐ's Theory: this syndrome included: *hòuhēi* 'thick-black' 厚黑, *heihouxué* Theory of the Thick and Black and lizongwu. I also performed collocation queries for four combinations of terms that were collocated within paragraph limits:1. *liǎnpí hòu-xīnhēi* 'thickfacedness' 脸皮厚 and 'heartblackedness' 心黑 2. *liǎnpí hòu-hēixīn* 'thickfacedness' 脸皮厚 and 'blackheart' 黑心, 3. *hòu liǎnpí-xīnhēi* 'thick-faced' 厚脸皮 and 'heartblackedness' 心黑 and 4. *hòu liǎnpí-hēixīn* 'thick-faced' 厚脸皮 and 'blackheart' 黑心. My queries across multiple databases (Literature/History/Philosophy (F), Political/Military/Legal (G), Education and Social Science (H), Electronic Technology and Information Science (I), Economics and Management (J) and news (N) articles published since ~2000) discovered over 6,959 articles. See Chu, Chin-ning, *Thick Face Black Heart: The Path to Thriving, Winning and Succeeding* (Beaverton, OR: AMC Publishing, 1992). Also Tony Fang, "Negotiation: The Chinese Style," *The Journal of Business and Industrial Marketing*, 21:1 (2006), 50–60.

62. Qīnglèi Liú, 劉青雷, *Science of the Thick and Black of Love: Love Actually Is Just a Type of Deception Àiqíng Hòuhēixué: Àiqíng, Qíshí zhǐshì yīzhǒng Piànshù* 愛情厚黑學：愛情，其實只是一種騙術 (Táiběishì: Shuǐpíng Shìjì Wénhuà Chūbǎn, 2001). Bīn Yú, 余斌, "Children's Science of the Thick and Black" *Yù'ér Hòuhēixué* 育儿厚黑学, *Childhood Education Yòu'ér Jiàoyù* 幼儿教育(7), 2015.

Chin-ning Chu, *Thick Face Black Heart: The Path to Thriving, Winning and Succeeding* (Beaverton, OR: AMC Publishing, 1992). Yōugēn Zhōu, 周優根, *Thick and Black Art of War: the Way of Success for a Troubled World Hēi Bīngfǎ: Luànshì Chénggōng zhī Dào* 厚黑兵法: 亂世成功之道 (Táiběi: Sānchóngshì Sìzhītáng Shūfáng Chūbǎn, 2000); also: Chin-Ning Chu and Huáng Wéiyù, *The New Science of the Thick and Black Sunzi Art of War Xīn Hòuhēixué zhī Sūnzi Bīngfǎ* 新厚黑學之孫子兵法. 1, 1. (Táiběi: Lianjing, 2005). Pòkōng Chén, 陈破空, *Zhongnanhai Science of the Thick and Black: Secrets the Chinese Communist Party Won't Reveal Zhōngnánhǎi Hòuhēixué: Zhōnggòng bùnéng Shuō de Mìmì* 中南海厚黑學: 中共不能說的秘密 (Táiběi: Contemporary Collection Yǔnchén Culture Affairs Ltd. Corporation Dāngdài Cóngshū "Yǔnchén Wénhuà Shìyè Gǔfèn Yǒuxiàn Gōngsī 當代叢書(允辰文化事業股份有限公司, 2009).

63. Geremie R. Barmé, *In the Red: On Contemporary Chinese Culture* (New York: Columbia University Press, 1999), 139.

64. 厚黑史觀, 體用.

65. Spiritual potency 靈修.

66. To strengthen the weak to resist the strong 抵抗列強，要有力量.

67. 忍与己之谓厚，忍于人之谓黑.

68. Ritual *lǐ* 禮.

69. *Self-interest sī* 私. It should be noted that the classical Daoist philosophers Lǎozi and Zhuāngzi advocated for a strategy of preserving the self according to the standard of natural human propensity (*tiānzhēn* 天真), simplicity (*pǔ* 樸) and a spontaneous flowing that they describe as *non-action* (*wúwéi* 無為), which was antithetical to the destructive this-worldly values of ambition, honor, fame, and glory. Daoists passively navigate through the world by letting it be (*zàiyòu* 'accommodating' 在宥, whereas pro-social Ruists try to make it better—the effects of the good intentions of which anti-social Daoists critique as destructive. "Sages who improve the world are few, whereas those that harm it many" 則聖人之利天下也少而害天下也多. *Zhuāngzi, Qūqiè* 胠篋.

70. My translation of these terms are interpretations informed by nuances encountered in *Theory*, and contrast with conventional translations of these terms by technical philosophers. *Empathetic response rén* 仁, *rightness yí* 儀, *brotherly tì* 悌 and *filial xiào* 孝 affection.

71. Officialdom literature *guānchǎng wénxué* 官场文学.

72. Expedient means *fǎ* 法 and technique *shù* 術.

73. *Rectification of names zhèngmíng* 正名.

74. Friedrich Nietzsche, *On the Genealogy of Morality*, trans. Maudemarie Clark and Alan J. Swensen (Hackett: Indianapolis/Cambridge, 1998).

75. Masters of the Hundred Schools 百家主子. Wén Zhǒng 文种, Fàn Lí 范蠡, Zhāng Liàng 张亮, Chén Píng 陈平, Yī Yǐn 伊尹, Tàigōng (Guǎnzi), Hán Fēizi 韩非子, Zhāng Yí 张仪, Sū Qín 蘇秦, Jiāng Ziyá 姜子牙.Kuǎi Tōng 蒯通 (221–206 BCE), King Gōu Jiàn of Yuè, 越王勾踐.

76. 老子言厚黑之體， 韓非言厚黑之用.

77. Arthur Waley's *The Way and Its Power: Lao Tzu's Tao Te Ching and Its Place in Chinese Thought by Lao Tzu.* Ames and Hall *Dao De Jing: A Philosophical*

Translation (English and Mandarin Chinese Edition) Ballantine Books; English and Mandarin Chinese Edition edition (December 30, 2003)

78. Clear-sighted lord 明君. The ruler's way 主道.
79. Hán Fēizi, *Wielding Power Yáng Quán* 揚權,"黃帝有言曰：「上下一日百戰。」下匿其私，用試其上；上操度量，以割其下。故度量之立，主之寶也；黨與之具，臣之寶也。臣之所不弒其君者，黨與不具也。故上失扶寸，下得尋常。有國之君，不大其都。有道之臣，不貴其家。有道之君，不貴其臣。" https://ctext.org/hanfeizi/yang-quan/zh.
80. Wiles and machinations *qùzhì yǔ qiǎo*去智與巧. Pleading that results in no harm to one's potency: 說情而捐精. 故去（泰）甚去泰，身乃無害.
81. 周秦諸子，表面上，众喙爭鳴，里子上，同是研究厚黑哲理. 周秦諸子的書，是厚黑學的經典。老子韓非子，知道厚黑的體用.
82. 忍与己之谓厚，忍于人之谓黑.
83. *Pierre Berton Show*, "Bruce Lee: The Lost Interview," 9 December 1971, 12:24. "The highest good is like water" 上善若水, Lǎozi, *Dàodéjīng*, Chapter 8, https://ctext.org/dao-de-jing#n11599 (accessed 11 May 2019).
84. 一部二十四史，可一以貫之：厚黑而已. Esoteric truth *bùchuánzhīmì*不傳之秘, *satori*-enlightenment *bùjué huǎngrán dàwù* 不覺恍然大悟, age-old secret of their success *qiāngǔ bùchuánde mìjué* 千古不傳的秘訣.
85. See translation Chapter 8.
86. See translation Chapter 8.
87. 盜跖. The term for robber *dào* 盜 puns with the term for way *dào* 道. The Chinese phrase *Dào yìyǒu dào* 盜亦有道 ([even] robbery has its way) implies a potential contradiction between moral and pragmatic valuation: Master thieves can be virtuosic even if morally bankrupt. Mǎn Gǒudé 滿苟得. "Bodily integrity is power" 身全之謂德. Hán Fēizi," *Explaining the Laozi" Jiělǎo* 解老, Chinese Text Project, https://ctext.org/hanfeizi/jie-lao, (accessed 11 May 2019). "For this the sagacious rules by emptying heart-minds, filling bellies, weakening ambition, strengthening bones," 是以聖人之治，虛其心，實其腹，弱其志，強其骨

是以聖人為腹不為目 Lǎozi, *Dàodéjīng* 3. "The sagacious act for the belly, not for the eyes," 是以聖人為腹不為目, Lǎozi, *Dàodéjīng* 12. https://ctext.org/dao-de-jing. "Understands his white while preserving his black," 知其白，守其黑, Lǎozi, *Dàodéjīng* 28. *Preserving one's black* refers in the *Dàodéjīng* to a strategy of survival by making choices that conform to the natural *Way* of one's authentic human propensity (*tiānzhēn* 天真), and not slavishly following the values of others (fame, honor, glory, nobility etc). For *preserving one's black* in the *Zhuāngzi*, see images of the crooked tree in *Zhuāngzi* 7, and the *Tree on the Mountain Shānmù* 山木. *Master of nourishing life yǎngshēngzhǔ* 養生主, https://ctext.org/zhuangzi/nourishing-the-lord-of-life. *Intactness and integrity* 保身,全生.
88. *Master of nourishing life yǎngshēngzhǔ* 養生主; nurturing life force *yǎngshēng* 養生.
89. Ruǎn Jí 阮籍.
90. Ruǎn Jí 阮籍 (210—263 AD) *Dàrén Xiānshēngzhuàn* 大人先生傳, in *Ruǎnsìzōngjí* 阮嗣宗集 "Presently they confuse sound by creating music, and distort form by making colors, changing the revealed appearance while internally concealing

feelings. They desire to acquire more, and cheat and con on behalf of fame. Oppression resulted after rulers were established, and theft was engendered after officials were appointed. Through rites and and conventions they bind the people. They deceive the simple by concealing their cunning behind their majesty. The strong leer in treachery and violence, and the weak are exhausted in servitude. They enable their covetousness through false moral integrity, and they are internally dangerous while externally empathetic." "今汝造音以亂聲，作色以詭形，外易其貌，內隱其情。懷欲以求多，詐偽以要名；君立而虐興，臣設而賊生。坐制禮法，束縛下民。欺愚誑拙，藏智自神。強者睽視而凌暴，弱者憔悴而事人。假廉而成貪，內險而外仁..." "How does (the great man) differ from the louse in the pants?" 何異虱處裈中乎?

91. Historical nihilism: "Just like General Secretary Xí Jìnpíng proclaimed: "We must establish in society the excellent norm of adulating the heroes and cherishing the martyrs. Regarding the heroic martyrs who sacrificed for our people and nation, we must always remember them, giving them the utmost glory and reverence." 正如习近平总书记号召的："要在全社会树立崇尚英雄、缅怀先烈的良好风尚。对为国牺牲、为民牺牲的英雄烈士，我们要永远怀念他们，给予他们极大的荣誉和敬仰。" Section: 坚决向历史虚无主义亮剑: "让英雄文化成为伟大时代的主旋律" *Qiushi* 求是 24 December 2018. Online at QSTHEORY.CN 《求是》2018/24, accessed 5 June 2019, http://www.qstheory.cn/dukan/qs/2018-12/22/c_1123888093.htm. Also: http://theory.people.com.cn/n1/2018/1224/c40531-30484502.html.

92. 聖人也，厚黑也，二而一，一而二也。莊子說：聖人不死，大盜不止。The point of this passage from Zhuāngzi is that the conception of what is morally undesirable is ironically the result of articulating the value of what is desirable or 'good.' Good and bad are two sides of the same coin. For Daoists, more fundamental than the moral order prescribed by Ruist sages is the ways of Nature.

93. 善與惡，何關與認?

94. 我著厚黑學,純用春秋書法,善惡不嫌同辭,據事直書,善惡自見。同是一厚黑,用以 圖謀一己之私利,是極卑劣之行為,用以圖謀眾人之公利,是至高無上的道德。

95. Lǐ Zhì 李贄 "Explanation of the Childlike Heart" 童心說, In *A Book to Burn and A Book to Keep* (*Hidden*), *Selected Writings*, ed. and trans. Rivi Handler-Spitz, Pauline C. Lee and Haun Saussy (New York: Columbia University Press, 2016); 76; 106–113. Tàizhōu sect: Tàizhōu xuépài 泰州學派.

96. 厚黑之訣。厚黑技術。

97. See translation Chapter 8.

98. Those who cannot release ambition and intent and nourish their lot, are all unacquainted with the (right) Way of life). 不能說其志意，養其壽命者，皆非通道者也。

99. *The Six Sheaths* 六韜. Cunning concealment *tāolüè* 韜略.

100. "The affairs of nature continue, soundless and odorless." *Zhōngyōng* 33 詩經·大雅·文王："上天之載，無聲無臭。"Also see Roger T. Ames and David L. Hall, trans. *Focusing the Familiar: A Translation and Philosophical Interpretation of the Zhōngyōng* (Honolulu: University of Hawai'i, Press, 2001), 115.

101. "The affairs of the nature continue, soundless and odorless." *Zhōngyōng* 33 詩經·大雅·文王："上天之載，無聲無臭。"Also see Roger T. Ames and David L. Hall, trans. *Focusing the Familiar: A Translation and Philosophical Interpretation of the Zhōngyōng* (Honolulu: University of Hawai'i, Press, 2001), 115.

102. 身為菩提樹，心為明鏡台。時時勤拂拭，勿使惹塵埃。菩提本無樹，明鏡亦非台。本來無一物，何處惹塵埃。"There is no wisdom tree; nor a stand of a mirror bright, Since all is void, where can the dust alight?" In as sense it says "There is no Buddha." At least there is no object within you, called your Buddha-mind, which is mirror-like, and which must be wiped clean. I have been unable to identify the translator of this verse.

103. See translation Chapter 8.

104. Mayfair Mei-hui Yang in *Gifts, Favors, and Banquets: The Art of Social Relationships in China* (Ithaca: Cornell University Press, 1994).

105. 我們用厚黑學史觀去看社會，社會成為透明體，即吧社會真相看出." "Only then can we propose ways of improving it. 就可想出改良社會的辦法.

106. *A small token of appreciation* 小意思 *xiǎo yìsi*, to strategically induce a positive response *gǎnyìng* 感應, extract social benefits by *lālā guānxì* pull strings, call in favors: 拉拉關係.

107. Particular circumstances *shì* 勢.

108. 要立於不敗之地. 先為不可勝，以待敵之可勝.

109. "Recommend College Students Establish a 'Career Thick-black Theory' Class" 建議大學開設"職場厚黑學"課, 17 November 2010：紅网 accessed 22 January 2018, http://job.chsi.com.cn/jyzd/zcht/201011/20101117/141644034.html; https://m.sohu.com/n/483649721/?wscrid=95360_2.

110. *Kànchuān chǒulòu rénxìngde chǔshì zhēnjīng* 看穿醜陋人性的處世真經. Lǐ Zōngwú 李宗吾, *The Orthodox Compilation of Theory of the Thick and Black: the Authentic Scripture that Exposes the Ugliness of Human Nature in Society* (*Zhèngzōng Hòuhēixué Dàquánjí: Kànchuān Chǒulòu Rénxìng de Chǔshì Zhēnjīng* 正宗厚黑學大全集：看穿醜陋人性的處世真經), ed. Gōng Sūnlóng 公孫龍 (Taiwan: Pǔtiān Chūbǎn: Xùshēng Túshū Zǒngjīngxiāo 普天出版：旭昇圖書總經銷, 2016).

Chapter 8

Thick Black Theory 厚黑學
Annotated Translation

INTRODUCTION

This chapter features my annotated translation of the Sìchuānese intellectual Lǐ Zōngwú's (李宗吾, 1879–1943 CE) *Theory of the Thick and Black* (厚黑學 *Hòuhēixué*), an article written during the demise of the Chinese Imperial age (1911), which has galvanized political and moral philosophy in contemporary Chinese societies since the turn of the twentieth century (see analysis in chapter 7). Lǐ, in this short essay on strategic culture, focuses attention on the roots of Chinese heroism and queries the authority, legitimacy, and apotheosis of heroic strategists in Chinese culture. Lǐ strategically uses a cultural genealogy to compel readers to re-interpret the cultural legacy in order to reveal the concealed—the true roots of power and meaning in human life. Written as hyperbolic satire, Lǐ demonstrates that Strategic Intelligence is paradoxical: it is the best and worst of humanity—its greatest hope and most potent threat.

I have discovered many inconsistencies in Chinese history—the conclusions about success and failure reached in the Annals are senseless, and the ethics taught by the sages do not tally up.[1] There must be some secret to success that has not been revealed by the ancient annalists and sages. At first, I was unable to penetrate their mysteries—as I thought about the characters from the Three Kingdoms period I became spontaneously enlightened to their secret—the secret of the ancients' success is nothing more than their *thickened face* and *blackened heart*.[2]

I continued to investigate success and failure in the Annals—these four words (*thick face, black heart*) indeed are everywhere. I then composed an amusing article, titled *Theory of the Thick and Black*, which I divided into three parts, *Theory of the Thick and Black*, the *Classic of the Thick and Black*, and the *Thick and Black Record of Instructions*.³

It was published in the Gōnglùn Daily in the first year of the Republic. This type of topic was most startling at the time and it caused a great uproar—my friends urged me to desist even before the second volume was published. I did not anticipate that the *Theory of the Thick and Black* would spread across all of Sìchuān—wherever I went people asked me to talk about it. After reviewing it soup to nuts, the audience invariably got it, nodding and confessing— "the reason I failed in such and such situation was that I did not practice *thickening* and *blackening*." People also remarked, "the reason that person has such an impressive reputation is because he thoroughly grasped the *Theory of the Thick and Black*." Sometimes even strangers whom I happened to meet asked me with a tone of surprise if I were that Lǐ that invented the *Theory of the Thick and Black*? Sometimes bystanders would speak up—"He is none other than that Lǐ Zōngwú who invented the *Theory of the Thick and Black*!" What is even funnier is that students writing essays in the national language unexpectedly used this noun, so you can see how far it spread.

At first, I just meant to write an amusing article—I never expected to incite such a reaction. I was caught completely off-guard and wondered if mass psychology had something to do with its enthusiastic reception. I finally discerned through extensive research that the art of *thickening* and *blackening* originated in the theory that mankind's original propensity is evil—and thus its contribution is equivalent to Wáng Yángmíng's *Innate Knowledge*, which originated from the theory that human propensity is good.⁴ The ancients said, "*Empathetic response* (rén 仁) and *rightness* (yì 義) are things inherent to natural propensity." I say, "*Thickening* and *blackening* are things intrinsic to natural propensity." Yángmíng said, "Filiality arises naturally in a child's feelings towards his father—brotherly love arises when a younger brother sees his older brother." This is very clear, logical, and irrefutable. I say, "when a child sees the cake in his mother's mouth, he will naturally take it for his own—likewise, the infant who is eating while being held by his mother will push his brother away when he approaches." This is also very clear, logical, and irrefutable. Yángmíng's teachings were welcomed by all, and so is *Theory of the Thick and Black*. Mèngzǐ's' theory contrasts with Xúnzi's theory of the human propensity toward evil, and *Theory of the Thick and Black* in like manner is the opposite correlative of Wáng Yángmíng's theory of *Innate Knowledge*.⁵

Exactly what is human propensity? I wanted to thoroughly investigate this. And so I explored books from the Sòng to the Qīng dynasties and found that their moral explanations were farfetched, incoherent, and incomprehensible—most vexing! I then threw away those books.⁶ Only after using the methods of physics to investigate psychology was I able to discern that mechanics and psychology are connected. We cannot discern if human propensity is inclined toward good or evil just like we cannot posit the good or evil propensity of water or fire.

If Mèngzǐ's and Xúnzi's theories are both biased, the *Theory of the Thick and Black* that I teach is naturally even more biased—the degree of my bias is just the same as Wáng Yāngmíng's *Innate Knowledge*. The reader who cannot both understand and practice the principles of the *thick* and *black* will ultimately fail. The reader will naturally understand this after reading my *Psychology and Mechanics*. But, even if we do not wish to practice *blackening*, we still must take precautions against people who practice *thickening* and *blackening* in our name—we must be aware of their black arts.[7]

THICKENING AND BLACKENING

Ever since I began to read I have always wanted to become one of the greatest heroes of history. I searched the Four Books and Five Classics as well as the philosophical writings of the Hundred Schools and the Twenty-four Annals—all to no avail whatsoever. I thought that the heroes of old must have had a secret that had not been revealed. Perhaps because my disposition was doltish, I simply could not discover it. Forgetting to eat and sleep, I sought it without ceasing. After a few years passed, one day I coincidentally remembered the characters from the Three Kingdoms era and I suddenly saw the light. Eureka! I got it! The secret of the ancients who became the greatest heroes was nothing other than *thickened face* and *blackened heart*.

Of the heroes of the Three Kingdoms, the exemplar is Cáo Cāo, whose excellence consisted of *heart blackening*. After killing Lǚ Bóshē, Kǒng Róng, Yáng Xiū, Dǒng Chéng, and Fú Wán, he then murdered the empress and the prince. He then boldly pronounced, "Better to strike first than be struck!" As for *blackened hearts*, truly his had reached the highest pinnacle. With such a capacity, of course he is hailed as the greatest hero of the age.[8]

The next to be considered is Liú Bèi, whose excellence totally consisted of *facial thickening*—he depended on Cáo Cāo, Lǚ Bù, Liú Biǎo, Sūn Quán, and Yuán Shào, scuttling all over the place living under their patronage with no sense of shame. He was adept at crying—whoever wrote *Romance of the Kingdoms* really described him well, like when he cried himself out of a hairy situation and transformed failure into success. And so the saying goes, *Liú Bèi's lands were won through tears*. He is also an example of a hero with great capacity.[9]

Cáo Cāo and Liú can be said to be the most outstanding—when they were in the pavilion face to face discussing heroism over boiled wine, one with the blackest heart, and the other with the thickest face, Cáo said, "You are no match for me and I cannot best you. Look around, out of all of Yuán Běnchū's people—they are petty and unworthy of our notice." Then he said, "You and I are the only heroes in the realm."[10]

In addition, there is also Sūn Quán who became Liú's ally and brother-in-law. He suddenly captured Jīngzhōu and killed Guān Yǔ.[11] Yes, he did *blacken* his heart like Cáo Cāo, but it was insufficient—his *blackness* was a bit less than Cáo Cāo's when he sued Shǔ for peace. Although he was about Cáo Cāo's equal, neither able to outdo the other, he unexpectedly became a minister subordinate to Prime Minister Cáo. Yes, he did *thicken* his face like Liú Bèi, but it was insufficient—like when he broke off relations with Wèi. But although he did not *blacken* as much as Cáo nor *thicken* as much as Liú, he did integrate both, and so one must regard him as a hero. The three of them all effectively expanded their capacity, and they could not but divide the realm at that time into three parts since it was a stalemate.

Afterwards, the Sīmǎ clan opportunistically took advantage of the situation and rose to power after Cáo Cāo, Liú Bèi, and Sūn Quán each had died in succession. Influenced by Cáo and Liú, they concentrated the arts of *thickening* and *blackening* to a consummate degree—their hearts, like Cáo's, were so *blackened* that they bullied widows and orphans. Their faces were so much *thicker* than Liú's that they felt no shame at all when their foes sent them a headscarf and insinuated that they were little girls.[12] When I read the part in the history about Sīmǎ Yì not being goaded through shame into action by provocation of the headscarf, I could not help slapping the table and cheering "Long live the Sīmǎs!" So, the realm could not but be united until this exact time—all of this is *affairs unfolding in due course*.

Marquis Zhūgé was an extraordinary genius in the realm and the greatest of three generations, but he was no match for Sīmǎ Yì. Although utterly determined to "strive until there was no breath left in his body," he was ultimately unable to gain an inch of the central plains, and rather suddenly spat blood and died.[13] Although he was brilliant as the king's counselor, he was no worthy opponent for the renowned adepts of the *thick* and *black*.

I repeatedly investigated these characters' affairs before discovering the age-old secret of their success. The one thread that runs through the Annals is nothing other than *thickening* and *blackening*. This can be corroborated by citing some examples from the Hàn dynasty.[14]

Take the case of the unrivaled heroism of Xiàng Yǔ the Great, head of a mighty host of warriors the din of which made their enemies scatter—why did he cut his own throat because the world looked down on him?[15] The reason he failed, according to Hán Xìn, was because of his *feminine sensitivity* and *masculine temper*—that about says it.[16] *Feminine sensitivity* signifies that there is something one cannot bear—a flaw originating from a heart that has not been *blackened*. *Masculine temper* signifies being easily goaded—a defect that originates from an insufficiently *thickened face*. Xiàng Yǔ was a hairs' breadth away from being Emperor himself—but since he could not bear it, he wavered when Xiàng Zhuāng's sword swiped at Liú's neck during the Hóng Gate banquet, and Liú Bāng unexpectedly escaped.[17] As for his failure at Gāixià, we do not know who would have been the victor if Xiàng had crossed the Wū River and staged a comeback. Instead, he hosted his own pity-party. "Although I forded the river westwards with 8,000 of my compatriots, none now return. Woe is me! How can I face their families? Even if they do not openly criticize me, how can I not but feel ashamed!" These words could not be more wrong! Not only did he grieve about losing face, but he also confessed that he felt shame. For crying out loud, what can be said about the stalwart's face or the hero's heart? With little thought to this, he said, "I am destroyed by Heaven, not through defeat in battle." But Heaven, I fear, cannot be blamed for this.[18]

Let's also investigate Liú Bāng's capacity for a bit. The Annals documented that Xiàng Yǔ challenged the King of Hàn—"All of these years of savagery in the realm—I challenge you to a duel to discern superiority."[19] The King of Hàn smiled and deferred, "I'd prefer to duel with cunning strategy, not with arms." I ask, where did the term "smiled and defer" come from? Two beauties were washing Liú Bāng's feet when Lì Shēng met him. When Lì Shēng criticized him as arrogant for the lack of protocol in meeting an elder, Liú quickly deferred.[20] Where did that come from? Also, with his own father—when an enemy threatened to boil his father alive, Liú merely asked for a bowl of soup to be sent. He pushed his children Xiào Huì and Lǔ Yuán off the chariot when fleeing the Chǔ soldiers.[21] He also did away with comrades Hán Xìn and Péng Yuè when they became potential rivals—*Stow your bow when the birds have flown; roast the hounds in the fire after the bunnies expire.*[22] Now let's ask about Liú Bāng's heart? Does it resemble Xiàng Yǔ's *feminine sensitivity* or *masculine temper*? The Grand Annalist recorded that Liú Bāng had a imperial dragon face and regal nose, and that Xiàng Yǔ had double pupils, but of the coloring of their hearts or the thickness of their faces, not even one word was written—it is rather a travesty of a history.[23]

In terms of *face* and *heart*, the manner that Liú Bāng especially differed from most people is what is called the *sage at ease*. This word *black* truly is *serenely walking the path from birth, seeking one's heart's desire without overstepping the bounds.*[24] He enriched his *thickness* with erudition—his teacher was none other than Zhāng Liáng, one of the three worthies.[25] Zhāng Liáng's teacher was the Gaffer of Yíshàng—their transmission lineage is impeccable. The story of how Zhāng Liáng received that book and the influence of the Gaffer on him is nothing but teaching Zhāng Liáng to *thicken* his face. Of this principle, Sū Dōngpō's *On Marquis Hóu* was very clear.[26]

Zhāng Liáng was astute—he immediately understood things when his teacher pointed them out, and so the Gaffer hoped he would become the royal tutor. These arts are marvelous beyond compare, and the dull-witted could absolutely not understand—the Annals relay that most of the courtiers could not understand when Liáng lobbied at court, only the Duke of Pèi was able to follow."[27] And so Liáng remarked, the Duke of Pèi has a natural knack"![28] One can see that this type of learning is related to one's aptitude. It is certainly difficult to find the brightest teacher and no less difficult to identify a clever disciple. When Hán Xìn requested the title of King of Qí, Liú Bāng seemed to misunderstand, but he totally relied on his master's guidance, like when a teacher at school corrects a student's work. Liú Bāng still occasionally made mistakes even though he was naturally intelligent—the profundity of this learning can be seen in this. With deep learning added to his aptitude, Liú Bāng destroyed the *five relationships* that had been passed down.[29] He was able to pacify the various heroes and unite the country because he purged it of *propriety, rightness, shame,* and *honor.* Lasting for more than 400 years and a few decades, the power of the Hàn only dissipated when the *thick* and *black* force dissipated.

At the time of Chǔ and Hàn, there was a person who failed because although he had the *thickest* face, his heart was *unblackened.* Who was this? The famous Hán Xìn. In enduring the shame of crawling, his *thickness* was not inferior to Liú Bāng's.[30] But he neglected to learn *blackness.* When he became the king of Qí, it would have turned out for the best if he had just heeded Kuǎi Tōng. But he always remembered Liú Bāng's generosity, and he rather hastily exclaimed, "I've worn his clothes, so I should bear his worries—I've eaten his food, so I should strive to the death for him." He was later decapitated in the Chánglè palace belfry, and his whole clan was exterminated. This truly was a consequence of his own doing. He sneered that Xiàng Yǔ suffered from *feminine sensitivity,* but one can see that he also failed because his heart had not been *blackened.* He knew this great principle and still failed. No wonder!

At the same time, there was a person whose heart was the *blackest* but whose face was not *thickened*—and he also failed. The story of Fàn Zēng is well known.[31] When Liú Bāng smashed Xiányáng, he abducted Zǐyīng, garrisoned his troops at Bàshàng and did not interfere with the populace. Fàn Zēng tried all types of maneuvers and stratagems to destroy him. Although his heart was as *blackened* as Liú Bāng's, he could not suppress his anger since his face had not been *thickened.* When Hàn used Chén Píng's stratagem to sow discord between Fàn Zēng and the King of Chǔ, Zēng angrily took leave. And then, upon returning to Péngchéng, he developed an ulcer on his back and died. Generally speaking, for people who are engaged in great affairs, what's the point of being easily angered? "If Zēng had not left, then Xiàng Yǔ would not have perished." If he could have patiently endured a bit, then Liú Bāng's vulnerabilities could have been identified. Fàn Zēng could have attacked at any time, but instead he left angrily—throwing away both his own life and Xiàng Yǔ's realm. A great affair spoiled over a trifle.[32] Sū Dōngpō called him an eminent man—now isn't that excessive?

According to the research about the art of the *thick* and *black* elucidated above, the method is simple, but the actual use is mysterious—small means result in small ends—great means in great ends. Liú Bāng and Sīmǎ Yì unified the world after mastering both. Cáo Cāo and Liú Bèi only mastered one portion, and they still were able to become the rulers of their own domain. Hán Xìn and Fàn Zēng also only mastered a portion, but being born at the wrong time they both fell to their contemporary Liú Bāng who integrated both the *thick* and *black*. However, while alive, they all relied on their capacities to win rank, glory, and an honored position in the Annals so that later generations could discuss their exploits and relish their stories. From this perspective, one can see that the arts of the *thick* and *black* serve one well.

Heaven itself has given us *face* and *thickness* is from within it—likewise in giving us a heart, *blackness* is intrinsic to it. Examining it from the outside, it is not remotely surprising to acknowledge that its surface is not wider than a few inches nor big enough to fill a pair of cupped hands. However, a careful look reveals that its *thickness* is limitless and its *blackness* incomparable. Merit, fame, riches, palaces, women, clothes, vehicles—all of these originate from the *thick* and *black*. The marvel of the producer of life is truly inconceivable! But to throw away their precious treasure as the dim-witted masses do can only be reckoned to be the stupidest thing in the world.

The arts of the *thick* and *black* are divided into three degrees. The first step is *thick as the great wall, black as coal*. Although the skin of the face is initially paper-thin, it grows from inches to feet and becomes as thick as a wall. Although the color of the heart is initially milky-white, it darkens from white to grey to darkest midnight blue until it approaches coal blackness. Having arrived at this juncture, this can be categorized as the rudimentary stage of the arts because a cannon can still raze the wall even though it has been thickened—the possibility of destruction still exists. And although coal is black, it is a loathsome color and people are not willing to come near it. So this can only be understood as the first degree.

The second degree is *thicken and strengthen, blacken and brighten*. People who have a proficient mastery of the art of the *thickening* are invulnerable, no matter how you attack them. Liú Bèi was just this sort of man—Cáo Cāo had no power over him. People who have a proficient mastery of the arts of *blackening* are like a shop sign that has lost its gloss—the blacker the sign, the more the customers.[33] Cáo Cāo was just this sort of man famed for his *blackened* heart—and the nobles of the central plains willingly submitted to his rule. This truly is *a heart that is glossy-black, a sign that is shining bright.* Although one has crossed the great chasm to get to the second degree, a mark with form and color is still visible—and that is why we can presently clearly see Cáo Cāo's capacity.

The third degree is *insubstantial thickness, hueless blackness.* The utmost *thickening* and *blackening* are such that in subsequent generations nobody will discern the *thick* and *black*. It is very difficult to arrive at this juncture, so we can only investigate it in the great sages and worthies of the past. Some people ask, "how can this learning be so profound?" I reply, "the Ruist text *Doctrine of the Mean* teaches that one cannot exhaust the *Way* until one understands the *soundless and the odorless.*"[34] Buddhists must understand "there is no wisdom tree, nor a stand of mirror bright" before they can attain the buddha nature.[35] How much more so for the arts of the *thick* and *black* which are occult secrets to success not revealed by the ancients! Clearly the final stage cannot be attained without achieving "formlessness and odorlessness."

In conclusion, from the time of the three kings to the present, of the countless successes of nobility, generals, heroes, and sages—there is not one that did not originate from this! It is in all of the books and the reality of it can not be denied. If the reader is able to follow the path of my instruction, then go personally investigate it. Naturally you will find this inexhaustible source everywhere, as clear as day.

THE CLASSIC OF THICKENING AND BLACKENING

Liú Zōngwú said,

What is not thin is *thick*—what is not white is *black*.[36] *Thick* and *black* refer to the *thickening* of the facial skin and the *blackening* of the heart in society. This Classic is the inner teaching passed down from the ancients. But because I fear discrepancies through time, I wrote them down for posterity. This book begins by exploring the *thick* and *black*, its middle the myriad things, and returns to the *thick* and the *black* in the conclusion. It can be unfurled to cover the whole world, and yet rolled up and stored in the heart and mind. Its significance is limitless and it is pragmatic. Those adept at reading and contemplating it will get something from it. It is inexhaustible even if you use it your whole life.

That which governs life is called the *thick* and *black*, drawing out the *thickening* and *blackening* is called the *Way*, cultivating *thickening* and *blackening* is called learning. One can not stray from the *Way* of *thickening* and *blackening* for even an instant. That from which one can stray cannot be the *thick* and *black*. For this reason, noble men feel angst about what is not *thickened* and uncomfortable with what is not *blackened*. Nothing is more risky than thinning or more fearsome than whitening. Therefore the noble man must be *thickened* and *blackened*. Not expressing pleasure and anger, sorrow and joy is called *thickening*—displaying these emotions without concern is called *blackening*. *Thickening* is the great root of nature—*blackening* is progressing along the *Way*. For those who attain the utmost *thickening* and *blackening*—the realm will be in awe and the gods and demons will tremble.[37]

Herein, I begin by revealing ancient occult secrets. I first show that the roots of *thickening* and *blackening* are heaven itself and are unchangeable—they are innate, and one cannot leave these faculties. I next discuss the critical importance of preserving and cultivating *thickening* and *blackening*. Finally, I explore the supreme attainment of the techniques of *thickening* and *blackening*. The novice who desires to study to this degree will both quest and find it within themselves in order to expel the external entrapments of *empathetic response* and *rightness*, and to cultivate the *thick* and *black* from the root. This is the crux of this classic—afterward, I will discuss other things in order to clarify the meaning of this.

> Zōngwú said, The *Way* of *thickening* and *blackening* is easy and difficult. Even the most simple commoners can know something of it, but as for its supreme attainment, even Cáo and Liú could not know it all. Although folks with a common level of intelligence can take a few steps on it, the supreme end was even beyond Cáo and Liú's capacity to reach. Cáo and Liú were vexed by the vast expansiveness of the *thick* and *black*, how much more so will it be for the average Joe?[38]
>
> Zōngwú said, "Everyone says, 'I am blackened,' but they clearly stand out when trapped in the coal pit. Everyone says, "I am thickened"—but they are destroyed when shot."[39]
>
> Zōngwú said, "The *Way* of *thickening and blackening* is rooted in the body, verified by the masses, and validated by the three kings. Having established it, it will be followed in the world, there will be certainty when seeking the spiritual, and future sages will be assured."[40]
>
> Zōngwú said, "The noble man emphasizes his root, for the *Way* presents itself as the root grows. Is not *thickening* and *blackening* what is fundamental?"[41]
>
> Zōngwú said, "When walking with two others, one is bound to teach me something. I identify and follow the *thickened* and *blackened*, and reform in myself that which is not *thickened* and *blackened*."[42]
>
> Zōngwú said, "Heaven gifted the *thick* and *black* in me. What has the world got to do with me?"[43]
>
> Zōngwú said, "In a village of ten homes, there are likely others as *thickened* and *blackened* as me, but they are not as persuasive as me."[44]
>
> Zōngwú said, "The noble man cannot take leave of the *thick* and *black* for even the span of a meal, even when in haste or distress."[45]

Zōngwú said, "If someone graced with Xiàng Yǔ's talent had *thickening* and *blackening*, Liú Bāng would not be worth mentioning."[46]

Zōngwú said, "Adepts of *thickening* and *blackening* will rule the world—those without will not even have a pot to piss in."[47]

Zōngwú said, "The five grains are wonderful things to eat. But they are like grass and weeds if immature. *Thick* and *black* need to mature just like that!"[48]

Zōngwú said, "The Ruists are merely the thieves of *thickening* and *blackening*. They seem to reside in *loyalty* and *sincerity* and seem to practice *integrity* and *honesty*, and everyone is pleased with them and they themselves are smug. But they cannot compete in the ranks of of Cáo and Liú, and so I call them thieves of *thickening* and *blackening*."[49]

Zōngwú said, "Do not wonder why some people are not *thickened* and *blackened*! Although one may have the most easily growable thing in the world, he will not be able to produce it if he only nurtures it for one day and then ignores it for ten.[50] Few indeed are those who can understand the *thick* and *black*! The moralistic philosophers show up as soon as I leave. How do I differ from them? That which I call the *thick* and *black* is the great *Way*—one cannot obtain it without the utmost ambition and focused study. I am the founder of the *thick* and *black* and say I take on two disciples. The first diligently focuses, only listening to me—and the other only listens to me while secretly desiring the reputation of sages and worthies, wholeheartedly awaiting the arrival of the moral philosophers. So, although they both study together, the latter is inferior. Is it on account of his aptitude? I say "nope."

Zōngwú said, "When some affair has gone awry, the nobleman reflects that he must not have been sufficiently *thickened*, and he therefore resolves to be *thicker*. If it goes awry again, he reflects that he must not have been sufficiently *blackened*, and so he resolves to be *blacker*. If it occurs once more, the noble man says "he who opposes me is an unreasonable beast." He therefore uses the *thick* and *black* to slay them like beasts, is there anything wrong with that?"[51]

Zōngwú said, "The *Way* of *thickening and blackening* is brilliant and high—it is like flying up to the heavens—seemingly reachable.[52] It is like a long journey, beginning from the low and then proceeding upwards.[53] If you do not embody the *thick* and the *black*, then you cannot use it at home, and you cannot make others use the *thick* and *black* if you cannot use it at home."

It was my intention to compose the *Classic of Thickening and Blackening* as a chant to make it more convenient for novices to remember. However, since there are many profound principles within it, I have added some explanations throughout.

Zōngwú said, "The *thick*?—it is that which never thins through friction. The *black*? It is that which cannot be whitened through cleaning." Later on, I changed this to "thick—thicker with friction; black—blacker through scrubbing." Someone asked me "where does this exist in the world"? I replied, "callouses on the hands and feet—the more you rub them the thicker they are. Moisten the dust on top of the coal—the more you wash it the blacker it becomes." If someone's facial skin is thin, it can be slowly thickened through gradual friction. A heart born black will not be *black* if it is subsequently covered by a layer of *empathetic response* (*rén* 仁) and *rightness* (*yì* 義) from teachers of morality and karma. The original form will only re-emerge if you wash those away.

Zōngwú said, "*Thickening* and the *blackening* are not extrinsic to me, but intrinsic to the body. Heaven produces people with the *thick* and the *black*, and it is what they like.[54] This can be verified—go ahead and find a mother who is eating while holding her child. That child will try to grab the bowl from the mother's hands, and the bowl will be broken if one is not careful. He will also try to grab the cake from the mother's hand. He stretches out his arm to grasp it as soon as he sees it and he will pop it in his own mouth. If the mother does not give it to him, he will stretch out his arms and try to snatch it out of her mouth to put it in his own. A nursing child will push and hit his older brother when he sees him coming towards him. All of these are examples of unlearned behaviors that occur before thought and are examples of innate knowledge and behavior. Those who can leverage and expand this type of innate knowledge and behavior can accomplish great things. Emperor Tàizōng killed his older brother Jiànchéng and his younger brother Yuánjí and then murdered their sons and usurped their concubines.[55] He also forced his own father to yield the realm to him. These behaviors were nothing more than leveraging and expanding on the childlike innate knowledge and behaviors such as snatching the cake from the mother's mouth or pushing away or hitting his older brother. While ordinary people have this type of innate knowledge and behavior, they do not leverage and expand on it like Táng Tàizōng did, and so he became the world's greatest hero. Zōngwú said, "in terms of the flavors the mouth enjoys, we are all the same. That which the ear enjoys hearing, we all enjoy. The beauty the eyes behold, we all share. As for the heart, is it not the same? What is common about the heart? That is called *thickening* and *blackening*. The special way that the hero leverages and expands his *face* and *heart* is what is common to all hearts."[56]

The principle of *thickening* and the *blackening* has now been laid out before you. Regardless, it has been suppressed by the Ruist and Buddhist theories in such works as the Response and Retribution Manuals and Hidden Merit Tracts.[57]

> Zōngwú said, "The trees on Mt. Ox were beautiful until the lumberjack cut them down—and now there is no new growth whatsoever. Herds also pastured there and further denuded the mountain. As for what was original to people, is it not the *thick* and *black*? He who ravages his *thickness* and *blackness* is just like the lumberjack to the trees—cutting it down day by day, his *thickening* and *blackening* will not survive, and it will therefore be insufficient to become a hero. This results in people thinking that they cannot be heroic because they had the *thick* and the *black*—but can this be reckoned as their original propensity? So, the *thick* and *black* will flourish if you cultivate it and wither if you do not."[58]

Zōngwú said, "Children will all snatch away the cake that is in their mother's mouth. People who can leverage their inexhaustible *thickness* and *blackness*—which is also nurturing the instinct to steal a cake from their mother's mouth—will became great movers and shakers. He who has not lost the innocence of the newborn is what we call "the great man." If one does not nurture it within himself, this we call "self-destruction.""

There is one type of gifted person who understands this principle and pursues it wholeheartedly on the sly. There is another type of fool who has already started down this path although he does not realize it. Zōngwú said, "Many indeed are those who use *thickening* and *blackening* without knowing why, through force of habit without reflection all of their lives."[59] Except for the *thick* and the *black*, all of the world's theories mislead the people. From the beggars who down on their luck vie with each other for more food, to the country's president—they all are *thick* and *black* at the root. The study of the *thick* and the *black* is vast and profound—those who aim to be adepts must engross themselves within it. One can begin to apply it after a year of study and achieve great success after three. Therefore, Zōngwú said, "If somebody hopes to master the *thick* and the *black*, satisfactory results can be achieved in a year and great results in three."[60]

THICK AND *BLACK* RECORDS OF PRACTICE

Some people have asked me, "If you have invented the study of the *thick* and the *black*, why have you often failed?[61] Why are your disciples' abilities greater than yours? Why are you inferior?" I replied, "That's not right." Generally speaking, inventors cannot usually attain the highest peak. Confucianism was invented by Confucius and he was the most advanced. Yán, Zēng, Sī, Mèng studied with him, but their learning was one level lower and Zhōu, Chéng, Zhū, and Zhāng's learning was lower than theirs—the further removed, the lower the learning.[62] And the reason is that the founder's ability is too great. Western science is not like that—knowledge is very rudimentary at the time of invention and becomes more and more profound with further investigation. The inventor of steam power became aware of the principle through a boiling kettle lid. The inventor of electricity realized the principle through the movement of a dead frog. Subsequent researchers created all types of mechanisms and uses that the inventors of steam and electricity could not have anticipated. One can observe in Western science that the latter is superior to the former, and that the student surpasses the teacher. My *Theory of the Thick and Black* is similar to Western science—I am only able to understand some of the principles about the boiling kettle lid and the movement of a dead frog—and I have to wait for subsequent researchers.[63]

Although my ability is clearly less than my students and I will clearly be inferior, in the future, they too will become inferior to the students who they are currently teaching. One generation surpasses the next and so the *Theory of the thick and black* naturally will flourish!

People have also asked me, "You have talked about how extraordinary is the *thick* and the *black*, why have you not accomplished some great thing?" I replied, "I would like to ask, what great thing did your Confucius accomplish? He taught about politics and about great kingdoms, but what did he actually accomplish? Master Zēng wrote the *Great Learning*, especially teaching how to rule the country and pacify the world—I'd like to ask what kingdom did he rule? Where did he pacify? Zisī wrote *Doctrine of the Mean*, explaining some objectives and means. I would like to ask, where actually are the objectives and means? You criticize me without having critiqued them in the same way. It is difficult to find a good teacher and even harder to learn his lesson. This type of supreme, profound, and exquisite art cannot be encountered in eons. You still doubt after hearing, and cannot help deluding yourself."

After reading the *Theory of the Thick and Black* that I published, the average Joe inevitably always asks me to provide a shortcut since "this teaching that you have is vast and profound and difficult for me to grasp." I replied, "What do you want to do"? He says, "I want to be an official and accomplish some great thing," because average Joes all think that they are great politicians. I then transmit to them the *Mantra of the Six Characters for Seeking Officialdom*, the *Mantra of the Six Characters of Being an Official* and the *Two Marvelous Arts Taking Care of Business*.

The Mantra of the Six Characters for Seeking Officialdom

The significance of the six words of the *Mantra for Seeking an Official Position* are as follows: 空 *kōng*, 貢 *gòng*, 沖 *chōng*, 捧 *pěng*, 恐 *kōng*, 送 *sòng*."

空 *kōng* Leisure

Kōng means at leisure, and there are two kinds—the first describes how to approach what you do. Because those who seek an official position must channel all of their effort to seek an official position, they must put aside all other affairs, including work and business, farming and trade. One must not read books or study or teach. The second signifies time—seekers of official position need to be patient and cannot be hasty. If it does not happen today, then perhaps tomorrow—and if not this year then next!

貢 *gòng* Worming In

This word is borrowed from Sìchuānese. Its meaning is equivalent to the word for "boring into" that occurs in the phrase "curry favor." "Worm your way in and worm your way out" is the same as "drill in and drill out." One must curry favor to acquire an official position—everyone knows that but it is difficult to do. Some people say, "the definition of *gòng* is that one must worm oneself in to a preexisting hole." That's wrong and only partially right. Worm in if there is a hole—but what does one do if there is no hole? My definition is "worm yourself in if there is a hole, but still get in if there is no hole. Enlarge the hole if you have one, and drill a new one if you do not!"

沖 *chōng* Toot Your Own Horn

Commonly called "bragging," or "blow the hat off 'em in Sichuanese." There are two types of the art of *chōng*—the first is oral and the second is writing. The oral also has two types, verbal performance in a public place and in front of leadership. Writing also has the two types of writing reports and other memos and recommendations.

捧 *pěng* Flattering

This is the word used for flattery. This is the behavior Huá Xīn exhibits when the Duke of Wèi enters the stage—this is the best model to emulate.[64]

恐 *kǒng* Threatening

This means to intimidate, it is a transitive verb. The principle of this word is very profound, so I will say something about it. Official position is a priceless thing—how can one lightly give it away? Some people totally focus on *pěng*, but to no avail—and this is because they lack the art of *kǒng*. All important officials have a soft spot—if you can identify and lightly press on the vital spot—he will become alarmed and an official position will be conferred. The disciple should know that the characters *kǒng* and *pěng* are used together; for *kǒng* adepts, even *pěng* is imbued with *kǒng*—for example, although bystanders think one is toadying up in front of leadership, he actually is secretly pushing the vital spot and the senior official will break out in a cold sweat when he hears him speak. *Pěng* adepts use a *pěng* imbued with *kǒng*. While bystanders see an unyielding spirit criticizing their superiors, actually the superior is so pleased that he goes weak in the knees. Seekers of office must carefully experience this, as the sayings attest, "investigate it yourself before you can," and "the master craftsman can only transmit the technique, not the ability." Most importantly, *kǒng* must be appropriately used—the target's shame will flare up into anger and opposition if it is misused—is that not contrary to the aims of the office-seeker? So, why bother? Do not lightly use *kǒng* unless you are have no other recourse.

送 sòng Gifting

This word means giving gifts, and it can be divided into two types, big and small. Big giving signifies giving packages of money, and small giving includes delicacies appropriate for hosting an official, such as spring tea or pork shoulder. There are two kinds of recipients—those who can directly confer position and those who cannot directly confer position but who can, nevertheless, help us.

Using these six words will ensure the extraordinary effectiveness of each. The decision-maker will reflect on this and say to himself, "So and so wants an official position. He has already spoken much (this is the effective use of *kǒng*), he has some type of relationship with me (this is the effective use of *gòng*), he has some talent (this is the effective use of *chōng*), and he is good to me (this is the effective use of *pěng*). But this guy is a bit crafty—he will make a stir if I do not get him settled (this is the effective use of *kǒng*)." Having reflected thus far, he will then turn his head to see the piles of opium or gold stacked on the table (this is the effective use of *sòng*). With nothing more to be said, he will elevate him and place him in a vacant position. At this point, the office-seeker's desires have been granted. He will then mount his horse and take up his position, practicing the *Six Word Mantra of Being an Official*.

做官六字真言 The Six Word Mantra for Being an Official

The six word mantra for being an official consists of "空 *kōng*, 恭 *gòng*, 繃 *běng*, 兇 *xiōng*, 聾 *lóng*, 弄 *nòng*."

空 kōng Emptiness

Kōng means emptiness. First, this signifies writing. All official writings, whether instructions, memos, or new policies, are so totally empty and subtle that it is hard to fathom the meaning. One is only suddenly enlightened after the policy is displayed on the public walls of various official agencies. Second, this signifies being wishy-washy and indecisive in taking care of business. Sometimes this also means a hasty decision while maintaining an escape route. If one finds that things are not turning out well, he can then evade the consequences by hastily retreating.

恭 gōng Deference

Gōng means bowing and groveling.[65] This is divided into direct and indirect forms. Direct is intended for one's higher ups, and indirect is for their relations, including family, friends, servants, and lovers.

绷 běng Supercilious

This is colloquially called being taunt and is the opposite of the word *gōng*. It describes how one is to one's subordinates. It is divided into two types. The first is through one's deportment as a great superior who must not be offended. The second is to appear to be dignified and full of wisdom when speaking. *Gōng* is not only used for superiors, but can also be used for locals on whom you rely—*Běng* is not necessarily only used for local commoners and subordinates on whom you do not depend. If you sometimes do not depend on your superiors, then you might as well use *běng* with them. If you have to rely on your subordinates or commoners, then one should adjust and use *gōng*. The principle I teach is dynamic—"use it well to master it."

兇 xiōng Ruthless

In order to attain my goal, have no misgivings whatsoever of destroying people and families, selling off children and wives. But there is one thing one should notice—one needs to hide *xiōng* under the ethical cover of *empathetic response* and *rightness*.[66]

聋 lóng Deaf

This is being deaf—"let them laugh and curse me, I'm still an official." But the word *lóng* also contains the sense of being blind. In terms of writing that is critical of the official, he merely closes his eyes and ignores it.

弄 nòng Cashing In

This is making money. "The dragon from afar makes its home its hoard"—the eleven words above are all for this purpose. *Nòng* is aligned with *sòng* of office-seeking—you get *nòng* if you *sòng*. What you need to be careful of with regards to *nòng* is that you get approval for official affairs if you are to be seen as successful. When you cannot obtain approval, then use your own money to send a gift upwards, there is nothing wrong with that. If you then receive approval, it does not matter how much—take full advantage.

I merely provided a rough outline of the twelve characters above and did not elaborate much of their quintessence. Those who are ambitious for office can use these as a means to personally investigate.

The Two Marvelous Theories for Taking Care of Business

The Art of Sawing Off the Arrow shaft

Once there was a person who was shot by an arrow. The "externist" doctor he consulted merely sawed off the arrow shaft that was sticking out and then asked for payment. When asked why he did not remove the whole arrow, he replied that that was the internist's job—go see him. This is a story that has been passed down.

Presently, the people in the civil and military administration who are really capable all use this type of method. Take writing memos and instructions for example. The superior responds with "Disagree with memo—kindly request county seat thoroughly investigate/solve. *Request Investigation* is "cutting the arrow shaft," and *the county seat* is the "internist." Or another example, "I would like to refer this up to senior leadership for action." Here, *leadership* is the "internist." Just like if someone asks me to get involved with a certain thing, I say, "I really concur with this, but let me first consult with so and so." *I really agree* is "cutting the arrow," and *so and so* is the "internist." Or, I'll take care of this part now, and the rest later. What is done *now* is "cutting the arrow shaft," the rest *later* is the "internist." In addition, there are other types of "sawing off the arrow shaft," such as sawing it off without mentioning the internist, or just deferring to the internist without even sawing it off. There are many types of these situations—think about it carefully and you will become aware of it.

The Art of the Tinker's Dam

A wok used for cooking was leaking, so the owner asked the tinker to come and repair it. The tinker first used a knife to scrape the black soot off the bottom, asking the owner to please light a fire so that he can burn away the soot. He took advantage of the host's absence to tap the bottom of the wok lightly with his hammer several times, which lengthened the crack. The tinker showed the wok to the host when he returned, saying "the crack in this wok is really long—I was not able to see it until I scraped all of the dirt off of the bottom with my knife. Now, I can only use steel nails to fix it." The host looked down in surprise, and replied, "great job, great job! I am afraid that this wok would be unusable if I had not met you today!" After the wok was repaired, the host and the wok-mender both parted merrily.

Duke Zhuāng of Zhèng connived with Gòngshū Duàn to engage in much unjust behavior before he dispatched troops to punish him.[67] This is called the art of the tinker's dam. History is full of such examples. Some people say, As for Chinese political reform—many places intentionally "spoil the flesh in order to get the cure." This is the art of the tinker's dam used by our reformers. Qīng dynasty officialdom generally used the art of sawing the arrow shaft—the arrow shaft and the tinker's dam have both been used during the Republic.

The two marvelous arts discussed above are widely known examples of taking care of business. No matter in the past or present, in China or abroad, all who have complied with this precedent have been successful, and those who violated it ended in failure. Guǎn Zhòng was a great ancient Chinese political strategist, and he used these two types of methods in managing affairs.[68] The Kingdom of Qí did not dispatch their troops when the Dí tribe attacked Wèi. Instead, they waited until Wèi had been totally destroyed before they started the just action of restoring the descendants of the perished kingdom. This is the art of tinker's dam. As for the battle of Shàoling, he used the fact that Chǔ did not submit a tribute to their liege as a pretext, but did not criticize the King of Chǔ for usurping the title of king. This is the art of sawing the shaft. At that time, Chǔ's power was far greater than Qí's. That Guǎn Zhòng dared to urge Duke Huán of Qí to dispatch troops to punish Chǔ can be said to be ruining things in order to fix them. Only when the Kingdom of Chǔ showed an attitude of resistance did he immediately saw the arrow off and finish the affair. The battle of Shàoling started with the art of the tinker's dam and finished with sawing the shaft. Guǎn Zhòng is called a great genius because he ruined the wok to mend it.

The generals of the late Míng dynasty allowed rebel bands to escape even after being surrounded. Although they originally planned to use the art the tinker's dam, the empire fell apart because the rebels could not be controlled. Because they could not mend the wok after ruining it, they are now called "muddleheaded ministers who harmed the empire."[69] General Yuè Fēi sought to recover the central plains and return the two emperors—he ultimately sacrificed his life because he tried to extract the arrowhead.[70] Likewise, Yú Qiān fetched Emperor Yīngzōng of the Míng dynasty back after being kidnapped.[71] This can also be seen as a case of extracting the arrowhead—and he also suffered the loss of his life. What for? Because he violated the principle.

When Wáng Dǎo of the Jìn dynasty was prime minister, he was unwilling to send out troops to punish a renegade.[72] In response to a letter sent by Táo Kǎn criticizing him, he replied, "Biding time, awaiting thee." After reading the letter, Táo sneered, "biding? he is doing nothing but abiding a scoundrel!" Wáng Dǎo's "biding time" in order to wait for Táo Kǎn is leaving the arrowhead in, especially waiting for the "internist." When the kingdom's worthies gathered at New Pavilion to grieve, Wáng Dǎo with deep feeling cried out "we need to rally for the the royal house and homeland, rather than snivel like the prisoners from Chǔ"![73] He had the semblance of loyalty, wielding an iron hammer to go mend the wok. But actually, that lovely speech was the end of it—the Huái and Mǐn emperors were trapped in the north never to return, and the arrowhead was never extracted. History remembers Wáng Dǎo as the Yíwú of East River because he resembled Guǎn Zhòng.[74] The reader that heeds and executes my techniques will assuredly become the greatest political strategist after Master Guǎn.[75]

CONCLUSION

I have now spoken at length, and there is no harm in my telling the reader the secret of success now that we have "harvested the gourds." To use the *thick* and the *black* one need to cover it with the morality of *empathetic response* and *rightness*, not leaving it nakedly exposed. Wáng Mǎng's failure was in exposing his *thick* and *black*.[76] If it had not been exposed for his whole life, I am sure that Wáng Mǎng would be in today's Ruist temple eating the offering of cold pork. Hán Fēi wrote, "covertly value, overtly castigate."[77] This method is most necessary. As for this *Theory of the Thick and Black*—one should hide it under your pillow and do not leave it out on the table. If someone should ask "Do you know of Lǐ Zōngwú?" You need only don a serious face and reply with, "that horrid person who preaches the *thick* and the *black*—I don't know him." Although the mouth says this, you must consecrate the place of the "Great Completed Ultimate Sagely Master Lǐ Zōngwú" in your heart.[78] If you can do this, you will rock the world in life, and in death you will indubitably be offered offerings in the Ruist temple. So, I am always elated when people curse me, responding that "my *Way* has been broadly put into effect."

One last point that I've already mentioned—you must cover their *thick* and the *black* with a moral layer of *empathetic response* and *rightness*, especially when you meet Ruist experts of the ethics of *empathetic response* and *rightness*. When you meet friends who discuss sexuality, there is no point in bringing up the ethics of *empathetic response* and *rightness* with them, is that not but inviting their disinterest? Instead, you should cover it with the words "sacred love." If you meet a Marxist, cover it with "class struggle and the "dictatorship of the proletariat," and he may even call you "comrade." In conclusion, cover your face with a layer of whatever suits those folks at any given time and place. Investigate your inner *thick* and *black* and you will cleave to the source no matter the myriad changes in the world. Those who have the heart to study it will understand.

NOTES

1. For most of Chinese history the Annals were considered as authoritative history.

2. The Three Kingdoms period (220–280 CE) refers to a period of conflict between the states of Wèi, Shǔ, and Wú at the demise of the Hàn dynasty. The *Records of the Three Kingdoms Sānguózhì* 三國志, composed in the third century in the genre of official history, influenced much subsequent cultural production, including popular sayings, and the enormously influential fourteenth-century Chinese

master novel, *The Romance of the Three Kingdoms* (*Sānguó Yǎnyì* 三國演義. The translation I refer to is Luó Guànzhōng, *Three Kingdoms: A Historical Novel,* trans. Moss Roberts (Berkeley: University of California Press, 1991).

3. Lǐ uses the conventions of orthodox Ruist genres, including the Late Imperial *Records of Instructions* to parody the authoritative tradition.

4. Wáng Yāngmíng 王陽明 (1472–1529 CE) was one of the patriarchs of a late imperial school of Ruism. Wáng's concept of *virtuous knowing* or *innate knowing liángzhī* 良知 refers to moral knowing that is innate in every human, but which can be blinded by selfishness. Because of *liángzhī*, everybody could become a sage.

5. Mencius Mèngzǐ 孟子 (fourth century BCE) and Xúnzi 荀子 (310–220 BCE) were Ruist philosophers with differing views of the world and the human. Mencius thought that humans are naturally inclined to virtue, and therefore a proper environment can help them reach fulfillment. Xúnzi saw the universe as ambivalent about humans; he thought that the human must be compelled to virtue. This passage is as funny as Chinese philosophy gets—analogous to the way in which Ruist orthodoxy naturalized the opposing views of Mencius and Xúnzi, indubitably influenced by the Chinese love of symmetry, Lǐ is ironically and shamelessly asserting a traditional type of authority to *thickblackology* because it functions as an opposing and yet correlative theory, the *yīn* to Wáng Yāngmíng's *yáng*.

6. Sòng 宋 dynasty (960–1279 CE). Qīng 清 dynasty (1644–1912 CE).

7. The word used *fǎshù* 法術 can be translated as spell, sorcery, and as means *fǎ* 法 and technique *shù* 術.

8. The ghastly murder of Lǚ Bóshē and his innocent family occurs in Chapter 4 of Luó, *Three Kingdoms*, 36–38. The execution of Kǒng Róng occurs in chapter 40, (Luó, 307). The scholar Yáng Xiū is executed in chapter 72 (Luó, 549–554); Dǒng Chéng's whole clan was massacred, chapter 24 (Luó, 188). Cáo Cāo executed the Empress and Fú Wán's whole clan in chapter 66, (Luó, 509).

9. Liú begins crying and sighing in chapter 1 (Luó, 8). In Chapter 38, Liú showed his "humble expression of personal feeling" by which he wept so much that his "tears wet the sleeves of his war gown and soaked his lapel" moving the greatest of Chinese strategists, Zhūgé Liáng. (Luó, 293). At the loss of Guān Yǔ, Liú "uttered a dreadful cry and fell unconscious to the ground." Chapter 77 (Luó, 589).

10. Luó, *Three Kingdoms*, 165.

11. Lord Guān is killed by Sūn Quán in chapter 77 (Luó, 584).

12. To goad Sīmǎ Yì into an open fight, Kǒngmíng (Zhūgé Liáng) sought to rouse him to action through the humiliation of questioning his masculinity. Chapter 103 (Luó, 801).

13. In Chinese culture, the name of Zhūgé Liáng is synonymous with virtuosic Strategic Intelligence. Zhūgé Liáng, also known as Kǒngmíng, dies in Chapter 104 (Luó, 806–807).

14. In many ways the Hàn dynasty (221–206 BCE) functions in Chinese discourse in the same way that Rome is foundational to Western civilization.

15. The story of the tragic hero Xiàng Yǔ is derived from Hàn dynasty historian Sīmǎ Qiān's 司馬遷 (206 BC–AD 220) *Records of the Grand Historian Shǐjì: The Exemplary Record of the Marquis of Huáiyīn Huáiyīnhóu Lièzhuàn* 史記·淮陰侯列傳.

16. *Feminine sensitivity* and *masculine temper* 婦人之仁，匹夫之勇.

17. The student of Chinese Strategic Intelligence would do well to study the strategies utilized in the scene of the Feast at Hóng Gate, because it provides an evocative description of strategic intrigue and battle in the social space, and a literary and historical exemplar of virtuosic duplicity. Zhāng Liáng encouraged Liú Bāng to attend the Feast at the Hóng Gate hosted by his frenemy Xiàng Yǔ, who, goaded by a defector from Liú (Fàn Zēng), wanted to kill him. Zhāng helps Liú overwhelm Xiàng's militarily superior force through the use of strategy. From Xiàng's own uncle Zhāng learns about his Xiàng's murderous intent, and he then not only manages to prove Liú's friendship to Xiàng, but he (1) uses a proxy (Fán Kuài 樊噲) to upbraid Xiàng, (2) uses Xiàng's uncle to defend Liú from an assassination attempt by Xiàng's cousin, and (3) bribes Xiàng and Fàn Zēng while Liú escaped. Chinese Strategic Intelligence is indeed a potent force, but it is not for the timid.

18. Here Lǐ echoes the Hàn dynasty historian Sīmǎ Qiān's 司馬遷 famous assessment.

19. The King of Hàn is Liú Bāng.

20. Lì Shēng was a "mad scholar" who lied that he was a drinker, not a scholar, in order to be admitted to see Liú Bāng, who was cavorting with beauties. Lì embarrassed and reminded Liú of his ultimate goal. The implication is that Lì's strategic criticism of Liú's inattention to protocol is a pretense. Sīmǎ Qiān 司馬遷 (206 BC—AD 220), *Records of the Grand Historian Shǐjì* 史記: 97: *The Exemplary Record of Lì Shēng and Lù Jiǎ, Lì Shēn—Lù Jiǎ Lièzhuàn* 酈生陸賈列傳.

21. Liú pushed his heirs off of the cart multiple times. After being gathered repeatedly, the driver told him that it was premature.

22. To rid yourself of allies who may become rivals after one has gained power. A quote associated with King Gōujiàn of Yuè, 越王勾踐.

23. Dragon face, and double pupils are the outward marks of great men.

24. An ironic inversion of Confucius. The Master said, "From fifteen, my heart-mind was set upon learning; from thirty I took my stance; from forty I was no longer doubtful; from fifty I realized the propensities of *heaven tiānmìng* 天命; from sixty my ear was attuned; from seventy I could give my heart-mind free rein without overstepping the boundaries." "吾十有五而志於學，三十而立，四十而不惑，五十而知天命，六十而耳順，七十而從心所慾不踰矩。From the *Analects of Confucius* 論語·为政. *The Analects of Confucius: A Philosophical Translation*, trans. Roger T. Ames and Henry Rosemont, Jr. (New York: Ballantine Books, 1998), 76–77.

25. One of the "three heroes of the Hàn" 漢初三傑, the legend of Zhāng Liáng relays that he received a special book of secret strategic knowledge (believed to either be the Tàigōng's Art of War 太公兵法 or Jiāng Ziyá's *Six Sheaths* Liùtāo 六韜) from a sage, the mastery of which would enable him to tutor the ruler and bring peace and prosperity to the realm. Sīmǎ Qiān 司馬遷, *Records of the Grand Historian Shǐjì* 史記: *Marquis Liú of the Hereditory Houses/Liúhóu Shìjiā* 留侯世家, Chinese Text Project, accessed 9 February 2019, https://ctext.org/shiji/liu-hou-shi-jia.

26. Sū Shì 蘇軾 (1037–1101 CE), also known as Sū Dōngpō, one of the most eminent scholars of the Sòng dynasty, wrote an article entitled *On the Duke of Liú/Lùn Liúhóu* 論留侯 in which he discussed the critical importance of the strategies

of overlooking trifling irritations in order to achieve the long game, and strategic patience while waiting for your opponent to exhaust their strength. Overlooking trifles also occurs in the *Analects of Confucius:* The Master said, "Impatience with trifles ruins great plans." 論語·衛靈公: 曰："小不忍則亂大謀。"事有大小之分. *Legge's translation:* The Master said, "Specious words confound virtue. Want of forbearance in small matters confounds great plans." *Chinese Text Project,* accessed 6 January 2019, https://ctext.org/analects/wei-ling-gong.

27. The Duke of Pèi is Liú Bāng.

28. *Records of the Grand Historian Shǐjì* 史記: *Marquis Liú of the Hereditory Houses/Liúhóu Shìjiā* 留侯世家, *Chinese Text Project,* accessed 9 February 2019, https://ctext.org/shiji/liu-hou-shi-jia. 良數以太公兵法說沛公，沛公善之，常用其策。良為他人者，皆不省。良曰：「沛公殆天授。

29. Ruist moral values.

30. Hán Xìn, one of three "three heroes of the Hàn" 漢初三傑, is famous in Chinese history for submitting to the humiliation of crawling under a hoodlum's crotch instead of killing him because he knew that great things were in store for him in the future. Sīmǎ Qiān 司馬遷, *Records of the Grand Historian Shǐjì* 史記: *Biography of the Marquis of Huáiyīn/Huáiyīnhóu Lièzhuàn* 史記·淮陰侯列傳. "淮陰屠中少年有侮信者，曰："若雖長大，好帶刀劍，中情怯耳。"眾辱之曰："信能死，刺我；不能死，出我袴下。"於是信孰視之，俛出袴下，蒲伏。一市人皆笑信，以為怯. *Chinese Text Project,* accessed 6 January 2019, https://ctext.org/shiji/huai-yin-hou-lie-zhuan.

31. See footnote 15.

32. "The Master said, clever words undermine excellence *dé* 德, intolerance of trifles undermines great schemes." 巧言亂德，小不忍則亂大謀. From the *Analects of Confucius* 論語·衛靈公, 15:27. *The Analects of Confucius,* 190. Sīmǎ Yì also cites this saying in *The Three Kingdoms,* chapter 103 (Luó, 798).

33. In old China, the background of shop signs were often lacquered black in order to highlight the characters. The wearing off of the lacquer over time signified that the shop was a good one because it was long-lasting.

34. "The affairs of the heaven continue, soundless and odorless." *Zhōngyōng* 33 詩經·大雅·文王："上天之載，無聲無臭. The *Classic of Poetry* says, "I cherish your brilliant virtue, which makes no great display in sound or appearance." Confucius said, "In influencing people, the use of sound or appearance is of secondary importance." The *Classic of Poetry* says, "His virtue is as light as hair." Still, a hair is comparable. "The operations of Heaven have neither sound nor smell." 56 Also see Roger T. Ames and David L. Hall, trans. *Focusing the Familiar: A Translation and Philosophical Interpretation of the Zhōngyōng* (Honolulu: University of Hawai'i, Press, 2001), 115.

35. A famous citation from the Chinese Chán (Zen) tradition.

36. This section devilishly parodies the classical Ruist tradition, subverting the orthodox interpretation by consistently replacing key words in each verse.

37. "What Heaven *tiān* 天 commands *mìng* 命 is called natural tendencies *xìng* 性; drawing out these natural tendencies is called the proper *Way;* improving upon this *Way* is called education *jiāo* 教. As for this proper *Way,* we cannot quit it even for an instant. Were it even possible to quit it, it would not be the proper *Way.* It is for this reason that exemplary persons *jūnzi* 君子 are so concerned about what is not seen,

and so anxious about what is not heard. There is nothing more present than what is imminent, and nothing more manifest than what is inchoate. Thus, exemplary persons are ever concerned about their uniqueness." *Zhōngyōng* 1. Ames and Hall, trans. *Focusing the Familiar*, 89.

38. "The proper *Way* of exemplary persons *jūnzi* 君子 is both broad and hidden. The dullest of ordinary men and women can know something of it, and yet even the sages *shèngrèn* 聖人 in trying to penetrate to its furthest limits do not know it all. The most unworthy of common men and women are able to travel a distance along it, yet even the sages in trying to penetrate to its furthest limits are not able to travel it all. As grand as the world is, people are still never completely satisfied." 第十二章 君子之道，費而隱。夫婦之愚，可以與知焉；及其至也，雖聖人亦有所不知焉。夫婦之不肖，可以能行焉；及其至也，雖聖人亦有所不能焉。天地之大也，人猶有所憾。 *Zhōngyōng* 12 Ames and Hall, trans. *Focusing the Familiar*, 92–93.

39. The Master said, "Everyone says 'I am wise,' but they are lured into snares, and know not how to escape." (人皆曰：『予知』；驅而納諸罟擭陷阱之中，而莫之知辟也。) *Zhōngyōng* 7. Ames and Hall, trans. *Focusing the Familiar*, 91.

40. "Thus, the proper *Way* of the ruler *jūnzi* 君子 is rooted in his own person, is corroborated by the ordinary people, and is compared with the *Way* of the Three Kings so there is no mistake." *Zhōngyōng* 中庸 29, 故君子之道。本諸身。征諸庶民。考諸三王而不謬。建諸天地而不悖。質諸鬼神而無疑。百世以俟聖人而不惑. Ames and Hall, trans. *Focusing the Familiar*, 110.

41. "Exemplary persons *jūnzi* 君子 concentrate their efforts on the root, for the root having taken hold, the *Way* will grow therefrom." 君子務本，本立而道生. From the *Analects of Confucius* 1.2 論語·學二篇 *The Analects of Confucius*, 71.

42. "The Master said, 'In strolling in the company of just two other persons, I am bound to find a teacher. Identifying their strengths, I follow them, an identifying their weaknesses, I reform myself accordingly.'" 三人行，必有我師焉。擇其善者而從之，其不善者而改之。 From the *Analects of Confucius* 7.22 論語·述而 *The Analects of Confucius*, 115–116.

43. "The Master said, '*Tiān* 天 has given life to and nourished excellence *dé* 德 in me—what can Huán Tuí do to me?'" 子曰：「天生德於予，桓魋其如予何? From the *Analects of Confucius* 7.23 論語·述而 *The Analects of Confucius*, 116.

44. "The Master said, 'There are, in a town of ten households, bound to be people who are better than I am in doing their utmost *zhōng* 忠 and in making good on their word *xìn* 信 but there will be no one who can compare with me in the love of learning *hàoxué* 好學.'"子曰：'十室之邑，必有忠信如丘者焉，不如丘之好學也。 From the *Analects of Confucius* 5.28 論語·公冶長 *The Analects of Confucius*, 102.

45. "Exemplary persons do not take leave of their authoritative conduct even for the space of a meal. When they are troubled, they certainly turn to it, as they do in facing difficulties." From the *Analects of Confucius* 論語·里仁, 4.5 :" 君子無終食之間違仁,造次必於是,顛沛必於是. *The Analects of Confucius*, 90.

46. "The Master said, 'If a person with talents more admirable than those of the Duke of Zhou is arrogant and niggardly, the rest is not worthy of notice.'" 子曰:如有周公之才之美，使驕且吝，其餘不足觀也已. From the *Analects of Confucius* 論語 · 泰伯, 8.11, *The Analects of Confucius*, 123.

47. "One who is fond of fame can easily yield power. But the loss of trivial things is clearly irksome to those who value getting." 好名之人能讓千乘之國。苟非其人，簞食豆羹見於色. Mencius Mèngzǐ: Jìnxīn (latter) 孟子: 盡心下: For alternate translation, see Bloom, 7B11, 158.

48. "The five grains are wonderful to eat, but they are akin to weeds if not full-grown. The same goes for empathetic response, which needs nurturing." 五穀者，種之美者也;苟為不熟,不如荑稗,夫仁亦在乎熟之而已矣. Mencius Mèngzǐ: Gàozi (former) 孟子: 告子上. For alternate translation, see Bloom 6A19, 131.

49. Here Lǐ cites two famous Confucian verses that discuss duplicity, moralism, and the despoilment of virtue *dé* 德. Analects 17.13 The Master said, "The 'village worthy' is excellence *dé* under false pretenses." 子曰：乡原，德之賊也. *The Analects of Confucius*, 207. And Mencius Mèngzǐ: Jìnxīn (latter) 孟子: 盡心下. For an alternate translation see Bloom 7B37, 165–166.

50. 雖有天下易生之物也，一日暴之，十日寒之，未有能生者也告子章句上·第九節. Mencius Mèngzǐ: Gàozi (former) 孟子, 告子上. For an alternate translation see Bloom 6A9, 127.

51. In Mencius' original formulation, the noble man does not contend with ignorant people because they are ill-informed. Mencius Mèngzǐ: Lílóu (latter) 離婁下:28. For an alternate translation see Bloom 4B28, 92.

52. 公孙丑曰：'道則高矣，美矣，宜若登天然，似不可及也；何不使彼為可幾及而日孳孳也？' Mencius Mèngzǐ: Jìnxīn (former) 孟子，盡心上. For an alternate translation see Bloom 7A41, 154.

53. The original verse in the *Zhōngyōng* discusses how harmony radiates from the self, to the family and beyond. "In traveling a long *Way*, one must set off from what is near at hand, and in climbing to a high place, one must begin from low ground: such is the proper *Way* of exemplary persons *jūnzi* 君子, *Zhōngyōng* 15. 君子之道,譬如远行,必自迩;譬如登高,必自卑 *Zhōngyōng* 中庸 15: 故君子之道。本諸身。征諸庶民。考諸三王而不謬。建諸天地而不悖。質諸鬼神而無疑。百世以俟聖人而不惑. Ames and Hall, trans. *Focusing the Familiar*, 95.

54. 烝民：民之秉彝，好是懿德. *Book of Poetry Shījīng, Dàyǎ* 詩經:大雅.

55. Emperor Tàizōng, founder of the Táng dynasty (618–907 CE).

56. 口之于味，有同嗜焉. *Mencius*, Gàozi (former) 告子上 : For an alternate translation see Bloom 6A7,125.

57. Response and Retribution Manuals *gǎnyìngpiān* 感應篇, and Hidden Merit Tracts *yīnzhìwén* 陰騭文. Both were pietistic texts that recommended good works as a means of reducing karmic debt and increasing positive outcomes. One can see an example of these syncretistic texts at https://archive.org/details/Treatise2014Edition, and https://archive.org/details/wenchang.

58. Mencius, Gàozi (former) 告子上. For alternate translation, see Bloom 6A8, 126.

59. 行之而不著焉，習矣而不察焉，終身由之而不知其道也，眾也. Mencius Mèngzǐ, Jìnxīn (former) 孟子, 盡心上. For alternate translation, see Bloom 7A5, 145.

60. "The Master said, "If someone were to make use of me in governing, in the course of one year I could make a difference, and in three years I would really have something to show for it."' From the *Analects of Confucius*, 論語·子路 13.10. *The Analects of Confucius*, 164.

61. This section parodies the *Records of Practice* compiled by the disciples of the Ruist patriarch Wáng Yāngmíng.

62. These are the most famous of the classical and late Imperial Ruist scholars.

63. A reference to a legend about James Watt (1736–1819 CE), the father of the steam engine, who was inspired from watching a boiling kettle. Luigi Galvani (1737–1798 CE) discovered bioelectricity when he compelled the legs of a dead frog to twitch through an electric spark.

64. Cáo Cāo is the Duke of Wèi. In Chinese tradition, the figure of the scholar Huá Xīn denotes someone who is excessively opportunistic, desirous of wealth and status over the virtues of loyalty and detachment. Huá Xīn is often contrasted with Guǎn Níng 管寧, a scholar unsullied by attachment to Cáo.

65. This phrase *xiéjiān chǎnxiào, bìngyú xiàqí* 胁肩谄笑，病于夏畦 refers to an ancient Ruist adage from the Mencius (滕文公下) which proclaims that the authentic, noble Ruist worthy should never fawn and toady to political leaders. For alternate translation, see Bloom 3B7, 67–68.

66. A clear reference to the value system the Chinese have called the *official standard guānběnwèi* 官本位 (as in the gold standard), and as *officialism guānliáozhǔyì* 官僚主義. Being an official is a standard by which all value is weighed, and all assessments made authoritative and legitimate.

67. Another example of royal fratricide and intrigue in Chinese history. In response to the plotting of his mother and brother Gòngshū, Duke Zhuāng of Zhèng (757–701 BC) strategically laid a trap for them. He bided his time to let his mother and brother flesh out their rebellion before taking definitive action.

68. Guǎn Zhòng (720–645 BCE) was a famous minister to Duke Huán of Qí 齐桓公 during the Spring and Autumn period (770–476 BCE), a period known for interstate intrigue and division. Chǔ was a rising power that threatened the power of Qí, so Qí created an alliance to attack one of Chǔ's vassals, ultimately forcing Chǔ to submit to status quo.

69. The instability surrounding the fall of the Míng dynasty was exacerbated by multiple rebellions and widespread banditry. One rebel group even managed to hold the capital for a year—the infighting further weakened the Míng state, enabling the Manchus to successfully invade.

70. General Yuè Fēi 岳飛 (1103–1142 CE) of the Sòng dynasty is one of the most famous generals of Chinese history. He was recalled to court while attempting to recapture the north from foreign invaders because the reigning emperor feared a threat to his regime if the northerners released the previous reigning emperor that they held hostage. Upon his return Yuè Fēi was executed.

71. The Emperor Yīngzōng was captured by a Mongolian force in 1449 CE, and his brother was made emperor. Yīngzōng was returned a year later. In 1457, when his brother became ill, a palace coup re-installed Yīngzōng, and his savior (and the protector of Beijing) Yú Qiān was beheaded.

72. Wáng Dǎo (276–339 CE) was an eminent political strategist of the Jìn 晉 dynasty (265–420), and Táo Kǎn was an exceptional general. *Jìnshū* 晉書: 66.

73. The Huái 懷 Emperor was executed in 313 CE after being held hostage for two years. Emperor Mǐn 愍 was executed in 316 CE. *Jìnshū* 晉書晋书·*Wáng Dǎo zhuàn* 王导传.

74. Yíwú was Guǎn Zhòng's title.
75. Master Guǎn Zhòng.
76. Wáng Mǎng 王莽 (45 BCE–23 CE) seized the Hàn throne, holding power for about 20 years, before the Eastern Hàn regained power.
77. Hán Fēi 韓非 (280–233 BCE) is an important political philosopher. Lǐ cites Hán's *On the Difficulty of Persuasion Shuōnán* 說難. In the passage cited, Hán argues for the necessity of kingly duplicity.
78. Confucius' title.

Conclusion

To recognize in the cultural identity of the strategist the theological, sociocultural, and psychological consequences of alienation, and to explore cultural and political subjectivity in terms of agency, power, and meaning, is to depart from the tone of most scholarship on strategy in the practical disciplines that seek to employ it.[1] Whole professions extol the strategically intelligent, and many use it to divine the hidden aspects of the present with an eye to managing the future. Conventionally believed to result in strategic advantage when used well, strategic practitioners claim that it is a better way that results in excellence, even though the range of deceptive devices used and level of invasiveness often appear questionable. Strategy, understood broadly, is not only valued for what it does with regards to strategic advantage, but for the worth it provides to identity when strategic advantage is realized. In short, Strategic Intelligence is a form of hope that aims to mitigate the alienation of the human condition, and the hermeneutic approach that I used in this book demonstrates the intimate and indivisible link between the cultural, the powerful, and the philosophical.

The questions that I wrestled with in the previous chapters include the following: What does it mean to be a heroic strategist? What exactly makes this identity justified, legitimate, and authoritative in culture? How does the identity of the strategist shape her orientation in the world? How does her worldview inform the types of knowledge she values, and the values which guide her actions? What might the identity of the Strategically Intelligent teach us about how to be in the world? Does Strategic Intelligence have virtues of its own? What is it exactly if not a type of meaning and a form of hope? Where does it come from? And how has it existed in the past?

What appears to be universally shared about Strategic Intelligence are strategic values, which are variables that can not be seen directly, and which are rarely explicitly articulated. The threat of finitude to an embodied being is modeled in human experience in the paradoxical metaphorological paradigm that *life is death*. The threat of foundational and fundamental insecurity, which I identify in the foundational stories that depict a zero-sum antagonistic environment, sets the condition for a human type of hope, a superior type of hope that I refer to as Strategic Intelligence. Although the paradoxical metaphorological paradigm is shared, the expression of various aspects of Strategic Intelligence in the cultures of different eras is uniquely conditioned by their psychology, culture, language, and history. In other words, the particularity of the antagonistic environment is what triggers the particularity of the cultural response. This insight leads us to two interesting conclusions.

First, to understand a foreign strategic culture, one must be able to understand the manner in which it creates meaning by interpreting how it discloses its strategic values in the extra linguistic and the extra conceptual—in stories, metaphors, and figures, and the unique ways in which it adapts from its own cultural legacy, or others. In this view, strategic culture as an analytic framework of a preexistent values-domain is qualitative and hermeneutic (interpretative), rather than quantitative and empirical. The same can be said for Strategic Intelligence, which is a type of practical decision-making (praxis) grounded in the appropriate interpretation of the meaningful parameters of radical flux and the contingent, rather than a stable, universal law. Because any present reality, which is always informed by its particularity, can never be exactly the same as the snapshot of a previous reality, the strategic (both as intelligence and culture) resists ultimate theorization.[2] Strategic hope is a form of experiential, practical wisdom rather than a theoretical type of knowledge.

Practitioners of various forms of Strategic Intelligence are those who hope to wrestle some value from a pre-existent situation that thwarts heroic meaning and understanding—intelligibility from mystery, pattern from chaos, stability from contingency, security from insecurity, identity from nought, and strategic advantage from ever looming disadvantage. Strategic Intelligence, in potentially reversing various types of asymmetry in human affairs, enables freedom and ambition by enabling strategic knowledge. As the American intellectual John Erskine (1879–1951 CE) wrote, "We really seek intelligence not for the answers it may suggest to the problems of life, but because we believe it *is* life."[3] The cultural history presented in this book demonstrates that nature favors neither the physically strong nor the rigidly virtuous, but rather the heroical and virtuosic strategic. The strategic approach to life, embodied life in particular, responds to a mystery that discloses itself neither as discourse nor concept. This first mystery we perceive as risk because it holds our potential at risk, and we name it threat.

Strategic Intelligence is therefore a response to both preexisting threats and threats that may arise *in* space and time, and *by* space and time. To claim a need for Strategic Intelligence is to acknowledge a fundamental poverty, of necessity at the level of existence, and because of this we invest Strategic Intelligence with the highest form of authority as a *mission* of historical importance, and an ultimately significant form of hope.[4] Those who have advantage hope to keep it—those who suffer from its lack hope to acquire it. Meaning and power, in this view, are always contested.

Embodied consciousness, aware of its poverty while shackled in Plato's cave, plays with reality the silent game of concealing and revealing being that is known to children in every era and every language, of *celabimus et quaeris*, κρυφτό, *nascondino, al escondite, grasp the hidden* (*zhuōmícáng* 捉迷藏), of hide and seek. We play this game because it is dramatic and fun, because hiding and finding bring both pleasure and the thrill of pain, and because hiding and seeking are aspects of the game of life itself. By playing this game, we come to know both the virtuosity of seeing without being seen, and the virtuosity of blinding others through concealment. In this game, participants take turns playing both predator and prey, hunter and hunted. And this is where we catch a glimpse of the paradox of life—that Existence hides and Becoming seeks, that Being hides and Existence seeks, that Becoming necessarily holds Existence at risk, that power is enabled and constrained by life, and that meaning and identity are held at risk by death. This implies that meaning and identity are always at risk, always contingent, always constrained—that meaning exists *in extremis*.

Boggling the mind and bewildering consciousness, this other cannot find rational embodiment in language or concept—mind therefore escapes the trap *strategically* by lodging, via imagination, in a fantasy of the bodiless infinite, while concealing both the provenance and limits of its own strategic machination—that the image of infinity is made finite by the mind imagining it, and the culture supporting it. As the myth of the Garden of Eden relays, deception is necessary and sufficient, and yet paradoxical—it is necessary and sufficient for human enlightenment, but through enlightenment humankind becomes aware that it has been deceived by itself. Strategic Intelligence then is the core aspect of humanity—through heroic deception mankind paradoxically both mitigates and enables its very alienation. This dynamic can only be approached obliquely through the tension and rich fecundity of the paradoxical metaphorical paradigm, that *life is death*. The threat is repressed, displaced, or sublimated. *Life is death* is a paradoxical metaphorical paradigm that functions like a blackhole that holds all within its forcefield—it shapes and leaves its trace in language and concept, while concealing itself from view. Having hidden its root beyond language and concept, Cultural Cryptology shows itself astute with regards to heroic meaning.

Cultural Cryptologists seek that which is hidden, and analyze sources not for truth or understanding primarily—what do eternal truths and understandings have to do with the necessity of survival and escape from entrapment? Strategists do not wish to understand it, and the matter of its truth is secondary to the manner of its encryption and the possibility of its decryption. Rather than understand it, strategists hope to open it, to order it, to compel it to reveal order, to dominate it, to consume it, and to use it to overcome—all in the name of strategic advantage. Strategists do it for the common good that is the body, the body that is metonymy for identity, for the *mission* of defending the bodily identity that is always held at risk—the personal body, the racial body, the sexual body, the family body, the religious body, the corporate body, the cultural body, and the national body. Strategists do it because power and meaning are core to identity, because identity is the face of life itself, which is essentially an assertion of permanence, and therefore a provocation and challenge to contingency.

Born in the necessity of the body, the strategic molds its own values with regards to what needs to be known through prudent deliberation, and how humans should act in the world. Navigating through a reality understood to be Becoming-which-holds-existence-at-risk does not yield to facile moral judgment. To hide and to seek—neither role is good or bad in itself; rather, one may be good at, or bad at, or with regards to. Informed by a logic of positionality, life dispositions itself opportunistically, interpreting the terrain for maximum adaptability, which results in greater advantage vis-à-vis one's co-gamers. A world view shaped by zero-sum existential threat justifies, authorizes, legitimates, and validates all forms of heroic defense. This may even include a preemptive defense which offensively delivers effects in the domains of human discourse and affect, such as setting verbal snares, camouflaging intent through indirection and misdirection, feints, subtlety, half-truths, dissimulation, and emotional manipulation. Strategists conceal their position discursively, attacking their foes through suasion, through question and dialogue under the pretense of truth and understanding like the Greek philosophers examined earlier, or through emotional manipulation delivered through poetic allusion, as explored in the examples of ancient Chinese strategists. These strategies are not only defensible, they are also heroically strategic.

The strategic aspect of rationality can ultimately only be grounded in paradox. Riffing off of one master of Strategic Intelligence, we cannot tell whether Strategic Intelligence is good or bad just like we cannot tell if fire or water are good or bad. Strategic Intelligence is either valueless, or it is paradoxically both good and bad, heroic and villainous. Strategic Intelligence can be wicked, monstrous, beastly, despicable, duplicitous, conniving, sneaky, backstabbing, naughty, *tiáopí* 調皮, and deadly. It can just as likely be prudent, practical, audacious, brazen, plucky, cheeky, cunning, and shrewd. Like all arts, it is a beautiful and wondrous sight to behold—but it is also pathetic, tragic, and comedic. We groan at the debasement of the underdog who uses underhanded tactics even as we cheer her on to glory! And we marvel at the strategic master of the long game who voluntarily accepts shame, humiliation, and utter degradation as a necessary condition for greatness. The suffering of the nadir of mortification sets the condition for the most glorious of ascents—the greater the nadir, the higher the flyer.

I have aimed in this book to stake out the contours of Strategic Intelligence as a core dynamic of our humanity, of human cultures and societies in general, and as a central root of moral, political and cultural philosophical analysis. Querying the identity of the heroic strategist enables us to explore the central questions of the humanities, including what does it mean to be human; how do humans create meaning and why; what truly is the highest human good; and what are the authorized and legitimated means one may use to obtain the good life? The answers to these questions are not only relevant to the practical fields of governance and business that seek to use strategy to attain strategic advantage on behalf of their stakeholders, but they also touch on key topics explored in multiple academic disciplines. For example, in the fields of Philosophy and Theology: to what degree do root metaphors dominate thought, value systems, and our political discourse? What does the reveal/conceal aspect of metaphors imply for a theory of truth? How might we resist legacy metaphors and open ourselves up to new vistas? In Political Philosophy: strategic thought is intimately linked to human agency, power, governance, and competition; what are the authoritative grounds for justice and order if everything is understood to be zero-sum? What does this imply for the values of equality and fairness in democratic civilization, and for human cooperation and responsibility? If my hypothesis is correct, that the leitmotif of entrapment is just one type of figuration of finitude, what does this mean for the Western cultural values of freedom and liberty, social, philosophical, and religious attempts to liberate and enlighten humankind, and for contemporary movements that aim to achieve social, racial, and economic justice? Is the strategic universal? If so, how has it existed and persisted historically in other world cultures? What are its mechanisms? To what degree is it culturally recursive or free flowing across cultures?

As Eurasian cultural data originating from two sides of the vast continent demonstrate, Strategic Intelligence emerged historically as a human response to the threat of finitude to life itself and as a form of hope that promises meaning, power, and strategic advantage. Born in human experience and memorialized by culture in the paradoxical metaphorological paradigm that *life is death*, the cultural identity of the strategist and her strategic values have been continuously transmitted in cultural products for thousands of years. These culturally authoritative sources have both validated a strategic orientation in the world which is a coherent way of life, and transmitted a worldview that enables the practitioner of strategy to overcome threat through the development of interpretation, foresight, and appropriate adaptation. The strategic aspect of reason is one of the most fundamental dynamics of human meaning, and the cultural transmission of strategic values constitutes a transcultural world view that continues to enlighten young princes and princesses to the actualization of their royal potential, through a heroically strategic way of being and acting in the world.

The question of Strategic Culture, then, is *WWSD?*
What Would the Strategist Do?

NOTES

1. Adapted from Katherine Ellison, *A Cultural History of Early Modern English Cryptography Manuals* (New York: Routledge, 2017), 8. "To recognize in cryptography the theological, social, and psychological consequences of cultural alienation is to depart from the tone of most scholarship in the history of cryptography as a discipline."

2. Rather than use theory philosophically as I have earlier as a bringing to sight, here I use theory in its contemporary sense as used by International Relations theorists in its sense as an analytic framework that adequately explains variables, and captures the requisite features and phenomena to the degree that it will correctly predict what will happen in the future.

3. John Erskine, "The Moral Obligation to Be Intelligent," in *The Moral Obligation to Be Intelligent and Other Essays*, (Indianapolis: Bobbs-Merrill 1921). Italic added for emphasis.

4. US Office of the Director of National Intelligence, accessed 12 January 2019, https://www.dni.gov: "Our mission is to *lead intelligence integration* and forge an *intelligence community* that delivers the most insightful intelligence possible." Underline added for emphasis.

Bibliography

WEST EURASIAN PRIMARY AND SECONDARY SOURCES

Accademici Intronati di Siena. *Gl'Ingannati The Deceived*. In *Commedie del Cinquecento*, Edited by Ireneo Sanesi. Bari: G. Laterza, 1912. Hathi Trust Digital Library. https://babel.hathitrust.org/cgi/pt?id=uc1.$b732928;view=2up;seq=320.

Adler, Alfred. *The Science of Living*. Edited by Heinz L. Ansbacher. New York: Anchor Books, 1969.

Adventures of Amir Hamza, Lord of the Auspicious Planetary Conjunction. Translated by Musharraf Ali Farooqi. New York: The Modern Library, 2007.

Aesop's Fables: A New Translation by Laura Gibbs. Translated by Laura Gibbs. Oxford: Oxford University Press, 2002.

Al-Hamadhání, Badí Al-Zamán Maqámát. *The Maqámát of Badí Al-Zamán Al-Hamadhání*. Translated by W.J. Prendergast. London: Curzon Press, 1973.

Alberti, Leon Battista. *Momus*. Translated by Sarah Knight. Cambridge, MA: Harvard University Press, 2003.

Alemán, Mateo. *Guzmán de Alfarache*. Edited by Julio Cejador. Madrid, Renacimiento, 1913. Reprint of Coimbra, edition published in 1600. Hathi Trust Digital Library. https://catalog.hathitrust.org/Record/006137328.

Ambrose, *On the Duties of the Clergy De Officiis Ministrorum*. Catholic Encyclopedia, New Advent, http://www.newadvent.org/fathers/34012.htm.

Ambrosio, Francis. *Dante and Derrida: Face to Face*. Albany, NY: State University of New York Press, 2007.

———. *Philosophy, Religion, and the Search for Meaning*. The Great Courses, 2013.

Appian. *The Punic Wars*. In *Appian. The Foreign Wars*. Translated by Horace White. New York: Macmillan, 1899, Perseus Digital Library, Tufts University.

Arend, Richard J. "Revisiting the Logical and Research Considerations of Competitive Advantage." *Strategic Management Journal*, 3 (24), 2003: 279–284.

Ariosto, Ludovico. *La Lena, Comedia*. Stampata in Vinegia: Per maestro Bernardino Vinitiano de Vitali (1535). Hathi Trust Digital Library. https://babel.hathitrust.org/cgi/pt?id=gri.ark:/13960/t3qv9vv2p;view=2up;seq=8.

Aristotle, Source language from Perseus Digital Library, Tufts University. Translations in *The Basic Works of Aristotle*. Edited by Richard McKeon. Translated by W. Rhys Roberts. New York: The Modern Library, 2001.

———. *Metaphysics*. In *Aristotle in Twenty-three Volumes*. Translated by Cyril Armstrong. London: W. Heinemann, 1933. Perseus Digital Library, Tufts University.

———. *Nichomachean Ethics*.

———. *Rhetoric*. Translated by Henry John Freese. *The Art of Rhetoric*, Loeb Classical Library. London: W. Heinemann, 1926. Perseus Digital Library, Tufts University.

Ashley, Kathleen M. and Pamela Sheingorn. *Writing Faith: Text, Sign & History in the Miracles of Sainte Foy*. Chicago: University of Chicago Press, 1999.

Attar, Farid ud-din. *The Conference of the Birds*. London: Penguin Books, 1984.

Augustine (Saint). Sermon 80, "On the New Testament." Translated by R.G. MacMullen. From *Nicene and Post-Nicene Fathers, First Series*, Vol. 6. Edited by Philip Schaff. Buffalo, NY: Christian Literature Publishing Co., 1888. Revised and edited for New Advent by Kevin Knight. http://www.newadvent.org/fathers/160380.htm. "Doctrine of the Atonement," *Catholic Encyclopedia*. Denver, CO: New Advent, 2000.

———. Augustine's *Sermon* CCLXV (d). Cited in ed. G. Morin, *Sancti Augustini Sermones post Maurinos reperti*. Miscellenea Agostiniana 1 (Rome, 1930), 662 (cf. PLS 2, col. 707). *Sermones* CXXX.

Aulén, Gustaf. *Christus Victor: an Historical Study of the Three Main Types of the Idea of the Atonement*. Translated by A. G. Hebert. London, S.P.C.K., 1970.

Barnouw, Jeffrey. *Odysseus, Hero of Practical Intelligence*. Boulder: Lanham: 2004.

Barrett, William. *Irrational Man: A Study in Existential Philosophy*. Garden City, NY: Doubleday Anchor, 1962.

Bauer, Wolfgang. "The Problem of Individualism and Egoism in Chinese Thought." In *Studia Sino-Mungulica: Festschrift fur Herbert Franke*. Edited by Wolfgang Bauer. Wiesbaden: Franz Steiner, 1979.

Becker, Ernest. *The Denial of Death*. New York: Free Press Paperbacks/Simon & Schuster, 1973.

Beowulf. Translated by David Wright. New York: Penguin Books, 1957.

Blumenberg, Hans. *Paradigms for a Metaphorology*. Translated by Robert Savage. Ithaca: Cornell University Press, 2010.

———. *Shipwreck with Spectator: Paradigm of a Metaphor for Existence*. Translated by Steven Rendeall. Cambridge, MA: MIT Press, 1997.

Boethius. *The Consolation of Philosophy*. Translated by W. V. Cooper, 1908.

Bosworth, Clifford Edmund. *The Mediaeval Islamic Underworld: the Banū Sāsān in Arabic Society and Literature*. Leiden: E. J. Brill, 1976.

Burke, Kenneth. *A Grammar of Motives*. Berkeley: University of California Press, 1969.

———. *A Rhetoric of Motives*. Berkeley: University of California Press, 1969.

———. *Language as Symbolic Action: Essays on Life, Literature, and Method.* Berkeley: University of California Press, 1966.

———. *The Rhetoric of Religion: Studies in Logology.* Berkeley: University of California Press, 1970.

The Cambridge History of Literary Criticism: Classical Criticism. Edited by George A. Kennedy. Cambridge: Cambridge University Press, 1989, Volume 1. *Catholic Encyclopedia.* Denver, CO: New Advent, 2000.

Cassian, John (Saint). "The Second Conference of Abbot Joseph." Chapter 20. Full translation at C. S. Gibson. From Nicene and Post-Nicene Fathers, Second Series, Vol. 11. Edited by Philip Schaff and Henry Wace. Buffalo, NY: Christian Literature Publishing Co., 1894. Revised and edited for New Advent by Kevin Knight, Catholic Encyclopedia, New Advent. http://www.newadvent.org/fathers/350817.htm.

Clement of Alexandria. *Stromateis.* In *The Fathers of the Church: A New Translation.* Translated by John Ferguson. Washington DC: The Catholic University of America Press, 1991.

de Quevedo, Francisco. *El Buscón,* In *Vida del Buscón.* Madrid: Ediciones de "La Lectura," 1911. Based on the Zaragoza 1626 edition. Hathi Trust Digital Library.ht tps://babel.hathitrust.org/cgi/pt?id=mdp.39015067208168;view=2up;seq=8.

Detienne, Marcel and Jean-Pierre Vernant. *The Cuisine of Sacrifice among the Greeks.* Translated by Paula Wissing. Chicago & London: University of Chicago Press, 1989.

———. *Cunning Intelligence in Greek Culture and Society*, Translated by Janet Lloyd. New Jersey: Humanities Press, 1978.

de Weever, Jacqueline. *Aesop and the Imprint of Medieval Thought: A Study of Six Fables as Translated at the End of the Middle Ages.* Jefferson: McFarland & Co, 2011.

Derrida, Jacques. *Donner la Mort.* Paris: Galilée, 1999. & *Littérature au Secret: une Filiation Impossible.*

Durand, Rodolphe. "Competitive Advantages Exist: A Critique of Powell." *Strategic Management Journal,* 9 (23), 2002: 867–872.

Ellis, Anthony. *Old Age, Masculinity, and Early Modern Drama: Comic Elders on the Italian and Shakesperean Stage.* Farnham: Ashgate, 1988.

Epictetus, *Fragments*, Perseus Digital Library, Tufts University.

Erskine, John. "The Moral Obligation to Be Intelligent." In *The Moral Obligation to Be Intelligent and Other Essays.* Indianapolis: Bobbs-Merrill, 1921.

"Fable," *Routledge Revivals: Medieval France, An Encyclopedia.* Edited by William W. Kibler, Grover A. Zinn. Milton Park: Routledge, 1995/2016.

Firdawsi. *Shahnameh: The Epic of the Persian Kings.* Translated by Admad Sadri. New York: Quantuck Lane Press, 2013.

Frye, David. Editor and Translator. *Lazarillo de Tormes & The Grifter: Two Novels of the Low Life in Golden Age Spain.* Indianapolis: Hackett: 2015.

Godfrey-Smith, Peter. *Philosophy of Biology.* Princeton & Oxford: Princeton University Press, 2014.

Gracián, Baltasar. *Oráculo Manual y Arte de Prudencia Oracle.* In *Obras de Lorenzo Gracian: Tomo Primero, que contiene El Criticon, Primera, Segunda y TerceraPartes, El Oraculo, y El Heroe*. Madrid:Universidad Complutense de Madrid, 1664. Hathitrust.

Gray, Colin. "Out of the Wilderness: Prime Time for Strategic Culture." National Institute for Public Policy. US Nuclear Strategy Forum. Publication No. 0004. National Institute Press, 2006. http://www.nipp.org/wp-content/uploads/2014/12/CSG-Strategic-culture-paper-Marheine-pub.pdf.

———. "Strategic Culture as Context: The First Generation of Theory Strikes Back." *Review of International Studies*, 25 (1) 1999: 49–69.

———. *What Should the U.S. Army Learn From History? Recovery From a Strategy Deficit*. Carlisle, PA: US Army War College Press, Strategic Studies Institute, 2017. https://ssi.armywarcollege.edu/pubs/display.cfm?pubID=1360.

Gregory of Nyssa (Saint). *Nicene and Post-Nicene Fathers*. Second Series, Volume V. Edited by Philip Schaff.

Griffiths, Paul J. *Lying: An Augustinian Theology of Duplicity*. Grand Rapids: Brazos Press, 2004.

Grünberg, Ludwig. *The Mystery of Values; Studies in Axiology*. Amsterdam, Rodopi: 2000.

Guicciardini, Francesco. *Ricordi Politici E Civili*. In *Opere inedite di Francesco Guicciardini*. Edited by Piero Luigi Guicciardini. Firenze: Barbèra, Bianchi e comp., 1857–1867.

Hale, David G. "Aesop in Renaissance England." *The Library*, 5–XXVII (2), 1 June 1972: 116–125.

Harrison, Robert Pogue. "Review: The Ambiguities of Philology Reviewed Works: *Cunning Intelligence in Greek Culture and Society*" by Jean-Pierre Vernant, Marcel Detienne, Janet Lloyd; *Les Maîtres de Vérité dans la Grèce Archaique* by Marcel Detienne. *Diacritics, JHU Press*, 16 (2) (Summer 1986): 14–20.

Hesiod. *Theogony*, and *Works and Days*. In *The Homeric Hymns and Homerica*. Translated by Hugh G. Evelyn-White. Cambridge, MA: Harvard University Press, 1914. *Theogony, Works and Days*. Perseus Digital Library, Tufts University. http://www.perseus.tufts.edu/hopper/text?doc=Perseus:text:1999.01.0129.

Hobbes, Thomas. *Leviathan*. In *Classics of Political and Moral Philosophy*. Edited by Steven M. Cahn, 2nd ed., New York/Oxford: Oxford University Press, 2012.

Homer, *Iliad*. In *Homeri Opera*. Oxford: Oxford University Press, 1920. Perseus Digital Library, Tufts University.

———. *Odyssey*. In *The Odyssey with an English Translation*. Translated A. T. Murray. Translator. Cambridge, MA: Harvard University Press), 1919. Perseus Digital Library, Tufts University.

Horace, *Satyrarum Libri*. Perseus Digital Library, Tufts University. http://data.perseus.org/citations/urn:cts:latinLit:phi0893.phi004.perseus-lat1:2.5.

Horovitz, J. "Traces of the Greek Mimes in the Orient." In *The Mediaeval Islamic Underworld: the Banū Sāsān in Arabic Society and Literature*. Edited by Clifford Edmund Bosworth. Leiden: E.J. Brill, 1976.

Huizinga, Johan. *Homo Ludens: A Study of the Play-Element in Culture*. Boston: Beacon Press, 1955.

Hume, David. "Of the Original Contract." In *Classics of Political and Moral Philosophy*. Edited by Steven M. Cahn, 2nd ed. New York/Oxford: Oxford University Press, 2012.

Hutton, Edward. *Florence*. London: Hollis and Carter, 1952.

Jacoby, Charles H. Jr, and Ryan L. Shaw. "Strategic Agility: Theory and Practice." *Joint Force Quarterly*. 81. Qtr2, April 2016. National Defense University Press. https://ndupress.ndu.edu/JFQ/Joint-Force-Quarterly-81/Article/702009/strategic-agility-theory-and-practice/.

James, William. *Pragmatism, a New name for Some Old Ways of Thinking, Together with Four Related Essays Selected from the Meaning of Truth*. New York: Longmans, Green and Co, 1948.

Jameson, Fredric. *The Political Unconscious: Narrative as a Socially Symbolic Act*. Ithaca: Cornell University Press, 1981.

———. *Postmodernism, or The Cultural Logic of Late Capitalism*. Durham: Duke University Press, 1991.

John of Damascus (Saint). *On the Orthodox Faith* Ἔκδοσις ἀκριβὴς τῆς ὀρθοδόξου πίστεως "Concerning the Divine Œconomy and God's care over us, and concerning our salvation." ΚΕΦΑΛΑΙΟΝ 45. Περὶ τῆς θείας οἰκονομίας καὶ περὶ τῆς δι' ἡμᾶς κηδεμονίας καὶ τῆς ἡμῶν σωτηρίας. Book 3, 1:45. https://babel.hathitrust.org/cgi/pt?id=njp.32101063614737;view=1up;seq=419. Translated by Henry Wace and Philip Schaff. New York: The Christian literature company;1890–1900. Also, *A Select Library of Nicene and Post-Nicene Fathers of the Christian Church*, Second series. https://babel.hathitrust.org/cgi/pt?id=njp.32101063614737;view=1up;seq=446.

John of Salisbury. *Policraticus*. In *Frivolities of Courtiers and Footprints of Philosophers: Being a Translation of the First, Second and Third Books and Selections from the Seventh and Eigth Books of the Policraticus of John of Salisbury*. Translated by Joseph B. Pike. Minneapolis: University of Minnesota Press, 1938.

Johnston, Alastair I. *Cultural Realism: Strategic Culture and Grand Strategy in Chinese History*. Princeton: Princeton University Press, 1998.

———. "Strategic Cultures Revisited: Reply to Colin Gray." *Review of International Studies*, 25 (3) 1999: 519–523.

———. "Thinking about Strategic Culture." *International Security*, 19 (4), Spring 1995: 32–64.

Kant, Immanuel. *Religion Within the Limits of Reason Alone*. Translated by Theodore M. Greene and Hoyt H. Hudson. New York: Harper, 1960.

Kierkegaard, Søren. *Fear and Trembling*. Translated by Alastair Hannay. Penguin Classics; Reprint edition January 7, 1986.

Kwan, Kai-Man, and Eric W. K. Tsang. "Realism and Constructivism in Strategy Research: A Critical Realist Response to Mir and Watson." *Strategic Management Journal*, 12 (22), 2001: 1163–1168.

Lakoff, George. *Moral Politics: What Conservatives Know that Liberals Don't*. Chicago: University of Chicago Press, 1997.

———. *Women, Fire, and Dangerous Things: What Categories Reveal about the Mind*. Chicago: University of Chicago Press, 1987.

Lakoff, George and Mark Johnson. *Metaphors We Live By.* Chicago: University of Chicago Press, 1980.
Lane, Anthony N.S., *Bernard of Clairvaux: Theologian of the Cross.* Collegeville: Liturgical Press, 2013.
La Vida de Lazarillo de Tormes. H. J. Chaytor, Editor. Manchester, The University Press, 1922. Hathi Trust Digital Library. https://babel.hathitrust.org/cgi/pt?id=uc1.$b256846;view=2up;seq=8.
Liddell, Henry George and Robert Scott. *A Greek-English Lexicon.* Perseus Digital Library, Tufts University.
Mabbe, James, 1623. *The Rogue or the Life of Guzman de Alfarache.* New York: AMS Press, 1967.
Machiavelli, Niccolò. *Discorsi Sopra la Prima Deca di Tito Livio, Discourses on the First Decade of Titus Livy. Letteratura Italiana Einaudi. Tutte Le Opere.* Edited by Mario Martelli. Firenze, 1971.
———. *La Mandragola The Mandrake. La Mandragola: Comedia / di Niccolò Macchiavelli Fiorentino. Venetia: Per Plinio Pietrasanta, 1554.* Hathitrust. https://catalog.hathitrust.org/Record/102323168.
Magnússon, Eiríkr and Eysteinn Ásgrímsson. *Lilja (The Lily) an Icelandic Religious Poem of the Fourteenth Century.* Ulan Press, 2012.
Map, Walter. *De Nugis Curialium: Courtier's Trifles.* Edited & translated by M.R. James. Oxford: Clarendon Press, 1983.
McCauley, Daniel H. "Rediscovering the Art of Strategic Thinking: Developing 21st-Century Strategic Leaders." *Joint Force Quarterly.* 81. Qtr2, April 2016. National Defense University Press. https://ndupress.ndu.edu/JFQ/Joint-Force-Quarterly-81/Article/702006/rediscovering-the-art-of-strategic-thinking-developing-21st-century-strategic-l/.
Mir, Raza and Andrew Watson. "Critical Realism and Constructivism in Strategy Research: Toward a Synthesis." *Strategic Management Journal*, 12 (22), 2001: 1169–1173.
Mirandola, Giovanni Pico Della. *De Dignitate Hominis Oration on the Dignity of Man.* 1496 CE. *Pico Project*, https://www.brown.edu/Departments/Italian_Studies/pico/index.html, accessed 14 Oct 2019.
Moloughney, Brian. "From Biographical History to Historical Biography: a Transformation in Chinese Historical Writing." *East Asian History, the Continuation of Papers on Far Eastern History.* Edited by Geremie Barme. Institute of Advanced Studies Australian National University, December 1992, #4. http://www.eastasianhistory.org/sites/default/files/article-content/04/EAH04_01.pdf.
Montiglio, Silvia. *From Villain to Hero: Odysseus in Ancient Thought.* Ann Arbor: University of Michigan Press, 2011.
———. *Wandering in Ancient Greek Culture.* Chicago: University of Chicago Press, 2005.
Moss, Candida R. *The Other Christs: Imitating Jesus in Ancient Christian Ideologies of Martyrdom.* Oxford: Oxford University Press, 2010.
Neville, Robert C. *Reconstruction of Thinking.* Albany: State University of New York Press, 1981.

Nietzsche, Friedrich, *On the Genealogy of Morality*. Translated by Maudemarie Clark and Alan J. Swensen, Hackett: Indianapolis/Cambridge: 1998.

Nizam al-Mulk. *The Book of Government or Rules for Kings The Siyāsat-nāma of Siyar al-Mulūk*. Translated by Hubert Darke. New Haven: Yale University Press, 1960.

North, Sir Thomas. *Fables of Bidpai (Pancatantra)*. London, Ballantyne Press 1570. HathiTrust Digital Library, https://catalog.hathitrust.org/Record/100654063.

Nye, Joseph. *Bound to Lead: The Changing Nature of American Power*. New York: Basic Books, 2013.

O'Leary, Philip. "Choice and Consequence in Irish Heroic Literature." *Cambrian Mediaeval Studies* 27, Summer 1994: 49.

———. "Magnanimous Conduct in Irish Heroic Literature." *Eigse* 25, 1991: 28–44, 59.

———. Verbal deceit in the Ulster cycle. *Eigse* 1986: 16–26.

Olmsted, Garret. "The Earliest Narrative Version of the Táin: Seventh-century poetic references to the Táin bó Cúailnge." *Emania* 10, 1992: 5–17.

Oppian. Translated by A. W. Mair. Loeb Classical Library. London: W. Heinemann, 1928.

———. *Cynegetica The Hunt (Κυνηγετικά)*.

———. *Fishing (Ἁλιευτικά Halieutica)*.

Ovid. *Ars Amatoria*. In *Amores, Epistulae, Medicamina faciei femineae, Ars amatoria, Remedia amoris*. Edited by R. Ehwald. Leipzig: B. G. Teubner. Perseus Digital Library, Tufts University, 1907.

Parmar, Aradhana. *Techniques of Statecraft: A Study of Kautilya's Arthaśāstra*. Delhi: Atma Ram & Sons, 1987.

Penman, Bruce. Editor. *Five Italian Renaissance Comedies*. Harmondsworth: Penguin Books, 1978.

Peet, Bill, Wolfgang Reitherman, and T. H. White. *The Sword in the Stone*. Burbank, CA: Walt Disney Home Video, 1963.

Pindar. *Nemean. The Odes of Pindar Including the Principal Fragments with an Introduction and an English Translation*. Translated by Sir John Sandys. Cambridge, MA: Harvard University Press, 1937. Perseus Digital Library, Tufts University.

Plato, *Laches*. Original source at Perseus Digital Library, Tufts University. Translations in *Five Dialogues: Euthyphro, Apology, Crito, Meno, Phaedo*. Translated by G.M.A. Grube. Edited by John M. Cooper, 2nd Edition. Indianapolis: Hackett, 2002.

———. *Meno*.

———. *Phaedo*.

———. *Republic*. In *Plato in Twelve Volumes: with an English Translation, Republic, Vols 5–6*. Translated by Paul Shorey. Cambridge, Mass: Harvard university press, 1935. Perseus Digital Library, Tufts University.

———. *Lesser Hippias*. In *Plato in Twelve Volumes: with an English Translation, Cratylus, Parmenides, Greater Hippias, Lesser Hippias*. Translated by Harold North Fowler. Cambridge, Mass: Harvard University press, 1926. Perseus Digital Library, Tufts University.

———. *Parmenides. Plato in Twelve Volumes: with an English Translation, Cratylus, Parmenides, Greater Hippias, Lesser Hippias.* Translated by Harold North Fowler. Cambridge, Mass: Harvard University press, 1926. Perseus Digital Library, Tufts University.

Plutarch, *De Pythiae Oraculis.* In *Plutarch. Moralia.* In *Plutarch. Moralia.* Translated by Frank Cole Babbitt. Cambridge, MA. Harvard University Press, 1928. Perseus Digital Library, Tufts University.

———. *Moralia, Conjugalia Praecepta.* In *Plutarch. Moralia.* Translated by Frank Cole Babbitt. Cambridge, MA. Harvard University Press, 1928. Perseus Digital Library, Tufts University.

———. *Moralia, De garrulitate.* In *Plutarch. Moralia.* Translated by W. C. Helmbold. Cambridge, MA. Harvard University Press, 1939. Perseus Digital Library, Tufts University.

Polybius. *Histories.* Translated by Evelyn S. Shuckburgh. London, New York: Macmillan, 1889. Perseus Digital Library, Tufts University.

Poore, Stuart. "What is the Context? A Reply to the Gray-Johnston Debate on Strategic Culture." *Review of International Studies,* 29 (2), 2003: 279–284.

Powell, Thomas C. "Competitive Advantage: Logical and Philosophical Considerations." *Strategic Management Journal,* 9 (22), 2001: 875–888.

———. "Strategy Without Ontology." *Strategic Management Journal,* 3 (24), 2003: 285–291.

Prost, Marco. "Female Cunning on the Edges of Chivalry in Gerbert de Montreuil's *Continuation to the Conte du Graal.*" In Selected Proceedings from 'On the Edge', March 2015. The Reading Medievalist. Volume 3. Edited by Mahood, H. University of Reading, October 2016, 40–60.

Remley, Paul G. "Muscipula Diaboli and Medieval English Antifeminism." *English Studies.* 70 (1), 1989.

Ross, Margaret Clunies. *The Cambridge Introduction to the Old Norse-Icelandic Saga.* Cambridge: Cambridge University Press, 2010.

Rufinus of Aquileia. "Commentary on the Apostles' Creed." *Catholic Encyclopedia.* Denver, CO: New Advent, 2000.

Russell, Jeffrey Burton. *Satan: The Early Christian Tradition.* Ithaca: Cornell University Press, 1981.

Śarma,Visnu. *The Pañćatantra.* Translated by Chandra Rajan. London: Penguin Books, 1995.

Scobell, Andrew. *China and Strategic Culture.* Carlisle, PA: Strategic Studies Institute/U.S. Army War College, 2002. https://www.globalsecurity.org/military/library/report/2002/ssi_scobell.pdf.

Shaughnessy, Edward L. *Unearthing the Changes: Recently Discovered Manuscripts of the Yi Jing (I Ching) and Related Texts.* New York: Columbia University Press, 2014.

Smith, Riggs Alden. *The Primacy of Vision in Virgil's Aeneid.* Austin: University of Texas Press, 2005.

Snyder, Jack L. *The Soviet Strategic Culture: Implications for Nuclear Options,* R-2154-AF Santa Monica: California: Rand Corporation, 1977.

Sophocles, *Antigone*. Translated by by Reginald Gibbons & Charles Segal. Oxford: Oxford University Press, 2003.
———. *Oedipus Rex*.
———. *Sophocles, Four Tragedies: Oedipus the King, Aieas, Philotectes, Oedipus at Colonus* Oxford: Oxford University Press, 2015.
———. Ajax. *Ajax*. Translated by Sir Richard Jebb. *Sophocles, the Plays and Fragments with Critical Notes, Commentary, and Translation in English*, Part 7, The Ajax. Cambridge: University Press, 1896. Perseus Digital Library, Tufts University.
Strauss, Leo. *The City and Man*. Chicago: University of Chicago, 1964.
———. *Persecution and the Art of Writing*. Chicago: University of Chicago Press, 1952/1988.
Tobriner, Marian Leona. Editor and Translator. Juan Luis Vives. *Introductio ad Sapientiam*. In *Vives' Introduction to Wisdom: a Renaissance Textbook*. New York: Teacher's College Press, 1968.
Treverton, Gregory F., Seth G. Jones, Steven Boraz, Phillip Lipscy. "Toward a Theory of Intelligence: Workshop Report." Rand Corporation, 2006. https://www.rand.org/content/dam/rand/pubs/conf_proceedings/2006/RAND_CF219.pdf.
Twelve Angry Men, MGM Studios, Sidney Lumet, Director, 1957.
Virgil, *Aeneid*. In *Virgil's Aeneid*. Boston, Ginn, 1923. Translated by J. B. Greenough. Perseus Digital Library, Tufts University.
Vives, Juan Luis (*Jo. Lodovici Vivis*) *Introductio Ad Sapientiam Introduction to Wisdom*. Edited by John Georgi Cottæ, 1704.
Warner, Lawrence. *The Myth of Piers Plowman: Constructing a Medieval Literary Archive*. Cambridge & New York: Cambridge University Press, 2014.
Wheatley, Edward. *Mastering Aesop: Medieval Education, Chaucer, and His Followers*. Gainesville: University Press of Florida, 2000.
Wheeler, Everett L. *Stratagem and the Vocabulary of Military Trickery*. Leiden: E.J Brill, 1988.
Williams, Bernard. *Truth and Truthfulness*. Princeton: Princeton University Press, 2002.
Wolterbeek, Marc. *Comic Tales of the Middle Ages: an Anthology and Commentary*. New York: Greenwood Press, 1991.
Wolters, Heather M.K., Anna P. Grome, Ryan M. Hinds. Editors. *Exploring Strategic Thinking: Insights to Assess, Develop, and Retain Army Strategic Thinkers*. Fort Belvoir, VA: U.S. Army Research Institute, United States Army Research Institute for the Behavioral and Social Sciences), Research Product 2013-01. https://ssl.armywarcollege.edu/dclm/pubs/Developing%20Army%20Strategic%20Thinkers.pdf.
Xenophon. *Apology*. In *Xenophon in Seven Volumes*. Volume 4. Cambridge, MA; Harvard University Press, 1979. Perseus Digital Library, Tufts University.
———. *On Hunting Κυνηγετικός*. In *Xenophon's Minor Works*. Translated by John Watson. London: George Bell & Sons, 1878. Perseus Digital Library, Tufts University.
———. *Symposium*.

———. *Memorabilia*. In *Xenophon in Seven Volumes*, Loeb Classical Library. Volume 4. Translated by O.J. Todd. Cambridge, Mass: Harvard University Press, 1923. Perseus Digital Library, Tufts University.

Vives, Juan Luis. *Introductio ad Sapientiam Introduction to Wisdom*. Edited by John Georgi Cottæ. Biblioteca Nazionale Centrale di Firenze (National Central Library of Florence), 1704. https://archive.org/details/bub_gb_UwWuXbKXKY4C/page/n35.

EASTERN EURASIAN PRIMARY AND SECONDARY SOURCES

Book of Poetry Shījīng 詩經. Chinese Text Project. https://ctext.org/book-of-poetry.

Book of History Shàngshū 尚書. Chinese Text Project. https://ctext.org/shang-shu.

Record of Officialdom Reformed Guānchǎng Wéixīnjì 官場維新紀. In *Chinese Popular Fiction Masterpieces Zhōngguó Tōngsú Xiǎoshuō Míngzhù* 中國通俗小說名著/世界文 庫, 四部刊要 Shìjiè wénkù. Sìbùkānyào. Táiběi: Shìjiè Shūjú 臺北：世界書局, 1–69.

Allan, Sarah. *The Heir and the Sage: Dynastic Legend in Early China*. Albany: State University of New York Press, 2016.

Ames, Roger T, and David L. Hall. Translators. *Focusing the Familiar: A Translation and Philosophical Interpretation of the Zhōngyōng*. Honolulu: University of Hawai'i, Press, 2001.

———. *Dao De Jing: Making This Life Significant; A Philosophical Translation*. New York: Ballantine Books; 2003.

Bāo, Tiānxiào 包天笑. *The Last Days of the World Shìjiè Mòrìjì* 世界末日纪. In *Compendium of Late Qīng Fiction Wǎnqīng Xiǎoshuō Dàxì* 晚清小说大系, Táiběi: Guāngyǎ Chūbǎn Yǒuxiàn Gōngsī 光雅出版有限公司, 14: 1–8.

Barmé, Geremie R. "The Greying of Chinese Culture." *China Review*, 13, 1992:1–52.

———. *In the Red: On Contemporary Chinese Culture*. New York: Columbia University Press, 1999.

Bauer, Wolfgang. "The Problem of Individualism and Egoism in Chinese Thought." In *Studia Sino-Mungulica: Festschrift fur Herbert Franke*. Edited by Wolfgang Bauer. Wiesbaden: Franz Steiner, 1979, 427–442.

Birrell, Anne. *China Mythology: An Introduction*. Baltimore: John Hopkins Press, 1993.

Broschat. Michael Robert. "Guiguzi: A Textual Study and Translation." PhD diss., University of Washington, 1985.

Cáo Xuěqín 曹雪芹. *Dream of the Red Chamber/Story of the Stone Hónglóumèng/Shítoujì* 紅樓夢石頭記, Volumes 1–5. Translated by David Hawkes. Penguin Classics, 1974–1986.

Chén, Pòkōng 陈破空. *Zhōngnánhǎi Science of the Thick and Black: Secrets the Chinese Communist Party Won't Reveal Zhōngnánhǎi Hòuhēixué: Zhōnggòng bùnéng Shuō de Mìmì* 中南海厚黑学: 中共不能说的秘密. Táiběi: Contemporary Collection Yǔnchén Culture Affairs Ltd. Corporation Dāngdài Cóngshū "Yǔnchén Wénhuà Shìyè Gǔfèn Yǒuxiàn Gōngsī 当代丛书允辰文化事业股份有限公司, 2009.

Chén, Tiānhuā 陈天花. *The Lion Roars Shīzi Hǒu* 狮子吼. In *Compendium of Late Qīng Fiction Wǎnqīng Xiǎoshuō Dàxì* 晚清小说大系, Táiběi: Guāngyǎ Chūbǎn Yǒuxiàn gōngsī 光雅出版有限公司, 14: 1–80.

Chu, Chin-ning. *Thick Face Black Heart: The Path to Thriving, Winning and Succeeding*. Beaverton, OR: AMC Publishing, 1992.

———. and Wei-yu Huang. *The New Science of the Thick and Black Sunzi Art of War Xīn Hòuhēixué zhī Sūnzi Bīngfǎ* 新厚黑學之孫子兵法. 1, 1. Táiběi: Lianjing, 2005.

Cohen, Paul. *Speaking to History: The Story of King Goujian in Twentieth-Century China*. Berkeley: University of California Press, 2010.

Confucius Kǒngzǐ 孔子. Original text from Chinese Text Project https://ctext.org/analects.

———. *Analects of Confucius* 論語. *The Analects of Confucius: a Philosophical Translation*. Translated by Roger T. Ames and Henry Rosemont, Jr. New York: Ballantine Books, 1998.

Crump, Jr., J.I. *Strategies: Studies of the Chan-kuo Ts'e*. Anne Arbor: University of Michigan Press, 1964.

———. *Legends of the Warring States*. Ann Arbor: University of Michigan, 1998.

Doleželová-Velingerová, Milena. Editor. *The Chinese Novel at the Turn of the Century*. Toronto: University of Toronto Press, 1980.

Fang, Tony. "Negotiation: The Chinese Style." *The Journal of Business and Industrial Marketing*, 21:1, 2006: 50–60.

Féng Mènglóng 馮夢龍. *Tales to Awaken the World Xǐngshì Héngyán* 醒世恒言, 卷三, *Màiyóuláng Dúzhàn Huākuí* 卖油郎独占花魁.

Goldin, Paul Rakita. "*Miching Mallecho:* The Zhanguo ce and Classical Rhetoric." *Sino-Platonic Papers*, No. 41, 1993, 23–24. http://sino-platonic.org/complete/spp041_zhanguoce_intrigues.pdf.

Guǐgǔzi 鬼谷子 Chinese Text Project, https://ctext.org, https://ctext.org/gui-gu-zi.

———. *Center Classic Zhōngjīng* 中經.

———. *Diminishing and Increasing Pattern the Numinous Yarrow* 損兌法靈蓍.

———. *Exigency Quánpiān* 權篇.

———. *Internal Constraints Nèiqián* 內揵.

———. *On Discernment Juépiān* 決篇.

———. *Plumb the Depths Chuāipiān* 揣篇.

———. *Pounce and Pin Fēiqián* 飛箝.

———. *Pressing into Cracks Dǐxī* 抵巇.

Graff, David A. "Brain over Brawn: Shared Beliefs and Presumptions in Chinese and Western 'Strategemata,'" *Extrême-Orient Extrême-Occident*, No. 38, La Guerre en Perspective: Histoire et Culture Militaire en Chine/War in Perspective: History and Military Culture in China. 2014, pp. 47–64.

Guo, Xuezhi. *The Ideal Chinese Political Leader: A Historical and Cultural Perspective*. Connecticut: Praeger, 2002.

Hán Fēizi 韓非子. Chinese Text Project, https://ctext.org. https://ctext.org/hanfeizi.

———. *Five Pests Wǔdù* 五蠹.

———. *Guarding Against the Inner [Court] Bèinèi* 備內.

———. *On the Difficulty of Persuasion Shuìnán* 說難.

———. *Polishing Jade Héshì* 和氏
———. *The Rulers Way Zhǔ dào* 主道
———. *The Two Handles Èrbǐng* 二柄
———. *Wielding Power Yángquán* 揚權
Hanan, Patrick. *Chinese Fiction of the Nineteenth & Early Twentieth Centuries*. New York: Columbia University Press, 2004.
Hansen, Chad. "Review of *Knowing Words: Wisdom and Cunning in the Classical Traditions of China and Greece*" by Lisa Raphals. *China Review International*, 1 (2), Fall1994: 219–228.
Heath, Tim R. *China's New Governing Party Paradigm: Political Renewal and the Pursuit of National Rejuvenation*. Burlington, VT: Ashgate, 2014.
Hsiao, Kung-chuan Xiāo Gōngquán 蕭公權. *A History of Chinese Political Thought*. Volume 1, Translated by. F. W. Mote. Princeton: Princeton University, 1979.
Jia, Wenshan. *The Remaking of the Chinese Character and Identity in the 21st Century: The Chinese Face Practices*. London: Ablex Publishing, 2001.
Jullien, François. *Detour and Access: Strategies of Meaning in China and Greece*. Translated by Sophie Hawkes. New York: Zone Books, 2000.
Lǎozi, *Dàodéjīng*. *Chinese Text Project*, https://ctext.org/dao-de-jing.
Lǐ Bóyuán 李伯元. *Living Hell* 活地獄 *Huó Dìyù*. In *Compendium of Modern Chinese Fiction Zhōngguó Jìndài Xiǎoshuō Dàxì* 中国近代小说大系, Nánchāng: Jiāngxī Rénmín Chūbǎnshè: Jīngxiāo Jiāngxīshěng Xīnhuá Shūdiàn 南昌: 江西人民出版社：经销 江西省新华书店, 1989.
———. *The Record of the Revealing (of the Reality) of Officialdom* (官場現形記: *Guānchǎng Xiànxíngjì*), (Nánchāng: Jiāngxī Rénmín Chūbǎnshè: Jīngxiāo Jiāngxīshěng Xīnhuá Shūdiàn 南昌: 江西人民出版社：经销 江西省新华书店, 1989). 1106–1112. Also: *Officialdom Unmasked*. Translated by T.L. Yang. Hong Kong: Hong Kong University Press, 2001.
Lǐ Zhì 李贄. "Explanation of the Childlike Heart" 童心說. In *A Book to Burn and A Book to Keep (Hidden)*, *Selected Writings*. Edited and Translated by Rivi Handler-Spitz, Pauline C. Lee, and Haun Saussy. New York: Columbia University Press, 2016.
Lǐ Zōngwú 李宗吾.*Collectania of the Thick and Black (Rambles) Hòuhēi Cónghuà* 厚黑叢話.
———. *Theory of the Thick and Black Hòuhēixué* 厚黑學. In *Hòuhēixué Dàquán* 厚黑學大全. Hongkong: Shànghǎi Túshū Gōngsī, year unknown.
———. *The Orthodox Compilation of Theory of the Thick and Black: the Authentic Scripture that Exposes the Ugliness of Human Nature in Society*, *Zhèngzōng Hòuhēixué Dàquánjí: Kànchuān Chǒulòu Rénxìng de Chǔshì Zhēnjīng* 正宗厚黑學大全集：看穿醜陋人性的處世真經. Editor Gōng Sūnlóng 公孫龍. Taiwan: Pǔtiān Chūbǎn: Xùshēng Túshū Zǒngjīngxiāo 普天出版：旭昇圖書總經銷, 2016.
Líng Méngchū 凌濛初. *Slapping the table in Amazement* 初刻拍案驚奇. *Slapping the Table in Amazement: a Ming Dynasty Story Collection*. Translated by Shuhui Yang, Yunqin Yang, Robert E Hegel. Seattle: University of Washington Press, 2018.
Liú Ān 劉安. *Huáinánzi* 淮南子. *Chinese Text Project*. https://ctext.org/huainanzi.

———. *The Huainanzi: A Guide to the Theory and Practice of Government in Early Han China*. Translated and Edited by John S. Major, Sara A. Queen et al. New York: Columbia University Press, 2010.

Liu, Kang. *Globalization and Cultural Trends in China*. Honolulu, University of Hawai'i Press, 2004.

Liu, Kang, and Xiaobing Tang. Editors. *Politics, Ideology and Literary Discourse in Modern China*. Durham, Duke University Press, 1993.

Liú Qīngléi 劉青雷. *Science of the Thick and Black of Love: Love Actually is Just a Type of Deception Àiqíng Hòuhēixué: Àiqíng, Qíshí zhǐshì yīzhǒng Piànshù* 愛情厚黑學: 愛情, 其實只是一種騙術. Táiběi: Shuǐpíng Shìjì Wénhuà Chūbǎn, 2001.

Liu, Ts'un-yan. Editor. *Chinese Middlebrow Fiction: From the Ch'ing and the Early Republican Eras*. Hong Kong: The Chinese University Press, 1984.

Lǔ Xùn 魯迅. *A Brief History of Chinese Fiction*. Translated by Hsien-yi and Gladys Yang. Beijing: Foreign Language Press, 1976.

———. *A Brief History of Chinese Fiction Zhōngguó Xiǎoshuō Shǐlüè* 中國小說史略. Reprinted- Hong Kong: Qingwen Shuwu, 1972.

———. Lǔ Xùn 魯迅, "On Face," *Shuō Miànzi* 說面子, 1934. http://www.saohua.com/shuku/luxun/qjtz/017.htm.

Luó Guànzhōng 羅貫中. *Sānguó Yǎnyì* 三國演義 *Three Kingdoms: A Historical Novel*. Translated by Moss Roberts. Berkeley: University of California Press, 1991.

McNicholas, Mark P. *Forgery and Impersonation in Imperial China: Popular Deceptions and the High Qing State*. Seattle: University of Washington Press, 2015.

Mencius, *Mèngzǐ* 孟子. Original text Chinese Text Project. https://ctext.org/mengzi. *Mencius*. Translated by Irene Bloom. Edited by Philip J. Ivanhoe. New York: Columbia University Press, 2009.

Metcalf, Michael K. "Book Review: *China's New Governing Party Paradigm: Political Renewal and the Pursuit of National Rejuvenation*," by Tim R. Heath, *Journal of Strategic Intelligence*, National Intelligence University, Summer 2016: 99. http://ni-u.edu/wp/csir/journal-of-stategic-intelligence/chinas-new-governing-party-paradigm-by-timothy-r-heath/.

Moloughney, Brian. "From Biographical History to Historical Biography: a Transformation in Chinese Historical Writing." *East Asian History, the Continuation of Papers on Far Eastern History*. Edited by Geremie Barmé. Institute of Advanced Studies Australian National University, December 1992, #4. http://www.eastasianhistory.org/sites/default/files/article-content/04/EAH04_01.pdf.

Parmar, Aradhana. *Techniques of Statecraft: A Study of Kautilya's Arthaśāstra*. Delhi: Atma Ram & Sons, 1987.

Pines, Yuri. *Envisioning Eternal Empire: Chinese Political Thought of the Warring States Era*. Honolulu: University of Hawai'i Press, 2008.

Plum in the Golden Vase Jīnpíngméi Cíhuà 金瓶梅詞話. *The Plum in the Golden Vase or, Chin P'ing Mei*. Five volumes. Translated by David Tod Roy. Princeton: Princeton University Press, 1997–2015.

Raphals, Lisa. *Knowing Words: Wisdom and Cunning in the Classical Traditions of China and Greece*. Ithaca: Cornell University Press, 1992.

Ruǎn Jí 阮籍. *Dàrén Xiānshēngzhuàn* 大人先生傳/ in 阮嗣宗集.

Shī Nài'ān, 施耐庵, *Outlaws of the Marsh* 水滸傳. Translated by Sidney Shapiro. Beijing: Foreign Languages Press, 2016.

Sīmǎ Qiān 司馬遷. *Records of the Grand Historian Shǐjì* 史記. Original Text at Chinese Text Project, https://ctext.org/shiji.

———. *Biography of the Assassins Cìkè Lièzhuàn* 刺客列傳.

———. *Biography of Fàn Suī and Cài Zé/ Fàn Suī Cài Zé Lièzhuàn* 范睢蔡澤列傳.

———. *Biography of Hán Xìn and Lú Wǎn/ Hánxìn Lúwǎn Lièzhuàn* 韓信盧綰列傳.

———. *Biography of Lì Shēng and Lù Jiǎ Lì Shēn - Lù Jiǎ Lièzhuàn* 酈生陸賈列傳.

———. *Biography of the Marquis of Huáiyīn Huáiyīnhóu Lièzhuàn* 史記·淮陰侯列傳.

———. *Biography of Scapulomancy and Yarrow Cleromancy/ Guīcè Lièzhuàn* 龜策列傳.

———. *Biography of Tián Dān/ Tián Dān Lièzhuàn* 田單列傳.

———. *Biography of Zhāng Yí/ Zhāng Yí Lièzhuàn* 張儀列傳.

———. *Marquis Liú of the Hereditory Houses/ Liúhóu Shìjiā* 留侯世家.

Waley, Arthur. *The Temple and Other Poems*. London, 1923.

———. *The Way and Its Power: Lao Tzu's Tao Te Ching and Its Place in Chinese Thought by Lao Tzu*. New York: Grove Weidenfeld, 1988.

Wang, David Der-wei. *Fin-de-siècle Splendor: Repressed Modernities of Late Qīng Fiction, 1849–1911*. Stanford: Stanford University Press, 1997.

Wang, Jing, *High Culture Fever: Politics, Aesthetics, and Ideology in Deng's China*. Berkeley: University of California Press, 1996.

Watson, Burton. "Introduction to Han Fei Tzu." *Basic Writings of Mo Tzu, Hsün Tzu, and Han Fei Tzu*. New York: Columbia University Press, 1964.

Wilhelm, Hellmut. "The Scholars Frustration: Notes on a Type of Fu." In *Chinese Thought and Institutions*. Edited by John Fairbank. Chicago: University of Chicago Press, 1964.

Wú, Jiǎnrén 吳趼人. *After the Holocaust Jiéyúhuī* 劫餘灰. In *Compendium of Modern Chinese Fiction Zhōngguó Jìndài Xiǎoshuō Dàxì* 中国近代小说大系. Nánchāng: Jiāngxī Rénmín Chūbǎnshè: Jīngxiāo Jiāngxīshěng Xīnhuá Shūdiàn 南昌市: 江西人民出版社:经销江西省新华书店 1988, 89–222.

———. *History of Pain Tòngshǐ* 痛史. In *Compendium of Modern Chinese Fiction Zhōngguó Jìndài Xiǎoshuō Dàxì* 中国近代小说大系. Nánchāng: Jiāngxī Rénmín Chūbǎnshè: Jīngxiāo Jiāngxīshěng Xīnhuá Shūdiàn 南昌: 江西人民出版社:经销江西省新华书店 1988, 7–264.

———. *Bamboozled Xiāpiàn Qíwén* 瞎騙奇聞. In *Compendium of Modern Chinese Fiction Zhōngguó Jìndài Xiǎoshuō Dàxì* 中国近代小说大系. Nánchāng: Jiāngxī Rénmín Chūbǎnshè: Jīngxiāo Jiāngxīshěng Xīnhuá Shūdiàn 南昌: 江西人民出版社:经销江西省新华书店 1988, 411–478.

———. *The Despicable History of Recent Society Zuìjìn Shèhuì Wòchuòshǐ* 最近社会齷齪史, also called 近十年之怪现状. In *Compendium of Modern Chinese Fiction Zhōngguó Jìndài Xiǎoshuō Dàxì* 中国近代小说大系. Nánchāng: Jiāngxī Rénmín Chūbǎnshè: Jīngxiāo Jiāngxīshěng Xīnhuá Shūdiàn 南昌: 江西人民出版社:经销江西省 新华书店 1988, 5–138.

———. *Living Hell Huó Dìyù* 活地狱. In *Compendium of Modern Chinese Fiction Zhōngguó Jìndài Xiǎoshuō Dàxì* 中国近代小说大系. Nánchāng:

Jiāngxī Rénmín Chūbǎnshè: Jīngxiāo Jiāngxīshěng Xīnhuá Shūdiàn 南昌: 江西人民出版社:经销江西省新华书店 1988, 315–572.

———. *Sea of Regret Hènhǎi* 恨海. *Compendium of Modern Chinese Fiction Zhōngguó Jìndài Xiǎoshuō Dàxì* 中国近代小说大系. Nánchāng: Jiāngxī Rénmín Chūbǎnshè: Jīngxiāo Jiāngxīshěng Xīnhuá Shūdiàn 南昌市: 江西人民出版社:经销江西省新华书店 1988, 1–88. Also translated as *Sea of Regret: Two Turn of the Century Chinese Romantic Novels*. Translated by Patrick Hanan. Honolulu: University of Hawai'i Press, 1995, 101–205.

———. *Uncanny Reality Witnessed over Twenty Years Èrshínián Mùdǔ zhī Guài Xiànzhuàng* 二十年目睹之怪现状. Běijīng: Rénmín Chūbǎnshè: Xīnhuá Shūdiàn Běijīng Fāxíngsuǒ fāxíng, 1959, 1–6.

———. *World of Folly Hútú Shìjiè* 糊涂世界. in *Compendium of Modern Chinese Fiction Zhōngguó Jìndài Xiǎoshuō Dàxì* 中国近代小说大系. Nánchāng: Jiāngxī Rénmín Chūbǎnshè: Jīngxiāo Jiāngxīshěng Xīnhuá Shūdiàn 南昌: 江西人民出版社:经销江西省新华书店 1988, 411–561.

Xǔ Zhònglín 许仲琳. *Romance of the Investiture of the Gods Fēngshén Yǎnyì* 封神演义. Hong Kong: Zhōnghuá Shūjú 中华书局, 1976.

Yáng Chūmíng 杨出明. *Late Qīng Fiction and Socioeconomic Transformation Wǎnqīng Wénxué yǔ Shèhuì Jīngjì Zhuǎnxíng* 晚清文学与社会经济转型. Shànghǎi: Dōngfāng Chūbǎn Zhōngxīn 东方出版中心, 2005.

Yang, Mayfair Mei-hui. *Gifts, Favors, and Banquets: The Art of Social Relationships in China*. Ithaca: Cornell University Press, 1994.

Yú, Bīn 余斌. "Children's Science of the Thick and Black" *Yù'ér Hòuhēixué* 育儿厚黑学, *Childhood Education Yòu'ér Jiàoyù* 幼儿教育, 2015.

Zhāng, Yìngyú. *Book of Swindles* 杜騙新書. Translated by Christopher Rea and Bruce Rusk. Translators. *The Book of Swindles: Selections from a Late Ming Collection*. New York: Columbia University Press, 2017.

Zhang, Xudong. *Chinese Modernism in the Era of Reforms: Cultural Fever, Avant-Garde Fiction, and the New Chinese Cinema*. Durham: Duke University Press, 1997.

———. *Postsocialism and Cultural Politics: China in the Last Decade of the Twentieth Century*. Durham: Duke University Press, 2008.

———. Editor. *Whither China: Intellectual Politics in Contemporary China*. Durham: Duke University Press, 2001.

Zhōu, Yōugēn 周優根. *Thick and Black Art of War: the Way of Success for a Troubled World Hēi Bīngfǎ: Luànshì Chénggōng zhī Dào* 厚黑兵法：亂世成功之道. Táiběi: Sānchóngshì Sìzhītáng Shūfáng Chūbǎn, 2000.

Zhuāngzi 莊子. Chinese Text Project. https://ctext.org/zhuangzi.

Index

Abu 'l-Qasim Firdowsi Tusi, 131
Abū Zayd, 102, 131
Achilles, 31, 40, 41, 60
Adler, Alfred, 26, 42
Aesop, 47, 52–53, 66, 132, 223, 225–26
Ài Wèiwèi, 135
Ajax, 40, 48, 65
Alberti, Leon Battista, 112
Alemán, Mateo, 109
Alighieri, Dante, 99
Ambrose of Milan (Saint), 83, 86
Ambrosio, Francis, 9, 13, 20, 121
animals, vii, 4, 6, 22, 26, 38–39, 47–59, 74, 81, 85–87, 97, 108, 130, 141, 144, 146, 162–63, 170
Aphrodite, 49
Appian, 98
Aquinas, Thomas (Saint), 84
Aristophanes, 52, 57, 72, 97
Aristotle, xiv, 31, 38, 40–41, 52–54, 60, 107
Artemis, 38, 47–49, 59, 99
Arthaśāstra, 132
Arthur (King), 22–23, 37, 104, 140, 166
Athena, 28, 32, 38–39, 47–48, 51, 73, 98–99, 130
Augustine (Saint), 83, 86–87, 106

Badi' al-Zamān al-Hamadāni, 102

Becker, Ernest, xi–xiv, 5, 9, 24, 121
Bernard of Angers, 85
Bernard of Clairvaux, 83, 87
Bishop Theodulf of Orléans, 83, 85
Blumenberg, Hans, 7, 9
Boethius, 97, 99–101
Bó Lǐxī 百里奚, 143, 144, 155
Book of History Shàngshū 尚書, 29, 42n11
Book of Poetry Shījīng 詩經 150n23, 214n54
Book of Rituals Lǐjì 禮記, 29, 42n11, 184n38
Bó Yìkǎo 伯邑考, 144
Bugiardini, Giuliano, 74

Camus, Albert, 121
Cáo Cāo, 136–137, 147, 151, 174, 177–78, 193–94, 197–200, 210n8, 215n64
Cassian, John (Saint), 83–84
Cháng'é 嫦娥, 137, 144
Charlemagne, 105
Chaucer, Geoffrey, 108
Chén Píng 陳平, 146, 173, 187n75, 196
Chinese Communist Party, 135–36, 160, 170, 176
Chiron, 48–49
Christus Victor. *See* Ransom Theory
Circe, 28, 40, 120

240 Index

Clement of Alexandria (Saint), 83
Confucianism. *See* Ruism
Confucius 孔子, 138–39, 177, 202–3
Courtier's Trifles, 103, 105–8
Cú Chulainn, 104
Cultural Cryptology, 10–11, 52, 135, 140

Daoism, 138, 167, 171–75
Darwin, Charles, 5, 13, 162, 164, 171–72
David (King), 75–78, 80, 84–85
de Montreuil, Gerbert, 104
de Quevedo, Francisco, 109, 111
Derrida, Jacques, 121
Der Stricker, 85
Descartes, Rene, 120
Detienne, Marcel, xiii, xiv
Diana, 98
Dinah, 74, 81
Doctrine of the Mean Zhōngyōng 中庸, 138, 177–78, 198, 203
ductus obliquus, 20n4, 53
Duke of Zhōu (Zhōugōng) 周公, 138–39, 144, 152n59
Duke Wǔ of Zhèng, 141

Egbert of Liège, 107
Ephraem (Saint), 75
Epictetus, 37
Érec et Énide, 104

fabliaux, 103, 108
Fàn Jū 范雎 (Fàn Suī 范睢), 143
Fàn Lí 范蠡, 173, 187n75
Fàn Zēng 范曾, 196, 197
Farid Ud- Din Attar, 131
Féng Mènglóng 馮夢龍, 146
Foucault, Michel, 121
Freud, Sigmund, 121

Ganelon, 105
genealogy, xii, 1–28, 63–64, 71, 80–83, 98, 108, 120

Geoffrey of Monmouth, 104
Geoffrey of Vinsauf, 107
Godfrey-Smith, Peter, 13
Gōujiàn of Yuè (King), 36, 50, 140–41, 173, 177, 180, 211n22
Gracián, Baltasar, 41, 112
Gregory of Nyssa (Saint), 83, 86, 88
Grünberg, Ludwig, 14
Guān Yǔ 关羽, 194
Guǎn Zhòng 管仲 (Yíwú), 139, 208
Guicciardini, Francesco, 41–42, 110
Gǔn 鯀, 140
Gustaf Aulén (Bishop), 88

Hamzanama, 131
Hán Fēi, 韓非, xvii, 129, 141, 143, 161, 166–67, 173, 175, 209
Hán Xìn 韓信, 137, 180, 194–97, 212n30
Hán Yù 韩愈, 129
harrowing of hell, 32, 88, 110
Heidegger, Martin, 121
Heraclitus, 31, 33–34, 39
Herakles, 54
Heriger (Bishop), 85
Herla (King), 106
Hermes, 28–29
Hesiod, 5, 29–34, 54, 64, 72, 86, 88, 100, 134
Hobbes, Thomas, 32, 120
Homer, 29, 32, 34, 36–38, 40–48, 64, 134
homo impotens, 36
homo ludens, 25, 33, 36, 42n6, 64
Horace, 56–57
Huáinánzi 淮南子, 136, 138
Hume, David, 5

Iskandari, 102–3, 110, 131

James, William, 14, 27
Jerome (Saint), 83–84
Jesus, 24, 32, 39, 72, 75, 80–82, 86–87, 90, 110, 130, 143

Jiāng Ziyá 姜子牙, 137, 144, 173, 177
John Chrysostom, (Saint), 76, 82–85, 89
John of Damascus (Saint), 83, 86, 88
John of Salisbury (Bishop), 105
Joseph (Jesus' father), 87
Joseph (Old Testament), 75
Judah, 74–75
Judith (and Holofernes), 77–78
Jullien, François, 134–37

Kant, Immanuel, 32, 71, 120–21, 168
Kautīlya, 132
Kierkegaard, Søren, 24, 121

La Chanson de Roland, 105
Lakoff, George, 9
Lǎozi 老子, 159, 167–68, 172–76
Lawrence (Saint), 83
Laxdœla saga, 104
Leo (Saint), 87
Líng Méngchū 凌濛初, 146
Liú Bāng 劉邦, 195–97, 200, 211, 212n27
Liú Bèi 劉備, 59, 136, 147, 174, 177–78, 193–97
Liú Yǔxī, 136
Livy, 97–98
Lǐ Zōngwú 李宗吾, xvii, 145, 148, 159, 167–81, 191–209
Lotus Sutra, 132–33
Lù Jiǎ 陸賈, 146
Lǔ Xùn 魯迅, 161

Machiavelli, Niccolò, 37, 41–42, 83, 97, 103, 108, 109, 111, 115–21, 142, 146, 168–69, 172, 179
Magi, 80, 89
Mahabharata, 132
Mǎn Gǒudé 滿苟得, 138, 175
Map, Walter, 105–6, 109, 141
Mary (Virgin), 39
Master of Demon Valley Guǐgǔzi 鬼谷子, 29, 142–43, 161, 167, 175
Medb, 104

Mencius\Mèngzǐ 孟子, 138, 177
Merlin, 22, 24, 47, 54, 80, 104
metaphor, xii–xiii, 6–19, 26, 30, 33–34, 36, 39, 41, 110, 130, 160, 218, 221
metic, xiii–xiv, 10, 17
metis, 28, 32, 39, 98
Milton, John, 120
myth, xii, 27–28, 30, 32, 34, 36, 54, 61, 64, 72, 87, 97–98, 137, 139, 143, 145, 219

Nausicaa (Princess), 37–39, 47, 99
Nestor, 40, 41
Neville, Robert, 15
Nibelungenlied, 105
Nietzsche, Friedrich, xiv, 5–6, 12, 14, 19–20, 120, 168, 169, 172–73
Nizam al-Mulk, 131

Odysseus/*Odyssey,* 28, 32, 34–64, 73, 98–102, 110, 112–13, 130–34
œconomia, 93–85, 118, 132
Oppian, 47–64
Origen, 83, 86, 88
Ovid, 104

Pañcatantra, 132
Parius and Lausus, 106
Paul (Saint), 81–85, 87, 90
Penelope, 37, 40, 48–49, 51, 113
Peter (Saint), 28, 82–84
pícaro, 109–14
Pico Della Mirandola, 115
Plato, 8, 27, 30, 32, 41, 48, 52, 54–55, 57–64, 84, 97, 100, 132, 134, 138, 142, 176, 186, 219
Polemus (god), 31
Policraticus, 105
Polybius, 33, 40
Polyphemus (cyclops), 37–38
Pope Francis, 89
Prometheus, 28, 31–32, 34–35, 54, 173
Pythagoras, 34, 56, 120

Qū Yuán 屈原, 163

Rachel, 74, 77
Ramayana, 132
Ransom Theory, 50, 79, 86, 88
Raphals, Lisa, xiii, 134
Reynart (the Fox), 108
ridicula (genre), 103, 107
Robber Zhí 盜跖, 138, 152, 175–77
Romance of the Investiture of the Gods Fēngshén Yǎnyì 封神演義, 133, 144
Romance of the Three Kingdoms (Sānguó Yǎnyì 三國演義), 129, 147–48
Rousseau, Jean-Jacques, 120
Ruǎn Jí 阮籍, 129, 175
Rubens, Peter Paul, 34–35
Rufinus of Aquileia, 86
Ruism rúxué 儒學/Confucianism, xvii, 137–41, 160–64, 166–67, 171–79, 198, 200–201, 209

Sadius and Galo, 106
Sartre, Jean-Paul, 121
Sceva and Ollo, 106
Scheler, Max, 15
Seneca, 115
Shahnameh, 131
Shāng 商, 138
Shùn the Great 大舜, 138–39
Sigrgarðs Saga Frækna, 104
Sīmǎ Qiān, 29
Sīmǎ Yì 司馬懿, 137, 194, 197
Siyasatnama (Book of Government), 131
Sly Peter, 107
Socrates, 37, 40–41, 48, 55–64, 80, 110, 138
Sophocles, vii, 41, 48, 58
Spinoza, Baruch, 120
Strauss, Leo, 10, 20, 61
Suí Hé 隨何, 146
Sūn Wǔ 孫武 (Sūnzi 孫子, Art of War), 3, 11, 15, 133, 169–70, 180

Sūn Wùkōng 孫悟空 (Monkey King), 144
Sū Qín 蘇秦, 142–43, 173
Sū Shì 蘇軾 (Sū Dōngpō 苏东坡), 195
Sword and the Stone, 21–25, 30–34, 39, 47, 53, 104, 120

Tàigōng Wàng 太公望, see Jiāng Ziyá
Tàizōng (Tāng dynasty), 175, 201
Tamar, 74–75, 130
Tāng 汤 (King), 138–39
Terence, 105
Thickblackology (厚黑學)12, 167, 169–75, 191–209
Thucydides, 54–55
Till Eulenspiegel, 107

Ummayad Shiekh Haroun al Rashid, 105
Unibos, 107

Vernant, Jean-Pierre, xiii, xiv
Virgil, 97–99
Vives, Juan Luis, 35, 41, 111
Völsunga saga, 105
von Clausewitz, Carl, 3, 9
von Goethe, Johann Wolfgang, 7

Wang, Jing, 135
Wáng Mǎng 王莽, 209
Wáng Yāngmíng 王陽明, 192–93
Wén (King), 36, 138, 140, 144–45
Wén Zhǒng 文种, 173
Williams, Bernard, 5
Wolterbeek, Marc, 107
Wú Jiǎnrén, 11, 164

Xenophon, 40, 47–49, 55–58, 61
Xiàng Yǔ 項羽, 195–97, 200
Xiāo Hé 蕭何, 137
Xí Jìnpíng 习近平, 135, 160, 168, 176
Xúnzi 荀子, 192–93

Yáo 尧 (King), 138–40

Yī Yǐn 伊尹, 143, 173
Yǔ 禹, 138–41, 144
Yuè Fēi 岳飛, 208
Yù Ràng 豫讓, 141

Zeus, 28, 31–34, 37–39, 49, 51, 54–55, 61, 63, 80, 87–88, 98, 130, 143, 173

Zhāng Liàng 张亮, 173
Zhāng Liáng 張良, 137, 146, 195–96
Zhāng Yí 張儀, 143
Zhāng Yìngyú, 146–47
Zhuāngzi 莊子, 138, 171–72, 175–77
Zhūgé Liàng 諸葛亮, 137, 194

Author Biography

Dr. Gino LaPaglia is a Washington D.C-based scholar-practitioner with expertise in East Asian Affairs and Cultural Studies. He received his doctorate from Georgetown University.

www.ingramcontent.com/pod-product-compliance
Lightning Source LLC
Chambersburg PA
CBHW050901300426
44111CB00010B/1336